JOE'S FRUIT SHOP & MILK BAR

JOE'S FRUIT SHOP & MILK BAR

Zoë Boccabella

ABC Books

The ABC 'Wave' device is a trademark of the Australian Broadcasting Corporation and is used under licence by HarperCollins*Publishers* Australia.

First published in Australia in 2015
by HarperCollins*Publishers* Australia Pty Limited
ABN 36 009 913 517
harpercollins.com.au

Copyright © Zoë Boccabella 2015

The right of Zoë Boccabella to be identified as the author of this work has been asserted by her in accordance with the *Copyright Amendment (Moral Rights) Act 2000*.

This work is copyright. Apart from any use as permitted under the *Copyright Act 1968*, no part may be reproduced, copied, scanned, stored in a retrieval system, recorded, or transmitted, in any form or by any means, without the prior written permission of the publisher.

HarperCollins*Publishers*
Level 13, 201 Elizabeth Street, Sydney, NSW 2000, Australia
Unit D1, 63 Apollo Drive, Rosedale, Auckland 0632, New Zealand
A 53, Sector 57, Noida, UP, India
77–85 Fulham Palace Road, London W6 8JB, United Kingdom
2 Bloor Street East, 20th floor, Toronto, Ontario M4W 1A8, Canada
195 Broadway, New York, NY 10007

National Library of Australia Cataloguing-in-Publication data:

Boccabella, Zoë, author.
 Joe's fruit shop and milk bar / Zoe Boccabella.
 ISBN: 978 0 7333 3382 8 (paperback)
 ISBN: 978 1 4607 0417 2 (ebook)
 Boccabella, Zoë.
 Italians–Australia–Biography.
 Immigrants–Australia–Biography.
 305.851094

Cover design by Darren Holt, HarperCollins Design Studio
Cover image: courtesy Boccabella family; background images by shutterstock.com
Inside cover images: courtesy Boccabella family
Author photograph by Megan Grenenger
Typeset in Minion Pro by Megan Daymond
Printed and bound in Australia by Griffin Press
The papers used by HarperCollins in the manufacture of this book are natural, recyclable product made from wood grown in sustainable plantation forests. The fibre source and manufacturing processes meet recognised international environmental standards, and carry certification.

Dedicato ad

Annibale, Francesca e Remo

Contents

Within a Name	1
A Small Beginning	3
The Flood	6
Get Your Pineapples!	10
From What Is Lost	14
Polenta	19
Semper Fidelis	22
Making *Limonata*	25
Palm Trees and *Fico d'India*	29
On Monte Circolo	34
Eggs in Purgatory	43
Sons of the She-Wolf	47
Applethorpe	56
Being Thirteen	60
Good Friday — 1939	65
Africa and Ceylon	72
New Boots	80
Cottonvale	86
Cursive Voices	91
Burnt Sugar	96
The Olive Peril	108
Tempesta	113
Rusty Earth Motes	121
Two Loaves of Bread	123
Girl on a Bicycle	132
Southern Italian Pasta Gravy	139
The Harvest	145

Western Creek — 1942	154
Western Creek — 2013	167
Storia Scomoda — Part I	174
An Inconvenient History — Part II	182
Good Luck to You, Daughter	189
Letters and Spaghetti	202
The Astoria Café	214
'Battle of Brisbane'	223
Tin Dwelling	229
Poppies	236
Australia Felix	246
Fruit Shop and Milk Bar	254
Vita Brevis	261
Stonehenge Boarding House	275
Moroccan Beans	279
An Unlikely Racketeer	286
Old-style Ice-cream Milkshake	294
Annabelle and Joe	297
The Late Shift	300
Birth …	306
… and Death	312
A Small Thread	323
Old Chums	328
Call This a Holiday?	334
The Descant Shifts	340
Cloudland	346
Elder Wisdoms	352
Orange Drink — 6d	361
Compendium of Structures	367
Author's Note	371
Acknowledgments	373

Within a Name

My grandfather's name was Annibale, but many people called him Joe …

It runs with a rhythm through my mind, almost like the line of a song. I can still hear my grandmother Francesca drawing out each syllable in her Italian accent as she shouted, *Ah-knee-bal-lee*, from the top of the back steps when she'd put the pasta on. And yet even as a little girl I understood Australians generally knew him as Joe.

Back in the 1940s, a friendly local had dubbed him with that name when he deemed 'Annibale' too hard to say. My grandfather seemed content with this, introducing himself as Joe to most Australians from then on. He accepted it in the same way he adapted to many changes when he migrated to Australia (though he wouldn't contemplate changing his surname). And being nicknamed or adopting a more Anglo-sounding first name certainly wasn't unusual for migrants starting a different life in English-speaking countries.

What's in a name? Depending on the language in which it is spoken, 'rose' can be *rosa, ros, roos, róza, růže* … A ruse. Behind a nickname, a name nicked. A person may remain the same regardless of whether a word more palatable to another tongue is found to identify them. Or perhaps the name partly shapes its bearer. I sometimes wonder what my feisty great-granny Maddalena would have thought, considering she chose the name Annibale for her firstborn. She farewelled a fifteen-year-old son, known as Annibale, from Italy in 1939, to be reunited in Australia, almost a decade and a World War later, with a grown man most people called Joe.

By then his life had become immersed in Australia. He had worked on fruit farms, cut sugarcane and waited tables in a Greek café. He'd overcome the challenging war years — when he was interned and later blacklisted — putting them behind him as he had the poverty he'd left in Italy; yet still carried those experiences as part of him, just as his birth place remained in his heart too. And by this time, he had a wife and a son of his own who was born in Australia, forever connecting them to this country where they were now citizens. Together they were realising the dream Annibale had brought with him to Australia — to open a business — as it happened, a fruit shop and milk bar.

It was a time when everything was changing and anything seemed possible. Life was tough but you could still chase your dreams.

A Small Beginning
Brisbane — 1946

They stood in the shade of an awning that spanned the footpath, gazing at 365 Ann Street. The shop frontage of white-painted brick was roughly fifteen feet across. On the right, several steps led up into the shop, and on the left was a shuttered window, without glass but with a large shelf area beneath it just right to display wooden crates of produce.

'It's small.' Francesca held the handle of the pram in one hand to keep it still as baby Remo kicked. She glanced again at the newspaper in her other hand, folded open to the ad offering a fruit-shop lease for three hundred pounds.

Annibale manoeuvred the pram to park it against the wall, out of the way. 'But there're lots of passers-by.' He moved towards the door, which the agent had left unlocked for them. With a faint frown, Francesca tucked the newspaper in her handbag and lifted Remo into her arms.

Inside smelled of seasoned brick and dust on wood. There were two small rooms with ten-foot ceilings, one in front of the other, connected by a doorway. Given the narrow opening, it would be impractical to use both rooms and the front room alone was too cramped to contain a fruit shop and milk bar. They realised it was not so much a shop as a hole in the wall. Annibale began tapping on the wall between the two rooms.

'It's too small, Annibale.' Francesca swapped Remo to her other arm to take his weight. 'We'll find something else.'

'Let's just have a look at the rest of it.'

At the back of the shop, Annibale's roving gaze alighted on a landing he realised could work well as extra storage space. Steps led down from it to a courtyard around the side and he began envisaging where he could stack fruit boxes and keep the bins. The courtyard had its own entrance from Ann Street: a lockable timber-framed door covered in sheets of corrugated iron. Still carrying Remo, Francesca followed Annibale through it and back out onto the busy footpath. Her eyes instantly went to the pram to make sure it was still there, and as Remo was starting to wriggle she put him back into it. Annibale drew up beside her and they stood looking at the area around them, silently assessing.

The shop sat in the northeast section of Brisbane's central business district, in a block of buildings owned by the Church of England. With St John's Cathedral a little further up the street on the same side, and St Martin's Hospital in between, churchgoers along with hospital workers and visitors would make up a large part of the passing trade. In the same building as the shop was the Speedometer Screenwiper Service, whose door opened directly on to the corner of Ann and Wharf Streets. Down the hallway that separated it from the shop was a photographer, WA Jones, who promoted his services by tacking up his portraiture in a glass-fronted case on the outside wall next to the shop. At the end of the hallway, stairs led up to a tailor by the name of Epstein and, directly above the shop, a boot repairer with the surname Bleakley.

Looking back along Ann Street towards the CBD, Annibale could see the clock outside Central Station across from Anzac Square. Across from the shop building stood a hotel on the corner of Wharf Street, and further along was a boarding house. Opposite, Annibale saw on the other side of Ann Street a hulking russet-brick building with sash windows and four tall garage doors, one open and revealing a blunt-nosed fire truck. His gaze moved from the Fire Brigades' headquarters to a row of shops including a chemist and a snack bar, with rooms to let above.

The footpaths thrummed with men in hats carrying Gladstone bags and women toting brown-paper-wrapped parcels trussed with string, some donning gloves, others tugging the hands of resisting children. Young men back from the war passed too, some with empty sleeves or trouser legs pinned up; migrants still wearing the dark, heavier fabrics of Europe strolled by, older men smoking, the reflection in their spectacles concealing their gaze.

Feeling a small flutter of excitement deep inside, Annibale knew he wouldn't regret talking Francesca into moving to the Queensland capital to try their luck, even though they had a six-month-old baby and could have made a life on her parents' Stanthorpe farm. Breathing in the jumbled scents of warm bitumen, meat frying in a Greek café, truck fumes and the sweetness of Brisbane's subtropical air, already Annibale knew he could never go back to life on the farm. He turned to Francesca, eyes blazing.

Francesca showed him how to write '6th June, 1946' in English after his name when he signed the contract. Later that morning, Annibale went in to work his shift at the Astoria Café and gave his notice, saying he would be starting up a fruit shop and milk bar. The Greek manager, Milos, put out his hand and wished him all the best. 'There'll always be a job for you here, but I doubt you'll need it.'

Annibale and Francesca opened the shop at the start of their third week in Brisbane.

The Flood
Brisbane — 2011

It has been raining for most of the summer — immense, sheeting downpours easing to a drizzle before returning to a monsoonal deluge. After nearly a decade of drought, when dam waters dwindled and severe water restrictions caused tanks to become commonplace in backyards, the inundation is a reminder that Brisbane borders the tropics. Humidity soars close to a hundred percent. Everything feels damp — clothes, carpets, bare skin, the pages of books. A rain-cloud pall hangs so dense it's necessary to turn on lamps during the day. The grassy area around the Hills hoist and the banana and coffee trees becomes a quagmire. Little waterfalls splash over stone garden walls. December 2010 has been Brisbane's wettest recorded since 1859.

Disturbing reports are airing in the media of wide swathes of northern Queensland in flood. Milk-coffee coloured waters inundate towns and properties. People flee in droves. Others refuse to leave. And now, in early January, rising waters are affecting at least seventy towns and more than 200,000 people. Stock and wildlife cluster on scant hillocks, stranded amid predominantly flat land, or are drowned, countless numbers washed away. We watch the news in awe and sympathy. And then it starts to dawn on us that some of that floodwater might be gradually heading south ... towards us.

A cousin, Marco, who lives in Italy, contacts me to say they've seen reports on the Italian news. He cannot quite comprehend the size of the flood or, for that matter, the size of Queensland. 'Is it true the flood is as big as France and Germany combined?' His slight breathlessness gives away his amazement.

The Flood

A feeling of pride and affection for the vastness of this country where I was born rises in me, despite its penchant for drought, flood, fire and cyclones. My Australian heritage has sometimes collided with my Italian roots. If Australia and Italy were two paintings, the Australian one would be vibrant orange, blue and green watercolours, perhaps associated with youth, even though the continent contains some of the oldest land on Earth. The Italian canvas would be in textured oil paint — magenta, gold, rich violet and emerald — applied with brush and palette knife. Paintings that, if hung side by side, would be quite different, yet each with their own appeal and beauty. I love the splendour and drama of Italia. At the same time, Australia has a powerful immensity, its freshness and harmony whispered on a breeze.

Our house on a hill, while battered during summer storms, is safe from flood, but not so my Italian grandparents' house in New Farm, a few streets back from the Brisbane River. Although Nonno Anni and Nanna Francesca have died in recent years, many of their belongings remain underneath the wooden house: boxes and trunks of things collected during sixty years of marriage and seven decades in Australia, as well as possessions brought from 1930s Italy. In the past, as a family together we have already spent time sorting and removing many treasured keepsakes and items of furniture, yet for various reasons much remains stored.

Less than two years ago, on April 6, 2009, an earthquake devastated the area of the Abruzzo where Nonno Anni is from. The family house in the village of Fossa that has belonged to my ancestors for centuries — where once we could stay, and where I began to explore my Italian heritage — lies badly damaged. Heartbreakingly, most villagers continue to reside in temporary housing away from the village. In Italy, my grandparents' belongings lie beneath fallen beams, terracotta roof tiles, plaster and thick, grey dust. Now floodwater threatens their remaining possessions in Australia.

Roger and I drive towards the house, both of us quiet. Nearing the river, we see rows of sandbags stacked at the fences and front doors of homes and businesses. Two men awkwardly manoeuvre a sofa down a short flight of steps. A child holds a carrier from which a puppy barks. I think how, for decades, authorities have claimed we wouldn't again have a flood of the magnitude of Brisbane's 1974 one because of the subsequently built Wivenhoe Dam — its capacity the equivalent of more than two Sydney Harbours. *Wivenhoe will protect us.* Even now, hearing the somewhat belated warnings on the radio, it seems unbelievable Brisbane will flood. Yet it's perhaps naïve, arrogant even, to think anyone can ultimately control nature.

In 1974, Nonno Anni and Nanna Francesca received a knock at the front door from two uniformed policemen warning them a big flood was coming and the power was about to be cut off. Nonno Anni told me he recalled looking past the officers at the clear blue sky, the sun shining, and he was incredulous. Today the weather is the same. After weeks of rain right up until yesterday, sunrays drum on soggy ground and bitumen flecked with leaf litter, creating rising steam. Cicadas, silent during the rainfall, stir into yammer. The rain is gone but the flood is still coming, walls of water gushing along creeks, spilling over causeways and dam walls, scouring riverbeds and spreading into an inland sea engulfing all in its path.

Driving down the slope of Brunswick Street towards the junction with Merthyr Road, I hear Roger's intake of breath. 'Zoë, there's already water covering the road.'

I see my grandparents' house beyond police barricades that are now blocking off the lower section of Brunswick Street. Muddy water seeping up from the river through drains and popped manhole covers laps at their driveway. Although my throat feels constricted upon seeing it, the percolating water is still shallow and I'm determined to get to the house, especially as we've agreed to meet my father there. We decide to try the lane at the back of the house.

In my childhood, this lane was pitted dirt. Nowadays it is sealed bitumen and named after three sisters — the Fuljameses — my grandparents' next-door neighbours for decades, and the only ones I'm aware of who lived on this block longer than Nonno Anni and Nanna Francesca, who themselves lived here almost fifty years. The lane is still open. We drive through tranquil water about twelve centimetres deep. With the car windows wound down, I hear the gentle splash as we ease by and can smell the briny river water.

My father is already under the house loading Nonno Anni's ute with boxes. We quickly embrace. His bleak expression conveys what we're all feeling. The floodwater on Brunswick Street is silently, insidiously, creeping up the short driveway. Roger places a rock at the waterline to gauge how fast it is progressing, so we can get the cars out via the back lane before the water rises too high. In houses all around, people are frantically moving belongings, leaving, or filling sandbags. There is so little time now. The water is on its way.

There are several makeshift rooms filled with possessions and furniture in the breezeway underneath my grandparents' house and not enough time or hands to save it all — my uncle and cousins are overseas. And with tenants occupying the upper level, all the three of us can do is save what we can and move items up onto shelves or furniture higher than the water might reach. Holding several of Nanna Francesca's 1950s and '60s Italian vinyl records, I pause to watch Dad and Roger hoist my great-grandmother's *baule*, or glory box — the large, woven trunk she brought by ship from Calabria filled with her belongings, including two sixteen-litre tins of olive oil — onto an old sideboard cabinet, itself sacrificed to the encroaching water.

I'd dearly love to save a pale-yellow 1950s kitchen dresser with leadlight glass doors and Nanna Francesca's glass-fronted cabinet still containing espresso cups, ceramic swans and hi-ball glasses, but the ute is full and trying to move everything is futile. As fast as we work, as much as we sweat in the heat and humidity, the floodwater ultimately beats us.

In two hours, it has risen two metres beyond where Roger initially placed the rock. It's time to leave while we can still get the vehicles out. As we walk away, I look back through the breezeway at the things we haven't been able to move. I know I'm sentimental, and combined with the emotion of what is happening it's starting to hit me: Brisbane is in flood. The items left behind are just possessions, but like the sentiment evoked when I first walked through the earthquake-devastated family house in Italy, it feels like I am losing some essence of my grandparents all over again.

The last thing I catch sight of is part of an old sign, wedged behind a floral banana lounge. I can just see in red perspex lettering the final A and R of MILK BAR.

Get Your Pineapples!

Joe²/dʒoʊ/, n. Colloq.
1. ~ a male personal name, variant of Joseph.
2. ~ a man; an average fellow.

Before the tram quite stopped, Annibale swung down from where he'd been standing on the running board, holding on. It was a perfect Brisbane day. Cloudless, no wind, the early-morning air crisp but the sun pleasantly warming as the day went on. Not that Annibale felt the cold, having grown up in winters in the Apennine Mountains of central Italy. Even in Brisbane's coldest months he rarely slung his suit coat over his usual cotton shirt and singlet.

He merged into the congestion of Roma Street around the fruit and vegetable markets. Men crowded footpaths as utility trucks inched forward in the traffic, drivers resting their right elbows on the edges of their open windows. Double-parked delivery trucks idled. Open-sided vans waited to be loaded. There was the occasional hollow clop of hooves on bitumen as a horse-drawn cart manoeuvred among the mayhem, the blinkered horse bouncing its head with unease.

Flanking Roma Street Railway Station, the produce markets housed a double set of railway lines down the centre of the hundred-yard-long building, along which produce freighted in from other areas of Queensland arrived. Some came from Stanthorpe, including apples and pears from the orchards of Francesca's parents in the nearby hamlet of Applethorpe. Brisbane's continued expansion had led to the opening of the Turbot Street markets opposite the original Roma Street hall, the two sites functioning as one big operation in the central business district.

Annibale milled around, chatting with other men; waiting, like everyone else, for the bell to toll at eight o'clock sharp, as it had almost every day since 1884 to signal the beginning of trading. With the first gong reverberating from the Town Hall clock down the road, the market bell pealed. The men surged inside. Vendors, with long aprons over their trousers and shirtsleeves rolled to the elbow, hollered: *Get your pineapples! Rowell and Connors. In from Nambour. Juicy pineapples! Just in! Potatoes from Lockyer. Best price for a sack! Always a seller!*

Timber signs painted with merchants' names hung above the stacked wooden produce boxes and hessian bags clumpy with potatoes. Annibale walked among discarded cabbage leaves on the concrete floor, past sacks of onions and ash-coloured smooth-skinned pumpkins, casting his eye over knobbly pears and mandarins wreathed in dark-green curling leaves. He'd decided that, given their shop's location in the CBD, it was best they sell only fruit.

The vendors yelled their prices in a fast singsong cadence he had to concentrate hard to decipher. Yet after just a few weeks of buying, he was becoming adept at haggling for the best price and was rapidly learning what was in season and which items always sold — he had to, for his business to survive. And he was already befriending some favoured merchants.

'What's your name, mate?' asked one of the sellers after they'd been negotiating for a bit.

'Annibale.'

'An ... what? Cripes, that's a mouthful! Where're you from?'

'Italy.'

'Eye-talian, eh? Tell you what, I'll call you Joe.'

Annibale shrugged and nodded. 'All right, call me Joe.'

'I'm Len.' They shook hands, grinning. 'You hear about the big hailstorm out west, Joe? Wiped out a lot of crops, poor buggers.'

'Hail is unusual this time of year.' Seeing Len's curious look, Annibale added, 'I used to work on a few farms out that way.'

'Yeah? Good to hear. You know how bloody tough it is.' In unison, they chortled, raised brows, nodded.

And even though Len had dubbed him Joe, he still marked Annibale's boxes of produce with his proper initials — *AB*, for Annibale Boccabella.

Hoisting two wooden cases of fruit onto his shoulder, Annibale would carry them on the tram back to the shop, returning to the markets straightaway to collect another two cases. While he was gone, Francesca served customers and arranged the new fruit into displays, moving back and forth to check on Remo in his pram. Until Annibale got permission to do some work on the inside rooms and build the milk bar, the shop was not much more than a footpath stall sheltered by the building's corrugated-iron awning, with the produce on rough-hewn shelves out front. Francesca and Annibale took shifts standing on the footpath to serve passing customers, their 'cash register' a work apron with a long front pocket in which they rummaged to give customers their change.

Stepping off the tram on his way back from the markets one time, Annibale recognised a dark-haired woman and her son coming around the corner from Wharf Street. They were part of a Greek family from Barcaldine who ran the Eton Private Hotel, where many out-of-town relatives of patients in St Martin's Hospital stayed. Recalling a little of the Greek Milos had taught him at the Astoria Café, Annibale smiled. '*Kaliméra. Ti kánete?*' The woman did a double take, and then her face lit up.

Midmorning, Francesca would duck back to the boarding house in Spring Hill with Remo in tow to do some chores, returning in the afternoon. The days were long but necessary to get the business established. Knowing he was working for himself, Annibale was content standing on the busy footpath for hours.

By late afternoon, shafts of sunlight slanted across the street between the buildings, slipping beneath the awning and casting the last of their warmth across his legs. In between serving customers, he stood beside his fruit stand gazing along Ann Street. Cars with noble front grilles, round headlights and bulbous curves cruised by. It seemed almost everyone had an automobile. He thought of his village, Fossa, in Italy, where one was fortunate if they owned a horse and cart. His family had only a donkey and Annibale smiled, thinking of Gina, this donkey that had grown up with him.

A siren sounded over at the fire station and men came running from all directions, donning their coats and brass helmets. A red-painted Mack truck barrelled from one of the big garage bays, one of the firemen ringing a bell furiously by hand. Annibale had witnessed a fire engine surge out and smash into a car almost in front of where he stood, but this one moved freely through the traffic, its pealing clang receding as it went on its way. His gaze flicked to the snack bar just up from the fire station, run by a man named George.

The day Annibale and Francesca arrived to open their shop, George had stood out on the footpath and stared with folded arms. He sold some fruit and drinks, but mainly sandwiches, rolls and pies, which Annibale had no intention of stocking. Annibale was still keen to incorporate a milk bar, though, and decided it was time to seek permission to knock down the middle wall between the two rooms to expand the shop.

He had to see an administrator from the Church of England in a building a few doors up, next to St John's Cathedral. 'You wouldn't believe it, Francesca,' Annibale shook his head, 'but the man I have to see is a Mr St John.' They both chuckled, not knowing to pronounce the name 'sinjin'.

The administrator gave them permission to do the work, provided it was all at their own expense. Confident with the financial risk, Annibale went ahead, getting in a couple of tradesmen to help knock down the middle wall, creating one larger space. Then he hired a friend, Serafino — who'd started up a carpentry business — to build shelving along two walls, a glass display case and cabinets with glass sliding doors.

Annibale and Serafino were inside sawing and hammering when Archbishop Halse swept in, his long robe stirring wood shavings littering the floor. Born in England, the Anglican archbishop was Oxford-educated and stood with a commanding bearing. He took off his hat, his pale bald head shining with perspiration in the humidity. Putting down their tools, Annibale and Serafino straightened, wiping sweat and dirt from their faces and hands with their handkerchiefs.

The archbishop held up his hand. 'Please, do not let me stop you. I heard you were making some changes. I was passing by and thought I would take a look.'

Serafino went back to sawing and Annibale showed the archbishop where they'd knocked down the wall. 'I'm putting in a milk bar,' he said, indicating the spot where a long refrigerated counter would stand.

Archbishop Halse shook his head. 'I admire your get-up-and-go. You know when to take an opportunity. That's why you migrants come to this country, isn't it?'

From What Is Lost

At the peak of the flood, Roger and I can see from a distance Nonno Anni and Nanna Francesca's house surrounded by still, murky water. It stands silent and empty, the tenants having evacuated to an emergency refuge set up at the showgrounds. The flood hasn't reached the top level of the two-storey structure, but in the breezeway beneath, my grandparents' possessions are submerged.

I recall Nonno Anni telling me about the clean-up after the 1974 flood: how a lot had to be thrown out or burnt, and how weeks afterwards, they finally located the source of an enduring stench — a dead fish wedged in the back of a cupboard. Being a toddler at the time, I have no memories of Brisbane's '74 flood, during which the water came even higher than in 2011, and after which my mother donated my baby clothes to flood victims. Yet from childhood I was fascinated to pore over black-and-white photographs of the event: the picture of my father and Nonno Anni in the floodwater in my grandparents' front yard; of Nanna Francesca peering from the front doorway, refusing to come lower than the top step. In one photograph that my father took, Nonno Anni is in the water, waving to a tinny overloaded with long-haired young people rowing along Brunswick Street. They cheerfully wave back to him.

Roger and I venture to a high section of riverbank near the New Farm reach where several others are watching the furious torrent. Friends and strangers talk to each other, everyone sharing the experience of an event that will become a significant part of Brisbane's history. My father is there chatting with the owner of a well-known Italian café. It never ceases to amaze me how almost everyone in the older Italian community appears to be connected through an intricate network of relations, friends, acquaintances and shared experiences. Although I have my back to them, unable to take my eyes off the racing river, I can hear their conversation — possibly as can everyone else on the riverbank. They initially discuss the flood, before — in typical Italian fashion — side-tracking to the latest on the Italian grapevine, which merges into collective reminiscence.

'I suppose you spent your time growing up working in the family business too.' My ears prick, hearing the tinge of resentment I've come to recognise in my father's voice for all the unpaid weekend, holiday and after-school work he'd had to do as the eldest child in a migrant-family business. I turn ever so slightly to see the café owner shaking his head and clapping his hand on my father's shoulder. 'Yep, the life of a child of migrants, eh, Remo?' My father's responding chuckle possibly doesn't sound hollow to the café owner.

The last remnants from the fruit shop and milk bar my grandparents ran for twenty-three years are now underneath muddy water. Like time, the flood is unstoppable, and like the opaque floodwater, time has made it difficult to see what lies beneath.

I look back to the usually lazy-paced river. Upturned boats and pontoons tear past, huge tree branches, furniture, steel drums, animal carcasses — all carried by the rapid flow out to Moreton Bay. These floods have taken the lives of forty people in Queensland, with another ten remaining missing, many swept away as tsunami-like water stormed through the Lockyer Valley west of Brisbane.

The flood has peaked and still the water keeps coming.

It takes two days for the water to drop. I'll never forget the smell of the slick, almost-black mud the flood leaves behind. It invades the nostrils — a primitive, earthy odour redolent of decomposition and the gagging acridity of chemicals. Even dry, it reeks. Flies crawl in swarms over the desiccated mud caked over everything that was in the floodwater's path.

My father finds a box of schoolbooks he and his younger brother wrote in during the 1950s, now a brick of congealed dark mud, unsalvageable. I'm not sure what happened to the sign from the fruit shop and milk bar. Most of my grandparents' possessions are lost or have simply disintegrated, even large items of furniture. I think of the people who died in the flood. We got off lightly.

*The small house sat
on an average street.
Unassuming dwelling
of thought and abode.
Buffeted by squalls
— shut,
seemingly empty.
Yet radiating light,
hinting at all
that may dwell
within.*

I flop onto the double bed in the spare room, causing the wooden bedhead to hammer softly against the painted fibro wall. It draws Nanna Francesca's gaze and I hastily flick my thongs onto the linoleum floor before putting my bare feet on the bedspread — one she brought back from Italy. It's the type with a raised, swirling cream pattern against a sage-green background, and has a border of tassels that almost brush the floor. I'm in my mid-teens, still in the phase of wanting to blend in and be 'more Australian'. Yet deep down I am mindful of my grandmother's feelings, even if I don't want to let her know that, and even though she tests me at times.

'… and then there's Maria Sandrini — now, her husband is Santo Sandrini and they had three daughters and a son: Concetta, Evelina, Silvana and Dino. Santo is a builder and Dino is now a plumber. He married a girl … now what was her name? Her family was from Campania …'

'Nanna, I don't even know who these people are.' I examine a sliver of white on the only fingernail I haven't yet bitten. She ignores me calling her Nanna; her desire for me to call her Nonna another tug-of-war between us.

'… Donata, her name was, and they had three children — Stefano, Guiliana and Franca. Now, Concetta married Mario Carboni and they had a son and …'

Nanna Francesca is a keeper of spoken histories, including the genealogy of most Italians she knows. Her recall is phenomenal, and frequent. My attention drifts on the hum of her voice and I chew at the nail, watching her fold towels and put them away in a silky-oak dresser with stiff drawers. She unconsciously talks and moves in a kind of spoken waltz, the thin leather soles of her shoes tapping lightly on the floral lino. This is the bedroom occupied by my great-grandparents, Maddalena and Vitale, when Nonno Anni and Nanna Francesca accommodated their parents, their two sons, and my grandmother's brother, Vincenzo, at their Brunswick Street abode during many of the years they ran their fruit shop and milk bar.

I glance at the cupboards and chests Nanna Francesca has cloaked in old floral sheets and further camouflaged with additional boxes and belongings stacked on top. Seeing me looking, she puts down a towel mid-fold and shuts the bedroom door, beckoning me over. The worn linoleum is cool beneath my feet. She lifts a sheet to reveal a petite wardrobe of dark timber. A small key releases the lock and a comforting scent of peppery wood. One side contains slatted shelves holding neatly folded linen, a faint soap fragrance lingering in material long ago washed in a boiling copper.

Nanna Francesca shows me her treasured linens, hand-sewn and embroidered with her mother's initials, likely to have been placed in a glory box in Calabria some time in the 1920s. I press close, the olive skin of our arms touching. As she moves, a waft of onions she's been chopping earlier combines with the rose-scented talcum powder she pats on after her morning shower. For a few minutes in this dim room with Nanna Francesca, I forget to be the teenager that I will shake my head remembering decades later.

'These are beautiful. You should get them out sometimes,' I say.

Nanna Francesca lets out a horrified half-yowl. 'They're only for *good*. These are very precious, you know.' She hustles me aside.

'I know, but you never get to see them ...' My mumble is drowned out by her Italian as she hurries to relock the cupboard door and drop the shroud back in place.

Two decades later, after my grandparents are both gone, I find the linens exactly as she left them that day, along with many beautiful soaps given to Nanna Francesca over the years for birthdays and Mother's Days — all saved 'for good'.

Nonno Anni wasn't overly concerned with the value of possessions or sentimental attachment to them. In the backyard, he used one of his mother's Abruzzese copper cooking pots to mix some type of mortar.

'Polenta mostly,' he says when I ask him what he ate when he was growing up in Fossa during the 1920s and '30s. 'And my mother killed a pig to get us through every winter. We'd raise it from a piglet. Sometimes lamb from her parents' butchery but that was only if we walked across the valley to Poggio. Ma collected greens from the mountainside. She'd give me an orange for Christmas …' His gaze is far away now. 'I can still see my mother stirring the polenta and bending over the fire in the kitchen in Fossa.' He shakes his head as if to clear the clouds of reverie and gets back to work.

When I first hold great-granny Maddalena's cooking pot, with its gently curving base perfect for nestling among coals, the copper has dulled to a brownish-grey tinged mint-blue. There are two side rings once used to thread a chain or handle — long gone — to hang the pot on a hook above the fire or lift it from the embers, depending on the dish being cooked.

With a small file, I carefully chip away twenty-year-old mortar stuck to the sides. Then I work my arm until it aches, rubbing a section on the outside with an old rag dipped in copper cleaner. Slowly, there emerges a warm gleam.

Polenta

Fossa, Italy — late winter, 1924

The water in the copper pot came to the boil and Maddalena threw in a handful of salt. She allowed the maize flour to sift through her fingers, falling into the water a little at a time, to make the polenta. Her other hand worked hard using a well-worn wooden spoon, preventing lumps from forming and keeping it from sticking to the bottom of the pot. Depending on the coarseness of the grain, it could take almost an hour of constant stirring for the polenta to achieve a solid consistency.

'What are you saying, Vitale?' She struggled to keep her voice even, venting her unease in the cadenced stirring.

'I spend every waking hour in those fields. For what? The little money we make is getting less and less. I need to be able to provide for you and Annibale. I need to uphold my honour.' Vitale felt the pressure of what people might say about him if he failed to provide, particularly after what had happened with his aunt.

As inheritance carved the farmland of many peasant families into smaller fields — the resulting reduction in crop yield plunging them ever further into poverty — more of the men in Fossa were migrating to other parts of Europe or as far as the Americas and even Australia. They sent back whatever money they could to their wives and children who remained in the village, while saving for them to emigrate also. Vitale's childless aunt, however, had promised her house and land to him and Maddalena for Annibale's future, unexpectedly raising their hopes of being able to stay — and then blighting them.

During her final frail year, the parish priest, Don Angelo, had convinced Vitale's aunt that earthly chattels were barriers to Heaven. He promised her that if she changed her will to leave her house and land to the Catholic Church, once a month he would say a Mass in her honour. And he did. Though Vitale didn't dare bring that up and risk sending Maddalena into another temper.

'Honour,' she said quietly, almost to herself.

'What did you say?'

She turned to him. 'What honour do we have after what your aunt did?'

'Lena …' They'd gone over this so many times. 'There's nothing we can do about that.'

'Not with Don Angelo living in her house.' The polenta got another swift beating.

'It was Zia's decision to do what she pleased with her estate. What can we do about it?' Vitale knew she understood as well as he that parish priests brandished a power no peasant could match, especially when the priest's brother was the head of the local Fascist division.

Hot from bending over the fire, Maddalena lifted her apron to wipe her forehead. *You've taken marriage vows*, she reminded herself, knowing he was building up to tell her his decision. And, sensing Vitale's underlying anxiety, she didn't burden him further by asking to be part of making that decision — but it was hard. She'd married Vitale when she was twenty-nine, considered an old spinster in 1923 Abruzzo. By then she had one broken engagement behind her, along with many years working in her parents' butchery and grain mill in Poggio Picenze. Maddalena knew her friends hadn't had the same freedoms she'd had, especially after her father, Emidio, died in the summer of 1919 and she'd helped keep the businesses operating.

Vitale Boccabella, a year younger than Maddalena, lived across the valley in Fossa, a stone village tucked into a hollow on the side of Monte Circolo. Like generations before him, he was a peasant and a farmer. None of the girls in the village wanted to marry the duty-bound Vitale and look after his ailing father Demetrio — who was not so much ailing as harbouring an addiction to wine. But Maddalena Urbani saw in Vitale a quiet man, calm, when she sometimes was not, and she was glad her cousin had organised the introduction.

Baby Annibale woke in his wooden box of blankets near the corner of the kitchen and Maddalena swiftly tended to him, re-swaddled him and got back to stirring the bubbling polenta before it stuck. Vitale watched the rhythmic movement of her back and shoulders. It still amazed him that she'd married him. There were times he'd thought he'd never have a wife. He wanted to stay with her, not emigrate.

Yet for too many dawns to count, as the sun came over the mountains on the other side of the valley, he traipsed along with the other villagers down to work on his small piece of land amid the jumbled chessboard of fields on the valley floor. And for too many harvests, the earnings were scant. His father had left the previous autumn with some other men from the village for labouring jobs down south, while Vitale stayed behind for the birth of the baby. However, he knew his time had come and feared how Maddalena would react, especially as they'd been married barely more than a year, with Annibale just a few months old.

He tarried, toying with the handle of his cup, which was filled with warm liquid from the chicory, rye and sugar beet she'd boiled up in place of the coffee they couldn't afford, for he knew the journey would begin the moment he uttered the words. Vitale took a final sip, wiped his mouth. 'As soon as the snow melts I'm going to head to France with Croce Innocenzi.' He kept his gaze on the fire, readying for her outburst.

'France?' She turned. 'Why not Sicily, like your father?'

He met her eyes. 'You understand that I need to go?'

'For Annibale's sake, if not ours. We've hardly enough to live on here.'

Vitale relaxed. 'Croce heard the French might pay more in wages.'

She nodded, not voicing her fears, her questions, how long he might be away. Many honourable men in the village had gone abroad to work and remained loyal to their families, but there were also those who simply vanished, finding new wives and lives.

'I'll keep the field going,' she said. 'And, Vitale,' her chin trembled ever so slightly, 'please write to me.'

He got up and kissed her on the mouth.

Annibale was almost a year old when Maddalena finally received a somewhat creased letter in the autumn of 1924. With impatient hands, she tore open the envelope, not noticing the stamps or return address. *I'm sorry it's taken so long to write,* Vitale began, *but I am in Australia …*

Semper Fidelis

Maddalena lay in bed watching the night sky, framed by the window, fade with the dawn light. It was too dim to reread Vitale's letter without lighting the oil lamp and she didn't want to risk waking Annibale. Not that she needed to read it again; the shock of the words was impressed upon her. Vitale was in Australia, the other side of the world. With little work in France and down to their last coins, he and Croce had jumped on board the ship *Ville de Verdun* to Australia, shovelling coal from Marseilles to Melbourne in exchange for their passage. Vitale was now working on a potato farm in the Victorian countryside.

With a sigh, Maddalena got up and turned around to make the bed. The word 'Australia' conjured feelings of strangeness and distance, of a land so far away it was impossible to envisage what it looked like. Vitale didn't say if he planned to stay for good. She couldn't imagine leaving the Abruzzo, the only place she'd known, for a new life on the other side of the world. What lay beyond the encircling Apennine Mountains was largely a mystery. Gazing at Annibale sleeping in his tiny bed, she sighed again, thinking how Vitale was altering their son's future also. One little foot had escaped the covers and she gently tucked it back under them.

She put on long, heavy socks, holding them in place by winding string around her legs. Her leather shoes laced, she drew up her petticoats and fastened her long-sleeved shirt before stepping into an ankle-length dark-green skirt. It was almost cool enough for a shawl but she buttoned on a fitted jerkin instead. Pinned to the hip of her skirt, a little bunch of tin charms — including a horn, a frog, a Pope's head with mitre and crozier, a closed hand with forefinger extended and a *gobbetto*, or hunchback, all dangling from a circle with the number thirteen within it — tinkled as she moved, warding off the evil eye.

She brushed her hair, a little greasy around the scalp, and gathered it into a ponytail, twisting it up into a tight net. Then she tucked her hair under a scarf, over which she placed her *tovagliola*, a long, scarf-like head covering, and put on top of this a piece of cloth she kept rolled into flat padding. Maddalena grabbed her copper *conca* from the kitchen and quietly eased out the front door without waking Annibale.

Outside, she placed the water vessel on top of the padding on her head, just like the other village women who, between five and six every morning, collected water for their households from the communal fountain fed by an underground spring. Maddalena heard a door close and turned to see her neighbour, Giovanna, carrying her *conca* on her head. She paused to allow her to catch up. Giovanna's husband had left for Australia the year before to cut cane in a place called Queensland and Maddalena told her Vitale was now in Australia too.

Giovanna gave a knowing smile. 'It does get easier, you know, the separation.' Already several women were queuing at the fountain and Maddalena and Giovanna joined the back of the line. 'It was hard when Stefano left for Australia because Savina had just been born,' Giovanna went on. 'But I got used to it.'

Maddalena nodded slightly, her *conca* staying balanced from years of practice since girlhood. 'I'll be fine.' It occurred to her that soon she and Vitale would have spent more than half their married life apart.

Giovanna eased her copper vessel under the running spout. 'All we can do is follow our husbands and make the best of it.' She hoisted the *conca* onto her head. 'No matter where you go, your home is always there waiting.'

On a stretch of farmland between the Australian Alps and the mercurial waters of Bass Strait, potato workers toiled in the fields, the crumbly soil spongy underfoot. The potato plants had withered and harvest was in full swing. Vitale dragged a potato hook towards himself in swift movements, the tines unearthing clusters of tubers. He bent to pick up the vegetables, placing them in a hessian bag strapped to his waist. Potatoes were the main Australian vegetable crop and the workers planted and harvested by hand, though they used horses to plough and mound the soil along the rows.

Vitale's right shoulder ached from the frequent motion of scraping back the soil. He paused, holding the worn-smooth timber handle of the potato hook in his left hand, moving his right shoulder in a circle to ease the fatigue. Fine mist eddied in the autumn chill of early morning and eucalypts covering distant hills soared with eerily finger-like gnarled branches pointing to the sky. The thought of Maddalena and Annibale back in Fossa elicited a physical ache that carried from the depths of his stomach right up his throat.

He sighed and went back to work. The last time he'd felt this despondent was when, at twenty, the Italian government had conscripted him to serve for five years in the Great War. Because he was from the Apennines, Vitale became one of the Alpini soldiers, trained to fight in steep, snowy mountains. He fought in a three-year campaign in the Alps against the Austro-Hungarian Kaiserjäger and the German Alpenkorps, hating every moment of it. The conflict, known as the War in Snow and Ice, had a 600-kilometre frontline through the highest peaks and glaciers of the Alps. Twelve metres of snow fell during the winter of 1915–16 and thousands of soldiers died in avalanches, their remains never recovered.

During one battle, Vitale found himself face to face with an Austrian soldier. Both had their bayonets raised but Vitale was in the better position. Realising this, the Austrian soldier threw down his weapon and begged for mercy. He reached into his tunic pocket and got out photographs of a young woman and two small children, pleading with tear-filled light-blue eyes. Vitale hesitated. He looked around, saw no one was watching, and told the Austrian to run — a decision he never regretted.

That moment was a world away from when his Alpini battalion marched off to war in their grey-green uniforms and distinctive felt hats trimmed with black raven feathers, all of them singing folk songs. He saw the similarity with his coming to Australia full of high hopes and bravado, thinking he could make a fortune, to be followed by the sobering reality. With his lack of English and education, the best work he could garner was planting and harvesting potatoes, sharing a small brick hut with other men like him. Vitale had barely any money to send to Maddalena and not enough to return to Italy. Poverty had conscripted him this time into abject toil, stranded far from home, unaware of the Great Depression looming.

Making *Limonata*

Lemons fill the kitchen sink. I lean in and take a deep breath. Their fresh, strident scent cuts through the sultry air. The closing days of summer are hot and still, making the last couple of months — when widespread flooding and then a massive cyclone wreaked havoc across Queensland — seem unreal. After all the rain, everything is thriving; the lemon tree gravid with fruit. I tie on a dark-green-and-white-striped apron that belonged to Nanna Francesca and begin cutting the lemons in half, their juice pooling on the chopping board. Sugar syrup cools in a saucepan while I squeeze by hand a dozen or so lemons. Each yellow fruit is sensuously bulbous, bringing to life Chilean poet Pablo Neruda's poem 'A Lemon'.

The jug of lemonade is cold when my father drops by on his way to run errands. I carry it and two glasses to the table. The lemonade is the shade of flaxen storm clouds. It's sweet, yet with an aftertaste tart enough to raise the brows and cause a grimace.

He stares as I pour. 'Where did you get that glass from?'

'Nanna.'

He gulps down the lemonade without comment, the fluted glass changing from cloudy to clear. I watch him turn the empty glass in his hands as though it is a rare archaeological find. A trickle of lemonade left in it spills on the tablecloth.

Bemused, I say, 'I only have two or three but take one, if you like.'

'No, no, that's fine.' He puts the glass down, though his gaze stays connected to it. 'I just didn't realise there were still some around. These glasses are from the shop.' He always refers to his parents' milk bar and fruit shop as 'the shop' — they all did. 'They're what we used to serve the orange drink in.'

'Are they really?' Thrilled, I pick mine up. The glass is thick, heavily fluted, more than sixty years old. I later get my old school ruler and measure the glass to be fourteen centimetres tall, six and a half across at the rim and five at the base. Shaped like a tapering blunt-ended zeppelin, it is small compared to the wastebasket-sized plastic cups some drinks are served in these days, and yet large enough to quench a thirst on a humid Brisbane day. The glass feels sturdy in my palm, the brim wide and smooth between my lips, like a fragment buffed by sea and sand.

'What was it like, working in the shop?'

My father stands up. 'The whole time I was growing up, Dad only closed the shop for a few days over Easter and Christmas. He opened from seven in the morning until ten or eleven at night. I was sometimes alone in the shop serving and taking orders from suppliers when I was just nine or ten. All those years of unpaid work …'

While I've heard this before, it jars with what I know of my father's usual character — generous with his time, a volunteer — making me suspect there must be something else behind his reaction. He is already at the front door; I'm trailing behind. I wave him off as he hoons away. Through the rear windscreen I see the silhouette of his balding head behind the wheel; it's similar to how his father looked as I'd watch him drive off, except Nonno Anni clung to the custom of wearing a hat — a holdover from the earlier decades of his life when that was the norm for men.

I've become used to my father's 'flight' option when faced with something he prefers not to discuss. It occurs to me I feel different in that I want to talk, to find out more about the past, particularly since my mother died. But I respect that at present he doesn't feel the same. I will bide my time and hope that some day Dad will be willing to talk to me about the fruit-shop and milk-bar days. While I've spoken to Nanna Francesca and Nonno Anni at length, there are always more sides to a story. I appreciate that the experiences of first-generation descendants of migrants — those born first in the 'new' country — can be quite different from those of the original migrants or the second- and third-generation descendants.

With care, I wash the milk-bar glasses. After drying the last one, I hold it up near the kitchen window, the fluted body picking up sunlight. Minuscule snowflakes of wear in the glass attest to its once having a life of being banged down on my grandparents' milk-bar counter, then whisked away and hand-washed for the next surge of customers. It may look like an unassuming 1950s glass, but for me it is suddenly infinitely more precious.

I drag a wooden chair over to the kitchen cupboard with roses of leadlight glass in the doors. Standing on the chair, I transfer the three glasses to the top shelf, almost out of reach. Somewhere they can be seen, but also saved … 'for good'.

On serene nocturne chords,
our forebears weave
into our dreams.
Invoking, entwining
yarns and threads,
of their lives, of our lives
part of us, we part of them.
And we awaken
knowing they made us,
wanting to know more
of what we are made of.

Nanna Francesca scoops chocolate and vanilla from the tub of Neapolitan ice cream into a small bowl for me, adding strawberry as well to her own bowl. Nonno Anni rarely has sweets for dessert; the long green skin of a Granny Smith and its core are left on his plate with a paring knife. He favours fruit after dinner, a habit stemming from the fruit-shop part of their business, while Nanna Francesca kept up the habit of ice cream or chocolates from the milk-bar side.

'You want me to hang it here?' Nonno Anni brandishes a hammer.

Nanna Francesca hurries the ice-cream lid back on. '*Aspetta.*' He waits and we hear the freezer door slam in the kitchen. 'Hold it up again.'

I slowly eat my ice cream, aware of Nanna Francesca's bowl of Neapolitan melting into swirls of pink, white and dark-brown as my grandparents quibble over the exact height at which to hang a large new picture. Nonno Anni bangs in a four-inch nail that goes through the white high-gloss painted fibro to the tongue-and-groove boards behind, making the whole house shudder. Nanna Francesca purses her lips and murmurs something in

Italian as he hangs the picture a teeny bit crooked. Then she remembers her ice cream and sits beside me, both of us looking up at the painting.

For years, the main picture on my grandparents' lounge-room wall above the Rank Arena television set on wooden legs has been a print of a snowy village scene of chalets and firs blanketed in white that could have been anywhere it snowed in Europe. It has hung there my entire life, as much a part of my grandparents' lounge room as the 1930s art deco clock, and somewhat comforting.

During the 1970s when I stayed over, Nanna Francesca and I would sit together, sometimes with a small tin of Quality Street chocolates between us, on the two-seater vinyl lounge. Her hand-sewn floral slip covers went skew-whiff as we sat for hours watching films like *The King and I*, *The Ten Commandments*, *The Sound of Music* — whatever Saturday-night epic was on television. Usually Nonno Anni was slumped in his armchair, TV screen reflected in his glasses, an occasional robust snore waking him before he dozed off again.

Sometimes my gaze strayed from the television set to the snowy village scene hanging above it, knowing it was there to remind Nonno Anni of Fossa, even though it looked more like where Heidi's grandfather might have lived in the Swiss Alps. Now, there is another picture on the wall — again a generic painted scene, but this one reminiscent of the Amalfi Coast, to remind Nanna Francesca of Palmi on Calabria's coastline. It's been purchased years after the snowy village, but it is bigger.

I see Nanna Francesca looking at it instead of the television and, possibly sensing my regard, she looks at me and we smile together. Having grown up on the Queensland coast, I can relate to her Italian seaside scene, though I have never left Australia. I am close to twelve and cannot remember the only instance I saw snow, at Mount Buller in Victoria when I was around two.

'Have I told you about the place where I grew up?' Nanna Francesca leans in, speaking low, so as not to wake Nonno Anni. I glimpse tears in the corners of her dark, almond-shaped eyes. 'I was happy. So happy.'

Palm Trees and *Fico d'India*

The house perched high on one of the cliffs of Calabria overlooking the Tyrrhenian Sea, the balcony affording a view up the Strait of Messina to Sicily where a lazy curl of smoky cloud hovered about Mount Etna. Francesca's tiny hands gripped the vertical railings on the back balcony of her grandmother's house, her face half-pushed through them to see the water, the metallic smell of the balustrade in her nostrils.

She loved watching the tall masts of the swordfishermen's vessels, the trade boats and the ferries chugging across to Messina port where her father, Domenico Solano, had left on the 'big boat', the ship *Caprera*, to go to Australia in June 1927. The wakes of the boats made patterns on the flat sea in the same way as when Francesca pushed her finger along her grandmother's tablecloth, pulling and scrunching a little at the material as her fingertip moved.

Palmi, the town of palm trees and *fico d'India* where she was born, sat on the Costa Viola, known as the violet coast for its lavender skies melding into a gentle indigo sea. Francesca had been barely sixteen months old when her father departed for Australia, leaving her and her mother — also Francesca — in Palmi.

Francesca senior had tried to avoid sharing her name with her daughter, a quirk brought about by following the Italian custom of naming a first-born girl after the paternal grandmother. Domenico was insistent they follow tradition and name their daughter for his mother, Francesca Rizzitano, but Francesca argued for her own mother's name, Soccorsa Misale. The debate raged for a week. Apparently, it was one of the very rare times Mico, usually a quiet man, raised his voice. The registering of the birth was delayed a week, the recorded birth date reflecting this, but the name was Francesca.

After Mico left for Australia, little Francesca and her mother — known as Cesca now to avoid confusion — moved in with maternal grandmother Soccorsa. Francesca's nonna had *il forno*, a wood-fired oven underneath the house, and was the baker for the surrounding houses. Francesca grew up inhaling the aroma of baking bread, often sitting out of the way in a corner to watch the women arrive with their dough on wooden trays or in baskets. Each smooth mound was marked with an initial or had a symbol cut into it to identify to whom it belonged. Francesca felt something — too little then to recognise it as pride — watching her grandmother wield a wooden paddle, hearing the smooth scrape as she took cooked bread from the oven. Her nonna's hands were sure and dusty with flour as she lined up loaves with crusts of crisp tawny gold on the table.

Cesca started Francesca at school early, just as she was turning four. Being the eldest of many siblings, Cesca hadn't been able to go to school and didn't want the same for her daughter. Not having learnt to read or write, she was frightened of being unable to keep in contact with her mother once she and Francesca joined Mico in Australia. Therefore, on top of Francesca's regular schooling, Cesca sent her to a retired schoolteacher for extra lessons.

'You need to read and write Italian so when we go to Australia you can write to Nonna for me,' she told her daughter.

'Okay, *va bene*, Mamma.' It was a fifteen-minute walk from the house to her school and Francesca carried a little port each day, her hair tied with ribbons and her shoes buckled up over white ankle socks that she took care not to get dusty. A torn crust, still warm, sprinkled with olive oil was handed to her for *merenda* when she got home each afternoon.

The wood oven made the house suffocatingly hot in the long summer months of the far south. Some evenings the three of them sat on the balcony overlooking the sea, shelling peas and feeling the breeze as lightning licked the horizon. In winter, the bakery room made the house cosy. A photograph sat on the sideboard: Mico in his navy uniform, cigarette in hand, still and silent, yet animated by the reflection of lambent firelight as the three females hand-sewed through the evening.

The three generations lived well together and Francesca felt loved and protected by her mother and her grandmother — robust maternal figures with well-endowed bosoms that made a soft, comforting pillow for her cheek when they took her in their arms for a cuddle. The two women filled the fissure left by the father she hadn't been old enough to remember and knew mainly from his solemn-faced photograph.

Mico stared across the paddock of immature apple and pear trees, over the pale soil to the boundary of his farm where thick scrub and trees formed a natural fence beyond the wire one. He'd cleared the paddock of the same vegetation, by hand, by himself, the scars of blisters still whitish on his palms. In the distance, beyond the tree line and the town of Stanthorpe that lay out of sight, flowed a series of low, humpy mountains, a much darker blue than the sky. It was a beautiful day and the farm was finally becoming the orchard Mico had envisioned throughout his years up in northern Queensland working as a cane-gang cook.

His leather work boots scrunched on gravel as he slowly swivelled to where the wooden house had stood, now an ash-blackened rectangle, burnt into the ground, the stove standing heroically among a few charred planks of timber and heat-twisted corrugated iron. Mico's guitar case and half-open port stuffed with all he'd had time to save sat not far away on a patch of grass.

'What are you going to do?' Tino, whose own farm was nearby, patted his friend's shoulder.

Mico dug into his pocket for his pouch of tobacco. 'Build another.'

Cesca became anxious as each year folded into the next. Mico wrote to say he had barely enough to keep the farm at Applethorpe going, let alone afford passages to Australia for her and Francesca. 'When are we going to Australia? Never,' Cesca lamented to her mother after Francesca was in bed and listening from under the covers in her corner of the room.

'*Piano, piano,*' — slowly, gently. Soccorsa knew her daughter must join her husband but she cherished having Cesca and granddaughter in her house, knowing once they left she would never see them again. 'I will pay you to work here.'

Cesca worked *il forno* with her mother and saved her money, determined to join Mico in Australia. She wanted to have more children and, at twenty-seven, decided she couldn't wait much longer. Seeing Cesca's resolve and knowing she would never be able to save enough, Soccorsa offered to pay the fares for her daughter and granddaughter to sail to the other side of the world and out of her life forever. A grateful Cesca at once got Francesca to write a letter to Mico, saying, *I've got the money. Send me the authorisation papers and we will come.*

Before Cesca and Francesca left Palmi, Soccorsa gave her daughter the studio photograph of the three of them taken the year before in the autumn of 1933. Soccorsa sat white-haired and sober-faced in the portrait, her dress snug around her middle, her purse between two work-worn hands more used to holding a wooden ladle or oven paddle. She wore the same dress, saved for church or 'special', to see Cesca and Francesca off at Palmi's train station. Watching her daughter and granddaughter board the train, for their sake Soccorsa was stoic, but her face puffed and strained with the effort of holding in her emotions. She collapsed after the train pulled away.

At Naples, Cesca and Francesca boarded the passenger ship *Romolo*. It was 1934, five years almost to the day before Annibale would board its sister ship *Remo* from the same dock. Cesca's single-minded determination to look to the future got her and her daughter through the emotional departure from Italy. Francesca was never sure if her mother wanted to leave Palmi or if she just wanted to be with Mico and made the sacrifice to go, but it taught her much about a woman's duty to her husband, a duty she knew she would one day assume.

They travelled the two-month voyage with one of Mico's cousins and her two-year-old boy, the four of them happy to have a cabin to themselves. The women enjoyed not having to cook, and the novelty of going to the ship's dining room, with good food laid out for them, was something that never wore off. Apart from washing their intimate garments in the little basin in their cabin, for the first time since she was six Cesca didn't have to work. It was to be the only vacation of her life. She chatted with the other women, and she and Francesca joined in organised games on the open deck, the two of them always close.

Standing on deck holding the railing, looking out over empty ocean to the seeming faint rise and fall of the horizon with the ship's movement, Cesca said to her daughter, 'We belong to the sea. That's why we're not seasick like some others. Smell that sea air. Doesn't it smell like being in Palmi?' It was the only time she alluded to what they'd left behind.

When the *Romolo* glided into Australian waters, Francesca was shocked to see the roiling grey ocean and a stark horizon below pale skies, comparing it with the mauve sky melding into a gentle indigo sea she'd been accustomed to in Palmi. The boat docked in Fremantle, then Melbourne and finally Sydney, where Mico was waiting. As they disembarked, Cesca suddenly became anxious to see him.

'There he is!' Cesca strained forward, clutching her daughter's hand, then letting go to embrace her husband. Mico almost lost his hat. After a moment, they stood back from each other and Cesca looked down at Francesca. 'This is your papà.' Her eyes were shining.

Having no memory of Mico, Francesca, now eight, felt like she was meeting her father for the first time. Her only connection had been hearing someone read aloud his letters to Cesca and later reading them to her mother herself. (It was only when she got older that Francesca realised her mother had cunningly made sure they didn't leave Palmi until Francesca had reached a certain competence in reading and writing Italian.)

Francesca felt her hands grow moist. 'Yes. *Va bene*, Ma.'

Mico came down to Francesca's height and gave her two kisses and a hurried cuddle. It would take time for them to become used to each other.

On Monte Circolo

The house where Annibale and his mother, Maddalena, lived stood opposite the church on a crooked lane in Fossa, their village overlooking the Aterno Valley, rimmed by the Apennines. Gran Sasso, the highest peak, emerged in the distance as Annibale gripped the copper drainpipe outside the school window he'd just climbed through, his boots making a crunching thud as he landed on the gravelly ground below. He motioned for his friend Luigi to follow, beaming at having outwitted their teacher who, as punishment for them distracting other children in class, had locked them in the classroom while everyone else went home for lunch.

Annibale was five years old when he started school in the autumn of 1929. Fossa had one schoolteacher, a bespectacled *signorina* who, upon discovering Annibale was left-handed, grabbed his left arm and tied it behind his back with a length of rope. 'You'll soon learn to do everything with your right hand.' She sounded kindly but her expression was cold. 'We can't have a disciple of the devil among us. Remember …' Her voice rang off like a warning and she pointed to one of two posters on the classroom wall: Mussolini's head, his eyes two black stones, a banner shouting *The eyes of* il Duce *are on every one of you!* Annibale's gaze slid to the other poster, which proclaimed *Mussolini is always right!*

Mussolini had come to power in 1922, a year before Annibale was born. The young boy had heard many grownups in the village speak of il Duce as an impressive ruler destined to make Italy a great and powerful nation as it was in Roman times, and providing a better life for everyone, so he also believed it. Each student had two notebooks, one for penmanship, the other for arithmetic, both covered in Fascist cant and cartoons, including a picture of a boy about Annibale's age with cropped hair — of a colour much fairer than any village boy's —

wearing a Fascist Youth uniform and backpack, and holding a small rifle fixed with a bayonet.

The government had rewritten all school textbooks with a Fascist bias. In storybooks, a character called Mussolini replaced popular heroes. Maths exercises started with sentences like, 'If Mussolini's house measured …', and for spelling bees, the teacher followed the curriculum, using words associated with fighting and crushing opposition, something many in the schoolyard, including Annibale and Luigi, took to heart with a philosophy of 'fists first, questions later'.

Annibale had no memory of his father. By the time the Great Depression hit Australia, Vitale had been working there for almost six years. He wrote to Maddalena saying it was impossible for him to bring her and Annibale out to join him, and that he was instead saving for his passage back to Italy. Even as a boy, Annibale detected that his mother's elation upon reading the letter was tinged with worry for their situation.

During the years Vitale was in Australia, Maddalena was raising not only Annibale, but crops of sugar beet and wheat in their field, as well as the piglet that she would slaughter in autumn to keep her and Annibale fed over the winter. She took their harvests to the grain mill, tended the grapevines, fetched water, did their washing in the stream down in the valley, cooked, chopped the firewood, kept up the household chores and roamed the mountainside collecting herbs in her upturned apron for concocting into her homemade remedies.

Each year as Annibale got bigger, he could help more, feeding the chickens, the pig and their donkey, weeding the poppies from among their crops, sometimes collecting and chopping the firewood. He tried to be good for his mother's sake, but often found himself in situations — shinning down the drainpipe and skipping school or stealing roasted chestnuts that burnt holes in his pockets. And then there was the drinking of the blessed wine …

Winter blasted the landscape. Early in the morning the flames in the fireplace were low and the cold pervaded the stone house. Annibale buried himself deeper in his blankets as Maddalena gently prodded him. With a great show of reluctance he got up. Rising in the dark to serve as an altar boy at early-morning Mass he felt was beyond the call of duty. He dressed hastily and washed his face. Maddalena pulled aside the blanket nailed over the front door to help keep the cold out and reached for the latch. She opened the door, hustling Annibale out, and quickly closed it again.

The frigid air smacked Annibale, chilling him to the bone. It was so cold it almost hurt to inhale, and he scurried through the snow, grateful it had formed a hard crust. He passed the stone inscription near the church reminding the villagers that snow had fallen unseasonably late between the seventeenth and twentieth of April in 1505. Winter's brittle hands could claw into these mountains and sometimes it was not until the sun gained enough strength in late spring that it gave up its hold.

In his haste to get out of the cold, Annibale banged the heavy church door behind him. A thunderous echo clapped throughout the stone building. Don Angelo looked up from the altar. 'Ah, Annibale, I think you have woken the whole village. We might have a bigger than usual turnout this morning.'

Annibale said nothing. Only a handful of villagers attended early-morning Mass, usually the old nonni, widows destined to dress in black from head to toe for the remainder of their time on earth. Their backs were bent from years of toil, wizened faces blank as thin lips swiftly mouthed a succession of Hail Marys and gnarled fingers worked well-worn rosary beads. Annibale steered clear of them after several had overzealously pinched his cheeks.

'Come now, no time for daydreaming.' Don Angelo beckoned Annibale to join him behind the altar. 'I need to show you what to do.'

Inside, the church was almost as cold as outside. Annibale's fingers were numb and clumsy. The brief walk through the snow would leave him cold and damp for the entire Mass. *Porca miseria, I'll have to come up with something good to get out of this*, he thought.

Don Angelo took out a key and opened a small cabinet. 'Annibale, this is where the blessed wine is kept.'

'Don Angelo said I won't be serving from tomorrow,' Annibale announced to his mother when he came back for breakfast on the third morning.

Maddalena frowned. 'Why not?'

'It's another boy's turn now.'

She watched Annibale continue to eat then took her dish over to the sink. Through the kitchen window she glimpsed Don Angelo leaving the church. Without a word Maddalena grabbed an extra shawl and hurried outside.

'*Scusi*, Don Angelo, won't you be calling on Annibale to be an altar boy any more?'

He paused. 'No.' Then continued walking.

She stumbled in the snow after him. 'It's just I know it would mean a lot to Vitale, and if Annibale could—'

'Signora Boccabella.' Don Angelo stopped and drew his cloak more firmly around him, seeming to rise in stature. 'Your son likes the wine too much.'

Mortified, Maddalena bent her head and darted home.

Annibale yowled when she gave him a whipping, but the following icy morning as he burrowed under his blankets instead of serving at Mass, he felt the belting had been worth it.

Annibale and Luigi shimmied down the drainpipe near the window of their school classroom then ran across the hillside to the vineyards, basking in the warm sun and laughing with the feeling of freedom. They played amongst the vines and when they heard their schoolteacher swinging the handbell for school to resume, they hid in an old stone hut. The church bells eventually tolled for the end of the day and Annibale and Luigi saw in the distance the other children trickling out of school. They made their way back up the mountainside to their homes, a little apprehensive at what they had done but also thrilled they had got away with it.

Maddalena was in the kitchen cutting up mushrooms when Annibale arrived home. He greeted her with a big grin. She smiled back. 'How was school, Annibale?'

'Ah, the usual.'

Still smiling, Maddalena walked over to the front door and locked it. Annibale gave a start. The door was seldom if ever locked. He made a move to run but she pre-empted him.

Maddalena grabbed the nearest thing to her, the broom, and chased him around the table. 'Where have you been?' she demanded, taking a swipe at him as he ducked out of her reach and ran around the other side of the table. '*Scamp!* Tell me where you've been.' Another jab of the broom. 'You think I like having that high and mighty teacher on my doorstep telling me my son's no good?'

With the door locked, Annibale had nowhere much to run to in the tiny house so he headed for his bed and scrambled underneath. Maddalena swooped, poking the broom in after him. Squashed up against the wall he avoided the violent thrusts but yelled out in pretend pain so his mother would think she'd punished him. Then Maddalena left the room and returned with some rope, brandishing it like a whip into the space between the bed and the floor. Grabbing the end of the rope, Annibale yanked it. Instantly his mother lost balance, falling hard on the stone floor. She let fly a string of curses then picked herself up and rubbed her hip. Kicking one of the bed legs in frustration, she went back to the kitchen, unlocked the front door and began cooking.

Annibale did not move. He listened to his mother clattering about in the kitchen. Soon the aroma of frying mushrooms wafted under the bed, teasing his nostrils. Not having eaten since that morning, his stomach was staging a vociferous demonstration. He wriggled across the floor on his back and out from under the bed, trotting out to his mother with a faltering smile.

Maddalena, her hip still throbbing, smiled back. 'No supper for you tonight.'

'*Porca miseria.*' He kicked the leg of the table.

'And I'll have none of that or you won't go to *She-Wolf* on Saturday either.'

Annibale looked alarmed. Along with Luigi and the other village boys of his age, Annibale was in the younger division of the Fascist Youth organisation, Sons of a She-Wolf. He loved attending the weekly meetings and had learnt by heart most of the Fascist songs.

'You can't stop me, Mamma, or il Duce will be mad at you!'

Maddalena rapped her knuckles on her own head and pointed to him.

With no doctor nearby, different villagers came to the doorstep seeking Maddalena's remedies, some travelling by foot from hamlets on other mountainsides and along the valley canals that older folk spoke of as once being a wending river. Annibale would sometimes watch curiously as his mother cooked up an acrid-smelling sludgy remedy and applied it to a person's boil with a poultice, or treated an obstruction in someone's ear with a warm tincture of wine in which she'd steeped green cannabis seeds. There was no dentist in Fossa either, and with toothaches and cavities common, she burnt dried hashish, yielded from her hemp plants, in a wide cup designed so that the sufferer could inhale the smoke for pain relief, enabling the extraction of a rotten tooth.

Annibale, meant to be doing his homework in the other room, watched through the crack between the not-quite-closed door and the doorframe as his mother removed the *malocchio* or 'evil eye' curse from a woman. Placing a pitcher of water, a saucer and an oil lamp on the kitchen table, Maddelena poured water into the saucer then took some olive oil from the lamp to drop into the water. Annibale listened as Maddalena spoke of oil staying in one droplet in the water or scattering into many droplets to disperse the *malocchio*, but he soon got lost and didn't understand what it meant.

'It's scattered,' Maddalena said with satisfaction. 'The curse is gone.'

The woman sighed in relief and Maddalena glared at the doorframe, making Annibale shrink back. She smiled at the woman, who was much happier now.

'I was a little afraid to come here,' the woman confided. 'I've never been to a village witch before.'

'Is that so?' Maddalena's eyes danced.

The minute the woman was gone, Annibale tumbled out of the bedroom. 'Mamma, is it true? Are you the village witch?'

'It's an honour, *caro*. Means my remedies are working.' She ruffled his hair. '*Santa Maria*, look at your ears.' Moistening a corner of her apron in her mouth, she tried to clean his ears as he hollered and squirmed. 'You finished your homework?'

When Demetrio returned from Sicily, Annibale stared, amazed that this giant man, stooping to come inside, was his grandfather. Demetrio smiled, putting out his big paw, and Annibale, with a grin that matched his large ears, shook it.

Demetrio was seven feet tall; Maddalena, four-foot-eleven. Together they told Annibale about the time Maddalena broke a stool over Demetrio's head for drinking all their wine stored in the cantina during the early months after she and Vitale had married. 'I thought I'd killed him!' she wheezed as she and Demetrio laughed so much their eyes were wet. 'No wonder I went to Sicily!' he added, sending them off into another round of laughter.

Annibale discovered his grandfather had many stories. He spoke of Garibaldi's men storming the Castle Ocre on the crag above Fossa, the chestnut harvest, bandits on lonely Abruzzo roads, how to maintain their farm tools, the earthquake of 1915 that crumbled the front of their house and the way the valley could flood, which was why the elders shook their heads at the younger folk starting to build houses down there. Over time, Annibale heard other stories, too, of Demetrio getting into a fight with the *commune* (council) which wanted to demolish his house after the 1915 quake, and of Demetrio picking up two men, one in each hand, and slamming them together; but these came from the lips of other villagers and he wasn't quite sure if they were fable.

During the long winter months, wind and snow buffeted the mountains, and sometimes they had to dig their way out of the house when a heavy snowfall piled up against the front door overnight. Annibale felt loved and protected by his mother and his grandfather — three generations living together in the small village in a stone house that had belonged to the family for centuries. He didn't miss the father of whom he had no memory, the father who was on a ship getting closer to Italy.

Early in 1930, when the snow had melted, Vitale carried a small, battered suitcase up the crooked lane to their front door. Annibale watched his parents embrace for a long while in the open doorway, thinking how his mother always yelled at him if he left the door open too long in cold weather and allowed the heat from the fire to escape the house. He saw his father's brows rise upon seeing the baby son he'd left was now a boy who'd evidently inherited Demetrio's height, something not passed on to Vitale. Awkwardly, Vitale patted Annibale's back — a little too vigorously — and turned to his father.

For Annibale, it was hard having his father back with them. The six-year-old found himself resenting him because everything seemed to change. His mother's stomach swelled as she grew a baby. And Demetrio, now eighty-two, began to get weaker. At the height of summer, he died. Maddalena flung the customary basin of water on the stoop for their tears. And while Vitale spoke to the coffin-builder about making a casket longer than seven feet, Maddalena sewed a shroud by hand. Annibale did as he was told and went to the *stalla* to feed the animals. He wept when no one was watching, his face buried in Gina's fur as the little donkey flicked her ears and regarded him with sombre eyes.

For weeks, villagers crossed the threshold to offer condolences for Demetrio and hear Vitale talk about what it was like in Australia, where many of their loved ones were. Maddalena moved about pouring wine and feeding everyone gathered around the table. On plates, scoopfuls of polenta shone bright yellow, soaking up rich *ragù* flecked with handfuls of the dried red chilli peppers they called *il diavolicchio*, 'the little devils'. She stayed near the fire, while their neighbours, mainly women whose husbands were abroad, hung onto Vitale's every word, his recollections of Melbourne and the Victorian countryside providing a tenuous link with their men.

'My husband is in Fremantle, did you see him?'

'Were you near Ingham? My husband is doing well there.' Giovanna dominated the conversation. 'Vitale, did you see my Stefano?'

'It's a Depression over there right now. All I could do was harvest potatoes. I was getting sixpence a bag. The lack of work is worse than here.' His lament tactlessly shattered some of their illusions.

Giovanna wouldn't be put off. 'That's not true. My Stefano is making good money cutting cane at Ingham. You go back there and you'll make a lot of money.'

'Yeah?' Vitale's gaze lifted to above her head where Maddalena stood behind her, holding a heavy copper skillet. Giovanna turned and Maddalena smiled. 'More polenta, Gia?'

The baby was to be born in February 1931, the impending birth and another mouth to feed sealing Vitale's destiny to return to Australia. Even with the little money that Demetrio had left them it would take another year to save his passage back. Once there, he would cut cane this time and send back whatever money he could to help keep his family fed while saving for their passages to Australia, a mission both he and Maddalena knew would take many years.

When Maddalena went into labour, Vitale and Annibale vacated the house, the midwife firmly shutting the door behind them. Father and son sat in the stable with the warmth of the animals. Watching Annibale set about eating his bread and salami with a will, Vitale felt a twinge. 'When I go back to Australia, it will be up to you to look after your mother and little brother or sister while I'm gone.'

'Okay, Papà.' The seven-year-old kept chewing.

He touched the top of Annibale's woollen cap. 'And one day you will come out to Australia, too.'

'On a big boat like you, Papà?'

'Yes, on a big boat. When you're older.' Vitale blinked swiftly several times.

Eggs in Purgatory

Morning sun streams through the casement windows, the small squares of etched lilac glass making patterns on the silky-oak dining table. I'm prone to getting up early, even when I stay awake until late. Dad gets up early too and, as has become our custom on Sundays, we set up the Junior Scrabble board on the dining table. Already, the box is showing signs of wear since I received it for my seventh birthday only a few months before. Dad reads the newspaper in between goes, and when he leaves the room to put the kettle on in the kitchen, I take a surreptitious peek at the downturned letters.

While Dad gets out the carton of eggs to make breakfast, I carry a wobbly cup of tea along the hallway to the front room of our workers' cottage, my dressing-gown belt trailing behind. Mum, pregnant with my sister, sits propped up in bed reading another part of the newspaper. She takes the cup and smiles, pours without fuss some spilt tea from the saucer back into the cup, dripping a little on the paper. An aroma of simmering leftover tomato sauce from last night's pasta curls down the hallway, luring me back to the kitchen. I arrive in time to see Dad leaning over a broad pan cracking eggs into wells he has made in the sauce.

In Italy, this dish has the name 'eggs in purgatory', the eggs being the souls caught between the tomatoes — purgatory — and trying to escape to heaven. I grew up knowing it by the somewhat less evocative name, 'eggs in tomato'. My father always made it with leftover pasta sauce, his mantra never to throw out leftovers, and over the years he has served it at breakfast, lunch and dinner. As I grew up, it didn't occur to me to ask about the origins of the 'eggs in tomato' into which we dipped crunchy bread. Decades later, when I mention to Dad that I discovered it also goes by the name 'eggs in purgatory', he, too, registers surprise.

'I'm guessing Granny showed you how to make it?' I say.

His face lights up at the mention of his paternal grandmother, Maddalena, who was like a second mother to him, with his parents busy running their fruit shop and milk bar. 'She did.'

I think back to a time I saw Great-Granny Maddalena cooking it at her house in Sargent Street, near the New Farm reach of the Brisbane River. Memory has a way of playing tricks but I believe it was around midday on her eighty-sixth birthday. The extended family were all to gather at the house that evening. Dad was dropping some things off for the party and I came along for the car ride, as kids do. We always entered Granny and Bisnonno Vitale's house by the back stairs, never the front. The back door opened straight into the kitchen and they mostly left it open.

Bisnonno Vitale sits at the 1950s metal-legged kitchen table, his walking stick leaning against his leg, his back stooped from years of cutting cane, farm work and labouring jobs. Granny Maddalena is at the stove, which fits into a corrugated-iron nook fixed onto the back of their timber house. Dad speaks only in Italian to his grandparents and translates to me that they've asked me how school is. Shyly, I say it is good. Granny takes my cheeks in her hands, which are like smooth, softened leather, murmurs something in Italian, and then leaves a moist kiss on my forehead. I continue to feel it as it dries, and I itch to wipe the spot but don't so as not to hurt her feelings.

She goes back to the stove where her eggs in purgatory bubble in a pan. Granny Maddalena always wears an apron over her dress, and stockings and shoes, even when she is at home all day, or digging in her broad vegetable patch in the backyard. Her hair remains long and she twists and pins it up above the nape of her neck in an old European folk-style I've not seen since. She always seems to have berry-brown skin, even in winter. At the time, I have no idea she was the village witch back in Italy.

After a swift exchange of Italian between Dad and Granny and I find myself sitting at the table opposite Nonno, both of us with forks in one hand, bread in the other, bowls of baked eggs in steaming tomato sauce before us. In the other room, under Granny's animated instruction, Dad shifts furniture, setting up for the party. The sauce of rich, intense tomato, velvet with olive oil, tastes almost sweet before savoury nuances take over. Bisnonno Vitale grunts, eyes me, slurps a mouthful. His glasses seem to distort and enlarge his eyes. I look down and break the yoke with my crust.

'*E buona?*' His question brings my gaze back up.

'*Sì*, Nonno. It's good.'

He smiles, coaxing one from me, too. Dad returns and wolfs the rest of my helping.

That night, about twenty of us noisily crowd the linoleum-floored lounge and dining room for dinner and, afterwards, birthday cake. I wear a party dress with a black cat brooch pinned to the front. Nanna Francesca carries out a platter of homemade biscuits arranged on paper doilies. Nonno Anni shakes his head at his brother, Elia, as they sit in conversation. Behind them, the wooden sash window is fully open on this warm March night. My uncle plays the piano accordion, injecting even more energy into the rowdy group. I wish he would go on playing all night. Nanna Francesca is beaming. Granny furtively presses two crisp green two-dollar notes into my hand. Bisnonno Vitale has another glass of champagne with the liqueur-soaked sponge cake, then gets up and walks without his walking stick.

By the time of the party, Granny's eggs in purgatory that I'd eaten at lunchtime would have been far from my mind. And yet, more than three decades later, the memory resurfaces and for a few moments brings back to life people dear to me, long gone. Perhaps it's true that, in a humble way, people live on when others cook the dishes they cooked. I think of Great-Granny Maddalena's frittata and, on my mother's Australian side of the family, of Great-Grandma Charlotte's scones that won second prize at the 1927 Ipswich Show — recipes cherished not only for what they create, but also for what they reveal of my great-grandmothers' everyday lives.

I watch Dad now, close to seventy, standing at his kitchen table holding one of Granny's cream bowls on a slight tilt, fork in hand, whisking eggs. And I recognise the same action I've watched Granny use in preparing her frittata, and Nanna Francesca when she'd mix eggs in which to dip pieces of meat before crumbing them.

He looks up, the stirring scratch of the metal fork on the ceramic bowl slowing. 'What made you find out about the eggs in tomato?' Dad, who mostly lives in the moment, is giving me a look conveying that sometimes we can be plains apart in our ways of thinking.

'I was recalling those Sunday mornings of Scrabble at Red Hill.'

His face splits into a smile. 'They were lovely, weren't they?' But deep in his eyes, behind the smile, there is sadness, reflecting the often rocky times, illness and loss that have touched the family in intervening years.

I give him a playful push. He lightly punches me on the arm. His eyes are now smiling as he resumes whisking the eggs. 'And by the way, I knew you were sneaking a look at those Scrabble letters.'

Sons of the She-Wolf

By the time Annibale turned thirteen, it was evident he had inherited some of his grandfather's height, though he'd never be so tall as to have to stoop to pass through the front entrance as Demetrio had done. Annibale retrieved his cap from its hook in the kitchen, pulled it on down around his ears and shut the door behind him. The door scraped and he made a mental note to tighten the hinges when he got home, having forgotten the day before. He went to the stable to feed Gina and get his tools.

'*Buongiorno.*' Luigi was passing by the bottom lane.

Like their fathers, grandfathers and great-grandfathers before them, the friends fell into step, heading from the village down towards the valley farmland. As they chatted, Annibale kept glancing up to a ridge on the other side of the valley, watching for the rising sun. Luigi appeared oblivious, yet Annibale watched for it every morning. It seemed to take an eternity, then suddenly the sun slipped over the far mountain peaks, saturating the valley in light. He raised his face to it. Upon reaching the flat road below the village, they parted ways towards their own fields. Annibale laid his bottle of wine on the bed of a shallow stream at the end of his field so it would be cool to quench his thirst later on, then got to work.

Neither he nor Maddalena had had any qualms about him leaving school when he was eleven to work their field. Many other boys his age, including Luigi, did the same, proud to contribute to their families' meagre earnings. Annibale spent most of his waking hours doing manual work — clearing, planting, weeding, reaping wheat with his sickle, taking grain to the mill, pruning, picking grapes, growing and harvesting sugar beet, tending the coppice of almond trees, repairing and making tools — the never-ending cycle of working on the land. He was looking forward to joining the village men for his first overnight chestnut harvest that autumn up near the 'great stone of Italy', Gran Sasso, pinnacle of the Apennines. While the slopes where the chestnut trees grew were mostly verdant, one side of the highest peak, Corno Grande, was partly covered by the Calderone glacier.

Sunday was the only day he didn't work; however, Annibale often chose to muck out the stable to avoid church. Maddalena never chided him for sometimes missing Mass, though she attended every Sunday, sitting in her usual pew. Don Angelo remained the parish priest and Maddalena was mindful of bowing her head along with the rest of the congregation when he dedicated the Mass to a certain villager. Vitale's aunt wasn't the only one in the village who had left an estate to the Catholic Church in exchange for the priest dedicating a monthly Mass, but hers was the house in which Don Angelo chose to live.

Maddalena wondered if Don Angelo would continue encouraging elderly villagers to bequeath to the Church their property until he could dedicate a Mass each day of the month. For more than a decade she'd kept her resentment carefully concealed, particularly with both her sons now attending the weekly Fascist assemblies led by Don Angelo's brother. Annibale knew Don Angelo lived in their aunt's house but he'd never been told nor suspected the house could have been his.

That night, after he had tightened the door hinges and eaten supper, Annibale went to bed early. He fell asleep quickly, lying on his back. Hearing his soft snores, Maddalena marvelled that they were pitched at the same note as both Vitale's and Demetrio's.

Tucking Elia into bed, she whispered, 'Be careful not to wake Annibale.'

'Yes, Mamma.'

Maddalena gazed upon her younger boy. Elia's ears stuck out and his eyebrows sloped down at the outer edges on the same downward angle as the corners of his thin lips. He was five, and each year he grew was a reminder of how long Vitale had been gone this time. Elia closed his eyes, holding in his hand, under the blanket, a pin he'd pilfered from Maddalena's sewing basket.

In the kitchen, Maddalena sat down facing the fire and picked up her hemming. The fire was only small, set from fallen branches and twigs collected on *commune* land, the common wooded area belonging to the village as a whole. Since the Middle Ages, villagers had been permitted to collect dead wood for their fires from the locale as long as no more than a *fascio di legna,* or 'bundle of sticks', considered enough to cook with, was taken per day.

It was against the law to cut down trees for firewood. People had felled so many in the past, the surrounding hills were almost bare. Even the coveted beech trees had become scarce, now mainly growing in the Abruzzo National Park, an area reserved the year Annibale was born. Beech wood had been excellent firewood, easily split, and it burnt for many hours with bright, calm flames. Nights were getting cooler. The local police officer checked the wood people were bringing back into the village to ensure they hadn't taken too much. Maddalena had heard that some people had started hiding wood, collecting it during the night.

A bellow from Annibale made her jump with fright. Elia started up a noise like a piglet, halfway between a squeal and a whine. She hurried in to find the boys wrestling.

'Stop it! *Lascialo stare.*' Maddalena tried to pull the brothers apart. 'Annibale, stop.'

'Only if he gives you back the pin.'

Elia was all innocence. 'Annibale picked on me.'

'He poked me when I was sleeping.' Annibale squeezed his brother's arm.

Maddalena was about to yell at Annibale to stop when Elia whimpered and handed her the pin. She chastised Elia but glared at her elder son. 'You're older. You should set an example.' Maddalena could tell by the look on his face Annibale thought her unfair.

He rubbed away a bead of blood on his ankle where Elia had jabbed him with the pin. 'I'm not his father. Papà should be here to set an example.'

She whacked the back of his head. 'Your father's doing his best.'

In the years since Vitale left, Annibale had become more and more cynical about the intermittent, meagre amounts of money his father sent to them. Unlike some men from Fossa who'd emigrated, Vitale gave no sign of buying his own farm or saving the passages to bring his family across by boat. Not understanding Maddalena's allegiance to her husband, Annibale went back to sleep, vowing that when he had a wife he would never be apart from her.

'He's lazy, Ma,' Annibale complained when Elia was out in the stable toileting. 'I'm doing his chores as well as mine. He needs a good smack.'

Maddalena eyeballed him. 'I'll take care of it, not you.'

Elia came inside and she looked him over, asking if he was well. He wriggled away, saying he was. 'Then you can go with Signore Nascia to collect firewood so I can cook dinner.'

They returned on dusk; Elia ducked inside and ran to his room. Gaetano Nascia stood at the doorway with both bundles of wood. Perplexed, Maddalena stood up from readying the fireplace, holding an andiron.

'Signora, that boy is bone lazy.' Gaetano shook his head. 'I know he doesn't have his father here to keep him in line — perhaps Annibale can give him a smacking.'

'If anyone does any smacking it will be me.' Maddalena took a step towards the door.

Gaetano spotted the andiron in her hand and stumbled backwards, dropping their firewood and half-tripping down the stairs. Annibale, sitting at the table, kept his face neutral.

She pointed the andiron at him. 'Bring in that firewood.'

A few days later, Elia drifted into a kind of malaise. He began coughing and complained of a headache. Maddalena placed her palm under the tuft of hair that hung over his forehead. *Mannaggia,* she cursed in her mind — *he's burning up.* She strove not to appear outwardly alarmed.

'Hop into bed.' She gave his hair a gentle ruffle. 'I'll bring you some hot milk.'

Annibale returned from sowing the wheat all day to discover Elia suffering a high temperature, chilly and weak. Maddalena applied a cold compress to Elia's head, wrapped his body and legs twice with a sheet wrung in cold water and then covered him with a warm blanket. Elia lay like that for an hour, and was then released for two. Maddalena began the process again every three hours, in between putting a copper 'priest warmer' of hot coals among the sheets. Annibale felt uneasy about having called Elia lazy.

Maddalena noticed Elia's temperature seemed to fall slightly in the morning and rise in the evening. He became more listless, lying prostrate in an almost vegetative state. Then a kind of delirium set in, his little fingers picking at the sheets. Suspecting nervous fever — the villagers' term for typhoid — Maddalena feared the cure was beyond her own remedies and told Annibale to fetch the *dottore* from L'Aquila, almost fourteen kilometres away.

'Take Gina,' she said. 'You'll get there faster.'

The doctor's form seemed to fill the room as he came in carrying a leather case, keeping on his dark knee-length coat. He took Elia's temperature, then examined his chest and stomach. The doctor looked into the distance, seeing instead with his fingertips as he gently felt Elia's torso. Elia whimpered when his distended stomach was pressed, bringing back the doctor's gaze. He stood up straighter.

'Signora, your son has a temperature of forty degrees. It's typhoid fever.'

Maddalena nodded, her suspicion confirmed.

'Keep up your treatments but don't give him any food. Boiled water only.'

'No food at all?'

'Not until he's well.'

The weeks dragged on. Though the delirium passed, Elia didn't seem to get any better. Giovanna stopped by and told Maddalena the little girl down the lane had typhoid too and was gravely ill. The two women stood at the bottom of the bed. Elia stared back at them with dark eyes sunk in their sockets.

'Why, he's shrunk to skin and bone!' Giovanna put her hand up to her mouth. 'Can't you give him any food?'

'The *dottore* said only boiled water until he's well. I want to kill a chicken and make him some chicken broth. My mother always fed it to us for sickness.'

'Do it, I say. Forget that doctor. A good *brodo di gallina* will do Elia good.'

Maddalena boiled the chicken whole. The smell of the soup pervading the house reminded her of how her mother kept a steaming pot over the fire for when her father returned from long walks hunting *cinghiale* — wild boar. The broth was soothing and invigorating, instantly banishing fatigue and cold. Maddalena spoon-fed Elia the first bowl, but by the next day he sat propped up against his pillow, eating the chicken broth on his own.

Giovanna stopped by again. 'He's certainly improved with food.'

'He's always loved his food.' Maddalena glanced up to the heavens but she smiled.

Giovanna put her hand on her friend's arm. 'Your mother taught you well.'

In the following year, 1937, a Fascist 'government man' from L'Aquila came to Fossa to paint a slogan on the wall opposite the church. Annibale and Luigi were among a small crowd of villagers who gathered to see what was happening.

'Does anyone have a ladder?' the man barked.

Annibale raised his hand. His *stalla* was the closest. Once up the ladder, the man used a stencil to mark out the slogan. Annibale was impressed. He'd never seen such large, neat printing on a wall. Inspired by Italy's invasion of Ethiopia the year before, the slogan bellowed in black paint: *Quello che dobbiamo conquistare c'interessa di più del già conquistato* — to convey 'We don't look back at what we've conquered but forward to what we will conquer'. Down on the road leading up into Fossa, the man painted on the side of a house, *Noi tiremo dritto* — 'We go straight ahead' — referring to the advancement of Italy. However, he painted the slogan at a curve in the road, making it literally impossible to go straight ahead at that point, eliciting chuckles among the villagers after he had left.

Since joining Sons of the She-Wolf — *Figli della Lupa* — when he was four, Annibale had remained a member of the Fascist Youth. By the age of eight, he was in the *Balilla* division participating in drills using scaled-down versions of Royal Italian Army service rifles and attending rallies and party-organised entertainment. The girls attended *Piccole Italiane*, which promoted motherhood and domesticity. 'Fascist Saturdays' were part of life.

Annibale had been proud to be one of four local youths chosen to sing for Mussolini at the opening of the Campo Imperatore Hotel near Gran Sasso in 1934. Wearing his uniform and black fez with a red band and tassel, the silver eagle and *Opera Nazionale Balilla* initials on the front, Annibale opened his mouth wide and sang with gusto as il Duce watched with a smile. By 1938, at fourteen, Annibale moved on to the *Avanguardista* division of the Fascist Youth and always wore pinned to his coat his Fascist badge — a blue shield and a single star with an eagle holding in its claws silver *fasces*. The *fasces* was a bundle of sticks and an axe bound tightly together representing power over life and death, an ancient Roman symbol adopted by Mussolini's regime.

'Mussolini is doing good things for this country,' Annibale said to Luigi as he led Gina, loaded with pine saplings, up the road out of Fossa and around towards the monastery Sant' Angelo d'Ocre sitting atop an escarpment.

Luigi, carrying a shovel over his shoulder, nodded vigorously. 'Il Duce is right to have us planting these trees.'

Teams of men were planting pine forests and Annibale guided Gina many times up and down the dirt mountain road to bring more saplings, enjoying the sun on his back, and the recurrent metallic ring of his shovel hitting dirt and chalky rock when it was his turn to dig. Most of the workers admired their leader, envisaging the firewood Mussolini's reforestation program would provide in the years to come. No one foresaw the forest still standing thick and tall almost a century later: a reminder of Mussolini's curious desire to create a tougher climate in the hope of producing a superior Italian race, since he privately disparaged his fellow citizens as too indulgent and lacking ambition.

At the end of the day Annibale returned Gina to the stable and refreshed her hay, then took the laneway steps back up to the house two at a time. As he came in, Maddalena looked up from the letter she was reading and watched him hang his faded cap on its hook. He sat down at the table and she pushed some wine towards him.

'That from Papà?' He wiped his mouth.

'You know, we've been married for nearly sixteen years and for fourteen of those he's been in Australia and I've been here.' She looked back down at the letter. 'He's just finished a stint cane-cutting and is back working on the farm in Stanthorpe …'

Annibale got up. He saw Elia poke his head around the bedroom doorway.

'Sit down, Annibale. There's more in the letter.' She waited as he pulled back the chair and sat down again. 'Your Papà has decided it is time for you to join him in Australia.'

'What?'

'The money he got cutting the sugarcane is enough to pay for your fare. You're almost fifteen, old enough to go on your own. You can both work to save for Elia and me to join you.'

'What if I want to stay here? If I had my own house …'

Maddelena cringed and refolded the letter. 'There's something you should know.' She hesitated. 'The house the priest lives in used to belong to your father's *zia*.'

'I know that …'

'She'd promised it for you.' Maddalena sighed. 'Until the priest got into her graces.'

Annibale stared, unsure if he'd heard her correctly. *I could have had my own house and land. Papà needn't have been away all these years.* The life he might have had dissolved as quickly as he glimpsed it. He stood up. She saw his left hand curl into a fist.

'Why do you think I never told you, Annibale? I only did now because I want you to see you'll be better off in Australia.' She chewed at the corner of her bottom lip. 'Don't do anything rash. Remember the priest's brother. Stay. Supper will soon be ready.'

A distracted wave as he went out was his only acknowledgment of having heard her.

It was almost dark but the sky still held a leaden hint of dusk as Annibale strode along the arcing lane towards the priest's house. His footsteps almost silent, his figure a flash of movement in the gathering shadows, like a bat winging through the village alleys and tunnels. He knew the power of a priest, but Mussolini's sentiment rang louder in his ears: *Better to be a lion for a day than a lamb for a lifetime.*

When he caught sight of the house, Annibale halted abruptly, all of a sudden seeing it differently. From where he stood, concealed in the gloom of a covered passageway, he envisaged coming home from the fields and pushing open the door to his wife placing a meal on the table, their children running to greet him. He could have climbed the short flight of steps up to that house every day, gripping the curly iron balustrade, well into his old age. For centuries, his ancestors had lived and died on Monte Circolo, and now he must go far away, his place in their village history as good as stolen.

Don Angelo's form passed a window, faceless with the light behind him. Unconsciously, Annibale stepped forward. *Soon I will be gone from this village.* He teetered, realising he couldn't leave his mother and Elia vulnerable to fallout from his actions, and at the same time hating the priest for getting away with what he'd done. *But I'll never forgive him.*

Or forget. He turned towards home, his steps slow, his thoughts galloping, determination flickering in the cinders of what was lost.

He was quiet when he returned and sat at the table. Maddalena studied his face as she spooned pasta *chitarra* and gravy into his bowl and let it be. Even Elia seemed to grasp the situation and got through the meal without having to be told to stop kicking the chair leg.

'When will I go?' Annibale asked as she collected their empty bowls.

'The ship leaves in early April.'

Maddalena felt relieved Annibale seemed willing to go. Since Adolf Hitler's annexation of Austria into Nazi Germany, rumours of another war had started to circulate. Vitale had always refused to speak to her of the horrors that sometimes woke him from sleep, but she knew they related to his years as a conscript during the last war. She didn't want Annibale getting grandiose ideas of heroism, leaving his father stranded in Australia, and she was grateful that at least he was too young yet for the Secret Police to recruit him from the Fascist Youth. Maddalena detected something had already changed in him since he'd learnt the truth about the priest's house. She'd seen the glimmer in his eyes. Yes, she decided, better for Annibale to be far away from Europe.

Applethorpe

After Cesca and Francesca arrived in Sydney, they went straight to Central Station, where Mico helped his cousin and her little boy board a train to Bundaberg. Then he, Cesca and Francesca spent a night in a boarding house. They'd missed their train because they'd had to arrange to transport Cesca's *baule* — glory box. This hefty trunk, almost the size of a table, was full of sheets, blankets, kitchen utensils, pots and two sixteen-litre tins of olive oil from the grove of one of Cesca's brothers. Rather than curse the *baule*, Mico was inwardly relieved, since he had barely the basics for them in the house.

Mico had arranged for Tino to pick them up from the train station in Applethorpe. Tino must have made two trips because he greeted them with their horse and sulky as well as his own horse and cart for the *baule*. Tino hadn't yet brought out his wife from Italy, and Mico vowed that when he did, he would help him in the same way.

'It's cold.' Cesca rubbed her arms, despite the coat over her dress.

Mico grunted with a nod, tobacco smoke trailing from his mouth and nostrils.

Sitting in the sulky between her parents, Francesca's hand found her mother's gloved one. She gazed at the new landscape in which they were to live. Her cheeks and nose felt numb in the winter air, the astringent scent of the bush creeping through her father's tobacco smoke. Seeing how thickly the bushland grew, so dense it almost hid some farmhouses, Francesca felt a little scared. It was a relief when their farm came into view and she saw a house amid cleared land, flanked by orchards. And yet the wooden house stood tall and alone, seemingly vulnerable compared with the concertinaed stone houses familiar to her in Palmi.

Once the creaking wooden carts and the horses stopped, it was very quiet. Tino helped Mico carry the *baule* up into the house, the two men tilting and manoeuvring it back and forth on the stairs and just scraping it through the open doorway. Then Tino left so he needn't have to light the lanterns on his cart to get home. Being late afternoon in June, the sun had already slipped behind the hills, leaving an orange smear low in the sky.

The wooden house echoed with their footsteps, and as the fire had been unlit for several days, it was cold. Mico went outside to chop some wood and came in to hear Cesca and Francesca's female chatter filling the rooms as they discovered the kitchen and dining area, one large bedroom and another small one. Smiling to himself, he got the fire going. By the time the bare wood-panelled walls began to warm, Mico had dinner on the stove. As Cesca and Francesca unpacked, the house was already beginning to take on the conviviality of a home.

It had been a jolt for Francesca when she first saw the stark horizon between the sky and ocean surrounding Australia. Yet she found that some of the flattened hills around Applethorpe with their thinned-out trees and dry grasses covering large stretches reminded her of how the Gioia Tauro plain behind Palmi could look when it failed to rain. She accepted that her father had made their home in the hamlet of Applethorpe but she struggled with the frosty winter, it being the coldest place in Queensland. And she missed the sea.

'Francesca, we must write a letter to Nonna,' Cesca told her when Mico was mending tools out in the shed. 'We will tell her how lovely everything is so she will not worry about us.'

Putting on clothes unpacked from her port, Francesca smelled a hint of her grandmother's wood-fired oven smoke amid the folds of material. Come wash day on Monday, all such traces of Palmi would be lost forever in the boiling water of the copper.

Within a week, Mico was taking eight-year-old Francesca in the horse and cart to the local school, returning to pick her up in the afternoon. After a few days she began walking more than a mile each way with two Australian girls from a neighbouring farm, Betty and Dorothy. Knowing only Italian, Francesca communicated with hand signals at first or got other children from Italy in her class to interpret for her. She was determined to learn English and began speaking and understanding simple phrases within the first fortnight, picking up more and more in her willingness to learn.

The schoolteacher, Mr Londy, was a staunch Catholic. Each Sunday he, his wife and three children rode bicycles the three miles from Applethorpe to church in Stanthorpe. His discipline in school was severe and the children made up a ditty they sang in private: 'Mr Londy goes to church on a Sunday, so he can belt the children Monday …'

Francesca kept out of trouble, though, and liked school.

'Mr Londy picked me for the basketball team!' she announced on her arrival home one afternoon, and Cesca and Mico exchanged glances over their petite daughter, smiling.

Instinctively, Cesca put her hand to her stomach. Within two months of arriving at Applethorpe she'd fallen pregnant. Hearing Francesca was happy at school, being reunited with Mico, and expecting a baby — all helped make her feel settled in their new home and life together. She missed her mother and the rest of her family back in Italy terribly, but she was where she should be. And this coming baby would be born in Australia and would begin to tie them more firmly to their new country.

In the same way Australia had once been a distant place described in Mico's letters, Palmi began fading like the sepia ink on Soccorsa's crackly pages of correspondence. Francesca missed Palmi and especially her nonna, but soon she had a little sister nine years her junior, and a new bicycle. While in Italy she'd learnt to read and write Italian so Cesca could keep in contact with her mother, since starting school in Australia she had become skilled at reading and writing English and now helped Mico with the paperwork for the farm. Mico could read and write Italian but still struggled to decipher English.

Francesca's days were a mostly pleasant cycle of school, farm duties, house chores, church on Sundays and a trip into town once a week, if it wasn't raining. Stanthorpe's main street was a gravel road lined with pepperina trees, and Mico would leave the horse and sulky at the blacksmith's while they went into Pierpoint's, which stocked everything from grocery items to clothing and department store goods like appliances and crockery. Sometimes, for a treat, the family went to the pictures at the Arcadia Theatre, something they never could have afforded to do in Italy. And on other occasions Italians in the district invited them to parties, Mico always bringing along his guitar. If it were a very special celebration, those hosting would kill and roast a steer. There was joyful eating, singing and dancing.

And so several years passed, each similar to the last, yet in contentment rather than abeyance, as before. For Francesca those early years in Applethorpe were happy, despite the frugality of their lives. Australia was clawing its way back from the Depression, with unemployment wavering between ten and fifteen percent. Swagmen who jumped the 'rattlers' looking for work from town to town along the railway lines often made their way out to the farm. Many swaggies were pleasant chaps despite their hard circumstances, happy to chop wood in exchange for a meal and a straw bed in the barn to spend the night on. But there were also those who felt angry and betrayed by Australia, particularly if they'd fought during the Great War. And then there were those who were bitter.

Francesca, now thirteen, was alone in the house, scrubbing the wooden kitchen table with Sunlight soap, when a silhouette darkened the glare of the open doorway.

'Got some money I could 'ave, girly?' The swagman's voice crackled like dry leaves; his eyes looked kind at first, but there was something unfriendly in the way they glinted under the brim of his hat.

'No speak English.' On instinct, she began backing away.

He kept coming towards her, then reached to grab her arm. Startled, she twisted away and ran into her bedroom, slamming the door.

When Cesca came back to the house there was no sign of the swagman; he had disappeared around the far bend of the road by then. She was puzzled to find the front door of the house and all of the windows shut despite the lingering warmth of the autumn day. Francesca emerged from her room and Cesca couldn't be sure if her daughter's eyes were puffy from tears or sleep. She held her palm to her forehead, assuming she must be coming down with something. Francesca felt unable to relay what had happened. It seemed better to keep the awfulness of her brush with danger to herself rather than infect her mother whom she loved so much with the distress of it, particularly as Cesca was early into another pregnancy.

Francesca kept the incident secret and outwardly returned to her usual self, but it affected her; from then on she kept the door and windows of the house shut much of the time. It also coincided with Cesca and Mico's announcement that she would have to leave school when the baby was born to help with her little brother or sister, as well as on the farm. Francesca was devastated, then relieved when Mr Londy told Cesca and Mico it was against the law to take their daughter out of school until she was fourteen. Inwardly pleased, Francesca relished completing the extra year of schooling. Yet it was a temporary reprieve from the changes 1939 would bring.

Being Thirteen

Bunting strung from the weatherboard school building across to the front fence flutters colourful triangles in the stiff breeze. A hand-painted banner hangs on the front wall: *Applethorpe State School, 1911–1986, 75th Anniversary*. Children run across the grass quadrangle yelling in play: some current students; others descendants of the older people who stand back and reminisce as they gaze at the school, perhaps seeing it as it was during their time as pupils there. Nanna Francesca tells us she attended within a week of arriving from Italy, more than fifty years earlier. More quietly, her brother Vincenzo adds that he went here at least four decades ago.

Several beach umbrellas thrust in the dirt with chairs scattered around them provide some shelter from the morning sun, but mostly people mill about — people like Nanna Francesca in her good dress and cardigan, handbag over one wrist, camera strap on the other, her hair still high from a hairdresser's appointment in Brisbane before we left in convoy for Stanthorpe. Nonno Anni led the way in their enormous Ford Falcon with bench seats, Nanna Francesca on the passenger side, Vincenzo in the back. My parents, sister and me sailed along behind in a pale-blue Fairmont, the similarly enormous vehicle as overdone as many things of the mid '80s.

'Zoë, *vieni qua*, have a look at me in this.' Nanna Francesca waves me over to join her in the shade of the school building.

At thirteen, I'm the same age Nanna Francesca was in 1939. She shows me her school photograph, ripped down the middle at some stage and stuck back together with sticky tape. There are thirty-six children of various ages in four rows. Most wear cardigans or coats, shoes and socks, but one little boy has no shoes in what must be cold weather. He sits beside a boy holding a slate upon which is chalked simply *Applethorpe, 1939*.

I look closely at my grandmother as a thirteen-year-old. She is slim, pretty, her smiling cheeks like two little apples, hair in a bob, somewhat windswept. I've always known her as so proper, corseted by tradition, following what is 'right'. In this photo she looks a little mischievous, someone with whom I think I'd like to be friends, and in that moment I experience a softening towards her.

'Why did you have to wear those pants?' she hisses. 'A long skirt or dress would have been much nicer. I hope you're not wearing pants to the Mass tomorrow.'

My face is surly in the photograph Nanna Francesca takes of the family lined up along the school fence. Zio Vincenzo nods at me in fellow feeling and says something in his whispery voice that I don't quite catch.

That evening after dinner, while we're standing on a freezing grassy area waiting for a fireworks display to commence, Nanna Francesca tells me how she loved school but had to leave to help on the farm and look after her little sister, who was about four, and her brother, a baby at the time, once she turned fourteen. Since the expectation now is for most students to finish senior, I'm somewhat dismayed and go quiet. School is something I take for granted, even resent at times. Perhaps she interprets my silence as lack of interest but, deep in thought, I'm wondering if I was asked to make the sacrifice she did whether I'd be able to do so with such acceptance.

Twenty-seven years later, almost to the very day in May of that Applethorpe School anniversary, something makes my gaze land upon a plastic box in the garage. I open it to find half a dozen of Nanna Francesca's vinyl records, mostly albums by Italian singers and musicians recorded in the 1950s and '60s. In those frantic hours as the floodwaters were rising back in January 2011, more than two years ago now, I'm not sure what made me grab these records as we were forced to vacate. In the past, I'd seen my father and his brother going through Nanna's collection, dividing up the albums, and these were the leavings, threatened by muddy water.

Thick dust on the long-stored cardboard record sleeves grimes my fingertips as I flick through them. And then something small falls from between two records. It's a slender publication, about the size of an exercise book, which Nanna Francesca must have received as a past student at the 75th anniversary of the Applethorpe School. I pick it up in amazement. It could have so easily been lost in the floodwaters. The pages have fused from years of damp but come gently unstuck. Five pages in, I stop turning, stunned to see a school photograph taken in 1934, the year Nanna Francesca commenced as a student there. Knowing that she and my *bisnonna* — the two Francescas — arrived in Brisbane when their ship, the *Romolo*, docked on June 3, 1934, I try to quell rising hope. *Was the school photograph taken after June 3 that year?*

Almost holding my breath, I scan the children's faces, impatiently skipping to the names below. She's there. Her surname is spelt 'Soland' instead of Solano, but she's there. Almost in the middle of the second row, a little girl in a white dress, serious-faced. I rummage in a drawer for my grandfather's magnifying glass. It's not a clear picture, but comparing her stance, her expression, with her school photo taken in 1939, she looks … lost. This is perhaps the only photograph of her as the eight-year-old immigrant — still learning English, adjusting to her new Australian life, missing her grandma in Italy. I suddenly wish I could whip back in time and rather than go quiet when Nanna Francesca was talking to me while we waited for the fireworks to start, I would ask her questions, many questions.

I recall bringing along my own camera on that family trip to Stanthorpe in 1986 — one that required manually winding on the film after taking each photo. Rifling through paper envelopes of my old photographs, I'm relieved to find, along with those in which I'm a surly thirteen-year-old, others where I'm smiling, my face open. From the top of the wardrobe, I pull down my scuffed port from grade two in which I keep all the diaries I wrote during my teenage years. I discover I had written on that trip how touched I was to visit my great-grandparents' Applethorpe farm for the first time. Why, as a teenager, did I feel the need to keep that part of me so hidden?

It was during my adolescence that the generation gap between Nanna Francesca and me stretched widest. Born into an era that encouraged self-expression, feminism and rejecting conventionality, I grew up when it was accepted that a female would have individual aspirations. Nanna Francesca came of age in a time when emotional restraint, conformity, duty and sacrifice of oneself, particularly if you were a woman, were expected.

It wasn't until her later years that she spoke to me of the swagman, and she was reticent even then. Although she gave the impression that the most she suffered from the incident was a terrible scare, the extent of what happened remained a mystery and, sensing her discomfort, I didn't press her. Besides, by then I'd had an incident of my own, which I was yet to tell anyone about. Some matters induce the same silence whatever the generation.

Not long after we get back from the Applethorpe School anniversary, I'm on my way to a piano lesson after school. I see rainclouds closing in, though the winter sun still carries some warmth. The walk from the bus stop takes about fifteen minutes. Many of the post-war houses in the neighbourhood are boxy: some well-kept, clean and nicely painted with neat gardens, while others have long grass, broken fence palings and peeling paint. It is at one of these neglected houses that I notice two young men sitting on the front steps. They stare and murmur to each other as I come closer. Shouldering my school bag a little uneasily, I avoid making eye contact.

One of them bounds down the steps. To my horror, he comes right up and falls into step beside me. I'm short, small. Close up he is big. Still walking, I don't look at him. He puts his arm around my shoulders. The weight of it on my schoolbag traps my right hand at shoulder height, where I'm holding the strap. I look straight ahead. *Keep walking*, I tell myself. He walks with me. I feel the grip of his hand on my arm.

The other man rises on the front steps in excitement. Before he even speaks, instinct warns me he is the worse of the two, the leader.

'Bring her here. *Drag her inside!*'

My heart is hammering but I don't show any sign of having heard, any emotion. The man beside me doesn't react. We are still walking, his arm around me. He starts laughing. A crazed, wheezing laugh, wet with saliva. I sense him lean in closer as though he's going to kiss me. I keep looking frontward, seemingly unaffected, as though nothing is happening. The grip on my shoulder loosens. He removes his arm, stops walking, and I continue going forward. I don't look back, don't alter the rigid carriage of my body. Only when I turn the corner at the end of the street do I glance to check and see they are not following.

I still have almost ten minutes before I reach my piano teacher's house. It starts to rain. I forget to put up my umbrella. Perhaps I'm in shock. Instead of going straight to her house, I go to a tap in the park directly opposite and wash my face and hands.

'Zoë, what are you doing? Quickly, come inside!' Gloria calls from her window.

It is raining heavily. She hands me a towel and a glass of water, shaking her head and calling me a 'silly sausage'. I smile and shrug, glad that I can sit and gather myself while the student before me finishes their lesson. My hands, hidden beneath the towel, have stopped trembling by the time it is my turn to play the piano, but I make many mistakes.

Half an hour later, my father, a schoolteacher, comes to pick me up after a staff meeting. I act as I would on any other day after school. Nor can I say a word to my mother about what's happened, though she gives me a funny look when she comes downstairs to the laundry and finds me cleaning my school bag with detergent and a scrubbing brush. When she returns to cooking dinner, I scrub the cover of every schoolbook that was inside my bag.

It took me almost twenty years to tell Mum what happened. By then she had terminal cancer and we were lying together on her bed one afternoon, swapping confidences about various episodes in our lives. I still don't know why it took me so long to tell her. A short time after sharing this story with Mum, I drove past the house and saw it was still dilapidated, the only derelict dwelling in the now gentrified area. It looked deserted. Those weatherboard walls not covered by graffiti were down to bare wood.

What happened could have been so much worse. To this day, I'm not sure what compelled me to keep walking, looking straight ahead, seemingly unperturbed. Was I calm or paralysed by fear, even though my legs kept propelling me forward? Would I have been better off kicking and screaming? Perhaps the first man never intended to do anything more than put his arm around me, despite the other one wanting him to drag me inside. I hope it was a one-off prank on their part and didn't lead to behaviour more sinister with other girls or boys. But this is probably naïve, wishful thinking. I know that now, as an older woman, I would speak up. But the thirteen-year-old I once was can completely understand why Nanna Francesca didn't mention the swagman for so long.

Good Friday — 1939

The day Annibale had to leave Fossa to begin his journey to Australia was Good Friday and Maddalena thought that just as the Madonna had lost her son on this day, she, too, was losing hers. She kneaded the Easter pizza that morning, mixing tears in with the dough. Annibale emerged from the bedroom, carrying his port.

He touched her shoulder. 'Ma, I'll be all right. Papà is there. We know from his letters he is fine.'

Maddalena wiped her hands on her apron. *But Vitale is many years older,* she thought. It occurred to her that father and son really didn't know each other very well.

'Here.' She gave Annibale a small photograph of his father, taken many years before. 'So you will know him when you arrive in Brisbane.'

They went out onto the front stoop to say goodbye. Annibale gave his eight-year-old little brother, Elia, a hug and told him to look after their mother. Then he turned to Maddalena.

She clung to him and wept. 'I'll never see you again.'

'You will …' Annibale tried to soothe her but Maddalena, usually so stoic, seemed inconsolable.

Maddalena found it harder saying goodbye to her son than she had to her husband. And in terms of time spent together, she'd known Annibale for more than a decade longer. Striving to put on a brave face she forced a smile, but as he stepped back from her embrace and began to walk away, a wail broke from her lips.

Annibale blinked back tears. *Just keep walking,* he told himself, *for her sake.*

Maddalena's wails reverberated off the tall stone houses lining the laneway. She rubbed her eyes, annoyed that tears were blurring her vision as she watched Annibale retreating down Via del Pallio to the waiting horse and cart. For years she had watched him walk the same cobblestoned lane — as a little boy on his first day at school; to the fields, tools over his shoulder, sometimes leading their donkey, Gina, on a rope. And now, a fifteen-year-old with a broad set to his shoulders, carrying a small case containing all he owned — walking down the street and out of her life.

Maddalena watched until the horse and cart went around the corner. Then she raced past the church over to Piazza Belvedere, and from the railings there she glimpsed the cart disappearing and reappearing among the rooftops below as it descended the road along Monte Circolo. Annibale, not realising she was there, failed to look up. She raised her hand in a wave, about to call out, but he was gone. Head bent, she slowly turned and walked back to the house.

Annibale sat in the back of the cart, legs dangling over the side. The driver was a man of few words, which suited Annibale as he took in his surroundings for the last time. Gran Sasso was magnificent that morning with its white peak resplendent against the clear blue sky. The fields, villages, canals and roads, all so familiar, passed by for the last time. He took a deep breath of the mountain air. He had no idea if he would ever be back. And yet he left a little of his heart behind.

At the train station in San Demetrio Ne' Vestini, excitement overrode some of his sadness. He was going to Naples, his first time in a big city, the first time he would see the sea. He chuckled to himself. *For the next couple of months I'll be seeing quite a bit of the sea.* His itinerary was all mapped out. From San Demetrio he'd catch a train to Naples, where the boat would depart early next morning. The shipping company arranged for passengers from outside Naples to stay in a boarding house near the docks the night before sailing. Annibale was expected there that afternoon.

As it was Good Friday, the tiny train station at San Demetrio was deserted. Annibale had never caught a train before. He heard it coming in the distance before he could see it and picked up his port in readiness. Gushing steam, the intimidating black engine roared into the station, carriages clanking behind. He climbed aboard the closest carriage. Looking around for a seat, almost losing his footing as the train jerked forward, he suddenly realised all the passengers were young men in military uniform — fresh-faced conscripted soldiers, some not much older than he.

'Uh, is this the train to Naples?'

The packed carriage erupted in resonant male laughter. 'This is a troop train. Next stop the military compound.'

Annibale ran back to the door. Too late. The train was already leaving the station behind. He felt sick. All around him the troops were rowdy, their high jinks punctuated with laughter; they were carefree, naïve, oblivious to the fact that in a short time they would be plunged into war.

He watched as the train sailed past station after station, platforms all deserted on this Good Friday, cursing himself for getting on the wrong train. The tracks took the train right through the open gates of the military compound, Ci Senti, coming to a stop inside its towering walls. Annibale jumped off with the rest of the soldiers and saw guards swinging the huge gates closed behind the train. As the engine noise and residual steam died down, the ensuing quiet was frightening. He looked around, spying a guard.

'Please, you need to let me out. I got on the wrong train.'

The guard looked Annibale up and down, noticing the Fascist Youth badge still pinned to his coat. 'I can't let you out. You shouldn't have been on a troop train.' The armed forces remained loyal to the King, not Mussolini, some of the military considering the Fascists social inferiors.

Annibale suddenly felt a long way from Naples and Fossa. Spotting another guard near the gate, he ran over to him. 'I've got to go to Australia.' He was almost wringing his hands. 'My father is expecting me. I'm going to miss the ship.'

The sentry exchanged glances with the first guard, who'd followed Annibale over. 'No one is allowed to leave here now.'

'But I'm going to Australia.' Annibale's voice was getting louder.

'What's happening here?' Hearing the commotion, an officer of the Secret Police came over, and as Annibale explained his predicament again, the officer eyed the Fascist Youth badge on Annibale's coat. 'Are you part of the Fascist Youth?'

Annibale stood straighter. 'Yes, sir!'

The officer rubbed his chin, then turned to the guards. 'Why don't you let him out?'

The first guard's eyes tapered with hatred. 'I have my orders.'

'Well, I'm Sergeant Russo of the Secret Police and I tell you to open this gate!'

There was an uneasy standoff. The guard's expression became murderous. He knew the Secret Police ranked higher than the military.

Sergeant Russo escorted Annibale out the gate to a nearby train station, explaining that soon there would be another train to Naples. He scrawled a note and told Annibale to present it to the conductor and everything would be all right. Annibale thanked him profusely and the officer smiled. 'You know it's lucky you were wearing your Fascist Youth badge. When I saw that, I knew you were one of ours. You should forget about Australia. We could do with you in Italy.'

Compared with the quiet, rural life of Fossa, Naples was wild. Annibale dragged his feet, dazed by the crowds and constant noise. New sights and sounds bombarded his senses: the hiss of espresso machines; chaos as cars, trucks and horse-drawn carts choked the streets; the bold gaiety of shopfronts and people shouting out; an unfamiliar upbeat local tune, strange-looking palm trees; and, of course, the sea. To Annibale, such a large body of water was almost inconceivable. Undulating and reflecting the rose-grey afternoon light, it stretched beyond the horizon. Barely a month ago snow had fallen up in the Apennines around Fossa, yet in Naples spring was already hinting at summer, the air warm, muggy.

The boarding house wasn't far from the port. Annibale saw the ship called *Remo* on which he was to travel looming over the dock; the same ship Vitale had sailed back to Australia on in 1932. It was hard to comprehend it would be his home during the long voyage to Australia. Seeing the imposing vessel keyed him up to leave. *I'm on my way.* He marched into the boarding house.

'Haven't you heard?' The boarding-house owner looked surprised. 'All sea travel has been halted. Italy invaded Albania this morning.'

The overcrowded boarding-house rooms reverberated with chatter about the possibility of war. An old man from Basilicata, who occupied the bed next to Annibale, told him the League of Nations was finding it impossible to keep peace. 'If only Italy had been treated fairly in the treaties signed at the end of the Great War,' he lamented. 'The Allies promised Italy territory for helping them win, then went back on their promise, giving us nothing. Now il Duce is in with Hitler, who is making all the decisions.'

It was the first time Annibale heard someone refer to Hitler as the dominant of the two leaders. Conditioned not to question Mussolini's greatness, Annibale was sceptical, but the old man insisted. 'Just weeks ago, Hitler moved his troops into Czechoslovakia.' He propped himself up on one elbow, adding fervently, 'And to keep up, now il Duce has invaded Albania.'

Confined to the boarding house with little to do, Annibale felt beleaguered by these developments. He thought of returning to Fossa to be with his mother and Elia, but then his father was waiting for him in Australia and the family had spent so much on his fare. The shipping company could give no indication of when the *Remo* would be able to leave, only that they could get the go-ahead at any time, and when they received the embarkation order they'd depart immediately. This left Annibale in a quandary. He counted his money: he had only enough for two more nights at the boarding house. Unable to afford the train fare home, he faced a long return journey on foot — almost two hundred and fifty kilometres.

The crowded dormitory was stifling. Annibale had heard enough disquieting talk from the old man from Basilicata and decided to go up to the flat concrete rooftop to look at the sea. A group of men lounged on the back steps leading up to the roof, smoking and talking. He threaded his way through the sprawled figures, creating a stir in his wake as they grumbled and shifted to let him pass.

Squinting against the harsh sunlight on the rooftop, he went over to rest his hands on the balustrade. The imposing old fort Castel dell' Ovo jutted out on a peninsula into the Gulf of Naples. As much as Annibale would have liked to go and look at it, he wouldn't risk leaving the boarding house and missing the embarkation order. Instead, he watched the sea, still fascinated. The colour of the water transformed with the changing daylight, shades of washed-out blue turning to jade, in constant motion, as if it were alive. The scent of the sea was so different to the mountain-forest air.

A ruckus started up behind him and Annibale turned to see half a dozen men cornering a teenage boy on the other side of the rooftop, hurling insults at him. Annibale wandered closer. The boy was scrawny, his lank hair falling over his face, hands jammed in his pockets. Overhearing that these Italian men were taunting this boy for being Albanian, Annibale bristled. He hung back to see if the situation would resolve itself. One of the stockier men gave the boy's shoulder a hard shove, almost knocking him sideways, and then raised his fist.

'Hey!' Annibale strode into the half-circle of angry men. 'He's not doing anything to you.'

'He's Albanian,' the stocky man sneered. 'Deserves what he gets.'

'Leave him alone.' Annibale held his ground.

The man smirked at the others then stepped up to him. 'You want a go?'

Annibale sized him up and shrugged. 'All right, then.'

The man deliberated then snickered. 'Forget it,' he said and sauntered away.

When the men had left, Annibale turned to the Albanian boy. 'I'm Annibale Boccabella. What's your name?'

'Pandi. Pandi Stratu.' He put out his hand, which was trembling a little. 'Thank you,' he said as they shook hands. 'Thought I'd get a good kicking.'

Annibale waved his hand in dismissal. They sat talking. He was surprised to learn that Pandi, whom he'd presumed to be about fourteen, was actually two years older than he was.

Pandi produced a small orange from his pocket. 'You going to Australia on the *Remo*?' He dug his thumb into the navel of the orange and tore it open, proffering half to Annibale who took it eagerly.

'If it ever leaves.' A trickle of juice ran down his chin. He wiped it roughly with the back of his hand, voicing his monetary concerns caused by the delay of the ship.

'I guess we could always find some work in Napoli if they tell us we're stuck here for a long while,' said Pandi. 'What's the name again of the town you're heading to in Australia?'

'Stanthorpe. What about you?'

'Biloela.' Pandi struggled to pronounce it. 'I wonder if they're close?'

With a shrug, Annibale raised his hands, palms up. 'At least we're both going to the same port — Brisbane.'

They stared at the hazy form of Mount Vesuvius that dominated the skyline behind Naples, then back at their similarly motionless ship chained to the dock.

Good Friday — 1939

Forty-eight hours later, with most of Annibale's money by then lining the boarding-house owner's pockets, Annibale reconsidered the journey on foot back to Fossa. A tantalising thought of returning to Sergeant Russo and joining the Secret Police flashed through his mind. Then, not long after, the boarding-house owner came in and announced with some disappointment that the captain had given the order to embark. Italy had captured Albania, successfully completing the campaign in just six days. The subdued passengers sprang to life.

Like an army of ants, they created a dark trail from the boarding house, along the dock and up the gangplank onto the boat. Annibale and Pandi discovered their sleeping quarters in the cargo hold, a crude dormitory of metal bunk beds stacked three high. It was full of male immigrants heading to Australia, many never to return to Italy. A blend of anticipation, hope and melancholy charged the air. New faces straightaway began to blur the memory of those familiar ones left behind.

Annibale and Pandi stood on deck, leaning on the railings, sea winds ruffling their hair, long after many of the other passengers drifted back inside. They watched Italy growing smaller in the boat's wake. Neither spoke, the emotions they were feeling almost too big for words. On the brink of manhood, they now had the responsibility of making their own way in the world, yet the boyishness they still possessed put eager grins on their faces. Annibale tried not to feel the pain of leaving his mother and Fossa. He concentrated on letting the thrill of the journey take over.

From deep within the bowels of the vessel there came a sound, soft at first, fluctuating on the breeze and vying with the waves lapping around the boat. As more voices joined in, muffled, sentimental singing reached their ears and the words of an old folk song that conveyed a melancholy goodbye enveloped the *Remo*. Annibale bit his lip as he watched the last visible speck of Italian land disappear from sight into the horizon haze. He felt his eyes getting moist.

'Must be the sea air,' he said to Pandi, who was wiping his own eyes. 'So salty.'

Africa and Ceylon

Something had woken Annibale up. He lay still, drifting between wakefulness and sleep, and then it occurred to him: no hum of the engines. The boat had stopped. He opened his eyes. Yesterday the boat had wended its way through the Suez Canal and into the Red Sea, flanked by Egypt and Saudi Arabia. They couldn't yet have reached their first scheduled stop at Colombo in Ceylon. *Something is wrong*, he realised, swinging his legs over the side of the bunk as the overhead lights came on in the windowless cargo hold.

'What's happening?' Pandi looked bleary-eyed.

Annibale shrugged. The air inside the crowded dormitory felt very warm and close.

'Listen up! Listen up!' All heads turned as one of the crew strode into the dorm, clapping his hands to garner attention. 'We're in East Africa, docked at Massawa in Eritrea. Due to military action, your journey may now end here.' Pandi and Annibale turned to each other in alarm as the crewman continued: 'I can't say at this stage how long we will be here. To conserve fresh-water supplies on the boat, the captain has advised that women, children and the elderly will stay aboard and the men will go to the town of Asmara. Gather your belongings and assemble on the deck straight after breakfast.'

Many passengers knew of the province of Eritrea and its population of about one million becoming a part of the colony of Italian East Africa due to Mussolini's well-publicised victory statements following the Italo-Ethiopian War three years earlier. Yet none of them expected ever to go there. The men walked down the gangway and immediately felt the heat intensify as they were exposed to the strong sunlight. They gazed with curiosity at Massawa's white and coral buildings, the architecture reflecting previous Ottoman and

Egyptian occupations. Most of the men had never seen dark-skinned people before, and they couldn't help staring at the Eritreans.

The railway line from Massawa to the highland town of Asmara was about 120 kilometres long, rising to a height of more than 2,000 metres above sea level. A crewman stood up in the carriage and proudly announced, 'The Kingdom of Italy built this railway line as part of the great empire our leader Mussolini is creating!' Through the sooty windows, Annibale watched the landscape transform as they left behind the coastal plains where, the crewman told them, lions, panthers and elephants roamed. The train gained speed over the Ethiopian plateau alongside a turbulent river, then slowed into the highlands. Nearing Asmara, they glimpsed cotton gins, gold mines and, to their astonishment, the unmistakably Italian-style steeple of a Catholic cathedral.

Again, their accommodation was a rudimentary dormitory with bunk beds, this time in a long hut on the edge of town. The ship's crew suggested they spend the day exploring Asmara and going to the marketplace. At the higher altitude, the temperature was less stifling but the Italians found the sun's rays hotter than they'd ever experienced. After some deliberation, Annibale and Pandi emerged from the dorm wearing their usual long pants teamed just with the singlets they usually wore underneath their shirts.

A crewman leaning against a wooden pole, one leg bent, fished in his pouch of tobacco, the corner of a cigarette paper held fast on the moisture of his bottom lip. 'Wear a hat or you'll get sunstroke.' He carefully pinched out a line of tobacco onto the cigarette paper. 'And put something on your arms or they'll get sunburnt.'

'What do you mean, sunburnt?' said Annibale. 'I never heard of it in my life.'

'Well, you'll know all about it when you get scorched and all your skin peels off.' The crewman ran his tongue along the tip of his tobacco paper and sealed his cigarette, smiling as he looked up to see two singlet-clad backs disappearing into the dorm.

Pandi pulled on his shirt. 'Geez, what kind of hell have they brought us to?'

With long-sleeved shirts buttoned up to the collar and down to the cuff, Annibale and Pandi headed out with a group of older men from the boat. Asmara's sand-coloured rectangular buildings had flat roofs and no eaves.

In the main street, towering date palms, with the dead fronds of their foliage rasping against silvery trunks, offered little shade in the searing heat. They were astonished to see a dark-skinned woman walking along naked from the waist up, breasts drooping to her stomach. Another had a baby suckling at her breast. One of the older Italian male passengers asked an African man to take a photo of them all. He handed over his camera and the man took off.

Coming across Cinema Impero, built in 1930s Italian art deco style, the group halted in surprise. They stood looking around, calling out to each other and pointing as they spotted more Italian businesses — Bar Vittoria, Ferramenta, Pasticceria. The same crewman who'd stood up in the train now boasted that Asmara was the main city of the Italian Empire in Africa, with more than half of the population of 100,000 being Italian. Annibale glanced at Pandi, but his friend appeared not to equate Italy taking over Eritrea with its recent acquisition of Albania.

Not far from the cathedral, they discovered the Shuq district, a commercial and workshop area, and entered the covered marketplace through a brick arcade. Stalls with fruit and vegetables stacked high were interspersed with workshops making and selling kitchen utensils, pottery, pans, baskets. Chickens squawked from cramped wooden crates, a worker was beating out a sheet of tin. Native women crouched on the ground grinding *berbere*, a local mix of spices; Annibale's nostrils becoming punch-drunk with the unfamiliar aromas of cumin, cardamom, fenugreek.

He and Pandi wandered from the rest of the group and happened upon bunches of an oblong fruit they'd never seen before hanging along bamboo poles. They were very cheap so they bought a huge bunch and took it back to the dorm. While the African sun slowly sank behind the hills, they sat on the verandah eating the bananas and tossing the skins, some yellow, some green, onto a fast-growing heap in the dirt.

'They're not too bad,' Pandi said around a gluggy mouthful. 'Some are even sweet.'

Annibale nodded. 'They fill you up.'

Their mothers had ingrained in them that they must fill up on food when they could, and as cheaply as possible. Being teenagers, often hungry, they systematically worked through the whole bunch. After a while, Annibale found the combination of the day's heat, the rich scents carried on the evening air and his gorging on the bananas was making him feel nauseous.

Pandi wasn't looking so well, either. The same crewman who'd advised them about sunburn strolled up. His eyes moved from the sheen of sweat on their faces to the pile of banana skins.

'You two eat all those?' The cigarette he'd just rolled slanted in wait between his fingers. 'You're meant to let the skins turn yellow.' He struck a match as the boys exchanged looks. '*And* you ate the whole bunch.' His chuckle wheezed tobacco smoke. 'You'll just have to wait for nature to do its work now, boys.'

Five days later, a young crewman turned up at the dormitory in Asmara with word from the captain that the threat of military action in the area had lessened, and there was a window of opportunity for the ship to leave. By the evening they were all back on board and heading out to sea.

Again the *Remo* was destined for the scheduled stop of Colombo, capital of Ceylon, one of the world's chief ports and a vital fuelling station for steamers on the Australian and Asiatic routes from Europe. Soon after the *Remo* anchored in Colombo harbour, dozens of flimsy rowboats appeared, dwarfed alongside the large ocean-going vessel. With the frequent anchoring of foreign ships, enterprising locals had taken to ferrying sightseeing passengers to shore.

Annibale and Pandi clambered aboard a rowboat with a group of men, the tiny vessel pitching with the weight of each additional body. The passengers and the Singhalese boatman couldn't understand each other, so the rower held up several fingers for the coins required, tucked them into a woven canister on a belt encircling his waist and began rowing. Thin and sinewy, he wore a length of fabric wrapped around his head. His brown face creased in a smile, revealing mainly gums studded with yellow teeth. He rowed swiftly, eager to return for more passengers. Under the burden of six men, the boat sat low in the deep water. With each oar stroke, Annibale watched seawater threaten to lap over the sides. None of them could swim. Their boatman continued to row, his black eyes twinkling.

Colombo's port area differed from that of Naples and Massawa, with lush large-leafed plants rimming lagoons notched into the south-west coastline. Being close to the equator, the air was as hot as in Eritrea but also very humid. Pandi likened the sensation to moving through watery air. It was the brink of the monsoon season, and billowing mauve clouds assembled en masse in the distance. Yet on the harbour the sun still shone, sparkling on the water like scatterings of silver coins. The European men had never seen such a tropical setting. Annibale heard one turn to another and murmur, '*Paradiso?*'

On the shore, spectacle and perfume assailed them. The port was busy with foreign travellers and locals, assorted languages creating an overlapping percussion of different rhythms, a cultural cauldron simmering beneath a forceful sun. A headscarfed woman thrust a knurled bitter-melon in Annibale's face, hawking in a rapid barrage as he tripped, caught off guard. Pandi slapped his thigh in laughter and they hurried to catch up with the others heading to the town centre.

The European business section of Colombo, with its broad avenues and colonial-style stone buildings several storeys high, contrasted sharply with some of the earthen streets and more modest structures within the Pettah district. In the district called Fort, Europeans wore dark suits and hats, parking their motor cars near building colonnades. Over in the Pettah area, Annibale and Pandi saw small shrines with wilting floral offerings and heady smouldering incense. Ceylonese of various ethnicities and religions moved about, mostly wearing flowing white garments. They made their way on foot, carrying baskets on their heads or tapping donkeys' backs with small sticks to encourage them to haul two-wheeled carts, the scene more reminiscent of Fossa to Annibale than the cars and suits of the European district.

The men walked past Khan Clock Tower into the Pettah markets. As in Eritrea, unfamiliar scents thrilled their noses as they passed sacks of turmeric, coriander, cinnamon and aromatic cloves. Seeing bunches of bananas, Annibale and Pandi hurried on. An elderly woman wearing a cloth over her head spooned fragrant rice into bowls made of halved coconut shells. Her movements reminded Annibale of his mother spooning polenta. He wondered what Maddelena was doing just then and an upwelling of homesickness threatened to overwhelm him. Pandi pushed him forward, not wanting to lose the others and miss their boat ride back to the ship.

Their stomachs rumbled at a stall cooking meat on sticks covered in sauce of a burnt-orange colour. Tempting as the aromatic food was, a warning rang in their ears from the ship's crew not to eat or drink anything ashore or they would get very sick. Captivated, they watched a man play a type of flute, charming a snake half-coiled, half-poised to strike near his dusty sandalled feet.

There was so much to take in it seemed they'd barely been ashore when the heat on their backs began to diminish. Annibale looked up to see the sun descending in a gingery sky. It was time to go. He, Pandi and the others went back to find the same man who had brought them ashore, believing they had already paid for their return trip in his rowboat. The man nodded in recognition when he saw them and they climbed aboard. But this time the Singhalese didn't begin to row straightaway. He prodded one of the older men, gesturing that more coins were required for the return trip. None of them had any money, and thought they'd already paid him anyway. The boatman threw down his oars, refusing to row. Suddenly the *Remo* seemed very far away. One of the older men told them to stay put. 'If he isn't going to row us out, he isn't going to get any other customers either.' Realising what was happening, the Singhalese shouted and pointed at Pandi's shirt for payment, Pandi being the most slender and closest in size to him. The older men hurriedly agreed.

Pandi opened his mouth to protest; it was one of only two shirts he owned. Annibale leaned over to him. 'Don't worry, he won't be getting your shirt. Make a run for it when we get to the ship. The crew won't let this chap on board.' They both felt bad but didn't know what else to do.

It was a tense ride back with no smiles this time. When the boat drew up to the *Remo*, Annibale clambered up the rope ladder and aboard, Pandi swiftly following. The boatman yelped and tried to pull him back by the legs, causing the rowboat to sway, those still on board hollering, but Annibale was already hoisting Pandi up by his arms. Their footsteps beat a thudding escape across the timber deck, a string of Singhalese curses volleying up from the rowboat below.

After almost two months at sea, Annibale and Pandi were eager to catch their first sight of Australia. The *Remo* rolled over the choppy grey waters of the Indian Ocean and they crowded on deck with other passengers beneath an overcast sky. A fierce wind whipped them and they held their hats with one hand, a railing with the other. Annibale gulped in the sea air as he gazed intently at the horizon. Land steadily came into view. Passengers who were moments earlier bantering and brimming with excitement stood stunned. One elderly woman, who hadn't wanted to come on this voyage at all, was openly weeping. They sailed alongside desolate coastline, scrubby, rugged … bleak.

'It has to be all right, surely?' mumbled Pandi.

Annibale nodded, lips pursed, but with misgivings about his father's judgment — Vitale's years of absence colliding uneasily with Annibale's phase of adolescence when criticism surfaced freely.

As they neared Fremantle, the land didn't appear so bleak and it became apparent that people flocked to coastal townships like moths to warm, bright light. Fremantle was the chief port of Western Australia for vessels plying the European and South African trade routes. Noise, smoke and activity along the busy docks area, emanated from iron foundries, a soap factory, timber mill, tannery, flour mill and brewery.

After the long voyage, passengers were keen to find out the latest Australian news, and were relieved to learn that the country was continuing to shake off the Depression, with businesses reopening and unemployment falling. Most passengers weren't due to disembark until the *Remo* sailed around to the east coast, but while the ship was docked at Fremantle, everyone had their documents processed by Australian customs. Afterwards a group of Franciscan monks came aboard to welcome them to Australia and prepare them a little for what to expect.

'There is one thing we must warn you about,' said one of the monks, his tone serious. 'Ninety-nine percent of the population is of English origin, and at times Australia can be a prejudiced country, so be very careful not to get into any trouble or to cause fights, even if you are provoked. Justice may not always occur in your favour.'

The monks gave them each a pamphlet setting out various common English words and phrases. Before they left port, Pandi flung his across his bunk in frustration, but Annibale was determined. *If I'm going to make money here, I need to know the language as best I can.* Much to Pandi's chagrin, once the boat sailed out of Fremantle, Annibale withdrew from some of the card games of *scopa* and *briscola*, and gave up playing quoits, turning his attention to learning English.

The *Remo* hugged the southern Australian coastline, many passengers succumbing to seasickness in the rough waters. They were so close to their destination, but the final part of their journey seemed interminable as the boat sailed around and up through the ports of Melbourne and Sydney. As they progressed towards Brisbane, Annibale put the English pamphlet aside and contemplated seeing his father again. He was eight years old the last time he saw Vitale. Now he was fifteen. *What will Papà think of me?* He considered whether he should tell his father he now knew about Don Angelo and the disinheritance.

At dusk on their last night on the boat, Annibale and Pandi stood leaning on the railings, just as they had done when the *Remo* sailed out of Naples two months before.

'Well, this time tomorrow we will be there.'

Annibale nodded. 'Are you staying in Brisbane?'

'No, my uncle is taking me to the train station straightaway. I wonder how far Biloela is? I hope the people are nice. It's not like we can get on a boat and go back home again.'

Annibale slapped Pandi's back. 'We'll just have to make the most of it, eh?'

He knew it was unlikely he and Pandi would ever see each other again, but didn't say this aloud. At that moment, apart from his father, Pandi was the only person he would know in Australia.

New Boots

'Papà! *Papà!*' Annibale could see Vitale waiting on the dock but a surge of people blocked him off. His father seemed to be looking straight through him, then he turned and walked away in the other direction. Annibale took another glance at his father's photograph and, with his port in his other hand, tried to make his way through the throng. 'Papà! Papà!' He waved frantically, his cries drowned out in swarms of people disembarking, reuniting or meeting for the first time continued to obscure Vitale's retreating form. The prevalence of dark coats and hats made nearly everyone appear the same. Luggage and cargo cluttered the wooden docks. Brisbane, the capital and main seaport of Queensland, as well as the largest river port in Australia, provided anchorage for the majority of ocean-going passenger ships and handled the state foreign trade passing through — chiefly outbound shipments of sugar, coal and the thousands upon thousands of wool bales stored in the mammoth red-brick wool-store buildings facing the water.

When Vitale didn't come back, Annibale was a little frightened. He had already bade Pandi farewell. The excitement of when the *Remo* first docked now ebbed away. In a new country, with little money, he suddenly felt very alone. 'He's gone,' he inadvertently said aloud.

A nearby crewman overheard him. 'What's wrong? You look worried.'

Annibale's words tumbled out in a rush. 'My father … I saw him on the dock, now he's gone. This is his photo. I don't know what to do. I got no money …'

The crewman patted his shoulder. 'This has happened to others before. Go back on the ship. When your father can't find you, he'll come aboard to ask if you were a passenger and then you'll see him.'

When Vitale eventually did come to find him, the first words that blurted from Annibale's youthful mouth, after seven years apart, were 'Papà, you didn't see me.'

Vitale did a double take, then furrowed his brows. 'Annibale … is it you?'

'Course it's me.' Annibale stood a little straighter, then thrust forth the photograph as proof.

Vitale scratched his chin, a slow smile expanding. 'I know it's you … I just can't believe how much you've grown.' The eight-year-old boy he'd farewelled in Fossa in February 1932 was now taller and broader than Vitale was. A surge of pride rushed through him that this boy, this man, was in fact his son. He reached out with awkward affection and they half-hugged. 'Let's go and buy you some new boots.'

Vitale wore the dun-coloured clothes of a farmhand. His eyes darted, wary amid the dispersing crowd. He rarely ventured to a city. From the wharves Annibale and Vitale walked about two miles into the central business district. This was the fourth continent Annibale had set foot on in almost two months, and looking to the distance through gaps between buildings, again he marvelled at how the landscapes differed.

This small, subtropical city rambled on low hills either side of the broad, winding river, with the main business area on the northern banks and the industrial area on the southern. Suburbs crawled towards the foothills of the Taylor Range. Annibale had never seen anything like the timber houses with wraparound verandahs built high on stilts, or 'stumps' as the locals called them. Vitale explained that they were constructed this way to catch the slightest breeze and to avoid flooding.

After so long at sea, Annibale felt a little wonky on his feet, but his father didn't seem to notice. Vitale asked all about Maddalena and Elia, and was relieved to hear they were both well. After that, neither of them seemed to know what to say. Annibale trailed his father down thoroughfares with names such as Edward, Adelaide and Queen, surprised how wide the streets were, and busy — but nothing like the chaos he'd witnessed in Naples. Thunderous gongs rang out from the Town Hall clock tower, competing with the rattle of trams and the occasional tooting of cars. Tall imposing buildings, many made of sandstone, lined both sides of Queen Street. Awnings hung over footpaths to protect pedestrians and shopfronts from both sun and rain.

Annibale understood little more than snatches of the English he overheard people speaking around him. He worried, *How am I ever going to speak this language?* It occurred to him that in Italy the sound of talk and laughter was louder, brash even. Intense conversations there involved much hand movement. Italians slapped each other on the back, and men sometimes walked arm in arm. He saw a woman cover her mouth as she stifled a laugh. Two men lifted their hats to each other in greeting, but did not speak or stop.

A sign saying 'Hot Dogs' caught his eye, as these were two English words he'd learnt. The tiny shop had a glass-fronted counter beside the footpath. Peering in, Annibale saw with vague alarm bright red sausages unlike any he had seen before.

Although the June winter air was crisp, the sun bit into his shoulders. 'It's quite warm for winter,' he said. 'Strange to have no snow.'

'Stanthorpe is colder.' Vitale rubbed one of his eyes that had got dust in it. 'Not like Fossa, though. It can occasionally snow in Stanthorpe too, but in Queensland they build homes for summer, not winter, so it can feel cold at night sometimes … ah, here we are.'

Vitale pushed open a boot maker's door and a little brass bell jangled. Annibale found himself in a cramped, dingy space that smelled of leather and shoe polish. The shopkeeper appraised Vitale's Italian accent and farm clothes, and his lips tightened. Annibale tried on a pair of rubber-soled leather boots, aware of the shopkeeper's glower each time Vitale spoke to his son in Italian. Annibale said he was happy with the first pair he tried, not wanting to stay in the shop longer than he had to. He watched Vitale hand over his money, seemingly oblivious to the shopkeeper's disdain. *Perhaps, after many years here, he doesn't notice it.*

Outside, Vitale said, 'I've got a room at a boarding house up in Leichhardt Street. We'll leave your port there then get something to eat.'

They climbed a steep street to their accommodation in Spring Hill. Observing his father's form — bent, it seemed, from physical work — Annibale's lips puckered to one side and in that moment he felt a little sad for him.

Vitale and Annibale slid into the booth of a Greek café. Not one of the big fancy cafés in the centre of town, but a more modest outfit on the fringe that

Vitale could better afford. It was fitted out in art deco style, inverted light shades cradling dead insects hung from a pressed-metal ceiling, marbled light bouncing dully off scuffed tabletops. Vitale helped Annibale with the English on the menu — *grilled steak, pork chops, fried fish, hot joint of mutton or pork, steak and eggs, mixed grill, sausages and onions* …

When the waitress placed their meals in front of them, Annibale looked down at his in wonder. The piece of fried steak, with its plump outer strip of golden fat, was the largest he'd ever seen, almost overhanging the rim of the ceramic plate. It came with boiled beans, discs of carrot and two slices of buttered bread. Annibale devoured it all.

The waitress came to clear their plates. 'Would you like any dessert?'

Annibale looked questioningly at Vitale, who translated: '*Dolci*.'

'We got apple pie, banana and ice cream …'

Annibale shook his head. 'No banana, no.'

'Two coffees,' Vitale told the waitress.

'*Caffè*?' Annibale looked at him in amazement. They could never afford it in Fossa.

'Australians mainly drink tea,' said Vitale, not realising Annibale hadn't tasted either.

In Italy it was only the richer people in urban areas who could afford tea and coffee. Other Italians still mostly boiled up *orzo* — barley — instead of coffee, and for tea they used *carcadè* — hibiscus flower — known in Australia as rosella, and introduced to Italy when Eritrea became an Italian colony.

The waitress slid big teacups and a metal pot of milky liquid mixed with chicory essence in front of them, neither Vitale nor Annibale realising it wasn't made from true coffee beans. Vitale reached into the table caddy of salt and pepper shakers and a bottle of brown sauce, drawing out a glass canister of sugar. Sugar was another thing they rarely could afford in Italy. Annibale poured a generous stream into his cup and took a sip. It was a strange taste: smoky, milky and sugary all at once. He gulped it down, Vitale watching.

Seeing his father's smile, Annibale felt a gnawing of guilt for sometimes resenting him. He suddenly hoped they could bridge the gulf that so many years apart had created between them — perhaps they could begin by railing against the priest together. 'Mamma told me I could have inherited Zia's house if not for Don Angelo.'

Vitale's eyes widened before his bushy brows crashed down. He moved uneasily in his seat. 'Some things are better left.'

'How can you say that?' The empty cup almost toppled off the saucer as Annibale leant forward. 'He stole from us. Not just money. We had to leave. How the Church can …'

Vitale looked around. 'Shhh. Plenty of people are in the same situation. In Italy it's hard to make money, especially for farmers like us. Don't ever speak ill of the Church.' He ran his fingers through his thinning hair. 'Cripes, I don't need this.'

Annibale tried a different tack. 'I've got a plan.'

Vitale reached for his wallet. He shook his head and chuckled but there was little mirth in it. Without a word, he got up to pay for their meal at the counter. Annoyed, Annibale waited for him outside. They began walking back to the boarding house in silence.

'Don't you want to hear my plan?'

Vitale hadn't realised his son was spirited, like his wife. He wondered if it was due to Maddalena bringing him up or if she had passed it on to Annibale with her blood. It had been so long since he'd seen Maddalena he'd forgotten what being around someone feisty was like. For Vitale it was exhausting. He sighed. 'What is it?'

'Well, to open my own business.'

Vitale thought of Maddalena's family running several businesses in Poggio Picenze. *It's in the blood then.* 'Annibale, our plan is to save the fares to bring Mamma and Elia here.'

'I mean after we've paid their passages. I'll work hard and save for a business.'

'It took me years to save the passage for you.'

'But that was the Depression, and there're two of us now.'

Vitale wasn't about to be swept up in a proposition put to him by a fifteen-year-old. When he was that age, he kept his place and minded his parents whose word had been law. Besides, for Vitale any room for dreaming had closed forever the day the Church inherited his aunt's estate.

'Son, you have to remember we are peasants.' He touched Annibale's arm. 'That's all we're ever going to be.'

'Maybe that's all you're going to be.' Annibale angrily shook off his hand. But he knew he was trapped.

Vitale inhaled to speak again but halted. It was then he realised they could never redeem the years as father and son they'd spent apart.

They went to bed early, each with his own brooding thoughts. The train to Stanthorpe was leaving at six the next morning. Annibale lay in a rickety bed that creaked with the slightest movement. Across the room he could hear his father snoring. The sounds of Brisbane winding down for the evening soaked through the boarding-house walls, the distant clang and rattle of a late-night tram, a bottle breaking. Annibale's eyes were wide in the darkness. He'd got so used to the ship engines lulling him to sleep that to be back on land was somewhat jarring. He felt an urgent yearning to talk to his mother, to explain it was hard to accept the authority of this almost stranger, his father. It was a frustrating position to be in, bound by duty yet winged with ambition. He wondered how Pandi was faring.

Cottonvale

A pale winter sun had barely risen when the train left Brisbane. Ignoring the steam and flakes of soot, Annibale perched at the open carriage window as the engine up ahead gave a shrill whistle and sluggishly moved forward. Once the train gained momentum, the laborious *chug chug* hastened to a steady *clack clack* until it seemed almost to be flying over the tracks. The built-up city area quickly gave way to spacious suburbs, melding into farmland and then bush as they headed southwest. Grey-green trees and rocks as large as cattle punctuated dry grass. Fences of wire held up by splintered timber faded to silver marked property boundaries, some taut, others unkempt, the posts slanting. Despite being fenced, the land retained an untamed feel, stretching to stumpy mountains. Compared with their small cultivated plots in Italy, Annibale was in awe of Australia's vast expanses.

'I've arranged for you to work on Carlo Benocci's farm,' said Vitale, when Annibale finally pulled his head back from the window.

Carlo had left Fossa in the late 1920s. A distant relation, he had sponsored Vitale when he came out from Italy the second time, but maintained the line between employer and worker.

'You'll help plant and pick their crops of apples, beans and tomatoes, as well as chop wood, mend fences …' Vitale gave Annibale a stern look. 'Whatever Benocci asks you to do, you do. Remember, never disgrace the family name.'

'How far is it to Stanthorpe?' Annibale asked.

'You'll get off at Cottonvale, about nine miles north of Stanthorpe. I have to keep going on the train to get back to the farm where I now work in Wallangarra. It's about thirty-five miles from you. They only gave me two days leave.'

'Oh.' Annibale couldn't quite hide his surprise, having assumed he and his father would both be working on the Benocci farm.

Vitale glanced down. 'You'll take my place. Benocci has two other men working on his farm. Young and strong, like you. Carlo prefers that.'

It felt strange farewelling his father again so soon. After seven years apart, Annibale had got to spend a mere twenty-four hours with him. He was learning swiftly that any final carefree shreds of his youth were firmly in the past.

'I'll write to your mother,' said Vitale, 'and tell her you've arrived safe.'

Carlo was waiting in the shade of a corrugated-iron awning jutting over the platform of Cottonvale Station, the wooden building barely larger than one of the train carriages. Annibale got off the train, and after they'd exchanged greetings, stood holding his port as Carlo and Vitale spoke through the carriage window. The train, huffing steam and powdery smut, heaved forward, the carriages clanging together as they lurched with the momentum. Vitale's eyes met Annibale's before he ducked his head back inside, the train carrying him onwards.

Annibale adjusted his grip on the handle of his port as Carlo sized him up.

'You're big,' Carlo said approvingly. 'You must take after your grandfather. Come on then.' He led Annibale to a Chevrolet utility parked out the front of the tiny station. 'The farm's only about a mile away but I thought I'd drive anyway. I'm still running her in.' His mouth twitched with pride as he eyed his new truck. 'Better than a horse and cart.'

They got in, crashing the big metal doors closed behind them. It was the first time Annibale had been in a motor vehicle. As they bounced along a dirt road, the truck vibrating noisily, Carlo told him the farm was fifty acres. 'I bought it from the bank with ten pounds deposit after I got naturalised. Previous owner, a returned soldier, had up and left.' He turned into Pozieres Road.

Annibale would later learn that the banks owned many of the properties around the nearby hamlets of Amiens, Bapaume, Fleurbaix and Pozieres as mortgagee in possession. Apparently, of five hundred farms in the area allocated to returned soldiers about sixty succeeded. 'I've heard people say some didn't like the work or the isolation,' Carlo went on. 'But that's life on a farm, isn't it? There is no life. You just work, sleep and eat.'

Annibale was getting an inkling of what lay ahead.

'You and the other workers get up at sunrise and work until eight o'clock when you have breakfast,' Carlo told him. 'Then back to work until one, half an hour for lunch and work again till sundown. In return, you get meals, lodging and twenty-five shillings a week.'

Annibale bit his lip. From what he'd heard on the ship, twenty-five shillings was slave wages. He was sure he'd been told that an average weekly wage was at least four or five pounds. It explained why Benocci could employ three workers. With a sinking feeling, he thought of his father working on this farm for years. *No wonder it took him so long to save.*

The Benocci house stood high on stumps. Tin window hoods with waves cut into their bottom edges overhung each casement. A metal tank towered on a platform next to the house, and the outside toilet was a makeshift structure built with off-cuts of timber. The family lived upstairs in the house and the workers slept in crude quarters in one room beneath. Annibale slid his port under the spare camp bed, wondering if it was where his father had slept for all those years. He forced down rising anger and resentment. It was only his second day in Australia.

Annibale met the other workers out in the paddocks. Gerolamo and Paolo were similar versions of each other — youthful, lean, diligent and somewhat timorous — too poor, naïve or new to Australia to do anything about their situation.

At the dinner table, Mrs Benocci dumped meagre helpings of vegetables on each of their plates. After a full day of physical labour, the workers' stomachs grumbled. Annibale had a voracious appetite at the best of times and was both the largest and youngest of the workers. He watched Mrs Benocci carve a roast chicken. When she asked which piece he'd like, he smiled, thinking he'd misjudged her. 'Uh, whatever you choose is fine.'

With a reedy smirk, Mrs Benocci plonked the chicken neck on his plate. The rest of the Benocci family burst out laughing. Annibale wouldn't give her the satisfaction of getting to him so he ate the neck, but Mrs Benocci wouldn't leave it at that. 'Since you like the neck so much, Annibale, I'll give it to you every time.' More laughter. The other workers pretended to chuckle but glanced at Annibale with sympathy.

The wood-fire stove in the kitchen kept the upstairs part of the house warm, but downstairs in the workers' quarters, their breath hung in the frigid air. Gerolamo told Annibale to wear two pairs of socks and some extra clothing, as the temperature went below zero at night. Annibale lay in his sagging bed seething, wishing he'd stayed in Fossa, pity colouring the resentment he felt towards his father for getting him into this situation. He managed to get warm beneath the blankets but his face and head felt cold. When he thought of Don Angelo snug in his soft bed in their *zia*'s house, Annibale's heart pounded.

The countryside was very quiet. Beyond the muffled snores of the others in the room the only outside sounds were the distant lonely bark of a dog that carried across the cold landscape, and at one stage the clatter of a night train. Annibale tossed and turned. *Papà's problem*, he decided, *is that he has no ambition*. Annibale disliked Benocci's methods but he couldn't ignore the fact that he'd purchased his own farm and had his family around him.

Most of the growing and picking of the apples, tomatoes and beans happened in spring, summer and autumn. That winter Carlo instructed his workers to clear more of the land. Only about half of the fifty acres was currently viable and come spring he wanted to plant more crops. Gerolamo and Paolo showed Annibale how they used a Trewhella click ('monkey') winch, which involved tying a steel cable high in a tree, and one of the men on the ground several metres away slowly winding the operator by hand to tighten the cable. As the tension in the cable increased, the treetop started to quiver, then, following several loud cracks, the tree would come out by the roots, at other times snapping at the main trunk.

Annibale picked up broken branches and tossed them onto a pile for burning. With the large trees felled, they grubbed out saplings with axe and mattock, adding them to the burn pile. Then the root-running began. As the newest worker, Annibale, armed with shovel and mattock, was the main root-runner, digging out the twisting, diving roots left by the severed trees. In the first shallow ploughing, roots were as dreaded as hidden stones, since both could easily break a plough and the ploughman's ribs on impact. Annibale kicked at the pale granite dirt. His lips felt chapped, his cheeks raw. Magenta-topped grass ran rampant. He thought of their patch of land in the valley below Fossa, small but well-worked, fecund. A cold wind tried to snatch his hat.

In the months that followed, Annibale became acquainted with the range of winter tasks that they'd be too busy to tend to during the harvesting and packing of summer. Clearing, ploughing, spraying and pruning — with Annibale removing all the cuttings. Giving the packing shed a long overdue coat of paint and replacing several boards eaten out by white ants, which also required poisoning. Fixing the gate and the fence of the fowl-run, and then laying out the seedbeds ready for planting.

Despite the onset of spring, the air was still cold, especially at night, and after dinner one evening Annibale had a huge pile of firewood to cut by the light of a nearby lantern. Soon covered in sweat, he stripped down to his singlet. He enjoyed the methodical task of chopping wood. The deep thud of axe on timber, the crack as it split, the hollow thwack as he threw another piece on the pile. Yet he felt tired mentally. His life was on hold. He despaired at the years it would take to save for his mother and Elia's passage. *Years of this,* he thought, attacking a log with the axe. *I gave up Fossa for this.*

'Annibale!' Carlo appeared at the back door of the house. 'Come in. *Now.*'

Frowning, Annibale doused the lantern and walked towards the back steps, buttoning his shirt. Mrs Benocci demanded the workers sponge-bathe before setting foot in her house, so to be called in while he was still covered in sweat was unusual. He was surprised to find Paolo and Gerolamo already sitting with the entire Benocci family, then became aware that everyone was concentrating on the wooden radiogram in the corner. The Australian prime minister, Robert Menzies, was making a broadcast.

'Fellow Australians, it is my melancholy duty to inform you officially that in consequence of persistence by Germany in her invasion of Poland, Great Britain has declared war upon her and that, as a result, Australia is also at war …'

Annibale, grappling with the English, wasn't quite sure what the voice on the radiogram had said, although the gasps of the others told him it must be serious. Then Carlo translated for him and Gerolamo, who also didn't understand as much English as Paolo and the Benocci family did.

'Mussolini has that pact with Hitler.' Carlo clasped his wife's hand. 'I fear we're about to be cut off from Italy.'

Annibale's thoughts flew to his mother. That would mean no sending back money to Maddalena for their fares, nor any correspondence, in fact.

Fossa was finished.

The war had started.

Cursive Voices

In a second-hand bookshop in the Blue Mountains of New South Wales, I come across a thin book titled, *The Fruitful Granite: An Orchard in Queensland*, by Hector Dinning, published in Brisbane in 1928. I ponder how many hands might have turned its pages, how many bookcases, bedside tables and boxes it might have rested upon — before it again travels, this time back to the city where it was printed. The print feels embossed on each creamy page, almost as if a typewriter has stamped out the words. I expect a 'how to' on establishing an orchard on the Granite Belt near Stanthorpe, thrilled to have found a book written around the time my great-grandfathers, Mico and Vitale, were working in the area.

The first line takes me by surprise. 'The war made diverse creatures of us,' Dinning begins, pulling me straight in. 'It transformed many a meek, pasty-faced clerk into a hard-swearing fellow, lusting for blood, impatient of any weapon but the bayonet.' Though Hector Dinning died in 1941, his voice springs to life from the page, relaying how he saw those with previously strong nerves return rattled from the First World War. How it tamed others who'd once been 'rough and wild'. And bred others who came back driven, in Dinning's words, to evolve something out of themselves. 'War was at bottom the great leveller.'

Prior to the First World War, Dinning led an academic life, 'interspersed with coaching and free-lance journalism of a sporadic sort'. After his four years as a soldier, including seven months at Gallipoli, he decided to settle in Stanthorpe and bought a farm growing apples, peaches and grapes, claiming to be one of many ex-soldiers craving a quiet civilian life in the open air, working as his own boss. His descriptions are of a place I am familiar with, though its 1920s version is unfamiliar to me — the coarse banter of the orchardists packing their harvests into train carts at the siding; a Nubian lion and a tattooed lady among the attractions at the annual show, to which people wore their best clothes; quiet winter nights as Dinning and his wife read by the fire, he at times writing his book on paper on his knee.

Driving around the area northwest of Applethorpe, I come across various hamlets: Amiens, Bapaume, Fleurbaix, Pozieres — names apparently requested by the Returned Sailors and Soldiers Imperial League of Australia for the tracts of land carved up for returning soldiers to begin new lives upon. The books I look up on the history of this area suggest reasons most ex-soldiers later abandoned the land were high interest rates, a lack of farming knowledge or dislike of isolation. There is no mention of what was then called 'shellshock', or suggestion that the names on signposts, which must regularly have been passed on trips to town, might have reminded the men of places where they possibly lost mates or witnessed atrocity. Even Dinning makes no mention of it. I can't help thinking of it every time I drive past one.

While the naming of these hamlets was to acknowledge the French locations of battles of the First World War that were significant to Australians, when the conflict was still ongoing, the hamlet now called Applethorpe was renamed from 'Roessler', along with many other places and businesses in Australia that bore German names. The Roessler family were original selectors who'd established the first commercial orchard of mainly apples and cherries north of Stanthorpe. However, with anti-German sentiment across Australia, in 1916 authorities decided it best to change the name of the area to the more benign Applethorpe — 'apple village'. I'm interested to find out what the original Indigenous name for this area was too, but it proves difficult to trace.

Dinning and his wife reading by the fire conjures a different image to that of my great-grandparents on their Applethorpe farm. Mico and Cesca's lives as peasants in Italy were, of necessity and lack of opportunity, far from the academic life Dinning had lived. For Cesca, poverty and her duties as an eldest daughter — required to look after her younger siblings while her mother baked — relegated her to a life of virtual illiteracy. All my other Italian great-grandparents — peasants born between 1893 and 1900 — benefited from some education.

I cannot say if there were books in Mico and Cesca's Applethorpe house apart from schoolbooks, yet they had music. On wintry fireside nights, before his wife and daughter arrived, Mico would take his guitar from its battered case and strum a song that reminded him of Italy. Later he was accompanied by Cesca and their children's singing. I'll never know my great-grandfather, never hear Mico's voice relaying his time on the Granite Belt, so I value Dinning's written voice, his account of this era. And I'm grateful that, like many families, my great-grandparents retold stories, so spoken histories were passed down through the generations — their scribe still decades from being born.

> *In flowing strokes,*
> *letters loop and join*
> *beneath my hand,*
> *coursing writing,*
> *cursive voices,*
> *rising and falling,*
> *overlapping on the page.*
> *The reader partnering*
> *the writer, sometimes*
> *decades, continents apart,*
> *breathing each voice to life*
> *and giving sound to those*
> *between the pages patiently,*
> *humbly, waiting to be heard,*
> *sometimes long forgotten.*

I dig out the notes I took when I began writing down my grandparents' stories and see the pages have tanned slightly with age. *Was it that long ago?* I count back seventeen years. It rattles me slightly. It's true what they say: as you get older the years seem to flit by with greater swiftness. The first day I sat down to properly interview Nonno Anni and Nanna Francesca — taking notes and recording their stories on a whirring tape-recorder I'd borrowed — curiously feels as if it was both a month back and a lifetime ago.

Nanna Francesca and Nonno Anni sit across from me at their kitchen table. She perches forward, leaning on the table's edge with crossed arms. He sits back, arms wide, palms flat and still on the tablecloth. Weeks before, when I told both my grandparents I'd like to begin recording the stories of their lives and that I might write about them one day, neither blinked. They'd nodded and shrugged, pragmatic. Now, as I turn my spiral notebook to a fresh page, the late-spring morning suddenly feels warm. A fug of silence fills the room, bar the chirrups of sparrows bouncing on the patio tiles just beyond the open back door. Nanna Francesca eyes the broomstick. I eye the portable air-conditioner she never allows us to turn on because it creates 'a cold draught'.

'I want to write down how it really was.'

Nanna Francesca, suddenly not so pragmatic, looks at me askance, yet Nonno Anni understands. The joys and successes of their lives as migrants carry in equal measure challenge and grief. Some happenings are especially difficult to talk about, but together we may bring them into the light, if we are all brave.

'Enough history is rewritten,' he says. 'I'll tell you how it happened.'

Nanna Francesca purses her lips. I know this must be hard for her with the Calabrese notion of keeping quiet, keeping your business within the family. And I am under no illusion that no matter how objective I strive to be, the leg rope of being a granddaughter holds me fast.

'Francesca, put on a fresh pot of coffee.' Nonno Anni smiles, giving me a wink that comes out as more of a double blink. 'You know, my father, he used to put a raw egg in his cup of coffee, sometimes a bit of red wine, pieces of bread, then he stir it all up.'

'Yeah?' My lips twist, dubious about how good that might taste.

I hear the click, tick, tick of Nanna Francesca lighting the gas hob. 'Zoë, get the cups.' She sounds abrupt but it is her usual no-nonsense manner more so than any tenseness.

I anticipate the interviews will span hours, be collected over days, months. But on this first morning, with the scent of instant coffee brewed on the stove — International Roast, of course — and Nonno Anni spreading crumbs from one of Nanna Francesca's jam-drop biscuits on the table, we begin to talk. And laugh. And get teary at times. Nonno Anni talks the most, Nanna Francesca filling in the gaps. He has always been a natural storyteller, and my grandmother's pragmatism returns. Like two lines of interplaying music, his voice is the dominant instrument, hers a constant background rhythm, adding, prompting, when the leading notes waver, sometimes a lilt rising above.

ZOË: *So, with the war, when you could no longer receive mail from Italy, you didn't know what was happening with your mother and Elia?*
ANNIBALE: *Well, what could you do? They were at the house and we were here. That's it.*
FRANCESCA: *They had to be safe in their own house, surely.*
ANNIBALE: *I wanted to get back to Fossa, though. I wanted some money to get home.*
ZOË: *You'd changed your mind about staying in Australia?*
ANNIBALE: *Well, you know … the language was hard and the people didn't like us much … Have you heard of the newspaper* Smith's Weekly?
FRANCESCA: *It was half and half. Half the people didn't like us with the war, you know.*
ZOË: *So what was it like when the war was on?*

Burnt Sugar

The cavernous packing shed usually kept the driving heat out, especially if a breeze swept through from one open end to the other, carrying the scent of dry grass. But January 1940 brought a heat so severe it permeated the densest shade, slowed whirring cicadas and made the creek run warm. Annibale's first summer in Australia coincided with the worst heatwave for decades in southeast Queensland. Day after day, the temperature climbed close to, and past, forty degrees Celsius, taking its toll in particular on the elderly and men working in the sun, with one hundred and twelve reported deaths. Accustomed to the bitter winters and mild summers of Fossa, it stunned Annibale that such an enervating heat could drag on for weeks and even kill people.

He worked in the shed alongside Gerolamo and Paolo, sweat running down their faces and bodies, dampening their clothes and plastering their hair to their scalps. They packed green beans into wooden boxes for transporting on the train to Brisbane — the beans destined to feed Australian troops. Although he was a naturalised Australian, the government had identified Carlo Benocci as an 'Italian producer' and stipulated he supply a hundred-weight of beans per month for the army, which bought them at a fixed price, and prohibited him from sending any of his produce to the Brisbane markets where the margins were more profitable. Apart from this, little had changed on the Benocci farm since the outbreak of war. In fact, the war had so far had minimal impact in Australia as a whole. Germany had paused in its conquest of Western Europe in the months following the defeat of Poland and very little fighting was happening.

'People I spoke to in High Street are calling it a "phoney war",' Carlo said after returning from collecting supplies in Stanthorpe. 'They think it'll soon blow over.'

Many older Australians, with the losses of the First World War still fresh in their minds, were hesitant about sending troops again to a war far away in Europe, although young men, disdainful of such caution, were enlisting. The Menzies government held off placing Australian forces and the economy on a war footing, but forbade pacifist groups such as the Quakers from holding meetings, and also banned the Communist Party and groups supporting fascism. Despite being a member of the National Fascist Party for most of his life, Annibale hadn't attended a meeting since leaving Italy and rarely set foot outside the Benocci farm. He thought of his Fascist Youth badge in the bottom of his port and wondered if he should get rid of it. Italy was not yet directly involved in the war, but Hitler and Mussolini's Pact of Steel alliance meant it was only a matter of time. And, unlike the Benocci family, Annibale and the other workers remained Italian citizens.

'I heard it costs five pounds to be naturalised,' moaned Gerolamo. 'How are we ever supposed to be able to afford that?'

Annibale had visions of police turning up at the farm to deport him from Australia. He'd return to Fossa almost as penniless as when he left. He decided he'd had enough of slave wages, freezing quarters and chicken necks. It was time to make his own way, but he knew he owed his father the respect of speaking to him first. He sent word to Vitale that he was coming to Wallangarra on the Sunday train.

'I'm going to Ingham to cut cane.'

Vitale was appalled. 'Annibale, don't be a fool. We have a plan.'

'Plan? It's impossible to make any decent money at Benocci's, let alone enough for Ma and Elia's fares. And even if we could, we can't write to them.' They could only hope Maddalena and Elia would be safe from the war due to the relative isolation of Fossa up in the mountains. 'We could get deported from Australia any day. I want to make a bit of money beforehand.' He didn't voice aloud to his father that he wanted to return to Fossa for good, that if the Australian government didn't deport him, he'd save for his fare home.

Vitale looked up at his son. During his year on the Benocci farm, Annibale had developed muscle and height, and at more than six feet tall he towered over his father. It struck Vitale anew that their long separation during

Annibale's formative years was always going to undermine his parental authority. He slumped down on a bench seat in the shade of Wallangarra Station's lengthy portico, staring at the tracks. The red-brick Victorian-style building was grander than most, being where interstate travellers changed trains between Queensland's narrow-gauge and New South Wales' standard-gauge tracks. Vitale was glad he'd met Annibale at the station rather than having this conversation in front of the others at the farm.

'What about Benocci? You can't let him down.' Vitale was unable to fathom Annibale leaving the relative safety of the farm.

'Papà, for more than a year now I've worked for his small wages.' Annibale thought his father was being unfair. He felt he'd done his duty. The war thrust the future into a kind of limbo and Annibale no longer felt obliged to continue working on the Benocci farm. 'I'm going to cut cane and make some real money,' he said. 'Why don't you come with me?'

Vitale shook his head. 'It's backbreaking work. Nearly did me in last time. I'm almost forty-six, getting old …' He sighed deeply. 'And if you honoured your father you wouldn't go.' Vitale heaved another sigh, more exaggerated this time and sneaked a glance under his bushy eyebrows. 'But don't you worry about me. You do what you think is right.'

It was stifling sitting in the train carriage heading north to Ingham, but watching the landscape transform into lush green seas of rippling cane filled Annibale with a pleasure he hadn't felt in a long time — *freedom*. In spite of it being autumn, as the train wended its way up the Queensland coast to the far north, the heat gradually intensified. Annibale jammed open the stiff window as far as he could but the hot air blowing in barely dried the sweat before it formed again. He could feel it beading in his hair and trickling down his neck. And yet, sitting on a shabby seat with one port containing all he owned, he was happy to be shaping his own destiny. Even if Vitale, when realising his son was going to defy his wishes, was stony toward Annibale as he tried to say goodbye. Annibale cringed, knowing Maddalena would be upset by their parting badly at such a time. But she wasn't in Australia.

It didn't help that in April, Germany blazed into action again, seizing Denmark and Norway, and pressuring Italy, which remained noncommittal, to honour its Pact of Steel and enter the war. Annibale had arranged a spot on an Italian cane gang with Stefano Tomasi, the husband of Giovanna, their neighbour in Fossa, to start in June for the 1940 cane season. He'd just given his notice to Benocci when it hit the press that Germany had invaded Holland and France. Britain was now under threat. The 'phoney war' was over. Australian troops were now fighting in the Middle East and the Mediterranean, mostly under British commanders, with many RAAF members also serving in Britain. The German *blitzkrieg* was crushing much of Western Europe, with British troops needing to be rescued at Dunkirk.

Italy entered the war, much to the distress and bewilderment of many Italian-Australians. Passengers and crews of Italian ships docked at Australian ports or sailing within its waters became the first Italian prisoners of war in Australia. The ship *Remo*, on which Annibale and Pandi had sailed to Australia, was detained in Fremantle. Its sister ship, the *Romolo*, on which Cesca and Francesca had travelled, had sailed from Brisbane, but was set on fire and scuttled out at sea by its crew just before they and the passengers on board were picked up by the Australian navy ship *Manoora*, and the men taken to a POW camp in New South Wales. Soon after, HMAS *Sydney* sank two Italian ships, one of them the *Espero*, with the *Sydney* staying to pick up more than forty Italian survivors before returning to Alexandria in Egypt.

The Italian migrants in Australia received such news with mixed emotions. There were Australians on neighbouring farms and in town with whom the Italians had been friends for years. Many of them assured their Italian friends nothing would change between them but others became distant and guarded. The war was causing racism to escalate, too. Migrants feared some Australians were turning on them. Annibale was venturing north during shaky times. Word travelled on the Italian grapevine that in North Queensland in particular, Italian migrants were bearing the brunt of racist attacks, including bashings. Vitale had written to Annibale before he left, making one last plea for him not to go.

A year ago, his parents' word would have been law, but travelling halfway across the world, enduring the Benocci farm and facing the uncertainty of war, Annibale felt entitled to make some decisions of his own. He was sixteen, his hands callused with work. Like all labourers, Annibale knew his survival and success depended on a strong body and stamina, both of which he possessed. He was thankful to have inherited some of his grandfather's height and his mother's astuteness. So far, they had got him on a train to Ingham.

The journey from Stanthorpe to Ingham's cane fields was the equivalent of traversing the entire length of Italy, from Sicily up to the very top of 'the boot'. Watching large tracts of land rush past the open train window, Annibale thought of Pandi. *This country is so huge I'll probably never see Pandi again*, he thought. Yet he wondered if Ingham was far from Biloela.

Situated on the floodplain of the Herbert River, Ingham's heat and high rainfall were perfect for growing sugarcane. Of its two sugar mills — the Victoria and the Macknade — the Victoria was one of the largest in Australia, each season processing millions of tonnes of cane, filling the air with a cloying, almost liquorice scent of molasses. Sugarcane was Queensland's most valuable crop, and in Australia second in value only to wheat. The Australian sugar crop, ninety-five percent of which Queensland yielded, was among the largest in the world.

Annibale had written to Stefano because Vitale had worked on the same gang with him in the early '30s. Stefano had since become the leader of a gang of Italian cutters and aspired to own his own cane farm one day.

'You right-handed or left?' Stefano asked after Annibale stowed his port under a spare canvas stretcher bed in the corrugated-iron shed the cane gang shared. Even the walls and windows were of corrugated iron, each window propped open with a stick.

'Well, left originally but I learnt to use my right. Both, really.'

Stefano handed him a cane knife, a wooden-handled oversized machete with a hooked end. 'It's harder to cut if you're left-handed. I'll show you how in the morning. Come on, we'll join the others for dinner and I'll introduce you to the rest of the gang.'

Annibale followed Stefano along a dirt trail worn through knee-high grass to another shed, which housed a crude kitchen and a trestle table with bench seats.

'Home-style *Italiano* cooking here, Annibale.' Stefano grinned, clapping him on the back. 'You'll remember my wife, Giovanna — well, I brought the family out from Fossa. It's lucky they got out here on one of the last ships before contact with Italy was cut.'

Giovanna clanged a lid halfway over a tall pot of boiling pasta and came around from the other side of the kitchen table. 'I bet finding us in Australia must be a great surprise.' She smiled, seeing the look on his face. For a moment, Annibale couldn't speak. Seeing Maddalena's close friend was almost like seeing his mother again for the first time in more than a year. She squeezed him tight and he inhaled the smell of onions along with a faint hint of perspiration. 'We were so lucky to get here before the war took off. I'm sorry but I don't have any news except your mother and Elia were both in good health when we left. I'm sure they are safe.'

'Yes.' Annibale found his voice again. 'I'm sure they must be.'

Stefano and Giovanna's daughter, Savina, not much older than Annibale, looked up from cutting a pile of carrots and gave him a nod and a discreet smile. He remembered her as more girlish when he'd left Fossa, but now she appeared … older. As Giovanna and Stefano chatted on, they seemed unaware of Annibale's gaze returning to Savina's bent head, her black hair in two shiny braids. Nor did they notice her eyes, their darkness almost glowing, venturing to meet his.

Annibale discovered that cutting cane meant working harder than he'd ever worked in his life. As Vitale said, it was backbreaking, dirty work. The cane-cutting season extended from June through to December, and although cutting began in the cooler months, the winters in Ingham were brief and Annibale was soon struggling with the heat. Sometimes they cut the cane while it was green with the 'trash' of leaves to slice off too. Other times they lit the fields, the energetic orange flames lashing at the black night sky. After these burns, Annibale quickly became covered in a slick mixture of sweat and soot as he cut the cane stalks left behind, but at least the snakes and rats were gone — and with them the risk of Weil's disease, an infection from rats that could be deadly.

Annibale's hands smarted with nicks and blisters that swelled overnight. His arms and back became stiff and ached. They cut under boiling sun or pounding rain. To keep motivated, he kept tallying up the shillings against his tally of tons, enjoying the satisfaction of earning decent money for his efforts. The cane was about seven feet tall and Annibale's height and build worked in his favour, his ton percentage high. Where he had earned twenty-five shillings a week at the Benocci farm, he was now averaging thirteen pounds each week, more than double the average weekly Australian wage. After long, strenuous days, the cutters slept soundly in their dormitory-style hut near the riverbank despite the oppressive heat, the clamour of crickets and frogs and the occasional possum plummeting from an overhanging tree branch and landing with a bone-jarring bang before scuttling across the iron-sheeted roof.

Since bringing Giovanna and the family out to Australia, Stefano had moved into a house in town with them, driving out to the cane fields each morning in his treasured second-hand Dodge ute. Giovanna came with him most days, sitting straight-backed on the ute's bench seat, her hefty bosoms resting over a big basket of food on her lap. Some days she asked Savina to accompany her to help with the cooking, and Annibale and Savina often managed to snatch some time to talk amid the overlapping conversations at mealtime. But generally Savina had to stay home to do the laundry and keep house, much to her and Annibale's disappointment. Giovanna didn't think it right for her youngest daughter to spend too much time around a bunch of mostly unmarried men, preferring to cook the meals for the men each day herself.

Annibale ignored the friendly jeers of the other cane-cutters and suppressed a smile at seeing the neat stack of shirts left by Savina on the end of his bed. The cutters washed their blackened, sugar-stiffened clothes on Sundays, bending them into kerosene tins of boiling water with slivers of kerosene soap. Savina had offered to wash Annibale's shirts and singlets, and though their material was faded and worn from much use, she returned them immaculately cleaned and ironed, and folded with much care.

Late one afternoon, his wet hair combed back, bath towel slung over one shoulder as he returned from the communal showers, Annibale saw Savina by the riverbank behind the kitchen hut. He had his dirty cane-cutting shorts and singlet tucked under one arm and hurriedly dumped them in the dormitory before heading back to talk to her. Like most Italian parents, Giovanna and Stefano would not permit an unmarried daughter to be in the company of a male without a chaperone, but Annibale reasoned the other cutters were frequently walking by on their way back from the showers and he could see Giovanna just inside the open kitchen window briskly kneading dough on the floured tabletop.

He found Savina picking cherry tomatoes from bushes staked with the whittled backbones of stripped palm fronds. She broke into a smile as he approached, glancing up at her mother's form framed by the kitchen window. As Savina continued picking, she and Annibale chatted together. From a distance, the young couple could have been examining one of the plants, heads bowed together, the late-afternoon sun accentuating hints of gold in their dark hair.

'Hoi!'

They both flinched. A group of men from an Australian cane gang stood on the opposite bank of the river, shirts tied around their waists, bare skin glistening with sweat.

'Shouldn't eat those if I were you,' one of them yelled out. 'Riverbank is full of snakes. Those tomatoes will be poisonous, growing where the snakes are.'

A few of the cutters laughed. Annibale and Savina looked at each other. They waved and continued picking. The Australians shook their heads and sauntered off. One kicked at the ground, billowing up river sand, and shouted, 'Mad dagos.'

Annibale turned to Savina. 'What does that mean?'

Holding her basket in one hand, she held the other above her forehead to shade her eyes from the sun, watching the men move into the distance. 'I'm not sure.'

That evening, as the Italian cutters tucked into plates of pasta flavoured with the cherry tomatoes, some cheese and parsley, Giovanna said, 'Oh, *mamma mia*, I had to go into town this morning to buy some sheets …' This prompted laughter among the cutters as, no matter how hard she tried, her pronunciation of the double 'e' always sounded like an 'i'. 'I always look first when I go to shops to make sure an older Australian is serving because some of the younger ones just laugh in my face at my accent. But, oh, when I found out what I was really saying to the Australians when I said "sheets" …' She pretended to cover the ears of Savina sitting beside her, giggling at the same time.

'The first few months after I arrived in Australia,' Stefano was not to be outdone, 'one day I went in to buy some eggs and I came out with an axe.' As they laughed, he added, 'I was too embarrassed to go ask again.'

'What's that they call a "dago"?' Annibale asked, ending the laughter.

Stefano frowned. 'Where did you hear that?'

'From one of the Australian cutters, across the riverbank.'

'If you're not born in Australia they've got it in for you,' one of the other cutters said. 'Especially now with the war on. I got called a dago and spat on the last time I was in town and all I was doing was walking down the street.'

'The Australians have nicknames for everyone.' Stefano threw up one hand as if to say, *What can you do?* 'Poms, froggies, yanks, chows, kikes, dagos. Sometimes they use them fondly, but many times they don't.'

'How about *Smith's Weekly*?' said another cutter. The newspaper was openly critical of Italians in Australia, regularly referring to them in print as 'dirty, dago pests'.

'I haven't seen it,' Annibale admitted.

'I kept this so I can show my grandchildren one day what we had to put up with.' An older cutter reached into a battered tea-chest in the corner, the copy fluttering onto Annibale's lap. Upon opening it, the first thing he saw was a caricature of an Italian as a hairy, snarling, limp-moustached figure wielding his cane knife like a weapon, snatching land from timid-looking fair Australians. Annibale had been unaware the economic success of some Italian settlers had become a cause of resentment for numerous British-Australians, particularly in sugarcane areas. He was starting to read some English and saw another article which criticised the accented speech of 'the Italian settler', along with Italian behaviour, eating habits and the darkness of their olive skin. When he got stuck on a sentence, Stefano translated for him, reading aloud, 'Italians are a greasy flood of Mediterranean scum that seek to defile and debase Australia …'

Annibale was stunned. And hurt.

Men swarmed into town on their day off, most going to the pub to slake their thirst from a week of cutting cane. As the war ratcheted up, many of the Italian cutters opted to crack open the brown bottles of beer back at their hut. Annibale drank beer at the hut too, becoming accustomed to the bitter taste of Australian lager, but after several months he longed for a change in surroundings. The early-summer heat was already stifling and it had been a hard week cutting. Several blisters on his palms had opened and bled, and his shoulders ached. He'd heard the other cutters praising the superior taste of a beer 'off the wood' at the pub, and he had never tried one poured straight from a wooden keg.

He walked into town on his own, unable to coax any of the other Italian cutters to join him in light of the latest spate of racial friction. Allied troops had attacked Italian troops in Egypt and Libya, and some local Australians were crowing about reports of 38,000 poorly equipped Italians being defeated and taken prisoner after just four days in the battle at Sidi Barrani.

The pub Annibale wandered into was an expansive wooden building with rooms to let upstairs and a bar, dining room and ladies' lounge downstairs. A wrap-around verandah on the top storey shaded the front footpath, the posts adorned with cobwebby wrought-iron lacework. In the main bar the windowsills were deep, their paint worn away by the many arms resting on them over the years, and the double sash windows were pushed high to let breezes in and tobacco smoke and spittle out. Men stood around or perched on stools. On the long bar counter two wooden kegs sat with taps facing barmaids who poured beers with just the right amount of foamy head, skilfully skimming the overflow into metal drip trays.

Still shy of seventeen, Annibale could pass for the lawful drinking age of twenty-one. His English wasn't fluent but he was starting to get by. Stefano had told him to ask for a 'pot' of beer, which to Annibale sounded strange. The fair-haired barmaid, her floral dress pulled taut across her breasts, didn't move at his request and he wondered if he'd said it wrong.

'A pot?' he repeated, somewhat uncertainly.

The barmaid's lips thinned. Then she almost smiled as she gave a nod. She lifted a drip tray and poured it into a glass, half filling it. Then she picked up the second drip tray, pouring until the glass brimmed with the murky dregs. She placed it in front of Annibale and held out her open palm. 'Sixpence.' Her remote blue eyes looked like they could belong to a doll.

Annibale was too shocked to speak. Anger surged through him. He picked up the glass and splashed the dregs in her face. Her shriek was shrill. An Australian cane-cutter leapt from his bar stool and was beside Annibale in three swift strides, issuing a hard punch to the jaw. Annibale punched back. The pub erupted with shouts and the scraping of barstools as everyone rushed to get a better look. Annibale kept punching the other bloke, getting several strong punches in return.

Two policemen pushed their way through the crowd and saw an Italian migrant punching an Australian. 'Come on! Break it up.' They waded in, grabbing Annibale.

The Australian stumbled backwards, caught by some of the onlookers. 'Bloody dago,' he panted, wiping his bleeding nose. 'You lot should get off back to your own country.'

Annibale strained forward but the two policemen held his arms fast.

'What's your name, son?' the older policeman asked.

Annibale looked from one to the other, the trouble he was in dawning on him. He spluttered out his name, still out of breath from the fight.

'Right, you're coming to the station with us.'

They started half-dragging Annibale towards the door. In his panic, his English began to fail him, his pleas becoming stumbled and peppered with Italian. He suddenly remembered the Franciscan monk's warning — too late.

'Hold on there a minute.' A clear Australian voice rang out through the pub.

Both police turned slightly, still holding Annibale. They saw old Bert standing before them, a respected member of the community, once a cane-cutter and now a plantation owner.

'Jim, this isn't right,' Bert said to the older police officer. 'I saw what happened. The Eye-tie is trying to tell you the truth. This barmaid here, Moira, poured him the dregs from the drip trays. Now this lad may have given her back the dregs but Keith here threw the first punch, and we all know Keith's been sweet on Moira for ages.'

The police officer let out a small sigh. 'Moira, what did you do that for?'

Hair still dripping stale beer, Moira straightened with a haughty air. 'Well, the boss said that when the pigs come in —'

'Moira, he's not a pig.' The police officer shook his head. 'He's a human being like everyone else …'

To them we are pigs? Annibale didn't hear any more. The grip on his arms slackened and he stood there, eyes fixed on his boots, feeling the crowd looking him up and down. He felt like an outcast. His only comfort was that despite an Australian causing the trouble, another Australian had got him out of it. Annibale realised how vulnerable he was in a country where he was in a minority, where the authorities believed a local's word before his own. Still, they let him go.

The Olive Peril

I hold the long, smooth handle of the cane knife. The wood was perhaps once a walnut colour, but has deepened with use and age, oiled with sweat and blood to a russet-brown the same hue as the machete-like blade now covered in a thin layer of rust. I tentatively touch the blade, still sharp more than seventy years after Nonno Anni cut cane. He once grew a few sticks of sugarcane in his backyard to show me what it was like. I remember his huge hands bending a long stalk above my mouth so the sweet juice ran in, both of us laughing as some ran down my chin, my father jostling so he too could have a taste.

For decades, the cane knife sat underneath my grandparents' house, among half-empty paint cans, tools, brown beer bottles full of homemade tomato *passata*, wooden fruit boxes, *ferratelle* 'waffle' irons, soft-drink crates from the milk bar, discarded pots and stacked chairs that were brushed free of cobwebs and dust whenever a party was held. For almost eight years of my life I was an only child, and had no first cousins, so with only adults in the family for company, I often drifted under my grandparents' house to play while the others were upstairs. Two storerooms and a huge laundry, as well as the garage, were each an Aladdin's cave for my imagination and perfect for creating stories. It began for me a lifetime of seeing what some might consider junk or clutter as a trove of treasure.

There were two cane knives originally and I'm grateful to have been given one of them long before the flood; that this portal to one story among many wasn't lost.

Rain is falling steadily from the night sky, but inside the library the air is dry and warm. A leathery, inky, dusty scent of row upon row of books pervades the quiet space, a reassuring smell. When I first sat down, I was one of many hunched over in separate wooden study carrels. The number of people here now is dwindling, a feeling of emptiness seeming to percolate throughout the study area and along the rows of tall bookcases. I rub my eyes, sore from hours of reading, and glance at raindrops trickling down the window.

Decades of material — newspaper articles, essays and the speeches of various politicians and authorities in Australia from the 1890s to the 1950s — disparages Italian migrants for being 'cheap labour', 'working longer hours than required to make more money', 'living frugally' and 'taking jobs from whites'. For having 'grease oozing from hair and complexions due to a diet based on olive oil'; for 'eating worms' (spaghetti) and 'bait' (calamari); for their 'stature', 'smelling different', and 'having a darker shade of skin'.

The material urges Australian women not to marry Italian men, not to have children with 'polluted blood'. I realise I am one of these said children. I look at cartoon illustrations published in the press right up until the mid-twentieth century that over and again depict Italian men as swarthy, moustached, leering, threatening. The printed pages of newspapers may be faded with age, but headlines and phrases jump out, too intense to fade completely: 'Olive Influx', 'Dago Menace', 'Olive Trash', 'Greasy Wogs', 'Olive Peril' …

And one of the fiercer spots for this sort of denigration was the Queensland cane fields — an area already notorious for decades of 'blackbirding'. South Sea Islanders were enticed, tricked or simply grabbed from beaches and kidnapped onto boats by 'blackbirders' who called themselves 'recruiting agents' and who worked directly or indirectly for Australian sugar plantation owners seeking free or cheap indentured labour. It was thought that white people couldn't (or shouldn't) tolerate working in tropical conditions, but black people could. This practice began in 1863, the year Abraham Lincoln declared the end of slavery in the United States, and would continue for the next forty years, with around 62,000 Pacific Islanders traded as human cargo — until the Queensland government brusquely sent them packing, even those with established lives and families in Australia who didn't want to leave.

With my elbow on the edge of the desk, I put my head on my hand. Black, white, olive, green — the cane grew tall and tasted the same regardless of who planted, cut and stacked it.

I walk a narrow trail
shadowed by tall sugarcane,
straining to see what stands
hidden to my left and right.
Churned earth connives
to trip me up.
The cane rustles in murmur,
impenetrable,
to the right and left.
Only the row's far end
is visible.
Same distance to go
forward or back.
The ancient blue sky,
licked by green cane leaves,
sees all, out of reach.

Sitting in the dim theatre with Roger beside me, our faces illuminated by stage light spilling from the performance of *Summer of the Seventeenth Doll*, I find myself thinking more of my Australian grandfather, Bob, as Ray Lawler's story of the seventeenth off-season for two cane-cutters unfolds. Grandpa Bob, Nonno Anni and Bisnonno Vitale all cut cane; Bisnonno Mico was a cane-gang cook. As far as I am aware, none of their seasons at the cane overlapped. When Nonno Anni was in Ingham, Grandpa Bob had already enlisted in the army (using his older brother Jim's birth certificate, since Bob was underage at the time). Yet Grandpa Bob cut cane just after the war, when there was still anti-Italian sentiment there. I decide to ask him about it when no one else is around.

I can hear him humming before I find him in his garage, where I've often sought him out at various times in my life, fixing or doing a service on his car. A tool lands with a metallic thud back in his toolbox and, looking up from underneath the bonnet of his car, he smiles to see me. 'G'day, love.'

The Olive Peril

Both Grandpa Bob and Nonno Anni have well-stocked garages full of tools, with various bits and pieces saved for reuse. Each has the knowledge — and preference — to fix or make things himself whenever he can, stemming from childhoods and young adulthoods during which they had little and made do. This similarity hadn't occurred to me until now.

'It was pretty competitive,' Grandpa Bob admits, when I ask him what he recalls of Italians on the cane fields. 'We wanted to cut more cane than the Italians, and I'm sure they wanted to beat us, too. Some blokes got annoyed, saying the Italians were taking our jobs, especially since we'd fought them in the war.' He straightens to wipe car grease from his hands on an old rag. 'You know, when I cut cane at Mirani, first we had to extend a narrow-gauge track from the main line out to the farm, and then push the small cane trucks into place — before we'd even cut any cane!'

He shakes his head, though his blue eyes are smiling in the corners. 'Cutting the cane was tough. The idea was to work up and down the rows, wrapping your arm around six to eight sticks at a time and cutting them at ground level. Then you tossed them on the ground with the tops all in one direction. When you'd cut and stacked four or more rows, you began "topping" the cane — lopping off the green tops. Then the loading onto trucks began. The cane trash — the leaves — had serrated edges, and I suffered cuts along my rib cage and around my ankles from it. And before you could take your aching body back to the barracks, the patch of cane to be cut the following day had to be burnt off.'

I notice he doesn't bring up the Italian cutters again, and never refers to them as being darker skinned. My wishful thought is that maybe it wasn't an issue for him, though I suspect more likely he doesn't want to hurt me by revealing an intolerance of other races earlier in his life, especially around the war years — long before his blonde daughter would fall in love with a dark-haired Italian. He could have made a careless comment as we chatted but instead he's acted with decency, knowing I must love my Italian grandfather as much as I do him.

In the 1940s, Grandpa Bob lived for a short time in a rented room above a row of shops on the opposite side of the road to Nonno Anni's fruit shop and milk bar, and while they would have passed each other frequently, they didn't know each other. Neither of them would have believed their lives would end up forever entwined with the marriage of their eldest children about twenty years later, especially as cross-cultural marriages were disapproved of at the time.

My grandfathers were both born in October 1923, three days apart, on opposite sides of the world. While Annibale grew up in the snowy mountains of Fossa, Bob mostly lived near the beach at Manly in Sydney. Annibale was dark-eyed, dark-haired and olive skinned; Bob, a contrast of fairness, had blue eyes and sandy hair. They were tall, about the same height, physically fit and strong. They worked hard in numerous jobs as young men before each establishing their own businesses with the assistance of their wives and achieving success.

Throughout his life, Bob liked watching cricket and football; Annibale rarely watched sport of any kind. Bob favoured meat and potatoes; Annibale, meat and pasta. Neither cared much for salad, nor were they churchgoers. They valued family, living an honest life. Both were quick to step in to defend or help a stranger, especially the underdog. Both patriotic men, their mother countries were on opposite sides during the war. They could so easily have chosen to shun each other, focus on their differences rather than their similarities. But they didn't, for the sake of two little girls, their shared granddaughters.

Perhaps most of us are more alike than we sometimes realise.

Tempesta

As the last stands of cane flicked and slanted in the breeze drifting over the emptying paddocks, Annibale contemplated what to do next. He was keen to work the following cane season but had about five months to fill in until then. Savina was inwardly pleased to hear he didn't want to travel all the way back to Stanthorpe for the off-season.

'I can't go back to earning twenty-five shillings a week,' he said to her under the cover of the boisterous conversations of the cutters gathering for the smoko of brown bread, cheese and sweet biscuits studded with citrus peel, which Savina and Giovanna had just hauled out to the cane field in old kerosene tins. He didn't mention that Benocci would have replaced him or that his father wasn't pleased with him. 'I need to find some farm work not too far away. Do you know if Biloela is near here? I have a friend, Pandi who—'

'Never heard of it.' She began to move away, sensing her mother looking at them. 'Just promise that you'll come back for the next cutting season.'

Stefano introduced Annibale to a man called Duncan Jones who had a property about forty miles away at Mount Fox. Duncan had been in Australia for many years, yet retained some of his English accent.

'So what work have you done, apart from cutting the cane?' Duncan's unblinking eyes looked him up and down.

'Well, I've worked on farms most of my life,' Annibale told him. 'We had a farm back in Italy and I've also worked on a farm at Cottonvale.'

Duncan nodded slowly. 'You're how old?'

'He's seventeen, but he's strong,' Stefano piped up. 'High tonnage. Cut more cane than some of the men.'

'Is that so?' Duncan scratched along his jaw.

'Look, I can do any work that needs doing,' offered Annibale. 'It doesn't worry me if I'm just fixing fences or something.'

With a slow nod, Duncan stuck out his hand. 'All right. Two pounds a week plus keep.'

Annibale clasped Duncan's hand in his own. 'Done.'

The landscape around Duncan's farm at Mount Fox differed again from the farms Annibale had worked on in Fossa and Cottonvale. An ancient volcanic eruption from the mountain that gave the area its name had blanketed the surrounding land in rich, fertile soil. Rainfall was high and everything from Duncan's crops of maize and sugarcane to the ever-encroaching bushland and subtropical rainforest grew lushly. As the men worked in the paddocks, large, flightless cassowary birds with black plumage and brilliant blue necks stalked and foraged in the bush beyond the fence lines. Insects kept up a dissonant percussion both day and night.

Lying in bed, waiting for sleep to come, Annibale thought of Fossa. The snow would be melting once again, with the valley about to burst into spring, a beautiful time of year. Elia would have grown. He envisaged his mother, wishing he had a photograph. Being unable to write to her while the war continued produced a dull ache that settled somewhere in the pit of his stomach. *If she had been my father, we would be in a different situation now. He still felt exasperated Vitale wouldn't come up and cut cane with him. We could be making so much more money between us.*

He allowed his thoughts to stray to Savina ... the curve of her calves below her modest dresses, the tiny mole on the back of her neck. He sighed and punched the lumpy pillow into a more comfortable form.

Duncan was Annibale's first non-Italian boss, yet, like Benocci, he kept his workers at a distance and rarely showed any warmth. The two other workers on the farm were also Italian cutters filling in during the off-season. They were a few years older than Annibale and both from another cane gang and the same village in Campania. It baffled Annibale that Duncan chose to employ Italian migrants. Duncan and his wife barely concealed their belief that migrants, Italians especially, were inferior to them. Though the Joneses had also immigrated, being from England they didn't consider themselves migrants since Australia was but one loyal part of the vast empire over which Britain ruled. Government propaganda easily influenced the couple, whose staunch belief in everything Menzies and Churchill said and did allowed no room for question.

Annibale saw Duncan sitting in the squatter's chair on the verandah, keenly reading *Smith's Weekly,* and wondered whether he might exploit his workers for being migrants, even though his wages were fairer than those Benocci paid. In time, he began to understand Duncan's real rationale for hiring them: he could feel superior to Italian workers in a way he couldn't with Anglo-Australians.

Duncan seemed driven by God, too, but a different type of God from the one Annibale had grown up with in Italy. Duncan's God was of the fire-and-brimstone variety, an unforgiving, punitive God, born out of the pages of a Bible he read from each evening. He took each word on the worn, tissue-like pages as absolute truth and wielded quotations like a threatening staff. Annibale found it difficult to endure Duncan's moralistic ravings about Hell and damnation, but he kept his mouth shut. He, the other workers and Duncan's tiny, listless wife sat silently through the readings and sermons Duncan tacked on to the saying of grace as the food on their plates grew cold.

Every Sunday Duncan and his wife went into town to go to church and every other Saturday they all went into town to get supplies. Duncan pretended not to notice that while his wife did the shopping two of his workers went to the pub, but he did observe that Annibale didn't join them, choosing instead to go for a walk or stay at the farm.

'The pub not for you then, boy?' Duncan said to him back at the farm after the midday meal, the other two workers having stayed on in town.

Annibale shook his head, not about to relay what had happened to him in Ingham.

'I'm going out shortly to have another try at killing a wild pig that's been running amok,' Duncan told him. 'Be good eating, too. You can come with me.'

They set off into the bush that began promptly where Duncan's property ended. The cassowaries hissed and scattered. Annibale followed closely behind Duncan as they trampled through native grasses, the occasional crisp snap of twigs loud under their work boots. They walked into a landscape of boulders and bottle-tree scrub lightly shaded by tall eucalypts peeling scraggly bark. A startled wallaby sprang from a patch of vine thicket lining a small gully and they heard it thump away, swiftly disappearing into the scrub. Annibale looked all around him and could see only bush. He had no idea of the way back to the farm.

Duncan held his rifle over his arm uncocked and Annibale carried a tall pole and a coil of rope. They had walked for about half an hour when Duncan drew them to a halt and motioned for Annibale to crouch down with him behind some low scrub. Duncan readied his gun, then put a finger to his lips. Annibale nodded and kept quiet. After a while he could feel his legs beginning to tire. The sun, despite filtering through the trees, was hot on his back. He carefully, quietly shifted his feet and continued to wait.

Presently, Duncan let out a soft grunt and drew his gun up to shoulder height and into firing position. Annibale followed the tip of the gun to see the hulking form of a wild pig picking its way through the bush. The sudden crack of the rifle was deafening. Annibale's ears were still ringing long afterwards. Duncan, all business, set about gutting the pig, leaving the innards where the unfortunate beast died, explaining it would be heavy enough to carry back as it was. He instructed Annibale to help tie the legs of the pig onto the pole so they could walk back in single file, each with a pole end across his shoulder and the pig carcass swinging between them.

They were about to lift the carcass when Annibale thought he heard the sound of crying. He paused, listening hard, thinking his ringing ears must be playing tricks. Then he heard it again.

'Okay, lift?' It was more of a command from Duncan than a question.

Annibale frowned. 'Hold on a minute. Did you hear that?'

'What?'

'Listen.' Both men stood with their heads tilted, straining to listen. And there it was … the unmistakable sound.

'That's a baby crying.' Annibale swung round, trying to work out which direction it was coming from.

'Nah, it's just a bird or something.' Duncan bent to lift the pig.

'It doesn't sound like a bird to me.' Annibale set off in the direction of the crying.

Duncan stood there a moment, then swore beneath his breath and followed.

Annibale stopped stock-still. Near the base of a tree, an Aboriginal baby lay covered in black ants. He stared in shock.

'Don't look at it.' Duncan's face was grim.

Annibale scanned the bush. There was no one else around.

'Do you think they just forgot him or something?'

Duncan shook his head. 'They've left it on the ant bed on purpose. Maybe cause it's a half-caste. It's their business. Come on, we've got to get back.'

'We can't leave this baby here!'

'What are we supposed to do with it? It's none of our business. Come on, time to go.' Duncan's voice was firm.

'But it's wrong. We can't leave him here!'

Duncan's eyes narrowed. 'I thought you understood English. I said it's time to go.'

Annibale looked at Duncan, then back to the baby again. 'It's not right.'

'Look, you're going to have to make a choice.' Duncan took his rifle off his shoulder. 'Now either you help me carry back the pig or you can stay here …' He caressed the trigger.

Annibale instantly grasped his meaning. They were far from anyone, deep in the bush. He stood there unmoving, distressed. Duncan roughly pushed him to start walking. Annibale realised his mouth was open and closed it. He could feel his feet moving, his back prodded, his boss behind him, but his mind and his heart remained at the base of the tree. Bile kept rising in his throat and he forced it back down, trying not to gag.

Wordlessly they shouldered the heavy weight of the pig, Duncan taking the lead, and carried it through the bush towards the property. As they walked, Annibale could hear the cries of the baby echoing throughout the bush long after the sounds had died away. He stared at Duncan's back with a mixture of anguish and hatred.

Before they got to the house, Duncan made it clear Annibale wasn't to say a word about it to anyone, threatening him with consequences if he did. He held his rifle as he said this. After the pub incident, Annibale knew most of those in authority would prefer to believe the word of an Englishman in his forties than that of a seventeen-year-old dago. The other two workers had returned from town and Duncan instructed them to help him butcher the pig. Annibale said nothing and went back to the workers' quarters to shower. For a long while, he stood beneath the stream of water and wept.

That evening when they all sat waiting to begin eating, Duncan opened his Bible. Annibale leant forward and picked up his knife and fork. Duncan's wife and the other two workers exchanged glances. The only sound in the room was of metal cutlery on china plate. Annibale kept his head down, chewing briskly. Duncan took a breath, fingered the leather bookmark and began reading aloud.

Scarred with self-recrimination and regret, Annibale remained haunted by images of a baby he wished he'd gone back to save. Nights were the worst when he couldn't sleep because of the sound. He covered his ears but still he could hear the baby's cries.

To get several crops out of one planting of sugarcane, it was common practice to leave behind stubble when harvesting. New shoots sprouted from this, becoming a 'ratoon' crop, which would be harvested for three or four years and then ploughed in before planting new setts. Duncan's ratoon crop was four years old and so it was ready to be ploughed in. While he usually hitched up the horses to pull the plough, this time Duncan had managed to borrow a tractor from a neighbouring property. He directed the two Campanian workers to do chores close to the homestead and told Annibale to stand behind him on the tractor to learn how to operate it.

Annibale's lips twitched, wanting to say no. Since the incident in the bush, he was desperate to move on but had to think carefully about what to do. He sensed Duncan was edgy, worried Annibale might talk, as he mostly kept him near at hand now. Only seventeen, in the middle of nowhere, a migrant in an area where racist attacks against Italians were escalating with the war — Annibale had to keep his wits about him. There was no one here to look out for him.

So with Annibale standing behind Duncan on the tractor, they chugged up and down the field, churning up the rich soil in their wake. As the afternoon wore on, storm clouds drew over the sky, creating an early twilight. The air was still and muggy. When the sound of thunder began, Annibale became keen to get back to the house.

Leaning forward, he pointed to the ominous sky. 'I don't like the look of that.' He had to raise his voice over the tractor motor.

Duncan cast a look up. 'It's a way off yet. I have to return the tractor tomorrow.'

The clouds rumbled closer. Annibale leant back, biting his tongue. Storms were vicious in North Queensland and could be upon you faster than you could prepare for them. They continued up and down the field. Flashes of lightning appeared, the clouds thundering. Annibale lifted his hat to wipe his brow, his clothes soaking with sweat from the increasing humidity.

Duncan applied the brake and Annibale almost toppled forward as they lurched to a halt. He sighed inwardly with relief as Duncan turned off the engine.

'You need to know how to use this so you can finish the field on your own.' Duncan jumped down from the tractor and Annibale's heart sank. 'Right, switch her on.'

Out of the corner of his eye, Annibale saw Duncan put his hands on his hips. He sat down in the driver's seat and tried turning the motor on. Nothing happened. There was the faintest hint of a breeze. Annibale felt the welcome coolness of it drift across his bare forearms, but the drop in temperature also indicated that the storm was almost upon them. He tried to turn on the motor again. Still nothing happened. All of a sudden, the breeze whipped up into a squall. Annibale tried the tractor yet again.

'What are you *doing*?' Duncan grabbed his hat before it flew off his head.

Annibale looked up to see the wind flaying the trees on the field perimeter, bending some of the smaller half-grown ones almost in two. Duncan climbed up and elbowed Annibale aside. He attempted to start the tractor again and again, trying to force the engine back to life. Swearing, he hit the steering wheel and jumped back down.

The wind was rushing past Annibale's ears. 'We should get back to the house. It's too dangerous out here now.'

Duncan's look was scornful. 'Have a bit of backbone, boy.' His shout barely cut through the screaming wind. 'It's not even raining yet. I'll have a look at the motor. When I give the word, pump the throttle and hit the switch — all right?'

The first drops of rain daubed lopsided circles on the metal body of the tractor.

'Try it now,' he commanded.

Nothing. Duncan fiddled with the motor again. Annibale lifted his gaze and saw a white haze of rain coming towards them. A crackle of lightning lit the sky, accompanied by thunder so loud that Annibale ducked involuntarily.

He felt the tractor vibrate. The motor made a rapid *prprpt* noise. Duncan yelled 'Maaaaa!' as he was hurled onto the dirt. He lay on his back, stricken and unmoving.

Annibale leapt down from the tractor. He went to grab Duncan, but as he did so he was thrown to the ground himself, the breath knocked out of him. Groaning, Annibale rolled onto his side and struggled to sit up. The sky opened into a downpour. Beneath the deluge, the freshly ploughed earth swiftly turned to mud. Annibale's rubber-soled boots — those same boots that his father had bought him back on his first day in Brisbane — sank ankle deep as he swayed to his feet. He knew Duncan was gone. Heavy rain poured into the man's eyes which stared lifelessly up at the sky. He had no pulse. In shock, Annibale thought, *He never finished ploughing his bloody field.* Then he turned and ran to get help.

The storm had dissipated to fine misty rain by the time the local police officer and an ambulance arrived. The Campanian workers stood sombrely watching as two men slid the stretcher bearing Duncan's covered body into the back of the ambulance. Annibale stood with his face downcast, his shoulders draped with a grey blanket that an ambulance officer had placed there. Duncan's wife, a small figure in a flower-patterned dress and lemon cardigan, was the picture of respectability, except that nicely groomed, delicate ladies didn't normally stand in rain and mud. One arm was folded across her slight frame, the other brought up to her face, her bird-like hand curved into a fist. A lone figure. There were no children.

'I'm sorry, missus,' the police officer said. 'It would have been quick. There's nothing anyone could have done.' He jerked his head towards Annibale. 'It's lucky this young fellow here was wearing rubber-soled shoes, otherwise he would have copped the same.'

Rusty Earth Motes

When I was young, my mother bought me children's books of Indigenous Australian stories, beautifully illustrated. I particularly liked a book called *Djugurba, Tales from the Spirit Time* — fourteen stories written and illustrated by Aboriginal authors and artists, and I still have my well-thumbed copy, published back in 1974. Another favourite was *The Quinkins*, from 1978.

I was captivated by the Indigenous myths and legends — telling of lush waterholes teeming with animals who helped or fought each other, bunyips, a witchdoctor outwitting two murderous giants, the tall and stick-like kindly figure of a Timara Quinkin, and menacing Imjim with red eyes and sharp fangs. A Sand Frog swallowed all the water across the land and became as big as a mountain, all the other animals yelling at him to give back the water so they could drink, too. Women turned into brolgas, and a bushfire taught the kangaroo to hop.

The richly painted red boulders and caves, yellow grasses and rust-coloured earth contrasted with indigo lagoons dotted with waterlilies, surrounded by shady trees against a horizon of low mountains. Tan-coloured scales of the giant serpent, Inganarr, slid past palm trees under skies of pale or deep blue, depending on the season. A family campsite, with dinner cooking over a fire, was a haven. The land looked untouched and idyllic. These stories of the Spirit Time were how, in a modest way, I became aware of and began to appreciate Indigenous culture.

Then as I got older I started to learn of entire Aboriginal communities having been violently wiped out or moved on, their lands snatched away with only a little given back more than two centuries later. Elders forced to be photographed in traditional dress. Entire tribes of all ages filmed and photographed naked. Women raped by men, both black and white. Babies left near snake holes or ant beds, sometimes rescued by relatives, sometimes not. Uneven battles. Land that remembers the sweat of its people, soaked with their blood. Stolen children. Stolen names. Stolen wages. Stolen remains. Stolen art. Segregation.

Many traditions, stories spoken, sung and danced, languages, agriculture and land knowledge of the oldest culture in the world ignored or stamped out. Health care almost non-existent. Literacy, education, freedoms, employment, the right to vote, to be in certain places — denied or curtailed. Apartheid, born in Queensland, before its exportation to South Africa. Recognition refused. So many dying without knowing justice. A war on the life force of a people.

I think of the richness of the Spirit Time stories I loved in childhood and feel tremendous sadness, anger and impotence.

'I still hear that Aboriginal baby crying sometimes at night before I go to sleep,' Nonno Anni says to me more than sixty years after the incident occurred.

The skin on the back of my neck prickles.

'I wish I could somehow go back and change what happened ...' He takes out his handkerchief and wipes his eyes.

Two Loaves of Bread

When the cane-cutting season started up again, Annibale resumed his spot in Stefano's gang. Savina found him preoccupied. She'd heard about Duncan's death — they all had — and she understood his not wanting to talk about it, but she suspected Annibale was keeping something else from her. He attacked the cane, content to be lost in the methodical actions of grip, cut, throw. The welts on his hands calloused. His tonnage and earnings increased. She noticed he didn't make such an effort any more to snatch conversations with her.

It had been more than a year since Annibale had spoken to his father, and feeling compelled to mend things, he wrote to Vitale and got a swift reply, healing the uneasy parting between them. Vitale said it was fortunate he'd received Annibale's letter when he did as he was about to start work at a different farm near Stanthorpe.

The owner, Giuseppe Rossi, is from Calabria, he wrote. *He has only daughters so he's taken on me with another but he's looking for one more if you're interested. Write back to let me know.* At the bottom of the letter, Vitale had started signing off then added, *The war won't reach up into the mountains to Fossa. Ma and Elia will stay safe.*

Annibale refolded the letter, not so sure. With campaigns in the Middle East resulting in Allied losses, Germany rampant in Europe and Japan advancing south, a heightened level of anxiety was gripping much of Australia. Civilians had to carry identity cards, and under the Australian government's *National Security Act 1939* all migrants of Italian and German origin were declared 'enemy aliens', even if they had been naturalised or were born in Australia. As an enemy alien, Annibale was fingerprinted, photographed, numbered and required to stay within the limits of the local police district. He also had to report to the police station once a week, walking into town to do so. There, the sight of men with shovels in hand, cigarettes on lips, digging trenches to be used as bomb shelters in the school playground amplified his sense of unease.

Not long after Annibale received Vitale's letter, Stefano, Giovanna and their family were still in bed in their house in town very early one morning when loud banging rattled the front door. His shirt half-buttoned, Stefano opened the door and several police surged inside. Savina screamed and jumped out of bed. Maddalena grabbed her and they huddled in a corner of the kitchen. The police turned beds and mattresses upside down, upended drawers over the kitchen floor and emptied glory boxes, strewing about embroidered linens. Stefano stood in front of his family.

'We're confiscating these.' A police officer held up the Tomasi family's camera and pointed to their radio.

Stefano stepped forward. 'But why? I don't understand.'

'You are well known in the local Italian community and might be disseminating information from the enemy.'

'No! Never. I'm naturalised. A British subject! I've been living here in Australia for more than twenty years—'

'Are you questioning our motive?'

Stefano shrank back. 'No, of course not—'

'I'll also need the keys to that ute out there. Because of your Italian origin you are no longer allowed to possess an automobile.'

Stefano sagged against the doorframe as he watched the police drive away in his beloved Dodge. 'It took me years to save for that ute.' His eyes searched Giovanna's for reassurance. 'I've never broken a law my entire life.'

'Come, Stefano. I'll make you a hot drink. Then we have to clean all this mess up.'

'How will I get to the cane fields?'

'Take the pushbike.'

'They took that, too.'

'Walk. It's war. There's nothing we can do.'

When they heard what had happened, Annibale and a couple of other cutters walked to the Tomasi family's house to make sure they were all right. Annibale saw Savina's hands were still trembling and she stuck close to her mother. Old Bert, the cane-cutter turned plantation owner who'd stood up for Annibale in the pub, also turned up after hearing of the raid.

'It's such a shame.' Bert shook his head as Giovanna swept up the last slivered remnants of broken dishes. 'Many Australians have lived happily alongside Italians for ages, but there's a particular group spreading trouble. I've heard some are soldier settlers from the first war whose farms failed. But plenty have got it in for Italians, especially if you're doing well.'

'Don't they realise I spent four years at the front in the first war, when Italy was an ally of Britain and France?' Stefano had his head in his hands. 'I fought *on their side!*'

'I saw the Paragon Café has put up a sign to say they're Greek, not Italian,' said Giovanna. 'Their son got attacked by some Australians who mistook him for Italian. No one wants to be seen as Italian. I thought we were lucky to get here before the war; now I wonder if we'd have been better off staying in Italy.'

Bert stood up to go, putting his hat back on. 'I heard several farmers are sacking any workers who are Italian. Keep your heads down. It could get worse yet, missus.'

Tensions remained high. In the name of patriotism some Australians began taking the law into their own hands. They intimidated and physically attacked numerous Italian migrants and vandalised Italian businesses. Then they ransacked several Italian cutters' huts, burning the few precious belongings the migrants owned. The respect and acceptance many Italians had earned through half a century of hard work were being dispelled in the hysteria of the moment. Annibale now went into town only to report at the police station. He had no war with Australians but the expectation that he was to support this new country wholeheartedly was complicated by local racist aggression and the fact that the Allies were currently bombing his birth country — where his mother and little brother lived.

The front page of the *Courier-Mail* contained the latest war news bordered by advertisements for Ovaltine, Three Sevens cigarettes and Malvern Star bicycles. Stefano read out that the Allies had bombed Naples, and one of the cutters became concerned for his young wife and child living there. The port area had been one of the main targets of the attack. Annibale thought of the boarding house where he had stayed beside the docks and wondered if anyone had survived. Again, he thought of his mother and Elia. With communications to Italy cut, it was all too easy to assume the worst or maintain a possibly false sense of hope.

The Australian government ramped up a program of alien internment, putting together lists of potential detainees, chiefly German and Italian migrants. Across Australia, police began taking them into custody. Annibale was stunned, having envisaged deportation rather than being made a prisoner of war. The initial targets around Ingham were influential members of the Italian community, the police arresting some businessmen and farmers and warning of heavy penalties should anyone protest against the internments. They hadn't yet interned any cutters in Stefano's gang but the constant uncertainty and stress were conniving to unravel tempers.

'We're seen as criminals,' Stefano complained. 'But what crime have we committed?'

Despite earning good money, Annibale's aim to start his own business looked so out of reach in the current state of affairs that it no longer seemed to matter. He turned eighteen, the day passing like any other, his grip on independence still tenuous, while Vitale's mild attempt to lure him back to Stanthorpe felt like ensnarement. Annibale was torn between honouring his father and honouring himself. The war stretched interminably ahead. Life in general remained suspended.

'Savina, this war ... I don't know if I'm going to be put away ... my father wants me to go back to Stanthorpe ...'

'Now you listen to me, Annibale,' she said in a low voice through the open window of the kitchen hut as she washed the dishes. 'You just keep your head down and cut the cane. You can't leave. If you do it will be the end of us.'

It didn't help his frame of mind when, the following week, rain began pouring and didn't let up. Days turned into weeks with no end in sight to the constant wet. In the shed where the cane-cutters slept, a wearing watery drumbeat pelted against the corrugated-iron roof and walls. They placed buckets throughout the shed along with kero tins, cups, empty food caddies — anything they could find — to catch the water dripping from the many leaks and emptied them often. The floor was gritty and wet.

Clothes, sheets and towels became damp and mildewy. When Annibale pulled back the covers to collapse into his stretcher bed, he discovered lime-green frogs between the white sheets. All the men's feet were beginning to suffer from working in sopping-wet socks and boots. The nearby creek rose, the water turning from clear to cloudy-brown. There was talk of flood.

Then the rain stopped. Annibale couldn't remember ever being so pleased to see the sun. He felt almost cheerful on the walk into town for his weekly report to the local police station. The ground remained soggy but everything was thriving and rinsed clean. Even the sky seemed a more brilliant blue as though freshly washed. Annibale took off his hat to feel the sun on his face. He rounded a corner and Giovanna almost barrelled right into him, tears streaming down her cheeks.

'Signora Tomasi, what is wrong?'

'They … they've taken Stefano. He went to report in like every week and they arrested him.' She cast a look over her shoulder at the police station. 'They said he's a risk because of the amount of money he has in the bank. But it's the money we've been saving for a cane farm. We were almost there.'

'Where are they taking him?'

'I don't know. They won't tell me anything.' Giovanna was distraught. 'They've put him behind bars. He's not a criminal. He only ever worked hard. Stefano wouldn't harm anyone. Oh *Dio*, what will become of us?'

Annibale looked from her to the police station. *If I report in, I risk being taken too. If I don't, I'm breaking the law.* He started backing away. He didn't even have a full minute to decide, fearing the police might be watching him through the window. Without a word, he turned and walked away from the police station, fast enough to create distance, slowly enough not to attract attention. Giovanna must have understood. She let him go without a word.

Annibale went straight to the army disposal store in town and bought a khaki cap, jacket and army bag. He raced back to the hut with his purchases. It was midmorning and everyone was out cutting cane. He grabbed the port from under his bed and transferred his belongings to the army bag. Then he took his port around the back of the hut to the riverbank. The river was still high and muddy from the prolonged rain. He threw in the port — the port that had travelled with him all the way from Fossa — and watched it toss on the swirling water. It floated several metres swiftly downstream before being swallowed by the murky torrent. He looked down at his Fascist Youth badge clasped in his other hand and threw that in too.

Back in the empty hut, he put on the khaki cap and jacket and shouldered the army bag. He'd seen Australian soldiers on leave in similar gear and hoped he could pass for one, as long as he didn't speak to anybody and reveal his accent. In the kitchen he grabbed two loaves of bread from the tin where it was kept and put them into his bag with his clothes. It would be a long trip to Stanthorpe. He left without speaking to anyone, hoping Savina would understand, but in his heart he knew that his leaving was ending anything between them.

Waiting on the platform for the train to Townsville was the scariest time. He looked around, not wanting to see police or anyone he knew. Ingham's community, though mostly itinerant, was small. He became aware of a man, perhaps fifty, leaning forward with his forearms resting on his knees, tamping tobacco into a pipe. He looked Annibale up and down. Annibale looked away, afraid eye contact might invite conversation. Smoke drifted along the platform towards him. He sighed, relieved to see the train approaching.

It was easier to blend in on the busy platform at Townsville during the half-hour until the train south departed. Not wanting to draw attention to himself or become engaged in conversation, he made a beeline for the men's room and shut himself in a cubicle. It was late afternoon and he'd not eaten since breakfast, but he decided to wait a little longer. He had two days of travelling ahead of him so the loaves of bread would need to last for all that time. He waited until he boarded the train to Brisbane before tearing the end from a loaf. Saliva flooded his mouth. The bread was dense, moist and crusty all at once. It eased the gnawing in his belly.

The train stopped intermittently and Annibale relied on water from drinking fountains at stations to slake his thirst. If by accident he made eye contact with anyone during these stops, he nodded politely and moved on. For two days, he sat tense with the fear of capture each time a train guard passed by or a conductor checked his ticket, the staccato *clack clack* of the train on the tracks plucking at his strained nerves.

Beyond the soot-smeared window, he saw a billow of white cockatoos take flight and disappear westward, unknowingly looking towards where Biloela lay, far out of sight. Annibale's gaze fell back closer, watching tawny scrub rushing past. He knew there could be no returning to Ingham, not while the war continued at any rate. Giovanna must have known he would leave. She would tell Savina. He felt sad and hoped she wasn't too hurt; that she understood his reasons.

In Brisbane, he had to change trains for Stanthorpe. With more than an hour to wait, he sought out a phone box, praying Giuseppe Rossi's farm had a phone and that the job Vitale had mentioned was still open. He dialled the operator to be put through, keeping his voice low lest someone overhear him and question an Italian apparently in uniform. His hand holding the receiver became slick with sweat as the operator took a while searching for the number. 'I'll put you through.' Annibale stifled a gush of relief. His fingers scrabbled among the crumbs in the bottom of his bag for more change.

The train arrived in Stanthorpe just after half past four in the afternoon. Before leaving the carriage, Annibale took off the army cap and jacket and left them under the seat. He walked down the hill from the train station to the main street. The humidity of Ingham was gone, replaced with the dry sweet-hay smell of the summer inland. Vitale had told him to go to the grocery shop, which had a phone, and ring the farm when he got there.

'Could you please make a phone call for me?' Annibale asked Gianni, the Italian shop owner. 'I need to let Giuseppe Rossi out at Applethorpe know I've arrived.'

Gianni went into a back room to make the call, returning with a smile. 'Wait out front. He's coming to get you.'

'*Grazie.*' Annibale turned, dithering by the newspaper stand.

Aware that many migrants couldn't read English well, Gianni said, 'Have you heard? America's been attacked by Japan. You can bet Australia's next. And with most of Australia's troops overseas defending Britain, it doesn't look good.'

A little shaken, Annibale thanked Gianni and went outside to wait. On December 7, 1941, while he had been travelling on the train down the Queensland coast, the Japanese had been bombing the American fleet in Pearl Harbor, bringing the United States into the war.

Even underneath the shop awning, the setting sun still had some force, reflecting off the dusty glass shopfronts, most closed for the day in the nearly deserted street. It occurred to him that the government hadn't confiscated the Rossi vehicle as they had Stefano's and those of other Italians. It seemed the internment push wasn't as frenzied here as up north. The thought made him feel he'd done the right thing leaving.

It was almost quarter to six when a farm truck trundled up with Giuseppe Rossi hunched at the wheel. 'Put your bag in the back,' he called through the open window.

Annibale did so and slid onto the bench seat, not even getting the door shut before Giuseppe drove off. He stole a glance at his new boss, who had a cigarette in one hand on the steering wheel, and he wondered what this job would bring. It was not far to Applethorpe, but during the fifteen-minute trip Giuseppe managed to lament the war, the weather, produce prices and that he had to hire help, cursing a lack of sons to run the farm. After two days of tense travel, Annibale's sense of propriety was almost threadbare, and he was quiet.

'You got different eyes,' Giuseppe remarked as they drove off the sealed road onto a bone-jarring corrugated dirt track. 'You look like a *zingaro*.'

Annibale let out a short, mirthless laugh and turned away. 'I'm no gypsy.'

He gazed at row upon row of apple and pear trees with the sinking feeling that his father had got him work at a farm similar to that of Benocci. Now on the run for not reporting to the police station, he had no choice but to stay and keep a low profile. *This war has been going for more than two years now,* he thought. *Surely it will be over soon.*

Vitale was waiting in the lodgings underneath the farmhouse where he and the other permanent worker, Claudio, slept. 'Why didn't you write and tell me you were coming down?' Vitale chided him without saying hello. 'They had to call me in from the fields for your phone call. It looked bad. You were lucky Giuseppe took you on just like that.' He zeroed in on the bag Annibale was cramming in under the spare bed. 'What bag is that? Where's your port?'

'It broke. This was all I could get.'

He wished his father would stop batting against him like an annoying moth. *I've been up north a year and a half and he hasn't even asked how I am or why I've come back. He only cares what others might be thinking.* There was no way he'd tell his father he'd evaded the authorities. Knowing Vitale, he'd encourage him to turn himself in, or do it for him. Absence had bred an almost pitying fondness for his father, but five minutes in his presence and Annibale was ready to get on a train back to Ingham.

Girl on a Bicycle

Giuseppe Rossi owned two parcels of land with a road running between them. Over a number of years he'd cleared it all, planting out the larger twenty-acre block with apple, pear and plum trees. On the seven acres on the other side of the road he grew a rotation of different vegetable crops. The family's high-set timber home nestled among the orchards, rambling and comfortable, with two potbelly stoves for the winter and a wide verandah on which to sit out front in summer. Nearby was a big packing shed with a fruit grader, a stable housing two draughthorses, and a lean-to chaff shed.

'You okay to handle a draughthorse and plough?' Giuseppe eyed Annibale.

He shrugged. 'Of course.' He didn't mention never having been near a draughthorse before and tried not to be alarmed by their size.

'People are starting to buy tractors, but I don't know …' Giuseppe rubbed the back of his neck. 'A bloke, Ellwood, in the district has taken on the Allis-Chalmers agency. He's sold quite a few, they say. But with petrol rationing now, a tractor's difficult to run. As it is, I'm mixing metho, shellite and kerosene in with petrol to make it go further for the truck.'

'Horse and plough is fine.' Annibale hadn't been on a tractor since Duncan was killed.

Remilda, Giuseppe's wife, had named their daughters for the saint day of their birth date (*onomastico*), giving them somewhat unusual names. Liduina, born April 14, and Aurea, born July 19, were still at school, while the eldest, Firmina — born November 24 and in her mid-teens — helped her mother with housekeeping and the vegetable patch. Giuseppe almost ignored his daughters, because they had not been born male. When not working, he sat on the front verandah smoking and reading the paper, oblivious to the chatty laughter of the quartet inside.

Firmina, closest to Annibale in age, had kind eyes and shadows of fine hair above her mouth and between her brows. He caught her looking at him while she unpegged the washing and he tended to the horses and he smiled, but wasn't tempted to stroll over to chat. The Rossis were even stricter than the Tomasis when it came to an unmarried daughter talking to an unmarried male and would expect a proper chaperone to be right beside them. The other worker, Claudio, who was a couple of years older than Annibale, had told him the Rossi family were from the same town in Calabria as he'd grown up in. And that back there it was believed a bachelor and spinster discovered alone together were presumed to be in an intimate relationship and expected to marry or risk bringing *vergogna* — shame — upon their families. Claudio had chuckled a little self-consciously and added he thought the idea old-fashioned and didn't agree with it himself.

Annibale thought of Savina and wondered how she and Giovanna were managing in Stefano's absence, but couldn't chance writing. He was most likely on a wanted list by now for not reporting to the police. Someone at the post office in Ingham might open the letter, see his name and turn him in, tracking him down by the postmark. *It's over between us now anyway*, he reasoned. *Savina said herself if I left it was the end.* He did feel regretful, though, for what might have been.

Unlike Mrs Benocci with her chicken necks, Remilda generously doled out pasta to her workers. She tossed it in whatever vegetables were ready for harvest in the kitchen garden, cooked down in a tomato *passata*. Meat was a scarce luxury. Annibale savoured each mouthful, his two-day train trip consuming nothing but bread and water still fresh in his mind.

'There is fruit for after,' Remilda said, but then she peered into the large serving dish that held the remains of dinner. 'There's probably enough pasta left here for half a bowl, though.' Her questioning gaze fell on Annibale.

He smiled, pushing his bowl forward and stretching his long legs out under the table to avoid the surreptitious whack of Vitale's boot.

'You can't keep eating all the leftovers,' Vitale started in when they retired to their quarters. 'It's embarrassing. These are times of war and rationing.'

'Boh! Nobody minds. Let me sleep. I'm tired.'

'A good son obeys his father. I won't have you ruining our name.'

'You work among the apple and pear trees all day and I know you eat the fruit,' Annibale retorted. 'I'm out ploughing the other paddocks, where there's no food.' He climbed into bed and faced the wall.

Vitale stared at his son's back. He became aware of Claudio shaking his head and smiling as he sat on his bed undoing his shoelaces in another corner of the large room. Muttering to himself and feeling old and outnumbered, Vitale got into his own bed, drawing the sheet up to his ear.

He had observed that whenever he and the others went to report at the police station, Annibale made vague excuses, citing errands to run and saying that he'd report in later. No one took notice except Vitale, though he never dreamed Annibale was evading the authorities, instead suspecting he was going to the pub or card games. He loathed his son's boldness, the effrontery of youth, but envied it at the same time. A shy man, Vitale had endured many lonely, challenging years both times he'd come out to Australia on his own, but he felt Annibale only saw how his absence as father and breadwinner had affected them in Fossa. Vitale wanted to articulate all this to his son but he didn't know how.

Mammoth granite rocks dotting the landscape drew in the heat and held it like giant embers. Everything slowly baked — the hardening soil, tussocks of blanched grass, the corrugated-iron roofs of the house and shed, men's arms and necks. The horses sweated, flicking their tails and blinking away flies. Cicadas screeched and the orchards drooped, exhausted by the heat and pregnant with fruit. During the drawn-out summer days, everyone longed for refreshing rain and yet feared the storms that might bring strong winds and hail to damage the ripening crops.

Annibale was alone as he headed back from the farthest paddock. Dust darkened by sweat was caked in fine lines on his neck and the insides of his wrists and elbows. As he neared the road separating the Rossi paddocks, he caught sight of a girl riding along on an old pushbike, her skirt flapping in the breeze to reveal her calves flexing and contracting as she pedalled. Something about her made him pause and raise a hand to shade his eyes. He watched her cycle to the neighbouring property, just able to make her out in the distance as she carefully leant her bike against the house and disappeared up the timber steps.

The apples and pears wouldn't be ready for harvest until February and March but the plums were ready in January. They strapped hessian bags around their necks and waists and carried wooden stepladders out from the shed. Giuseppe manoeuvred one of the draughthorses, pulling the cart in as close as he could for the men to empty the full hessian bags into crates on the back, and then he joined in the harvest himself, pausing to move the horse on as necessary. Everyone wore wide-brimmed hats, except Claudio.

'I want to get a little sun. Girls like it when your skin glows,' he said, prompting guffawing from the others.

After a while, Claudio began to sing 'Santa Lucia'. Soon the other three men joined in, their resonant voices drifting among the plum trees, despite the war, family far away, the hovering threat of internment. Vitale even smiled under his hat as they came to the chorus.

Annibale was singing with gusto, up a ladder reaching for plums on a tree close to the road when he saw the girl on the bicycle pedalling towards him. His singing became softer, distracted. He could see her dark hair rippling to her shoulders from under her straw hat, catching the breeze as she rode. Her right hand gripped the handle of a basket of eggs that hung from a handlebar. Their eyes connected and she waved to him with her free hand as she went past. He waved back, swivelling to keep looking as she rode on. She wore a pale-lemon dress with short sleeves and a floaty skirt, her legs moving with the lissomness of a teenager. Annibale watched until she disappeared from view.

'Who lives on the farm next door?' he called to Claudio.

'Mico Solano and his family.'

'Where are they from?'

'Calabria.' Claudio wiped the sweat from his brow. 'I'm going back in. Won't be long.'

'What for?'

'I need a hat.'

'Hey, he needs a hat!'

'What about all those girls who like your skin to glow?' Giuseppe teased.

'What girls?' muttered Vitale. 'The ones in his head?'

'I might be seeing a girl tomorrow,' Claudio yelled over his shoulder.

'Yeah, and tomorrow the barber cuts all beards for free.' Vitale's face was deadpan but his eyes crinkled. The others laughed as Claudio legged it towards the house.

Remilda paused before ladling out the pasta. 'Tino Benito has invited us all to his daughter Pina's sixteenth birthday on Saturday.' She smiled at the burst of anticipation and cheerfulness around the dinner table and began dishing portions even more generous than usual. It had been a long while since most of them had properly celebrated a birthday and it was a good excuse for a get-together after so long without a social event. 'It's late in the afternoon, after harvesting, and will finish early so we get home by eight o'clock curfew.'

Since the Australian government's *National Security Act* had labelled them 'enemy aliens', a curfew required that Italian and German migrants remain in their houses between eight pm and five am. With this restriction, the prospect of a gathering with neighbours, even for a few short hours, was out of the ordinary and exciting. Annibale was thinking that it had been years since he'd attended something social.

'Do you think it is safe?' Claudio's worried look quietened the chatter around the table. 'I mean, aren't gatherings between Italians banned now?'

'But it's a birthday party.' Remilda could see her daughters' concern and stared at Giuseppe, willing him not to say they should stay home.

He looked over at Vitale, who seemed set to back up a refusal. But the hopeful faces of the others made Giuseppe yield. That or possibly fearing Remilda wouldn't let him come near her in bed if he stopped them going.

'It will be okay.' His words set off a gush of relief and happy babble. 'Who else would even know about it?'

It was the end of January 1942 and no one from the Rossi farm or the neighbouring properties had been interned. Annibale knew that had he stayed at the cane fields, he wouldn't be so lucky. He thought of the intimidation and attacks on Italians that had occurred in the weeks before he fled Ingham. The Rossi family seemed unaware of the frequency and intensity of these happenings and Annibale didn't want to alarm them or cause Giuseppe to change his mind about the birthday party. Yet, inside, he felt on edge. It had been almost two months since he'd reported for his weekly check-in at the police station.

The Rossi family and their workers walked together in fading light up the dirt road to the Benito farm, Claudio and Annibale carrying a weighty boiler of Remilda's pasta between them. Remilda and her daughters had donned belted cotton dresses with hemlines below the knee. The men wore clean, pressed work clothes. Giuseppe carried a mandolin.

The sun, though hovering low, still had some bite to it, and the armpits of the men's shirts were sweat-darkened by the time they reached the Benito house. Two excited dogs came bounding up to them, jumping towards the boiler of pasta. Remilda cried out and Annibale and Claudio lifted it above the dogs' heads. Tino appeared, wiping his hands on his handkerchief, and ushered them all into the fruit-packing shed where they were setting up.

'We invited Solano and his family, too,' he told them, dabbing sweat from his neck. Remilda and Giuseppe had expected as much, knowing Mico Solano and Tino had been friends in Applethorpe for years.

Annibale looked over to see a couple of men moving trestle tables into the centre of the big shed with its floor of compacted earth. The women swooped in, flinging tablecloths across the battered tops and marking out places with plates, glasses and cutlery. Though he'd never seen her up close, Annibale immediately recognised the girl who'd ridden by on her bicycle. Despite her diminutive size, her presence was strong, her dark, almond-shaped eyes hinting at the Arabian influence in southern Italians.

She'd pinned her hair to one side with a barrette, her curls brushed into thick waves that hid the back of her dress collar. When she moved, a tiny gold cross on a delicate chain around her neck caught the light. Her complexion was even, her nose slightly rounded with a little beauty spot on one side. When Tino made the introductions she barely spared Annibale a glance, greeting him with the same polite smile she gave the other workers.

Eighteen of them sat down to a repast of Remilda's *fettuccine* in *passata* and Mrs Benito's rich rabbit stew sweetened with carrots, along with bread baked in *il forno* — Tino had built the wood-fired oven himself — and pizzas mostly topped with the Solanos' home-grown vegetables and a tomato slurry to moisten the hard crust. Tino opened several flagons of wine he'd made with table grapes and the somewhat rugged drop helped the gathering along. Annibale tucked into the food. The Calabrese dishes were different from the ones his mother used to cook, but just as flavoursome, even if the rabbit had a few too many tiny bones.

Francesca sat at the other end of the table. She stayed close to her mother, Cesca, attending to her siblings, a sister, Soccorsa, aged about seven, and a little brother, Vincenzo, who was two or three. Cesca got out dessert, which she'd transported in a big cooking pot: doughnut-like little dumplings called *zeppole* and *crostole* — twisted ribbons of sweet, crusty pastry. Annibale sank his teeth into a *zeppola*, one eye on Francesca. She looked up, and for a moment he caught and held her gaze. An inkling of feeling radiated between them. Vitale saw, his thick brows furrowing together.

Everyone sang 'Tanti Auguri' for Pina as she blew out the candles on a sponge cake and then there was still a little time before curfew for some dancing. Giuseppe retrieved his mandolin and Tino brought out his piano accordion. Mico tuned his guitar, his eyes half-closed as smoke puffed from the cigarette perched on his lips. Together they launched into some lively folk songs. Tino's five-year-old son, Alfio, strummed madly at his ukulele, unknowingly drowned out by the others. Having never danced in his life, Annibale remained in his seat between Claudio and Vitale, clapping along and watching the others.

'Annibale, why don't you ask one of the girls to dance?' Remilda called.

He looked up with a start, his gaze moving from Firmina to Pina and then Francesca, who looked equally uncertain. 'Oh, I've got a headache. Maybe next time,' he said feebly.

'I will.' Claudio jumped up, putting out his hand for Francesca to take.

Vitale leaned in close to Annibale, his murmur releasing a stale whiff of wine. 'You did the right thing. You can't dance with her. You're just a worker. A stray. Claudio is the son of friends of the Solano family. Besides, Francesca is a Calabrese.' He sat back with a determined nod. 'You need to find an Abruzzese girl.'

Tight-lipped, Annibale sat clapping and watching.

Southern Italian Pasta Gravy

Roger and I wake in a small cottage near Stanthorpe to discover a light scumbling of frost has settled outside during the night, turning the landscape piebald, patches of white among olive green. As he pours lukewarm water over the car windscreen, I crunch across the grass in buttoned-up coat, scarf, gloves and beanie pulled tight, enchanted by spiderwebs that look like crystals and leaves frozen to glass, in the manner of someone who has always lived in the subtropics. Having grown up with biting winters in the South West Slopes region of New South Wales, Roger is a little more blasé.

We drive towards the main street of Stanthorpe, past the motel once run by Italians my grandparents knew, past Pierpoint Motors and the post office clock tower, and on through the other side of town, heading out towards Applethorpe and the farm that once belonged to my great-grandparents Mico and Cesca. Before we left Brisbane, I spoke to my father on the telephone and was surprised to learn he'd recently been back to the farm with his uncle, Vincenzo.

'I asked the people living there now if we could have a look around and we were there quite a while,' Dad told me. 'It's incredible. Even the shed my grandfather built is still standing, though it's showing signs of wear.'

Fantastic, I'd thought, hoping to see it again. I hadn't been to the property since our family trip to Applethorpe for the 1986 school reunion, and the cool dimness of Bisnonno Mico's shed remained a treasured memory.

'It's not the same Italian family who owned it when we had lunch there in the '80s,' Dad added. 'If you're going there, I wouldn't go in and ask to look around — I think by the end of our visit they were happy to see us go.'

From the other end of the telephone, he couldn't see my disappointment. 'So was the farmhouse the same or have they changed it?'

'Ah, I don't really remember.'

'Maybe we could get together soon and you can tell me more about the farm? We could talk about the times you worked in the shop, too.'

'Yeah, we could do that, some time …' His voice sounded vague, distracted, then he said he had to go.

Pensive, I replaced the beeping receiver in its cradle.

It's freezing when Roger and I get out of the warm car. Not wanting to intrude, we stand on the opposite side of Ellwood Road to the farm. A little over sixty years ago I could have walked straight inside the kitchen into the arms of my great-grandmother. Yet time and death make me a stranger.

I gaze along the empty road conjuring the image of a small party of workers and a family walking in neatly pressed clothes to the neighbouring farm to celebrate a birthday in 1942. I think how my grandparents couldn't dance together that night, recalling their explanation from our interviews.

> FRANCESCA: *My father wouldn't have let me dance with strange people anyway. It wasn't like Annibale was one of our friends' sons or someone like that.*
> ANNIBALE: *I was a stranger. A stray, you see? Somebody with different eyes.*

Only now does it occur to me that it was such a curious thing for my grandfather to say.

An icy wind is gusting over the empty paddocks — Mico's hand-planted orchards were ripped out some time ago. It whips around us, scouring my cheeks and the tip of my nose pink. Perhaps it's the bitter coldness prodding my clothes or the bleakness of the day that makes me feel a little empty. For all the seasons they spent on this land, the laughter, living and hardships they experienced here, there are no ghosts of my family to see or feel. Only wind creating an eerie soughing in some nearby pines and aging timber dwellings that one day might fall, and then there will be nothing in the landscape to say my relatives lived here at all.

Southern Italian Pasta Gravy

Three things survive my great-grandmother Cesca — photographs, monogrammed linens, and her way of cooking pasta sauce. A southern Italian, Nanna Francesca called this tomato-based pasta sauce 'gravy', confusing to me as a child, considering my Australian mother called a deep-brown liquid accompanying a roast 'gravy'. It might also be called *ragù, bolognaise, sugo, passata* or even *pesto*, according to the region in Italy a family comes from and the way the mostly grandmothers and mothers cooked. The expectation of a certain flavour passed down, a legacy perhaps not even consciously realised at times.

I have a little notebook, no larger than my palm, of recipes Nanna Francesca kept. It still has a supermarket price sticker on the front — 52¢. She has written on the cover *Cooking Book 1980* in handwriting similar to my own. I didn't inherit my mother's beautiful penmanship. Instead, it seems that in the same way I inherited the shape of my grandmother's hands, Nanna Francesca also passed down to me a haphazard scrawling way of writing that struggles to keep to the lines.

The recipes have titles like 'Mrs Cicchetti *ferratelli*', 'Mrs Broglio *crostole*', '*Zippole* Calabrese', '*la Pignolata*', 'Lucia *ferratelli*' and 'suppa', a combination of English 'soup' and Italian '*zuppa*'. Lists of ingredients also appear in a mix of English and Italian.

Crostole Lucia	Suppa Minestrone Giannina
plain flour	*chicken stock*
3 eggs	*1 patata*
3 tablespoons sugar	*1 carota*
essenze vanilla	*pumpkin*
essenze limone	*celery*
2 cucchia olio	*cipolla*
2 cucchia brandy	*1 cup lenticchini a bagno*

Those she cooked most often (usually sweets) are revealed by splotches or oil spots on the page, many of them recipes exchanged with women at the Italian club — the *Associazione Nazionale Famiglie degli Emigrati*, or National

Association of Migrant Families. Some women brought along sweets they'd made at home that could sell for a dollar a plate to help raise funds to keep the organisation going. Each woman had her specialty, depending upon where in Italy she'd been born — *ferratelle, crostole, frittelle, cannoli* — and always generous serves.

I'm reminded of this, years later, hearing an Australian war bride speak of how homesick she and others like her were after they'd immigrated to the US, having married American GIs they'd met in Australia during the Second World War. With no Australian club to go to in America, they often gravitated towards British ones, but sometimes they'd organise special Australian gatherings and bring along plates of lamingtons, patty cakes and meat pies to reminisce. These Australian-born women had found it just as hard relinquishing being Australian citizens (though they were still considered British subjects up until 1948) as did the migrants who came to Australia in giving up the nationality of their birth countries.

I recall Nanna Francesca and her younger brother, Vincenzo, together cooking what they called *zippoli* and *sfogliatelle* (also known as *zeppole* and *crostole*, again the names varying between different areas of Italy), just as their mother, long gone, had done. The conversation of the siblings was peppered with companionable squabbling, at times in English, at others switching to hushed Italian, making me wonder about what or whom they might have been nattering.

When Nanna Francesca taught me to cook some of her savoury dishes, there was never any pen or paper. These memorised recipes were measured by hand, tasted to adjust to what was 'right' — a flavour inherently known from years of eating her version of a dish; knowing, say, if a tomato pasta sauce was 'too green', served too soon rather than simmered for hours for flavours to develop. She never spoke of her pasta sauce as being her mother's recipe and it didn't occur to me to ask her before she died. I can only assume it must have been.

It is almost eighty years since Bisnonna Cesca arrived from Calabria and first cooked her tomato pasta gravy in the humble kitchen of a farmhouse in Applethorpe. I wish I could know how closely the sauce I cook now takes after hers. It would be lovely to think that it is a connection to not only Calabria and Nanna Francesca, but also a great-grandmother I admire but never got to meet.

I invite Zio Vincenzo over to lunch on his seventy-fourth birthday and cook it for him, knowing he's had years of eating his mother's and sister's pasta sauces. In expectation, I watch as he lifts the first mouthful to his lips. He chews and slowly smiles.

Porta aperta per chi porta,
chi non porta ... parta pur.
Italian tongue twister
Keep doors open for people who bring something,
those who bring nothing ... can leave.

The next time Roger and I come to Stanthorpe it is the height of summer. We meander through the town's heritage museum where there is an Italian section among the displays. An old basket press, once used for crushing grapes to make wine, instantly draws Roger. I stand before two trunks that travelled in a ship from Italy along with the hopes and fears of the migrants who'd packed them. Even for those who didn't have a large number of possessions, it must have been hard to choose between items accumulated over a lifetime or handed down for children and a household, and pack into the confines of a trunk roughly a metre long and half a metre wide.

On a table next to the trunks is an old set of scales, calibrated in pounds, donated and once used by a Mr A Patti on his fruit stall. I cannot see anything to indicate his story and as I look at the scales, battered with use, I find myself thinking of my own grandparents' initial fruit stall on the footpath in Brisbane's Ann Street, and I wonder if Mr Patti's start in business was similar. It seems a common thread running through so many migrant experiences: a long journey, making a 'new life', growing produce, selling food, serving food — growing, sustaining, giving back.

Along a hallway, I come across a framed drawing of the Pierpoint store in Stanthorpe where Nanna Francesca's family shopped. It's a little like the 'Olesen's Mercantile' in the *Little House on the Prairie* books by Laura Ingalls Wilder — the main store in town that sold almost everything or could order it by catalogue. Pierpoint's, with its pretty two-storey weatherboard building, corrugated-iron awnings and attic windows in its peaked roof, is long gone. This is the first time I've seen a picture of it.

Included in the drawing is a dwelling next door with a sign painted on its gable: *1882 S. Pierpoint, Blacksmith and Wheelwright, Ironmongery*. This is the blacksmith, Nanna Francesca had told me, where her father left the horse and sulky while they shopped at Pierpoint's, had lunch and sometimes went to the Arcadia picture theatre, the trip to town a treat and a change from everyday life on the farm.

Late in the day, Roger and I discover another set of scales at the deserted Stanthorpe railway station, these once used for weighing crates of produce. While he becomes absorbed in working out the mechanism of the scales to measure his body weight, I wander along the platform and sit on a bench in the shade.

The afternoon is still hot. A dry breeze stirs my hair and the long, sun-bleached grass growing between the train-track sleepers. I think of Nonno Anni arriving at this station in December 1941, leaving behind on the train a khaki cap and jacket, the threat of internment in Ingham. Then I think of the next time he had to come back to this station and the train he was forced to board.

The Harvest

In early February, clusters of apples blushed gold and rosy clung to the leggy branches of the orchard. Annibale glimpsed Giuseppe walking through the trees, rubbing his hands as one would on a frosty morning, before disappearing towards the house. Looking across the orchard laden with apples, Annibale wondered if there'd come a time when he'd be an owner rather than just a worker. He felt an apple hit his back and swung around, annoyed.

'Oi! I'm not picking them all up on my own,' Claudio called out to him.

'Righto.' Gripping an old kerosene tin, Annibale picked up the apple Claudio had thrown and added it to the tin. Apples stung by fruit fly fell to the ground, and to stop the pest spreading they picked up the bad ones every few days and threw them into a pit at the far end of the property. They were due to harvest next week and he was glad it meant the end of picking up rotten fruit, a task that seemed to fall to him and Claudio as the younger workers.

Annibale was on his own heading back to the shed when he saw Francesca walking towards the house, wheeling her bicycle beside her. He raised his hand in a wave and they exchanged greetings. Up close, Annibale stood almost a foot taller than her.

'I just came over to borrow some hessian bags,' she said. 'We're caught short.'

'You're harvesting now? We're not until next week. I can get the bags for you.'

Francesca looked dubious. 'I'd like to speak to Mrs Rossi first.' She laid her bicycle on its side and, somewhat primly, went around to the back steps.

When she came back, Annibale was standing with an armful of hessian bags. Francesca gave him a look. Mrs Rossi had told her to go into the shed and help herself. Part of her had hoped Annibale would be gone when she returned; the other part leapt to see him waiting for her. She was careful to keep this hidden from him, though.

'I only need a few.'

'Here you go.' He peeled off several bags and handed them to her.

'Thank you.'

He watched her roll them up then pick up her bicycle and put them in the basket. 'How old were you when you came to Australia?' he asked her.

Francesca blushed right up to the roots of her hair. 'Eight.'

'Did you come straight to Applethorpe?'

'We've always lived here.' She began wheeling her bicycle down the long driveway towards the gate, Annibale ambling beside her.

'So you went to school here in Australia?'

Francesca took one hand off the bicycle and carefully tucked a tendril of hair behind her ear. 'Well, Italy first, then Applethorpe. I had to leave to help when Vincenzo was born.'

'So you can read and write in both Italian and English?' he asked, mindful of only being able to do so in Italian.

'My father only reads and writes Italian,' she admitted a little stiffly, 'so when we send the fruit and vegetables to market I do the consignment notes and the cheques and forms for the bank.' Her voice trailed off and she looked ill at ease.

'I should let you get back.'

'Yes. I …' She didn't want to put him off, but despite the other workers nearby she felt uneasy talking to him without someone to officially chaperone. 'Thank you.'

The gravel road crunched beneath the bicycle tyres as she pedalled towards home, feeling Annibale's eyes upon her. She took a deep breath of summery air fragrant with apple orchards and sun-cooked grass, permitting herself a tiny smile. She'd once overheard Mr Rossi telling her father he thought Annibale had gypsy eyes, but she didn't agree. She felt quite taken by the shining dark hazel eyes of the tall Abruzzese.

By three o'clock the next afternoon, the sky was so gloomy Remilda had to turn on the light in the kitchen. Unsure if they should continue their chores, the workers gravitated towards the house to find Giuseppe standing on the front verandah, agitatedly watching the brewing storm. Annibale had never seen a sky so dark that it merged with the distant, forested hill line. The air was still, almost viscid. A strange half-light brought things into sharp focus. The grass appeared almost like straw; the wall of the wooden shed, grainy.

Giuseppe swore and lit a cigarette. 'Claudio, shift the truck in underneath the shed. Annibale, tether the horses.'

The truck engine puttered into life and Claudio reversed it into the depths of the shed.

Coming back up the steps to the verandah, Annibale heard Vitale say, 'It looks green.'

'*Porca miseria*.' The curse exited Giuseppe's lips on a gust of cigarette smoke. 'I didn't want to say it but it does, doesn't it?'

Looking again at the storm clouds, Annibale noticed patches of an eerie pale green among the brooding mass of purplish-grey. He turned to his father.

'Green means hail,' Vitale said before he could ask.

Annibale's gaze flew to the orchards laden with apples and pears, the crops of beans and cabbages. A door banged somewhere inside the house.

Remilda came out, looking at the sky. 'I'm worried Lidi and Aurea won't make it home from school in time.' It was more than a mile's walk away. 'Giuseppe, should we —'

He raised his arm. 'Here they come now.'

Aurea's voice reached them first. 'They let us out early, Mamma.'

'*Sbrigati*. Inside.' Remilda tramped halfway down the front steps to hurry them.

As the storm closed in, they saw the first flickers of lightning.

'We should start picking,' said Claudio. 'Doesn't matter if we get wet.'

'Don't be a fool.' Giuseppe shook his head. 'You could get hit by lightning.'

'I've seen it happen.' Annibale stared at the sky. 'The man didn't survive.'

He didn't say any more, and no one asked, but Giuseppe and Claudio exchanged glances. Vitale regarded his son, yet said nothing. The wind lifted their hair. 'Here it comes.'

Annibale saw rain seeming to march across the paddocks towards them. A bright flash scrawled a serrated line across the sky and someone gasped. Seconds later, a loud explosion of thunder rattled the windows. Remilda and the girls stayed inside; the men, on the verandah, getting damp from the mist brought in by the driving rain, their eyes drifting to the orchard.

The first hailstones hit the tin roof above them with heavy clunks, as if someone was pelting rocks. Then the sky released hail with a roar. Giuseppe slumped and put his head in his hands. Within several minutes the ground was white. The sound of a window smashing set Remilda shrieking. The men looked at each other. Giuseppe jumped up and ran inside, the others following close behind.

They lost all the apples and pears, as well as a whole crop of cabbages. One of the house windows was broken and some of the rustier sections of the water tank were punctured with sizeable holes. The neighbouring Solano and Benito families fared slightly better, having already harvested their apples and pears, but both lost tomato crops. Only the Benitos' potatoes survived and about two-thirds of the Rossis' beans. Remilda put on a brave face, pointing out that at least the nets had saved many of the beans, but Giuseppe struggled.

Late at night when everyone was in bed, Annibale thought he could hear weeping somewhere upstairs. He looked over at Vitale and Claudio. They both appeared to be fast asleep. For a brief time that summer, Annibale had felt almost content. The storm sweeping through snuffed that out and brought a reminder of how uncertain life actually was.

'I'm going back to the Benocci farm.'

Annibale stared at his father. 'Why? What for?'

'It's best if I go. I'm the oldest. Carlo said he'd take me back on. One of his workers was interned — Paolo, I think.' Vitale massaged his eye sockets with his thumb and forefinger. 'Giuseppe can't afford us all. He looked relieved when I said I'd go.' He pulled out his port.

Annibale wondered if Vitale had also overheard the crying. He put his hands on his hips. 'Benocci doesn't pay too good, I reckon.'

'Shush. You can't say that about people you're related to.'

'You can if it's true. Papà, it's just one hailstorm. There'll be other crops.'

Vitale shook his head and picked up his folded singlets, placing them into a corner of his port. *As usual,* he thought, *my son cannot see that what I am doing is for him.* Annibale was the last hired at the Rossi farm so he should be the first to go. Vitale knew Benocci paid little, and since Annibale had left to cut cane he'd felt awkward asking him to pool their money. Saving for the ship passages for Maddalena and Elia was a hope Vitale was letting go of. His new plan was to save enough for a ticket for himself to return to Italy for good after the war, though he kept this to himself. *If Annibale stays in Australia or returns to Italy that is up to him.* Deep down he knew he'd never been able to tell Annibale what to do. His son would always have an independent streak and the same determined character as Maddalena.

Annibale and Vitale said a collected, almost detached, goodbye. As Giuseppe drove him away in the truck, Vitale looked back at his son turning to talk to Claudio and he wondered when they'd cross paths again. He never told Annibale he was almost glad to be returning to the Benocci farm. It was where Maddalena knew he'd been working for a number of years before the war and he felt it gave him a connection with her, even if somewhat tenuous. Though he'd almost convinced himself all would be well, it had been two and a half years since they'd had any contact. His heart ached, not knowing how Maddalena and Elia were faring.

They had barely sat down at the dinner table when Remilda announced to everyone, 'Gianni was interned today.'

Annibale remembered the kindly grocery shop owner who rang the Rossis for him when he arrived back in Stanthorpe. Gianni hadn't seemed a dangerous type.

'Where did they take him?' Annibale asked.

'Who knows? Probably Brisbane. Off to one of the camps. And for what?' Remilda shook her head. 'He's run that grocery shop for over twenty years. What will happen to it?'

'I've heard what happens.' Claudio tore some bread off his slice. 'If the business isn't shut down, it's operated by a "controller" appointed by the court.

They put the profits in a trust fund and Gianni's family get a wage to live off from that, but only after the costs of looking after the trust are met. Depends if you get a decent controller or a crook.'

'Any one of us could be next.' Giuseppe was dismal.

A silence fell over them. In newspapers, officials proudly touted the current round of internments undertaken by the Queensland government to be the largest campaign to date. At the same time, members of various patriotic groups were calling for the internment of every male Italian or German migrant, some also seeking to include women and children.

No one knew whose door the police would knock on tomorrow. Nearly every Italian household, including the Rossis', had suitcases packed. Annibale felt edgy wondering what would happen if the authorities caught up with him. He hadn't reported to the Ingham police for almost three months. Part of him hoped that if they'd been unable to trace him by now they might never find him, but it was no longer only influential Italians or potential dissenters police were locking up in internment camps. All males of Italian heritage were being targeted.

After dinner, Annibale and Claudio sat on the back steps, the warm summer darkness alive with insects. Claudio sucked on the last of a cigarette, smoke trailing straight up in the still air. Annibale wondered what Francesca was doing right now. He thought of his mother and Elia, then his father. In a way, he was relieved Vitale was no longer around to witness the authorities catching up with him, should it occur. He hoped they'd spare his father, an older man with little money. Like Stefano, Vitale had fought on the same side as the Allies during World War I.

'All we can do is go along with whatever happens.' Claudio placed the end of the cigarette under his shoe to put it out. 'No point getting too worked up about it.'

Annibale nodded. He gazed into the distance towards the neighbouring Solano property. 'You danced a fair bit with Francesca at the Benito party.'

Claudio tapped his nose. 'She's a lovely girl.' He got up, throwing his box of matches up in the air and catching them in the same hand. 'Funny you mention her.' He shook his head, chuckling at Annibale's confused look. 'It's Saint Valentine's Day today.'

Annibale forced a laugh. 'Who can worry about that stuff? Any day we could be interned.'

'I'm off to bed.' Claudio sidled past. 'Don't worry. Everything will be okay.'
The next day, Singapore fell to the Japanese.

Australia was stunned by the fall of Singapore. The Japanese took more than 100,000 Allied soldiers prisoner, including 15,000 Australians, many of whom would die in brutal circumstances. A profound sense of fear and despair pervaded Australia. The country was too vast to defend properly. Australian troops were on the other side of the world fighting for Britain.

With the fall of Singapore, the new Prime Minister, John Curtin, directed Australian troops in the Middle East to return home to defend Australia. Britain's Prime Minister, Winston Churchill, overruled the decision, ordering Australian troops to Burma, also under Japanese threat. Churchill was prepared to let Australia go and allow it to fall to the Japanese in favour of protecting British interests. Unable to accept this, Curtin demanded Australian troops return to Australia. It was the first time an Australian leader was firm in rejecting such a demand from Britain. After several years — and previous wars — fighting and dying to defend the mother country, Australian troops were now returning to defend their own country — 46,000 of them.

Four days after the fall of Singapore, Darwin was bombed. The warning sirens sounded just one minute before Japanese bombers pounded the city. By sundown on February 19, 1942, at least 243 people had been killed, more than four hundred others injured, twenty-three Australian aircraft had been destroyed and thirty-one vessels sunk or damaged, including three warships and five merchant ships. The bombs levelled most of Darwin.

Concerned the rest of Australia might panic, the government banned release of details of the attack under its censorship laws. In Stanthorpe, the only news was a small article in the *Courier-Mail* newspaper the day after the bombing. Giuseppe made Firmina read it aloud to the others around the kitchen table, translating the English into Italian as she read.

'Darwin was bombed twice yesterday by Japanese warplanes.' She tugged at her collar, self-conscious. 'Ninety-three bombers with fighter escorts took part in the raids, the first on the Australian mainland. Four raiders were brought down. Damage to property was considerable. There were some casualties.'

A heightened frenzy surrounded civilian internments, once again mostly focusing on Italian migrants. Official figures would later reveal the number of civilian Italian migrant internees to be more than triple those of German or Japanese origin. Many German migrants avoided recognition, having changed their surnames to English names. This had occurred particularly during World War I when thousands of ordinary German-Australians, some the third generation of their family to have lived in Australia, had been interned, harassed and had their livelihoods ruined by anti-German sentiment. For the Italian migrants who had settled in Australia between the wars, there was little they could do to hide their accents, olive skin and dark hair and eyes that marked them out as Mediterranean.

Whenever Remilda and Giuseppe went into town for supplies they came home adding more names to the growing list of local Italians interned. Police rarely gave a reason and, lacking education and fluent English, most migrants felt unable or too scared to question them. Annibale was nervous. Every morning he headed out to the fields, working hard to put aside a succession of bleak thoughts. With youthful optimism he tried to convince himself they all might escape internment — but such hope was in vain.

He was with Claudio and Giuseppe picking the beans not damaged by the hailstorm when two police officers emerged among the plants with pistols drawn. 'Hands up! Which one of you is Giuseppe Rossi? Under National Security Regulations you are being interned.'

Giuseppe opened his mouth but no sound came out. They took him in his dusty farm clothes. He didn't even have a chance to see Remilda. The police ordered him onto the back of a truck with half a dozen other Italians from the district. As they drove away, Giuseppe hung his head. Annibale and Claudio looked at each other and rushed to the house.

Remilda and Firmina were out the back washing clothes, mother by the copper, daughter at the wringer. When Annibale and Claudio bounded up to tell them what had happened, Remilda let out a wail. 'He doesn't even have his port!' She pushed past Firmina, who was in tears, and ran to the house. 'We have to take his port to him at the police station.'

Annibale was glad the younger daughters were at school rather than see this happen to their father, though he wondered how they were going to be when they got home that day to find him gone. Claudio drove Remilda into town with the port. Annibale and Firmina could do little else but go back to the beans and the washing, both of them shaken.

That night, Annibale lay awake in the quiet darkness, too wound-up to sleep.

Suddenly Claudio spoke from the other side of the room. 'I'll never forget Giuseppe's face behind bars at the lockup. He looked … broken.'

A couple of days later, Annibale and Claudio were in the adjoining patch of beans when the police arrived again. Annibale looked at Claudio. 'Well, it's me or you now.'

They took Claudio. A few days after that, a boy on a motorbike delivered a telegram to Annibale, ordering him to report at the Stanthorpe police station by eight o'clock that night. *Pack all your belongings. You won't be coming back.*

When he was ready to leave, Remilda clutched Annibale to her breast for so long he felt embarrassed. 'I sent word over to the Benitos. Tino is coming to drive you into town.'

'Thank you.' Annibale wondered when Francesca would hear what had happened. He asked Remilda, 'Are you going to be all right here?' With so many of the Italian men interned, finding labour was becoming critical and numerous farms and businesses were starting to fail.

Remilda put her arm through Firmina's. '*Certo.* Us women are going to keep this farm going, aren't we, Firmi?'

Western Creek — 1942

12th March, 1942

At the police station, the sergeant greeted Annibale. 'Who's been a naughty boy then?'

'Beg pardon?'

'Someone hasn't reported in at Ingham where he should have for three months now.'

Annibale was silent.

The sergeant came up close. 'Tell me, who do you want to win the war?'

Annibale held his gaze. 'If my mother and your mother were having an argument, who would you want to win?'

'That your answer? Well, that's why you're in here.'

He was effectively a prisoner of war. The full impact hit Annibale as a constable led him to the lockup at the back of the police station. He joined a dozen others in farm clothes, neither Giuseppe nor Claudio among them. After a while a constable brought the internees sandwiches. Then the sergeant came to address them. 'All the camps are full.' His tone was brisk. 'So you're going to a new camp. An "internee special" is coming through here to take you tonight. We need to process your papers, so form an orderly line … *orderly*, I said.'

The men, mostly farmhands, were marched in the dark at gunpoint along High Street and up the hill to Stanthorpe's railway station. On the internee special all the windows were barred, the doors on the side away from the platform sealed. Herded aboard, they joined more Italians picked up in surrounding towns, including Texas, Inglewood and Yelarbon. By then it was almost ten o'clock, yet some Australians gathered on the platform to jeer — yelling, swearing and spitting at them. A young Italian bared his bum through the train window. Several internees laughed, though the older ones shook their heads. Annibale guffawed but didn't think it did much for their cause.

The train set off into the night on a slow circuitous route, stopping at stations to pick up more internees. As the lack of information and growing apprehension began to affect everyone, the atmosphere inside became tense. Mostly there was quiet, the internees peering out the windows, wondering where they would end up.

Long after midnight the train limped to the end of the line in Millmerran, steam drifting into darkness. The internees were unloaded into the autumn night air. Not far away, near the cattle yards, a convoy of army trucks was lined up. As he climbed into the back of a one, Annibale got a brief glimpse of the town further up the road, shut up, silent in the moonlight, the townspeople unaware. Then the soldiers tied the canvas flap down and the men, with their luggage, sat cramped in the dark.

Filled to capacity, the trucks lumbered through the rest of the night. A pungent smell of damp canvas mixed with the odour of sweat from crammed-in bodies. No one spoke. The late hour and monotonous drone of the engine made Annibale drowsy but he nodded off only until his head lolled forward, jolting him back to wakefulness. Hours went by. The only indication of the time was when the blue-grey light of early dawn penetrated a tiny slit in the canvas. Annibale looked around in the dim light and pulled his knees up to his chest.

The internees were thirsty, hungry and tired by the time the sun was well and truly up and the trucks finally came to a stop, the unexpected jerk causing the men and their possessions to lurch forward.

A soldier threw open the canvas flap at the back. 'Everyone out!'

Annibale grabbed his bag amid the jumble and scrambled off, blinking in the sudden glare. The camp was a dusty clearing bordered by scrubby bush, pine forest and, down an embankment, a snaking creek. Three soldiers held back large dogs that strained at the leash.

'See this gum tree?' The shout of another soldier made them all look over to where he was pointing at a lone stunted eucalypt. 'Anyone goes past that and you will be shot. See that other tree over there …'

There hadn't been time to surround the makeshift camp with the usual barbed-wire fences. After pointing out the boundary lines marked by different landmarks including the creek, one of the soldiers nailed to a tree a roughly painted sign repeating the warning to internees that the guards would shoot anyone who passed that point. It was in English and German.

In the stark sunlight, Annibale saw Gerolamo, with whom he'd worked at the Benocci farm, and they exchanged relieved looks. The soldier in charge indicated a stack of pale canvas tents and rough-cut sapling poles then told the internees where to pitch them so they formed rows with a lane between. It was two men to a tent. Annibale and Gerolamo swiftly paired up.

As the army trucks chugged away in a haze of dust, the bush became quiet bar the *chink chink* of tent pegs being hammered into the earth. The soldiers left to guard the camp, accompanied by a horse and several dogs, pitched their own tents outside the camp boundary. They ordered the internees to dig a rough latrine. They also gave them four large sacks of rice, corned beef, some pots, tin plates and other basic army supplies, and told them to make a roster for cooking their meals over an open fire in the area they called a 'galley' — four posts pounded into the earth with corrugated iron on three sides.

By the time the sun sat directly overhead, Annibale was sitting on the ground next to Gerolamo, scraping up sloppy rice from a tin plate. The cooking fire sank to ashes, trailing wisps of smoke towards a clear sky. He looked around the clearing of thin grass bordered by trees they couldn't seek shade from, since the trees stood beyond the invisible line the men couldn't cross. A lone crow cawing from the heights of a pine tree distracted his gaze.

Then he glanced at Gerolamo. 'How was my father when you left?'

'He was interned not long before me. Didn't you know?'

'No.' Annibale faltered. 'I didn't.' He felt thrown, hating the thought of police holding Vitale in a lockup. His law-abiding father didn't deserve that. Vitale had spent most of the past twenty years toiling on Australian land. It occurred to Annibale that for the first time he and his father didn't know of each other's whereabouts.

At night, the contrast between camp life and the everyday life they'd previously known sharpened as the men adjusted to sleeping with only a layer of canvas separating them from the outside world. The voices and coughs, burps and sneezes of others carried from tent to tent. Night birds and animals rustling in the nearby scrub sounded closer than they were. The sound of the wind picking up and creaking the trees, the reverberation of distant thunder, a solitary splash in the creek, one of the army dogs giving a restless bark — tent life was already beginning to immerse them in the land.

Day 2

The creek water held some of its summer warmth but it was still quite cold. Annibale crouched waist-deep, rubbing the soap along his arms and under his armpits, over his chest and body, and then tossed it across to Gerolamo who did the same before throwing it on to the next man. The gritty sand felt good beneath his feet. He bobbed under the water, washing the soap from his hair, and resurfaced, turning his face up to the late-morning sun.

'Right, you lot, out of the water! Next lot in!' The soldier, who looked barely out of training, kept one hand on the rifle over his shoulder as the naked internees moved from the water to the beach of the creek.

Annibale swiftly dried himself and dressed, leaving his feet bare to walk back up to the tent, taking care to avoid the ant beds camouflaged amid stretches of hard earth.

As their group neared the series of white tents lining a rough lane, Adro, one of the older men, called out, 'Hey, from now on we call this street Via Veneto!'

Everyone laughed, knowing of the famous street in Rome, and the tongue-in-cheek name stuck.

Day 15

Late-afternoon sun behind the trees made the branches appear black and threw the camp into shadow as Annibale and a few others scouted around the boundaries for firewood. Annibale glanced at the guard watching them. He looked about the same age as himself, eighteen. His name was Clement Huber. Their eyes met fleetingly as Annibale bent to pick up another stick. He saw no malice in the gaze. The soldier even seemed hesitant, as though the mantle of guard rested uncomfortably upon him.

Day and night, the Australian soldiers armed with guns and spotlights and dogs nearby, watched the internees but they didn't ill-treat them. There was a rule that the guards were not supposed to talk to the internees and vice versa. To Annibale, some young soldiers who sat or stood at sentry duty on their own for hours seemed lonely, possibly longing to have a chat. On occasion some did, though they were careful not to befriend the internees. Annibale looked again at the guard. Clement jerked his head, indicating Annibale should take his armful of firewood back to the galley.

Day 48

'Why can't we have visitors?' Adro asked the soldier in charge one afternoon. 'Criminals in jail are even allowed a visitor now and then. My daughter is sick. I need to know how my wife is going with the farm.'

'The location of the camp is classified. We're too far out for contact anyway,' the soldier said and looked a little uneasy. 'I have my orders,' he added helplessly.

Adro regarded him for a moment, his dark eyes sad, then nodded and went to his tent.

Day 72

They collected water for drinking and cooking from the creek upstream from where they bathed and washed their clothes, not that they were bathing in the creek now anyway. Winter was almost upon them, and with temperatures plummeting each night the water had got very cold. Annibale carried two metal buckets up to the camp, keeping his pace swift but careful not to slosh water over the sides. He poured some into a pot which another man had set to boil over the fire. They would return a little to the buckets and dip a rag washer in to have a kind of sponge bath.

Life in the camp had become a routine of meeting the necessities for daily living — water for consumption and cleaning; firewood for cooking and warmth; food, shelter, sleep. Sometimes for entertainment the internees sat in their tents and played cards. Annibale felt resentful, being forced to be there, but he also knew it could be a lot worse. This was a time of war; he accepted that. He wondered what the latest war news was — they all did — but the soldiers relayed nothing of life beyond the camp. Between themselves, the internees began to speculate whether the Japanese were making their way across Australia towards them ... and what might happen if they turned up at the camp.

'I guess we just have to wait and see who is going to be boss, the US or Japan,' Annibale said to Gerolamo, who nodded and continued biting his thumbnail.

Day 86

Annibale was inside the tent putting on his shoes and socks when he heard the howl go up. He gave a start, hastily tying his shoelaces, thinking some type of wild animal had penetrated the camp. Another wail sounded as he burst out of the tent and he realised it was a man.

Gerolamo, returning from the latrine, approached shaking his head. 'Adro's daughter died. A soldier just gave him the message. They won't let him out to attend the funeral.'

Day 100

The creek that had held summer rains when they'd first set up camp shrank in the dry winter. In some spots it barely flowed a few centimetres wide. They had to be careful where they collected water and made sure they boiled it before drinking. At times, the soldiers allowed the internees to walk for exercise within a mile radius of the camp, but mostly there was nothing to do but sit for hours. Annibale felt the boredom acutely. He was in his prime — fit, healthy, strong. It was frustrating to think of the work he could have been doing instead. He wondered how Remilda and her daughters were as they tried to keep the farm going on their own. He thought of Francesca.

Annibale and Gerolamo sat together, their heads in the scrap of shade provided by the pegged tent flap, their legs in the sun. An hour after lunch and the half-moon was high in the vibrant blue sky, the sunlight that warmed their legs also shining on the side of the moon. Annibale looked down at his hands, parched and cracked, skin taut across the knuckles from the dry winter air. His lips and the skin around his nostrils were sore and split. He savoured the midday sun. At night, the temperatures sank below zero, even lower if a wind blew up, shuddering tents and penetrating looser joins in the canvas.

Day 115

'You can take the option of doing work during your internment for the Forestry Department,' the soldier in charge announced to the internees first thing after breakfast.

Annibale glanced at Gerolamo, then at the nearby pine forest, and promptly volunteered.

For almost four shillings a day he cut timber and made firebreaks. It wasn't a full wage; but it wasn't so much the money — Annibale preferred to be working rather than sitting around all day. While it was often strenuous, he found the thud of an axe into a trunk, the final crack before a tree fell, satisfying after being constrained in the camp. The pine trees were tall and thickly clustered. When a breeze rushed through the tops of the needled boughs it made a lonely susurrant sound overhead, but down at ground level, the forest floor was a commotion of chopping and the occasional male voice calling out.

Day 126

Between them, the internees had a mandolin, a guitar and a handmade piccolo. The soldiers allowed the Italians to have singalongs, as long as they weren't rowdy.

Day 149

The internees had created their own routine where they shared their tasks fairly and had an understanding with the guards, and for around six months it had worked well. Then another influx of prisoners arrived, swelling their numbers. Some of these men had suffered severe beatings from Australians up north and out west. Others had been rounded up into overcrowded police cells with inadequate bedding. They were in no frame of mind to be part of the congenial structure the initial prisoners had worked to establish in the camp; a few were angry, but mostly they were exhausted and overwhelmed. Within this new group of internees was a staunch Fascist called Salvatore.

'Pray for the Japanese to invade soon,' he encouraged the group at dinner on his first night in the camp. 'They *will* come and liberate us and then we can get out of here!'

Annibale scanned the faces of the other internees, but none of them seemed particularly roused by Salvatore's discourse. Most of them were family men, worrying about their wives and children and getting back to their farms. Then he noticed an older skinny man sitting apart from the group. With his head down and his arms crossed over his body the man looked exhausted, his food pushed to one side, untouched. His shoulders stooped in a way that prompted Annibale to go and speak to him.

'The food isn't the best but you'll feel better if you have some.'

The man started and looked up in bewilderment. 'A-Annibale?'

It was Annibale's turn to register surprise. He looked closer and saw the man wasn't old at all. 'Pandi? Pandi, what happened to you?'

Pandi laughed hollowly. 'Where do I start?' He wiped his nose with the back of his hand. 'I got picked up in North Queensland ages ago. They didn't have enough of us to fill the internee train, so for weeks I was in the local lockup with a lot of other blokes while they picked up more to intern. At night we crowded into the cells and slept on straw. During the day, they put us in a tiny exercise yard where we could barely move. One day we were given raw pasta to eat and when someone asked for a drink of water they sprayed a hose through the bars.'

Annibale said nothing but Pandi saw his look of incredulity and went on, 'Our suitcases were impounded upon arrival, so for ten days we were forced to stay in the clothes we'd been wearing when we got arrested. The jail didn't have facilities for so many inmates, so we could only wash and shave once a week. When Salvatore and a couple of his lot arrived it turned ugly. Salvotore and two others beat up some blokes pretty bad. I overheard the police saying they couldn't risk someone getting killed, so they sent us here.'

'Did your father get picked up, too?' Annibale asked.

'He died a few months after I got to Biloela. His heart, they think it was.' Pandi shook his head. 'I wish I'd never come to Australia.'

They were both silent. Annibale hid his unease at finding his friend so depressed and aged. Pandi could have been no more than twenty-one or -two.

'But you're Albanian,' said Annibale. 'You shouldn't even be in here.'

Pandi shrugged. 'They think I'm Italian.'

Annibale put his hand on Pandi's shoulder. 'Wait here, I'm going to ask one of the soldiers if you can bunk in my tent.'

Pandi watched him approach the soldier, Clement Huber, whose ears stuck out a little. The ensuing conversation also caught the interest of Salvatore.

'It's all fixed,' Annibale said as he returned.

Salvatore's shadow fell across them. 'You friends with those Australians?'

'I was just sorting it so my friend could be in my tent. Don't worry about it.'

'Don't worry? *You* should be worried. Aren't you a Fascist?'

'Yes.'

'Go tell them that.' Salvatore jerked a thumb towards the guards.

Annibale shook his head. 'I'm not stupid.'

'Oh, I get it. We're stupid to have our views, are we?'

'No, but what good is it to express them now?'

Salvatore stared at Annibale for a long moment. Not about to be intimidated, Annibale had his fists ready.

'What's going on here?'

Pandi was relieved to hear a soldier's broad Australian accent.

'Come on, move along, we don't want any trouble tonight.'

'No trouble,' Salvatore smiled, sauntering off with his hands in his pockets.

Satisfied, the soldier moved on. But as soon as his back was to them, from a distance Salvatore pointed a finger at Annibale and mouthed, *You'll keep.*

Day 167

They woke to an unfamiliar dawn light. Annibale's throat was dry, his eyes scratchy with the grit of fine dust. He peered out the flap of the tent into a red haze. At first he thought the forest was on fire, yet there was no hint of smoke. Blustery winds had stirred up thousands of tons of dry red earth in the Northern Territory and South Australia, driving it across Queensland, blanketing the land in dust. With the climbing sun, the light changed from red to orange.

Throughout the morning, the dust storm silently passed over them. When Annibale rubbed his hands together, they felt like they were covered in talcum powder. Around midday, the sun and dust bathed the camp in a whimsical golden light and in the mid-afternoon it dulled to a grey-brown, like the blankets on their canvas stretcher beds. The wonder had worn off and the dust-filled air was becoming tedious for both guards and internees. As much as they tried to protect their belongings, it seeped in through cracks and folds, covering everything.

'Just when you think it can't get worse,' muttered Gerolamo, shaking out his blanket.

'This is terrible.' Pandi sounded close to tears. 'I can't take much more.'

That night, Annibale lay awake listening to a gusty wind flapping the canvas and making the sound of the sea in the gum trees. Through a crack in the door of the tent, he could see the perimeter trees bending in the darkness. The air was dry and cold, the temperature plunging as the dust storm finally passed. Annibale had to sleep hunched up, too tall for the scratchy blanket to cover him completely. If his feet stuck out, they froze; if he covered them, his chest got cold. He and some others had sewn together hessian sacks to make extra blankets and he got up and retrieved one for himself, throwing another over Pandi's scrawny form.

Day 198

After the dust came the rain. A great swathe of cloud drew in from the southwest and they didn't glimpse the sun for close to a fortnight. The endless rain on the tent made the interior canvas walls moist and mildewy. By the light of a kerosene lantern Annibale, Pandi and Gerolamo sat inside playing *briscola* with Italo, who had brought the pack of Italian playing cards out with him from Trieste. Clement Huber stood guard in the downpour, rifle at his side. Sitting on the edge of his stretcher bed, Annibale could see, just outside their tent, Clement's boots shiny with rain in the darkness. He shook his head. At the end of the hand, he got up and lifted the tent flap. Clement looked at him through droplets of water falling from the brim of his soggy hat.

'This isn't right,' said Annibale. 'You can't stand out there in the rain all night. Come inside for a bit and sit with us.'

Clement hesitated. 'We're not supposed to talk to you.'

'We're just playing cards.' Annibale shrugged. 'You can come in just to dry off.'

Clement thought for a moment, his eyes searching. He glanced around the tent, then smiled. 'Maybe I will come in for a minute. Thanks, mate, this rain is the pits.'

Day 211

With improved weather, the internees were employed in the task of cutting bull-oak wood for burning in charcoal pits to power gas generators. During this time Annibale noticed while they were working, several Australian military officers came to inspect the internment camp. They silently assessed the internees then left, and life within the camp continued unchanged.

Day 224

The creek water was still chilly but it was good to be able to immerse himself again after months of washing using the bucket of water. Annibale dunked his head under and resurfaced, shaking out the droplets from his hair before smoothing it back with his fingers. It was his nineteenth birthday today. In Italy, his birthday had always marked the seasons getting colder; now the weather was warming up. He thought of his mother, wondering if she would be thinking of this day. She had no idea where he was. Neither did his father.

Clement, the soldier, had quietly turned twenty-one three days before.

Day 235

Salvatore also took the opportunity to work in the forest, and when he joined them Annibale was on his guard. Taunts and fistfights he could handle but he knew Salvatore was more underhanded than that. Despite his previous warning of *You'll keep*, it wasn't Annibale who provoked his ire but another of the internees, Pino, who'd had enough of Salvatore's Fascist talk. The two of them had argued on and off all day as they worked and just after dinner that evening Salvatore and Pino jumped up in the light of the fire. They circled each other in the semi-darkness like panthers before leaping into a punch-up, fists flying. Shouts went up from the other internees, who moved back to give them room. One of the two soldiers on duty fumbled for his whistle to alert the other soldiers eating dinner by their own fire beyond the perimeter.

There was a flash from Salvatore, mirrored by Pino also drawing a knife. For several minutes chaos engulfed the camp, soldiers and internees scrabbling around, not knowing what to do to stop the fight. A gunshot rang in the night air, stalling the fight as everyone, including Salvatore and Pino, froze. The soldier in charge yelled. Another confiscated the knives. Salvatore and Pino were each led away bleeding to be patched up. Again, the camp became quiet.

Day 241

Smoke prickled his nostrils long before he could actually see the fire and Annibale stopped hacking away at the firebreak he'd been creating. He straightened, looking around to see where it was coming from. Others around him were doing the same, unsure what was happening. The guards had said back-burning wouldn't begin before they finished the firebreaks. Annibale's boots crunched over fallen pine cones, slipping slightly on the dense carpet of russet pine needles.

'*There!*' someone shouted, gesturing frantically towards an orange glow coming towards them at an alarming rate.

At the same time the whistles of the soldiers shrilled, followed by shouts of 'Everybody out! Back to camp. Everyone out! *Now!*'

They grabbed their tools and bolted, those Italians who'd lived in Australia long enough to know how rapidly the bush could go up leading the retreat. Much of the forest would burn before the rural fire service had time to assemble and appear with their water-laden trucks, sirens clanging. Returning to the camp in groups, depending on how far into the forest they had been working, the internees assembled for the required head count. Annibale saw Salvatore return, soot smudged. He grinned when Annibale caught his eye.

'Everyone form into lines and keep silent,' a soldier shouted. 'This is serious and no one is moving until we get to the bottom of it.'

Salvatore's face was insolent as the soldier called him over and told him to empty his pockets, including his cigarettes. 'Where are your matches?'

'Lost 'em.'

The soldier scowled. 'You haven't heard the end of this. Everyone to your tents. Get out of my sight. Now!'

The fire was relatively small, burning out after a few miles. No one was hurt but damage to the forest and wildlife was serious. It was never ascertained who lit the fire, but the soldiers realised they had a growing problem on their hands. The fire had revealed the secret location of the camp to the residents of Millmerran, most of whom had been unaware it was only about sixteen miles from their town. Considering their long drive through the night to get there, the internees were also surprised to learn they had been so close to a town all along and weren't as isolated as the soldiers had led them to believe.

Once they became aware, some local residents concerned for their safety, complained and petitioned for the removal of internees from the area. A severe wartime labour shortage clinched it. The Queensland Co-ordinator-General of Public Works directed that interned aliens employed in state forest projects at Western Creek, Monto and Inglewood be deployed to build roads around Ravensbourne, areas west of Roma, south of Charters Towers and near Clermont. The end of 1942 marked the shutdown of the temporary camp at Western Creek.

Day 254

As they were packing up, Pandi was called away to speak to the soldier in charge. He returned to the tent with a look of bewilderment and gladness. 'They're letting me go. Said they found out I shouldn't have been here in the first place.'

Annibale continued rolling up his bedding. 'Well, that's true.'

Pandi eyed his friend, suspecting it was Annibale's doing. 'I think I'll head to Brisbane. Look for work. It's a shame you can't come, too. You reckon we'll see each other again?'

Annibale stood up, arching his back to stretch out some soreness. 'Who kno—' He stopped, seeing Pandi's hopeful face. 'No, you know what, we probably will one day.'

Western Creek — 2013

Dear Ms Boccabella,
Thank you for your request for records relating to an internment camp in Western Creek, Queensland ... I have checked our collection and have not identified any records relating to the above subject. I regret we could not be of more assistance on this occasion ...

Dear Ms Boccabella,
Thank you for your enquiry regarding your grandfather's internment during the Second World War ... I have searched our catalogues and have not been able to find any records relating to him or this particular camp ...

Dear Zoë,
Unfortunately, we are unaware of any records regarding an internment camp at Western Creek. Two very long-serving employees of the Millmerran office (one of whom worked for twenty-three years at the State Forestry Department before coming to Council twenty years ago) were both very surprised to learn of an internment camp out that way and have never seen any records relating to same ...

Dear Zoë,
Thank you for your enquiry relating to the internment of Annibale Boccabella. A preliminary search proved unsuccessful amongst the collection archives ... Unfortunately, I could not find any mention of the temporary camp at Western Creek, Queensland ...

And then ...

Dear Zoë,
You are right about the big secret and the camp. Very few in this town knew anything about it . . .

On a cold winter's morning, we drive west. In the early light, heavy fog saturates the landscape, obscuring paddocks and hills and swirling in our wake along the almost empty highway. I glance across at Roger. It feels a little like times past in Italy, especially when I think back to setting out cross-country in Basilicata and Calabria. Except this time we are heading towards Western Creek in Queensland, Australia.

I feel drawn to see where my grandfather spent almost a year in an internment camp, and yet there is something else. A niggling feeling that has risen from various authorities having been unable as yet to locate any records relating to the internment camp at Western Creek or to those interned at that spot. Perhaps it is a need to find the camp not just for Nonno Anni, but also for all the men who were there, most of whom by now would have died. It seems remiss for its existence to be buried, forgotten — for the men interned, their loved ones who were affected at the time, and also the young soldiers who treated the internees fairly within the parameters of the situation, something that was not the case for many Australians in prison camps overseas.

The fog dissipates with the rising sun. Through the flood-ravaged Lockyer Valley and the Darling Downs, out west along the Gore Highway, there are constant roadworks. Several floods have washed away roads, large tracts of broken bitumen resting across paddocks or seemingly vanished. There are 760 kilometres of roads under reconstruction just in this area. From Brisbane, the five-hour round trip out to Millmerran stretches to eight.

On the plains, I look out the window across land reaching flat and empty to a horizon so distant that trees blur at the skyline. Under a high winter sun the landscape looks grey and brittle, and still there is a raw beauty to it. The railway track runs parallel to the Gore Highway, and I think of Nonno Anni travelling along here by train, locked aboard the internee special. And then the effort to keep the internment-camp location a secret from both the residents of Millmerran and the internees; the soldiers driving the internees in the back of canvas-covered army trucks around the surrounding countryside for hours. I hear Nonno Anni's voice ... *We travelled all night. We didn't know where we'd finish up.*

The Millmerran and District Historical Society and Museum is a well-organised set-up with several historic buildings, including a small school, a post office, machinery shed, creamery and shepherd's hut, all staggered around the neat lawns of the property. As Roger and I wander among exhibits in the rooms of the original council chambers, I find myself hoping there might be a small cabinet displaying photographs, perhaps a diary or implements from the internment camp, though it seems unlikely, considering the authorities seem to have no record of the internees being in this area.

I walk into a room filled with war memorabilia, mostly connected with the Australian army, and I recall that many young men in this area joined up to fight in the Second World War. Young men just like Grandpa Bob, who told me he'd been keen to 'do his bit'. I am mindful it was a very frightening period for all those in Australia, whatever their cultural background and circumstances. The internment story is but one of so many wartime stories, just and unjust, some horrifying in their violence and loss of life, others inspiring.

A large picture of Queen Elizabeth as she looked perhaps fifty years ago hangs on one wall; on the other, a Nazi flag. While there is nothing to indicate the nearby internment of 'enemy aliens', tacked above several old axes in another display is a photograph of government forest workers at Western Creek in 1940, two years before the camp came into existence. I gaze at it for some time thinking it may have looked similar when Nonno Anni undertook work there for the State Forestry Department.

I have high regard for local historical societies, set up with decency and pride by hardworking, usually older, volunteers to commemorate the history of their area. As correspondence built up from authorities, including the National Archives, State Archives and the Australian War Memorial, to advise that initial searches could provide no official records of my grandfather's internment or the camp at Western Creek, it was through contacts provided by Millmerran's historical society that anecdotal evidence began to emerge.

> Mr —— was a local man put in charge by the State Forestry Department to supervise the internees working in the forest. Mr ——'s son said his father said very little [about the camp]. Only that there were some tough fellows and knives were sometimes drawn. Mr —— has passed away.

> It's funny you should mention that camp. A little while back, an older gentleman was asking the same thing. At the time, I searched all our books and documents including our local government archives and I couldn't find anything about people being interned in this area during the war.

> The local Greek café owner often said he was very bitter about how his relatives were treated on the Greek Islands by Italy. However, [as the camp was shut down] some of the townspeople were amused to see him go to the Police Station yard with food items from his café to sell to the Italians when the internees must have been gathered for transport.

> During the war, an internment camp for war internees was established in the Western Creek Forest. It appears that it was a well-kept secret. Mr —— [our neighbour] at Turallin worked on the Forestry and was put in charge of some of the inmates to work in the forest. My knowledge of the camp came from rumour and it gained credence from talking to Mr and Mrs —— [our neighbours]. So I can only claim anecdotal evidence of the camp.

> Oh, there was definitely an internment camp out at Western Creek. A number of people in the town knew but no one talked about it. Even now. Funny. It happened so long ago.

I am grateful that several current and past residents share these stories with me, particularly as it appears that the internment camp at Western Creek is still a sensitive subject more than seventy years after its closure. Still, the evidence I have of the internment camp remains anecdotal. Nonno Anni told me it happened. The family of the local man who supervised the internees in forest work agrees he said it happened. A soldier who guarded the camp admitted he was there, despite his military record making no mention of it. Nonno Anni even had four black-and-white photographs of him and other internees in the camp. It could be argued that the photographs of men standing in front of tents or sitting with musical instruments or holding work tools with bushland behind them could have been taken anywhere. I don't have anything official to say the internment camp at Western Creek existed.

And then, while Roger and I continue browsing the exhibits at the Millmerran Museum, the woman behind the front desk with whom I made inquires upon our arrival seeks me out.

'I think I might have something for you about the camp, only very small, in a history of the town put together by a local man who served on the Millmerran Shire Council for many years. It is just one line, though, marked 2nd April, 1942.'

She hands me several typed pages and I scan through the entries.

18th September, 1936 — *The butter factory was opened, with a public holiday declared.*
2nd February, 1939 — *Alsatian or German Shepherd dogs banned in the shire.*
2nd April, 1942 — *Council decided to remove all directional signs in the shire due to the threat of invasion. It was also reported that a camp of alien internees had been established at Western Creek.*

Technically, it is still anecdotal evidence but at least it is something in writing, and by a local who worked for years for a government authority. I am grateful and thank her.

'May I have a copy of this? And the name of the person who collated it?'
'Of course.'
'We're going to head out to Western Creek, to find where the camp was,' I say as she hands me a copy.

She stares. 'Really? Well, there's nothing much out that way, it's kind of in the middle of nowhere. I don't think anyone is quite sure of the exact spot where the camp was.'

'Right.' I don't admit to her or to Roger that I don't feel so sure myself.

We drive along Saleyards Road and stand among overgrown grasses at the end of the old railway line. It was here the internees were unloaded in the night. I feel a pang of protectiveness for the teenager, Annibale, and the grandfather whom I loved. I give in to it for a few moments and then stifle the feeling, striving to be as neutral as possible to understand the internment camp from various perspectives: that of non-Italian Australians, frightened the migrants might rise up and turn against them; of young guards, some teenagers or not much older, following orders with sympathy and without; and of Italian-Australians, some resentful but accepting, others angry, all suffering the personal cost borne also by their families.

Back in the car, Roger looks across from the driver's seat.

I refold the map. 'This road bends around, and at the end of it we turn left.'

Driving out of Millmerran, I regret not having thought of bringing Nonno Anni here to show me while he was alive. Through studying different maps, knowing it was about twenty-five kilometres from the town, and Nonno Anni having explained much of the camp, I initially felt certain of finding it. Yet now, as the farmhouses thin and the dirt road winds into scrub, I feel increasingly unsure.

We are mostly silent as we travel along. The scrub becomes thicker. We judder over a cattle grid and enter a forest of tall trees. A wooden sign points an arrow to Western Creek, a metal one proclaims the area to be state forest. We cross a bridge and get out, taking a first look at the creek, low on water, milky green and curving below.

Back hurtling along the dirt road, I inch towards the edge of the seat, clutching the dashboard, my gaze swooping left and right. 'Slow down a little,' I murmur.

'This road goes for miles.'

'I know but I need to see …'

It's all trees, growing tall with thick scrub in between. With a sinking heart I realise it all looks the same, on both sides of the road. What was I thinking? I've dragged Roger out here on a wild goose chase. What did I expect after more than seventy years? This camp consisted of tents for twelve months. How could there be any clue to its whereabouts?

Roger glances at the odometer. 'We're about twenty k's from Millmerran.'

'Yes.' My throat feels dry.

Then, a few minutes later, nearing a fork in the road, I hear myself telling Roger to stop the car. We get out. Closing the car doors sounds loud in the quietness of the forest.

'Which road should we choose?' Roger can't help eyeing the car covered in dust.

'Perhaps neither.' I'm walking towards an area on my left, the only bit of clearing I've seen so far. 'For some reason, I feel like this could be the spot.'

'Of the camp? It's been cleared by cattle, I reckon.'

'Even the trees? Even though we came across a cattle grid?' I do doubt myself, though. Instinct usually serves well if I'm mindful enough to perceive it but I need more proof of the camp's site than just a feeling. Besides, as far as I can see there is no sign of the creek that Nonno Anni described as being nearby.

I walk alone into the clearing. The half-moon sits at a tilt, rising in the afternoon sky. I shiver. This is the spot. I'm almost sure of it. Without a word I walk deeper into the clearing, towards the tree-lined far boundary about a hundred metres away. The almost honeyed scent of the surrounding bushland fills my nostrils. I cross hard-baked dirt and then stop. My breath catches. Twenty metres ahead of me the land falls away. Down an embankment, concealed from the road, is Western Creek.

Staring at cloudy green water, low in the winter dry, and the beach of creek sand I know I cannot be sure, but I feel in my heart this is the place. It is very quiet except for a lone crow and the sound of treetops stirring in the nearby forest. A breeze that doesn't quite reach to where I am.

Roger quietly comes up beside me. 'Look out, you're almost standing on an ant bed.'

I look down at compacted, stippled earth, ants going about their business.

The sun tracks above. Behind it, the moon follows its own arc in the blenching sky. I'm not sure how long we stand by the creek. Sometimes talking, sometimes silent, listening. The occasional splash as we take turns throwing stones in the water. We don't see another soul.

Before we leave I take several photographs of the area, and as we drive away I keep looking back at the clearing through dust kicked up by the car.

It is a long drive back along the dirt road, over the flat highway and empty plains, through the gap in the mountains where the bellbirds call, back towards home and the humid sea, bringing some of the western dust with us.

Storia Scomoda — Part I

'Dad took us out to have a look at where the internment camp was, back in ... now let me see, I think I had started uni, so it would have been about 1964 or '65.'

I stare at my father. No one has ever mentioned this to me before.

He asks me about my own trip to Western Creek. 'So what did you see out there?'

'Before I say, can you tell me what you saw when you were there?' I ask him. 'I just want to make sure I ...'

He shrugs and nods. It's the first time we've sat down and talked, just the two of us, for a long time. To me it feels like warming in morning sun after a nippy night, wanting to make the most of it, aware the sun will soon shift again. He tells me of the trip his parents made with him and his brother out to Millmerran. When he estimates it having taken about half an hour to drive from the town out to the camp location at Western Creek my hope rises, the jigsaw beginning to fit. He describes the lonely area I saw, the regenerated scrub in the clearing.

'I don't recall a creek but then again it was quite dry when we went.'

'Did you walk in from the road?' He may not have seen the creek if they didn't walk across that clearing.

'No, we didn't walk very far in,' he says.

It still doesn't give definite confirmation but I'm feeling more confident. I'm about to tell Dad what I saw when he continues speaking.

'I have this vague image of standing where two dirt roads meet ...'

There is only one spot along one road that distance from Millmerran where there is a fork in the road. Nonno Anni is no longer alive, but by having shown my father the location in about 1964, he confirms for me in 2013 where the internment camp was.

'Actually, I'm sure I would have taken my camera on that trip,' says Dad. 'I'll start looking through my old photos and let you know if I get lucky.'

The seventy-year-old manila folder is speckled with age and dulled to a fawn colour, grimy in places where the hands of police and army officers held it. It is so well thumbed that the edges are cracked and nibbled, the worn cardboard spine mended with strips of masking tape that have fissured and curled with time. INTERNMENT INFORMATION is handwritten in black block letters on the front, underlined in red pencil. There are several codes scribbled in various inks, and then in different, thick-nibbed handwriting, underlined five times, is the word SECRET.

Hundreds of dog-eared pages are inside and I begin scanning each one for any reference to the internment camp at Western Creek, Nonno Anni or Bisnonno Vitale. Since the trip out to Western Creek, I have renewed determination to find some official evidence of the camp, searching again via the National and State Archives, Australian War Memorial, the State Library, shire councils and both district and Italian historical societies. Anywhere I might find some proof not solely anecdotal. Some of the faded type and handwriting requires a lot of effort to decipher. There are dozens of previously classified files now publicly available.

Immediately it becomes obvious that the Australian government, through the state police forces and the army, collected information on a range of residents. While people of Italian, German and Japanese origin attracted the most scrutiny, numerous nationals of more than thirty other countries were watched too. With a real fear of fascism at this time, this included British subjects born in Australia who were involved in fascist or communist organisations or the nationalist Australia First Movement.

The surveillance began surprisingly early. In relation to those of Italian origin, there is an urgent memorandum sent to every inspector throughout Queensland by Police Commissioner CJ Carroll dating from before Italy had entered the war. It refers to attached lists of Italian enemy aliens in each area and requests that 'reports should be furnished of every Italian, both naturalised and not naturalised, who it is considered should be interned'. With both sexes and also the descendants of Italian migrants included, it occurs to me that under Australia's 1939 *National Security Act* I would have been classified as an 'enemy alien'.

In March 1942, Police Commissioner Carroll declared enemy aliens 'the scum of the earth' who deserved no clemency. The Queensland Premier, William Forgan Smith, readily agreed. Recognising the personal prejudice of these two men, Catholic Archbishop James Duhig spoke out in opposition to the campaign against Italians, saying their deprivation of liberty was 'unjustifiable on the grounds of national security or public good'. In response, Forgan Smith cabled Prime Minister John Curtin, demanding the internment of all Italian-Australians, whether they were born in Australia or not.

The zeal with which Forgan Smith demanded the internment of every 'enemy alien' in his state provoked a curt rebuke at one point from the federal government. Arthur Calwell, chairman of the Aliens Classification and Advisory Committee, pointed out that Queensland internments — already doubling those of other states — involved 'too much racial and other prejudice' and that 'a right sense of proportion' needed to be exercised. I think back to being a teenage first-year university student yet to learn such history, blithely walking into my first lecture in a grand building named 'Forgan Smith'.

I happen upon a once-classified document titled *Movement of Aliens in Stanthorpe District*, and realise Nanna Francesca's family, Nonno Anni and Bisnonno Vitale were among those being monitored as part of the 'Italian alien population'. There were '84 naturalised British subjects of enemy origin' and '44 enemy aliens' in Stanthorpe, according to one of many counts taken. It is reported when Italian families gather for a picnic in case they are conspiring. Also noted are Italian migrants' visits to town and interactions between farms. One intelligence document reveals a local bank manager disclosing the movements of money in the bank accounts of Italian settlers.

A list of eighty-nine names of farmers in the district records them as having contributed to an appeal. These 'Italian compatriots' were donating money to a woman of Italian origin whose husband died, leaving her and her four children in 'very poor financial circumstances'. I scan the list and see the name of Nanna Francesca's father, 'D Solano', among the ten-shilling contributors. I have been searching for 'Boccabella' and it is the Solano side that comes up. So far there is nothing about Western Creek.

A few pages on I come across several neat hand-drawn maps. The second one stops me still. Marked by a shaded box titled 'Salano' is my great-grandparents' farm. Though the mapmaker has misspelt their surname, it is unmistakably their property. The road is clearly marked, as is the watercourse to the southwest and Applethorpe siding where they'd load their produce onto the train, as well as the local school Nanna Francesca and her siblings attended. On the same map, shaded boxes and names denote other farms in the area too. Direct routes to the farms of Italian migrants have been dotted out. It is a little sinister to think of Nanna Francesca's family being watched. Police, army and government officers would have seen nothing more than a couple with a teenage daughter and two younger children, keeping to themselves and working their farm.

I turn the page to a piece of correspondence that, unlike the other reports, has no names or signatures, though it has been officially stamped and initialled as a 'certified true copy'. It looks to be an instruction to an informant.

> *A simultaneous search of all alien properties in your area is contemplated and your full and urgent cooperation is sought ... On the map, every red circle represents a farm ... very carefully put alongside each, the names of the Italians on that farm, underlining the name of the Italian you consider should be searched ... it is essential to have the name spelt correctly, and the proper address, otherwise the warrant is not valid ... The Military Authorities can arrange for the supply of petrol, but is it possible for cars to be loaned by local residents? ... in order to preserve the secrecy of your identity ... you will not be asked to participate in the search, 24 hours notice will be given when the zero hour has been arranged. This will probably be very early in the morning. In the interim, any further information you have would be appreciated.*

What made Bisnonno Mico one of the fortunate few not to face internment? Nanna Francesca said perhaps it was because he was quiet, older, naturalised and kept to himself. Most likely, he was simply lucky. There were many other men — older, unassuming and law-abiding like Bisnonno Vitale — arrested and detained for several years.

Handwritten letters from citizens-turned-informants pepper the files. Some writers reveal themselves to have nursed long-held grudges. Others appear to have genuinely wanted to be helpful, believing they were doing their duty in good faith. The informers were both men and women.

> *I suggest X might be worth investigating. I don't know anything definite against him but Italians frequently visit his home ...*

> *Y made a remark to his wife, Z, in Italian while in the shop. When the shop owner, Mrs A, requested he speak English as she couldn't understand Italian, he is supposed to have said, 'You will soon have to understand it.'*

> *Last Friday evening at the patriotic concert, Italians B and C were accompanied by seven strange men who are said to be new arrivals from the north. Afterwards they all went out to the Yugo Slav's place ...*

> *D had coffee in the dago refreshment room, knows them all and is willing to give some valuable information. He says E and his wife, F, are cunning and need watching ...*

Newspaper clippings printed around this time further illustrate anti-Italian fervour with headlines such as 'Residents Seek Internment of Aliens', 'Demand for Internment of Enemy Aliens' and 'Poppa Has His Rifle Hidden in the Sugarcane' — this one an article referring to Italian migrants as 'Poppa Minestrone', and 'arrogant and smirking'. In another clipping, a man described as a 'Digger' complains of 'British quislings in our midst who are prepared to give the Mussolinites every protection'. The heightened threat of impending invasion, especially in northern Australia, reasonably enough drove fear among residents concerned about the ultimate patriotism of migrants. However, other documents reveal this was used as an excuse by some who, long before war was declared, already resented Italians in Queensland for 'taking over the sugar industry' in the north, and 'increasing the size of their properties' to gain a 'monopoly of vegetable growing' on the Darling Downs in the southeast of the state.

National Archives lists as at 2013 …

Internment camps in Australia during World War II:
- *Cowra, Hay and Holsworthy (Liverpool), NSW,*
- *Enoggera (Gaythorne), QLD,*
- *Harvey and Rottnest Island, WA,*
- *Loveday, SA,*
- *Tatura (Rushworth), VIC.*

A number of other smaller or temporary camps include:
- *Bathurst, NSW (1939),*
- *Long Bay, NSW (1939–41),*
- *Orange, NSW (1940–41),*
- *Dhurringile near Murchison, VIC (1939–40),*
- *Parkeston, WA (1942).*

Camps solely to accommodate prisoners of war:
- *Yanco, NSW, Marrinup, WA, Brighton, TAS,*
- *Murchison and Myrtleford, VIC.*

I turn to war diaries kept by members of the Australian Army units responsible for internees in Australia throughout the Second World War. These records are available from the Australian War Memorial's archives and I seek out entries made during 1942 when the internment camp at Western Creek was in operation. I don't immediately find any mention of Western Creek, yet I get a glimpse of life for internees across Australia …

- *Approval given for internees to write one letter per month subject to censorship.*
- *Latrines have no fly screens and some internees have succumbed to dysentery.*
- *Approval for internees to be photographed in groups and for prints (maximum of two per internee) to be supplied to such internees on*

payment of despatch to relatives if they so desire or for retention with their impounded effects during their internment.
- The privilege of sending 3 Xmas cards is a very small concession to grant to internees and is felt to be in keeping with the general policy of humanitarian treatment established by the Commonwealth.
- Local [Italian] internee, Mr X, has died, apparently from violence and internee Mr Y is under arrest.
- Provide Photostat copies of all forms (with copy of the internee's photo attached) of each internee moved away from his parent camp for employment in a detached work camp.
- The transfer of German women and children from Camp J to Camp K has been completed.
- With reference to the escape of [Italian] internee L, information has been received from H.Q. that the internee's body has been recovered from the River Murray, death being apparently due to drowning.
- Restriction to amount of luggage an internee may bring.
- Approval for additional riding horses for mounted patrols guarding outside work parties.

In another formerly secret file I come across a typed government document titled *Summary of Internments*, outlining the numbers of enemy aliens taken in Queensland as at 31 May 1942; they had been rounded up in Cairns, Townsville, Mackay, Rockhampton, Maryborough and Brisbane. It shows that almost three thousand people were arrested at this time, and while the number of Italians exceeded two thousand there were also many other nationalities interned whose numbers are listed under the headings *Germans, Austrians, Albanians, Bulgarians, Finns, Yugoslavs, Spanish, British, Romanians, Japanese, Hungarians, French, Russians, Swiss, Czeck, Eston, Poles, Danes, Lithuanian.*

This summary also reveals that 154 of these internees were women, dispelling some long-held notions that women were spared. Further on, I discover children were also interned. While I cannot locate an official number of those interned, a document titled *Internment of Children of*

Internees includes reasons for the practice, such as when one or both parents was interned and there was no one suitable or available to care for the children in their parents' absence. Other such children were sent to live in orphanages or children's homes during the internment of their parents.

The official total number of resident 'enemy aliens' of various nationalities interned in Australia during the Second World War differs between government documents, academic and history books in the same way that many war figures such as battle casualties, civilian deaths and land army volunteers can fluctuate. Totals of Italian internees I find range between 7,163 and 6,982 and 5,716 and 8,100, which roughly equates to between 15 and 20 percent of the Italian migrant population of about 40,000 in Australia then. In comparison, the United States interned 10,905 mainly Italian-born 'enemy aliens', or about 0.27 percent of the Italian-American population, which was said to exceed four million at the time.

With varying official figures and no record yet found of the Western Creek camp, I ponder whether the internees who were in 'temporary' camps are included in the total figures, and how many 'secret' camps such as Western Creek existed.

An Inconvenient History — Part II

I had expected it would be relatively straightforward to obtain a copy of Nonno Anni's internment record. A helpful reference library assistant tells me they are a popular subject of genealogical searches. But despite continued investigation, neither I nor various research assistants are able to find any mention of his name or of the camp at Western Creek. They are as puzzled as I am. I'm told a likely explanation could be that, in the authorities' haste to round up internees in early 1942, files were not properly kept. Or the files have since inadvertently been archived under a name unrelated to the camp, or not catalogued at all. My search appears to have come to a standstill.

I try a different tack and locate the army file of the young camp guard Nonno Anni talked about. Huber is not his real name; his name, also of German origin, was more uncommon, making him easily recognisable, so I have not used it. Only one military record contains this name. There is no mention of the camp on his service record, although there is a vague reference to an interval in Brisbane that covers the dates Nonni Anni said he was at the camp. I wonder if it's possible that the secrecy surrounding the camp at the time has resulted in no mention of it even on his record — but that seems extraordinary.

In a curious twist, this camp guard and Nonno Anni ended up living most of their lives in the same suburb, a few streets apart, and recognised each other. I shared classes in both primary and high school with the guard's grandson. On a high-school camp he insisted on carrying my backpack for most of a nine-kilometre bushwalk, chatting with me as we hiked. Friends teased me that he was keen but somehow I knew there was nothing in it. When we got in touch years later, he was happy and successful, living in Sydney with his partner, both of them key organisers of a float in the annual Mardi Gras Parade. How free our lives seemed then compared with those of our grandfathers when their paths crossed at Western Creek in 1942.

A State librarian contacts me to say they have found a small newspaper article mentioning an internment camp near Millmerran. At the time of its publication, Nonno Anni would have already spent two weeks in the camp.

ITALIAN INTERNEES

> Fifteen Italians who formed [a] portion of a batch of a conscripted labour corps and who arrived at Millmerran on Friday night en route to a camp broke camp. They were intercepted by the military guard and returned to camp. They pointed out to the forestry officer that they refuse to carry out the work allotted to them and that they did not intend to remain in the bush. The Millmerran police were communicated with and the aliens were arrested and brought in for subsequent internment. They then left Millmerran under military and police escort.
>
> The *Western Star and Roma Advertiser*, Friday, March 27, 1942

The librarian adds that they cannot find any other mention of the internment camp. A copy of this newspaper clipping together with the single sentence included in the history of Millmerran put together by the local councillor remain the only written items I've been able to obtain that mention the camp, and even so the news article does not mention Western Creek. I'm hopeful that in the future I or someone else will find some official record. Surely there is a file somewhere, but after months of searching it remains elusive and I must concede defeat for now.

For some time after the war ended, it seems no one spoke much of the internment. Even decades later, when I talked to Nonno Anni about it, he began by showing bravado and joked that it was his first holiday since travelling out on the boat from Italy, his making light of it hinting at how he'd come to handle with the ordeal. He went on to admit he felt sad he had lost those years when he was in the prime of life. Then he'd shrugged and intimated *what could you do?* He seemed philosophical, knowing that everyone was asked to make sacrifices because it was wartime, aware the broader community was affected, not just him and the other internees.

The fate of Italian migrant men in Australia during the Second World War panned out in roughly three ways. Some Australian-born Italians saw active service defending Australia. Others remained living and working in the community, sometimes due to the Catholic Church vouching for them. And then there were those sent to Australia's internment camps and the Civil Alien Corps (CAC), their incarceration varying in duration — some sent to help on farms when produce shortages began to occur; others forced to work years in CAC labour gangs, my Bisnonno Vitale included.

Nonno Anni insisted the soldiers guarding his camp treated him well, and he was fortunate to remain strong and healthy despite the crude living conditions and lack of sanitation in his camp. While being interned left its mark on his life, the carapace of youth perhaps shielded him a little. I believe it was harder for Bisnonno Vitale. Some people seem to be born into a timeline of challenge. Vitale was twenty when the First World War began, the prime age for conscription, and he served on the side of the Allies for the entire duration of the conflict. Next came the Depression and living away from his family for years at a stretch. And then, not long after, came the Second World War and years of internment and working in the CAC. By the time he was released he was over fifty.

Numerous Italian migrant women who were left to survive as best they could during their husbands' internment faced their own challenges as they grappled with running farms on their own or with small children — some to discover later that their husbands had been despatched to provide help on non-Italian-run farms. These women are inspiring, often having shown great strength and endurance as they toiled in the fields and taught themselves to drive or use machinery and sold their produce. At the same time they continued with their domestic chores in an era when doing the washing could take an entire day.

While most internees and their families quietly got on with their lives after the war ended — sometimes taking years to recover financially — a few found the experience too much.

'There were some men from the camp who didn't do too well after they got out.' Nonno Anni sighed and refolded a paper serviette, tucking it under the saucer of his empty coffee cup. 'Some returned home to find their farms empty or sold. There was one I know whose wife had killed herself. A couple of the men, they suicided. But that was kept quiet. People didn't talk about that sort of thing much. Most pretended it was an accident.'

'Because of the stigma at the time?' I asked.

'They wanted a Catholic funeral and burial. Priests wouldn't do it for a suicide.'

Enclosed in a yellow Kodak paper sleeve foxed with age, the white-bordered black-and-white photographs remain in perfect condition. Taken on my father's box Brownie camera in the mid '60s, the photographs capture the trip out to Millmerran and Western Creek when Nonno Anni took his wife and sons to show them where the internment camp had been. I recognise a picture of the town's main street, deserted in the middle of a summer's day. Nonno Anni walks down the wooden steps of the Millmerran Court House. A group of brumbies runs through the bush. And then, a photograph taken by Nanna Francesca of Nonno Anni and his two sons at the site of the internment camp at Western Creek.

I get out the magnifying glass. The three of them stand with their arms around each other, my father in the centre. They are all smiling. Nonno Anni has one hand on his hip, almost defiant. He would have been in his early forties, my age now. My father is about nineteen, his brother perhaps eleven or twelve. They all look happy, on a family daytrip. And yet this was the spot where soldiers kept Nonno Anni against his will for almost a year. Perhaps the self-assurance I read in his stance is to convey that the experience didn't beat him. He went on to run his fruit shop and milk bar, he married, had sons. I wonder if returning to the spot was in some way cathartic. Or was his aim to show his sons so that, in a time when no one spoke about it, what happened wouldn't be forgotten.

Recalling that day, my uncle describes to me having seen the skeletons of tents on the site of the camp — rough sapling poles that once had canvas slung across them with ropes attached to pegs. The image makes me catch my breath. The family was there more than two decades after the camp closed; is it possible the sapling tent poles still stood? Bill Garner describes in *Born in a Tent* a camp site Henry Lawson erected at Cape Howe in 1910 that was for years a landmark, locals proudly calling it 'the poet's camp'. Fifteen years after Lawson pitched the tent, his mate Edwin Brady rode past and found the ridgepole was rotting, yet the sapling side poles remained intact.

There are only three photographs in the Kodak sleeve taken of the site of the internment camp — the one with the father and sons standing in the foreground with a little of the clearing and some trees behind them, and the next depicting the site on its own. The third shows Nonno Anni standing alone beside what is unmistakably the skeleton of a tent, the sturdy sapling centre pole upright and the ridgepole showing signs of rot. Just like Lawson's tent frame.

I study the photographs closely, comparing them with those I took of the spot almost fifty years later, and with the few photographs taken within the camp in 1942. Unfortunately those taken in 1942 show very little of the landscape, focusing more on the internees. No two photographs taken in 1942, 1964 or 2013 are quite alike, but there is something familiar in the trees, the baked earth and wispy dry grass. If only one of the older photographs showed the creek, then I could be certain.

A few weeks later, I'm looking at the photographs once again when something makes me reach into the sleeve for the negatives. I discover a negative for a photograph not among those printed. It shows Nonno Anni and Nanna Francesca standing together, and in the background is the Western Creek embankment. I recognise the spot immediately, the stretch where Roger and I stood casting rocks into the water.

Further confirmation comes not long after when I have the opportunity to interview a Millmerran local, then in his nineties. I do not immediately mention my link with the camp, though my surname is likely a giveaway. Jack tells me that in 1942 he was working on the cattle property Western Creek Station, which shared a boundary with the area of state forest that contained the internment camp. The cattle fed right up to this boundary, and when Jack came to check them he often saw the men in the internment camp and even spoke to them.

'Italians. They could speak English in a sort of a way. Though I couldn't always understand them very well. I only had a little bit to do with them, talking at the boundary line, but they seemed nice fellows. A lot of them were fairly young. Sometimes I saw them sitting around the camp; other times they were working in the forest. I remember the galley kitchen with galvanised iron on three sides, a billy hanging to boil over the open fire. All the tents lined up. Roughly built bush toilets. Very rough living.'

'Did you go into town often?' I ask him. 'Were you aware of people in town knowing of the camp or was it a secret?'

'I went in on horseback occasionally, if you had to buy new clothes or run an errand or something. No, I don't think the camp was a secret in the town. Well … actually many were surprised to find out about it afterwards.'

'Do you remember the exact location of the camp?' I get out a map of the area.

'Oh, I know it clear as day. It was down the creek 'bout two mile from the homestead, near a fork in the road.'

'The Turallin–Western Creek Road?' I pinpoint the spot on the map.

'You got it. Yep, that's the spot, where the road forks and one road heads to Goondiwindi eventually and the other you can get to Tara.'

'And the creek is about a hundred metres in from the road?' I add, to be sure.

'Spot on.'

Smiling, grateful, I thank him.

Any sign of the camp may be completely gone now, but I seem to have come to, or very close to, its site. I wish Nonno Anni could have known that I went there.

ZOË: *Were you angry you had to be there? Or did you just accept it?*
ANNIBALE: *Well, I mean to say that …*
FRANCESCA: *That's the way it had to be. My father, he could have been put in there.*

ANNIBALE: *With the army, you had to accept it. They were like a storm wall. We didn't do anything. The only thing was you had to be there, that's all.*

ZOË: *You must have resented being taken away?*

ANNIBALE: *You resented.*

FRANCESCA: *But you know, it's war, so you really don't, you know?*

ANNIBALE: *It's war, what could you do?*

ZOË: *Did you talk amongst yourselves? Say this isn't right?*

ANNIBALE: *Between ourselves. That's all. We just had to sit, one way or the other, until the war finished. Here, let me show you some photographs I have of us in the camp … That is a group of us. That is us beside our tent. See Venice Street [Via Veneto] and our washing hanging on a rope? [Chuckling] And that is me, the day we left the camp.*

ZOË: *The army give you that suit, did they?*

ANNIBALE: *No, no, they give you army clothes to wear while you worked in the forest. But also, we had everything we'd brought with us. Because the police said take all your belongings because you won't be coming back.*

ZOË: *So after you left Western Creek, did you return to the farm you'd been working on?*

ANNIBALE: *No, no, they just moved us to Pikedale. I work on a road gang, building a new road. About five hundred of us.*

Good Luck to You, Daughter

The internees, mostly Italians, arrived on the back of army trucks at scrubland near Pikedale, about twenty-one miles west of Stanthorpe. They stood in the good clothes they'd donned to travel in, holding a suitcase or bag each, which for many of them contained all they owned. This time they would be living in prefabricated dormitory huts the army had set up, the officer in charge informing them, 'You'll each get eighteen shillings a week for food and six shillings a day building roads.'

After putting away their belongings, they congregated in road gangs, back in their work clothes, the December sun already hot on their faces. The army needed inland roads to be traversable during the wet season, and thousands of internees would provide the labour needed to both build and upgrade hundreds of miles of routes snaking across western Queensland and northwest to the Northern Territory.

They started each new section of road by clearing the land of brush, trees, stumps and boulders. Even with a stump-puller, this could be a slow process. Once they had cleared the debris, the levelling began with a Caterpillar angle-dozer that operated by day and, using hurricane lamps, at night. In its wake, men stepped in with rakes and hoes to remove jutting stones too large to remain in the road base. Then they added drainage ditches. A layer of small stones, clay and hard gravel followed, all spread by shovels.

The men cooked their food over fires in cut-off steel drums and the army provided medical treatment and tools, plus fuel and oil for the equipment. Like many of the internees, Annibale acquired a navy singlet that with time, sweat and sun faded to mauve-grey. His bare arms and an arc of skin below his neck tanned deep-brown. The timber grip of his usual shovel was smooth in his toughened hands. It was an existence: the clink and scrape of rocks and gravel guided by the tip of his shovel; the rapport and camaraderie with the other internees.

Gerolamo called out, 'Hey, I need a hand with an easy job over here. Who's the laziest? Put your hand up.' Several hands went up, going along with the joke.

They turned to Carlo, whom they called '*Culo*' — meaning bum — because it sounded similar to his actual name and because of his tendency to stay sitting on his.

'Hey, Culo, why don't you have your hand up?' someone called.

Carlo slowly smiled. 'Too much trouble.'

They snickered then fell quiet until the next excuse for some banter came around.

The war and the roadworks dragged on. Then one day the soldier in charge made an announcement that gave Annibale a flicker of hope for the future. 'There are a lot of farms in the area with a shortage of workers. If you want to work on them on weekends you can register and pay four shillings for a permit. We'll grant you leave from six o'clock on Friday nights through until Monday mornings at eight, when you must be assembled here to be counted. If anybody is not back by then, the police will come looking for you.'

There was a mixed reaction among the internees. Some thought it a bit rich having to purchase a permit to work on the same farms that many had worked on before the government forced them into internment. Others didn't want to work seven days a week without a break. But Annibale immediately wrote a letter to Mico Solano asking if he could work on his farm. When he received a reply in the affirmative, Annibale went straight to the officers' hut.

The officer in charge leant back in his chair, bending his head a little to size Annibale up over the top of his spectacles. 'I remember you …' His voice slowed as recognition dawned. 'You were among those internees working when the fires were lit up at Western Creek.'

Annibale's heart sank. 'I never lit that fire.'

'I always thought it was that Salvatore ratbag we sent out further west but there wasn't any proof.' The officer smiled. 'So, you want to go and work on which farm?'

Annibale made the twenty-five mile trip to the Solano farm in the back of an open-air truck, sitting among other internees heading to the same area. Although he'd met the Solano family at the Benitos' gathering, this first Friday night that Annibale arrived at their property for weekend work was when his real acquaintance began.

They rearranged chairs for him to join them at the table. It was a welcoming and homely kitchen bathed in lemony light. Cesca scuttled around, sweat shining on her face, her corpulent figure in a long dress designed more for modesty than the summer heat. A wedding band ringed one of her sausage-like fingers and a gold cross hanging on a chain around her neck rested on her bust that in turn rested on her stomach. She asked Francesca to cut the bread after telling Annibale they had their own *forno* that a neighbour, Signore La Rocca, had built for them before he moved out to Amiens.

'You know La Rocca? No? *Va bene.*' Cesca gave the pasta gravy simmering on the stove a quick stir, banging the wooden spoon five times on the side of the saucepan. 'You know, Annibale, my mother had a similar oven in Palmi. She could bake ten doughs at a time.'

'There was one occasion I got five pizzas in our oven —' Mico spoke up, stopping when Cesca gave him a look and said something Annibale didn't catch, though he got the sense she considered the kitchen and *il forno* her domain.

Annibale glanced at Mico. Reserved, tall and slim, with a well-built chest and muscled arms from farm work, Mico had a small brown mole on his right cheek and thick hair he brushed straight back. He rolled his own cigarettes, which he chain-smoked. When he offered him one, Annibale shook his head, never having liked cigarettes or their acrid smoke. Cesca went into the other room to tend to three-year-old Vincenzo and Mico told Annibale that a woman from Piedmont had taught him how to cook for a cane gang up north and he quite enjoyed cooking, especially puddings.

When Cesca didn't immediately return, Mico leapt up to check the boiling pasta, extracting a strand with the wooden spoon and biting it. 'It's about ready,' he said to everyone and no one in particular. 'Soccorsa, finish your homework now. We're about to eat.'

Annibale had almost overlooked Soccorsa at the table. Francesca, quiet as she grated some cheese, mostly drew his eye, though he was careful not to make the others aware. More than a year had passed since he'd seen

Francesca and he noticed she'd grown her hair longer. Cesca carried in Vincenzo and saw Mico lifting the pot of boiled pasta off the stove. She furrowed her brows.

'Here, I'll take Vincenzo.' Annibale put out his arms.

'Oh, *grazie*, Annibale.' Cesca went over to mix the pasta Mico had already drained.

Vincenzo reached out his hand, straining to touch Annibale's face. Annibale tilted his head back slightly, bouncing the little boy on his knees and making him chortle.

Francesca smiled. 'I'll put him in his highchair now.'

'He's getting a bit big for it.' Cesca placed a large bowl of pasta in the centre of the table.

'How are the Rossis?' Annibale asked halfway through the meal.

'Oh, Remilda and the girls have been working, working.' Cesca beamed. 'Mico offered to help them but they didn't want it. I'm so proud of them.'

Annibale thought of Giuseppe always cursing his lack of sons and felt pleased.

'They kept that farm going on their own,' continued Cesca, 'working at night as well as day sometimes. I'm glad they got a couple of internees to help them now.' She took a sip of water. 'You know, Firmina even learnt to drive the truck.'

'I think I'd be too frightened to do that.' Francesca carefully wiped leftover sauce on her plate with a piece of bread. 'It will be up to my husband to drive.' Her cheeks flushed.

Pretending not to notice, Annibale suppressed a grin and reached for a piece of bread.

'Annibale,' Mico moved his empty plate sideways and lit a cigarette, squinting from a smile, smoke or suspicion, Annibale couldn't tell, 'tomorrow we start the apples.'

There was a lot of work to do in the orchard, the two men systematically picking along the rows of trees. Annibale longed to talk or sing to help pass the time and alleviate the monotony, but Mico was content to puff quietly on a cigarette, pausing every so often to roll a new one. From his vantage point up a ladder, Annibale noticed movement in the distance, near the house. A utility truck was nosing up the dirt driveway, Cesca and Francesca emerging to meet it. Two men got out. Something about their animated gestures made Annibale pause. Francesca hung back behind her mother.

'What is going on there?' Annibale asked.

Mico broke from a reverie and turned, narrowing his eyes to peer into the distance. 'We've had a few different men coming around asking if they can marry Francesca.' He turned back to keep picking. 'Ever since she turned sixteen, they've been coming. A friend of her godmother's is trying to fix Francesca up with this fellow, Pasquale, but Cesca doesn't want it. They won't tell us his age but he's at least thirty-five and wants a wife straightaway and Francesca is just seventeen. I think that's him talking there now.'

Annibale noticed Cesca fling her arm out as though she was telling the men to leave and they wouldn't. He placed his foot down a ladder rung ready to go and intervene, but the two men got into the utility truck. They drove back to the road, then lingered, surveying the farm, before the driver put the truck into gear and accelerated.

A little while later, Cesca came out to the orchard, Francesca and Vincenzo in tow. 'I've told Francesca not to go one step anywhere without me,' she said.

Francesca sat down under a tree to finish hemming a dress by hand, keeping an eye on Vincenzo, who was playing with a toy animal she'd sewn from material scraps.

Mico sighed, the tip of his cigarette coming to life. 'What did they say this time?'

'He said he won't take no for an answer. He'll abduct her if he has to.'

Both Mico and Annibale snapped around.

She gave a tight nod. 'And what can we do if he does? The police won't do anything. Pasquale will just say she's meant to be with him. And we can't speak the English to object.' Cesca wiped perspiration from her temples. 'He said he saw her at the siding when we sent the last consignment to Brisbane and next time he'll take her.' She looked down at Francesca, whose head was bent. 'Not one step anywhere without me, Francesca, you hear?'

'Yes, Ma.' Francesca's eyes met Annibale's, then darted back to her sewing.

Annibale returned to the top rung of the ladder, unnerved. In between stripping the branches of fruit, he stole glances through the leaves at Francesca. He liked that she was a combination of contradictions: small but robust; demure, yet at times feisty; tearful with both sadness and happiness; sometimes fearful, other times no-nonsense. And he admired the way she handled the business side of her parents' farm, appreciating she would be a valuable partner to have in business as well as life. Such a thought gave him a glimmer of hope he might resurrect his dream of one day setting up his own business. *Perhaps in Stanthorpe's High Street … this war cannot go on forever.* He contemplated Pasquale's kidnapping threat.

By early autumn in 1943 the pelting sun had baked the grassy hills flaxen, bringing the dark-leaved trees that flecked the landscape into sharp focus. Each day the kingfisher-blue skies arced clear all the way across to the distant hills. Francesca shadowed her mother as promised. Then late one morning they saw Pasquale parked in his utility truck on the road, sitting watching them.

Cesca gazed back at him. 'Francesca, go into the house.'

Francesca ran up to her room and peered through a gap between the curtain and the window frame. Her hands trembling, she tried not to think what might happen if Pasquale abducted her, forcing her into marriage. She understood that if he got her alone, she'd have no choice but to marry him. If not, she would bring shame upon her family. Francesca knew what she really wanted, but staying mostly by her mother's side she had to mask her growing fondness for Annibale. She saw Pasquale drive off and went back outside.

Cesca and Francesca had started that Saturday morning churning washing in the boiling copper with a wooden paddle. Then they wound each item through the wringer before rinsing it in a tub of clean water. They had almost finished hoisting all the clothes through the wringer again when Cesca turned pale and clammy.

'I feel a bit strange,' she murmured.

She was almost fainting as Francesca helped her mother up the steps and inside, knowing it was heatstroke again. Cesca wouldn't consider removing her petticoat and stays to get a bit cooler and more comfortable.

'Drink this.' Francesca pressed a glass of water into her mother's hand and got a moist washer for her forehead. 'I'll finish the washing. You rest in here for a while.'

'But Pasquale …'

'It'll be fine, Ma. You'll hear me if I yell out and I think Annibale is in the shed.'

It felt unusual to be alone. Francesca began hanging out the washing. A slight noise made her start. She looked over her shoulder and saw a magpie hopping along the ground, foraging in the grass with its beak. The farm was quiet. She relaxed a little.

The flames beneath the copper were out by the time Francesca fastened the last wet garment to the line. She stood back, feeling satisfaction at seeing the washing sway in the breeze, the wire lines bowed under its weight. It was almost lunchtime and Annibale emerged from the shed. He motioned for her to wait. Francesca wished she wasn't standing so close to the washing, anxious he'd pick out which were her undergarments on the line. However, Annibale was oblivious, hesitant, his eyes flitting several times to the house. She almost bent to pick up the empty washing basket.

He finally spoke in a rush. 'Francesca, I want to ask for your hand in marriage.'

In that moment, Francesca saw that her life so far — watching her mother and grandmother, learning to cook, sew, wash, help raise her younger siblings, even learning to read and write Italian and English — had been preparing her for this. Joy rose within her, carefully tempered, as taught by her mother and grandmother.

'That would be good, yes. But you've got to ask my parents.'

She sounded so matter-of-fact. Then Annibale glimpsed tears of happiness she couldn't quite contain. He smiled, exhaled, awkwardly patting her shoulder with affection.

A fortnight after Francesca agreed to marry him, Annibale was yet to ask Mico for his permission, let alone the authorities. He'd rarely felt much fear in his nineteen years, yet he knew this was the biggest decision he would ever make — choosing the person to share his life, his confidences, his vulnerabilities. Once he married Francesca, he'd be with her forever. He feared Mico not giving his permission.

As the days stretched by, Francesca couldn't help confiding in Cesca about Annibale's proposal. The years they spent in Palmi without Mico kept them close, each going straight to the other to discuss anything significant. 'It's a good idea.' Cesca beamed, her foot pausing on the treadle of the Singer. 'We wanted someone like him, someone young and strong.' They spoke in whispers, even though the rest of the household was already in bed.

By late on Sunday afternoon, Annibale was mindful of being due back at the camp and didn't want to let another week pass without speaking to Mico. He'd never forgotten the Benitos' party when Vitale told him it was best not to dance with Francesca. He could still hear the starched tone in his father's words ... *You need to find an Abruzzese girl.* It filled Annibale with irritation. He didn't worry so much about north or south, or which region someone was from in Italy. As far as he was concerned, they were all as one now in Australia. His parents not knowing about his plan to marry was perhaps an advantage of wartime, rather than a drawback.

He found Mico in the packing shed. Annibale took a deep breath, barely noticing the familiar scent of wooden crates, hessian sacks, damp compacted earth and drums of fuel. A swallow flitted in through the big open door and up into its nest in a high corner. It caught Mico's eye and the tip of his cigarette came to life, an amber glow as he mumbled about getting a broom to knock the nest down, though he never did. His eyes rested on Annibale. Sunlight from the doorway behind him cast Annibale's face in shadow, but Mico knew the time had come. Cesca had prepared her husband. He lit a fresh cigarette and waited.

Annibale launched into what he had to say. 'Signore Solano, I want to ask ... would you give your consent for me to marry Francesca?'

Mico looked him in the eye. 'My only request is that you marry as soon as possible; none of these long engagements that last two or three years.' He moved the cigarette from his right hand to his left and put out his hand.

Annibale looked down and clasped it eagerly, breaking into a relieved grin. Mico chuckled and gave him a pat on the back.

Annibale had heard about internees obtaining permission to marry. It was possible to get a month of leave to do so. During 1943 as the war slowly turned in favour of the Allies, the Australian government was beginning to relax its detention of internees, even if refusing to liberate them completely due to lingering public resentment. However, a shortage in food production throughout Australia was prompting the authorities to quietly release internees from camps to recommence work. So Annibale felt hopeful about getting authorisation to marry.

In the officers' hut Annibale encountered the same soldier who'd organised his work pass to the Solano farm. 'The thing is, Mr Boccabella, being under twenty-one you need permission from your parents to marry.' The officer drew his spectacles towards the tip of his nose to better see over them. 'I take it that's not good news.'

'My mother is in Italy. We haven't had any letters from her for more than three years now, and my father is interned here in Australia but I don't know where.' Annibale almost wished the officer would bend the rules rather than contact his father.

The older man sighed, his chair squeaking as he sat back, pondering the situation. Then he leant forward, pushed back his glasses and picked up a pencil. 'Give me his name and where he was picked up and leave it with me. I'll see if I can track him down to get a letter to him.'

The officer couldn't disclose to Annibale that he later discovered Vitale had been sent to work on a road gang in the Northern Territory, nor that the only means of communication from Queensland were the weekly airmail service and the telegram service via South Australia. However, he did let on that, with the roadworks near Pikedale nearing completion, Annibale's camp was soon to move out to the Northern Territory. If Annibale didn't get Vitale's permission and approval for his leave by then, he would have no choice but to go. It was an anxious wait. Then, just as the Pikedale labour camp was closing down, Vitale's signed permission form came back. There was no personal message attached. Within a week, Annibale commenced his month of leave. Maddalena would have no knowledge of her son's marriage.

The Solano family and Annibale climbed up into the Chevrolet truck — Mico, Cesca and Francesca in the cabin; Annibale, Soccorsa and Vincenzo sitting in the tray at the back, hanging on to the wooden slats behind the rear windscreen. It was the Solanos' only vehicle. Painted in a white circle on the door of the driver's side was 'D. Solano, Applethorpe, STH QLD', something the whole family was proud of, but especially Mico. They drove up the highway to Warwick, a larger town than Stanthorpe and about thirty-five miles north, Vincenzo beaming into the wind.

First stop was to Pigott's department store in Palmerin Street, next to the imposing sandstone post-office building. Vincenzo delighted in watching the Lamson pneumatic-tube cash service: the cashiers placed a cylinder of money in the tube and it went shooting off on a rush of air up through pipes over their heads to the general office. Next to the furniture area and mail-order catalogue section — a major part of the store's business — were the manchester and dress departments, including tailoring and dressmaking workrooms. Here they purchased a wedding dress, veil and white shoes for Francesca, and a suit for Annibale. At the jewellers, Annibale bought a plain gold wedding band for Francesca.

The hands on the Town Hall clock were edging towards one o'clock when they sought the black tiled façade of a Greek café nearby. With Annibale bringing up the rear, they filed in through fly strips hanging across the doorway and all jammed into one of several wooden booths lining the length of one wall. Along the opposite wall stretched a long counter divided into different sections. Foiled chocolates in the confectionery section caught Francesca's eye.

Gold lettering on a mirror proclaimed 'Homemade Icy-Cold Lemon and Orange Drinks'. Vincenzo was intent on the milk bar, admiring the whoosh of the chrome soda fountains where a man stood making foaming ice-cream sodas and milkshakes in tall glasses. The sizzle of hot oil frying sounded like a waterfall in the back kitchen, an aroma of battered fish and lamb chops mingling with the almost smoky scent of toasted sandwiches coursing through the café. Cesca eyed the approaching waitress and told the others to hurry and decide what to eat.

After lunch, everyone visited the public restrooms in the Town Hall before the return journey. Francesca and Annibale were the first to meet back outside on the footpath, and alone for a moment both were self-conscious.

Seeing Francesca's eyes dip beneath the brim of her straw sun hat, Annibale felt a sudden rush of protectiveness.

'I will take care of you, Francesca,' he said. 'Everything will be good.'

'Yes, we—' She abruptly lapsed into silence as her father joined them.

Mico noted his daughter's pink cheeks and gave Annibale a look.

'Right then.' Cesca reappeared with Soccorsa and Vincenzo. 'Off home.'

Annibale lifted the two children into the back of the truck and climbed in after them. They sat among the shopping packages and supplies, except for the veil wrapped in brown paper that Francesca insisted on holding in the cabin. Mico accelerated down the long road between Warwick and Stanthorpe. The wind tore through Annibale's hair, roaring past his ears. Gazing at the pale golden paddocks and contorted gum trees, his beaming smile now matched Vincenzo's.

'I will not conduct a Nuptial Mass for an enemy alien.' The priest looked up from Annibale's papers and jerked his head towards Francesca. 'This poor girl cannot be married to someone who will be back in an internment camp within the month. No. I won't do it.'

It wasn't enough the Church took my aunt's house and land, Annibale thought with bitterness as they left the presbytery. *Now they won't conduct my wedding.*

Francesca recalled all the times she'd sat in a pew watching other girls in the district walk down the aisle in their wedding finery. She had been thinking, *Now it will be my turn,* but suddenly it seemed her chance was being put on hold. 'I suppose we'll have to wait until the war is over,' she said, close to tears. 'We must have a church wedding and Saint Joseph's is the only Catholic Church in Stanthorpe.'

Annibale spent the evening stewing, but the next day he came to the breakfast table and announced with defiance that they would marry in Brisbane. 'And not just in any church — we'll go to the cathedral.' His motive was two-pronged. He wanted to show up the priest who wouldn't marry them and he was determined to get to the city. Although he didn't say as much to Francesca, he hoped that if he could get a job in Brisbane he might not have to return to the road gang.

The war had been going for three and a half years and no one could predict how much longer it would last. Not wanting the engagement to stretch on for years, especially with Pasquale lurking in the background, Mico and Cesca agreed the wedding could be in Brisbane, though not without some concern. A fortnight earlier, on May 14, a Japanese submarine had torpedoed an Australian hospital ship, AHS *Centaur*, causing the loss of 268 lives, including eleven nurses, as the ship sank. The incident occurred about ten miles off the east coast of Stradbroke Island, adjacent to Brisbane, and residents feared an attack on the city next.

'They'll only be gone a few weeks,' Mico assured Cesca. 'It will be all right.'

They decided that Mico, the only one with a licence, would drive Francesca and Annibale to Brisbane, while Cesca stayed and looked after the farm, Soccorsa and Vincenzo. For Annibale, embarking on such a momentous event without his family was a circumstance of war. His ambition to make his own way in the world had resurfaced with the opportunity of going to Brisbane, and it made him impatient to leave. For Francesca, though, it was devastating. She and Cesca were so close she couldn't imagine getting married without her mother in attendance. She'd always assumed she'd marry in the district with family and friends present, and a meal and dancing at the farm afterwards. But she stifled her disappointment and upset, regarding it as another lesson in duty.

For most of that autumn the heat of summer persisted, then transformed almost overnight into the brittle chill of impending winter. Opening the port she had not used since travelling from Italy to Australia, Francesca caught a faint scent of wood-smoke from her grandmother's house. For a moment, she longed to be back in the seaside village of Palmi and her nonna's embrace. Yet in her heart she knew she'd never see Nonna again. Cesca came in and they murmured together, packing the port along with their tears and snapping it shut.

'Remember, a woman should always be available to her husband when it comes to marital relations.' Cesca held Francesca's face in her hands. 'Keep safe and write to me.'

Outside, the others were waiting by the truck. Mico already sat in the driver's seat, smoking. Annibale took Francesca's port and put it in the back.

Cesca held her tightly. 'Good luck to you, daughter.'

Francesca's chin trembled. She nodded, unable to speak. Annibale helped her into the cabin and clambered in behind. The door closed with a rigid thud. Vincenzo and Soccorsa ran alongside the lumbering truck waving their handkerchiefs, both stopping at the end of the driveway, arms still in the air. Cesca continued to stare long after the dust settled on the road.

Letters and Spaghetti

In Brisbane they lodged at a boarding house on Astor Terrace in Spring Hill. Francesca dressed for the wedding in her father's room and would later undress in Annibale's room. She fastened the clasp of the chain and gently touched the locket her mother had given her. It rested upon the modestly high sweetheart neckline of her wedding gown. She stood in front of the mirror in her long white dress and veil.

Mico knocked then came in and saw her tears. 'What's the matter?'

'I want Mamma to be here.'

'None of that. We're going to the church now and the boarding-house lady is fixing a nice supper for us after. Come on. The taxi will be downstairs in a minute. Wash your face.'

The Benitos' daughter Pina, who'd married and moved to the city and whom Francesca knew from school, was her bridesmaid. Pina had helped Francesca choose her bridal flowers, a spray of white blossoms and cascading deep-green foliage. The trailing effect of the bouquet matched Francesca's floor-length veil, which floated delicately around her like a fine haze. One white flower was pinned to the buttonhole of Annibale's black suit, matching his white shirt and bowtie.

To their relief, one of the priests at the Cathedral of Saint Stephen had agreed to marry them, despite Annibale being an internee. Half a dozen people gathered to witness the ceremony, including the son of the boarding-house owner who stepped in as Annibale's best man. The couple uttered their vows, their young voices taking flight, echoing up into the high arches of the cathedral. When Francesca looked into Annibale's eyes, trained on her with an almost imperceptible hint of mischief, she felt something deep within her flutter. At that moment, her nervousness melted away.

In their sole wedding portrait, luminous and serious-faced, Francesca looks straight into the camera lens. Beside her, Annibale, smiling, gazes sideways at his new bride.

The next morning, straight after breakfast, Francesca and Annibale stood on the footpath waving as Mico left for Stanthorpe. Even after they lowered their arms, Francesca continued to watch the Chevrolet disappear around the corner into the traffic, the last of her father's tobacco smoke fading away. She'd given him her bridal bouquet to take back to her mother. Sensing Annibale watching her, she smiled and nodded, knowing her life was with him now.

They set off arm in arm, walking downhill along the wide curve of Edward Street, looking across at the sound of a tram clattering along one of the double sets of tram tracks in the middle of the road. Steam drifted up from behind the elongated building of Central Station and across its clock tower. Along the centre of Ann Street, brick and concrete bunkers with air holes dotted along their sides stood ready should Brisbane be bombed. A group of middle-aged women, all with ornate brooches pinned to their long coats, ran a footpath stall raising money for the Comforts Fund that sent chocolate, tobacco, warm socks and other items to troops serving overseas.

By the time Annibale and Francesca reached the junction with Adelaide Street, the sunshine was intermittent, blocked by sandstone buildings, some as high as ten storeys. The city had a festive air, with flags fluttering from shopfront awnings. Cars beeped. A paperboy hollered. The Town Hall clock rang out. Wartime songs flowed from cafés. There seemed to be American sailors everywhere. They stood around in twos and threes, smoking or whistling, chiacking among themselves. Others escorted young Australian women with bright lipstick and hair tumbling in perfect rolls from beneath their hats.

Francesca gripped the crook of Annibale's arm, liking the feeling. Amid the bustle, she felt protected. It was the first morning they had woken up together, and whenever their eyes met Annibale grinned and Francesca bit her lips, trying not to smile too much. It seemed as if the whole world might be looking at them. Her new wedding ring still felt foreign, her thumb often creeping across to touch it. Only a few days before she'd been a teenage girl helping her parents on the farm; now she was a wife and strolled the city streets with her husband, unchaperoned. Their honeymoon stretched deliciously ahead.

They passed a shop window containing a display of iced cakes and freshly cut roses, a sweet bakery scent escaping out the door. The watch and clock shop smelled of oil and wood, a deep-throated grandfather clock chiming the hour late as they walked on. A café sign promising waffles with warm butterscotch sauce beckoned. Francesca felt hungry, though they'd had breakfast only an hour before.

'First we need to find a justice of the peace to witness my signature,' she said.

Annibale nodded. 'We could ask at the post office.'

Having married an unnaturalised Italian internee, Francesca was required under the *Nationality Act 1920* to declare her intention to retain Australian citizenship. She snapped open her purse and fished out the neatly folded document entitled *Declaration by a British Woman, Who Has Married an Alien, that She Desires to Retain While in Australia or any Territory, the Rights of a British Subject*. At the post office, the JP who witnessed her signature was a bespectacled older man. Upon seeing the form, he regarded Annibale sternly before signing. Pretending not to notice, they thanked him and moved on to lodge the form at the required government office. Coming back outside into the soft winter sunlight, they felt free to enjoy their honeymoon.

'To start with,' said Annibale, 'let's get something to eat.'

In the Botanic Gardens down by the river, more air-raid shelters loomed. Catching a waft of the briny water, Francesca could smell salt in the air for the first time since she was eight years old.

'I can't wait until we're allowed to send letters to Italy again and tell Nonna I am married now,' she said as they walked across an expanse of grass towards the zoological part of the Gardens. 'You must want to tell your mother, too.'

Annibale nodded without saying anything. He'd noticed before that she assumed everyone they knew back in Italy would come through the war unscathed. He was unsure if it was due to naïvety or her not wanting to contemplate what might be happening there. Either way, he thought it best to stay silent. There'd been reports in the press of Italy's south copping heavy bombing by the Allies, and even then the extent of it wasn't detailed.

The subject was dropped as they saw monkeys, emus and wallabies, and he was glad she was distracted. 'Cripes, look at this,' he said, as they stood before a giant tortoise brought to Australia by a friend of Charles Darwin ten years after Darwin captured the reptile in the Galapagos Islands in the 1830s. 'Who would've thought this would end up here?'

Annibale and Francesca marvelled at the ornately gilded walls and ceiling murals of the Gothic foyer. The Regent Theatre in Queen Street catered to both live shows and the picture screen, and was the best in the state. It was the first time Annibale had been to a picture theatre, and Francesca had only been to the modest theatre in Stanthorpe. The grandness of the Regent took both of them by surprise. Inside the foyer, the theatre's milk bar was doing a frenetic trade, the long counter almost hidden by theatre-goers sipping milkshakes through straws from footed parfait-style glasses, spooning froth from ice-cream sodas and buying little boxes of chocolates. Annibale kept glancing back down to it as they walked up the grand marble staircase to the auditorium.

They'd scarcely settled in their seats in the second tier when a majestic white-painted Wurlitzer organ appeared to rise magically from the orchestra pit in front of the velvet curtain covering the screen. The organist, dressed in a tuxedo, his hair slicked back, took his seat. Music from fifteen ranks of pipes flooded the room, penetrating everyone's chests and causing the massive central chandelier to sway a little.

Gripping the arms of his seat, Annibale stared around the vast auditorium that could seat more than 2,500. It was fast filling up as well-dressed ushers led people to seats. Young men in blue uniforms with brass buttons on the chest held trays strapped over their shoulders, hawking ice creams, sweets and cordial drinks in waxed paper cups. Amber light cast by numerous smaller chandeliers caused the gilded walls to glow, almost lantern-like. Annibale noticed the suspended crystal pendants vibrating as the organ pummelled out an old First World War tune, 'Pack up Your Troubles in Your Old Kit-Bag'.

'Vivien Leigh,' said Francesca as much to herself as to Annibale, squinting at the Fantales wrapper to see if she'd correctly answered the quiz question on it and chomping vigorously on the chewy caramel chocolate.

Before the film commenced, instead of 'God Save the King', the American national anthem was played in honour of the American GIs in Brisbane, earning the derision of several Australian diggers in the audience. A few rolled-up chocolate wrappers whizzed through the air amid the jeers. Yet by the time the newsreel and preliminaries were over and the feature film commenced the theatre quietened and everyone sat peaceably in the darkness, cigarette smoke drifting up through the shaft of light from the projection box.

'Where should we go for supper?' A tawny glow from the Regent sign made Annibale's eyes appear a lighter hazel.

Francesca stepped to the side of the footpath as people coming out of the theatre surged around them. 'There's the place that made those nice toasted sandwiches.'

'Excuse me.' An American GI tapped Annibale on the shoulder. 'Are you Italian?'

Annibale and Francesca exchanged glances.

'We overheard you talking Italian.' The GI gestured to three more Americans in uniform, his dark eyes animated, smiling. 'We're Italian-Americans.'

They stood chatting for a while, the theatre crowd continuing to disperse around them.

Then the first GI, Frankie, said, 'Why don't we find a café and get something to eat?'

Annibale looked at Francesca, who nodded. 'Why not?'

'I wish we could find somewhere in Brisbane that serves spaghetti.' Another of the GIs, Tony, clutched his stomach. 'I'm really missing it.'

'Well, we've got a Primus stove in our room at our boarding house,' said Annibale. 'Francesca cooks pasta on it. Do you want to come back and join us?'

Back at the boarding house the little party was very merry, all twirling forkfuls of pasta. There was only a couple of chairs, so an upturned wooden fruit box served as another seat, while others sat on the edge of the bed or the floor. Francesca was glad they had a kitchenette with enough crockery and cutlery for the six of them, and that just the day before she'd purchased a small bottle of olive oil from the chemist, the only shop that sold it.

By half past ten, the landlady thumped on the door and told them all to stop singing.

The Italian-American GIs began popping by every other night. Having learned of Francesca's sweet tooth, they brought with them some American Hershey chocolate from their Post Exchange, or PX, a type of retail store that sold only to the US military.

'Can you write in English?' Frankie asked Annibale, wiping his pasta bowl clean with a piece of bread. 'I want to write home to Mamma in Massachusetts but I can only write in Italian. The censors cut up my letter, saying it must be in English.' He popped the bread into his mouth.

'Francesca can,' said Annibale. 'She could write it for you.'

Frankie looked at her questioningly, still chewing, and she shrugged. 'Of course.'

In return for Francesca's letters and spaghetti, the GIs took her and Annibale to see a vaudeville show at the Cremorne Theatre across the river from the city. Then they came back to Edward Street and ate at the Shingle Inn, where Francesca and Annibale first saw lemon meringue pie, introduced to cater for homesick American GIs. Annibale shook his head but, encouraged by Frank and Tony, Francesca decided to try it. Not so long ago she'd been tailing her mother each day so Pasquale would not catch her unchaperoned; now being the only female surrounded by males full of high jinks made her feel a little heady and she set aside some of her usual reserve.

She eyed the fluffy meringue atop quivering lemon custard as the waitress placed a tall piece of the pie before her. 'It's really light,' she said around a mouthful. 'Light and sweet.'

The GIs laughed and clapped, making Francesca blush.

Annibale leant over, brandishing the fork with which he was eating a meat pie and gravy. 'Here, let me have a taste.'

On Saturday night, Frankie suggested they go to a dance hall called the Trocadero Dansant, though once there Annibale refused to dance. Instead, he and Francesca sat and ate supper in one of the alcoves, watching almost a thousand couples whirl around the dance floor to the seven-piece brass band and pianist playing under the half-domed stage. Francesca tapped her feet inside her shoes, wishing Annibale would dance with her, not realising he didn't know how. Everyone around them was making the most of life, kicking up their heels in the face of wartime danger. Francesca watched amazed at men in American uniforms teaching the Australian girls the jitterbug, many Australian soldiers amongst the movement too, though many more hovered together in groups, watching. Annibale encouraged Francesca to dance when Frankie asked, so she shyly agreed, letting him swing her around the burnished sprung-wood floor.

The next day the GIs received word they were heading to a campaign in the Pacific.

Stickytaped to the window of the café were two notices scrawled on pieces of fly-specked paper: 'Austerity Meals Here' and 'Waiters Wanted'. Annibale suggested to Francesca they go inside for lunch. Oblivious to his motive, she read the menu as he glanced around. Heavy plates clunked down on wooden tabletops over strains of 'Blueberry Hill' and the purr and occasional clamour of overlapping conversations. An aroma of gravy hung in the air.

Annibale waited until their meals were in front of them. 'This place is looking for waiters. I'm thinking of applying.'

Without looking up, she continued slicing her piece of roast chicken. 'I thought we were going back to the farm.'

Annibale was all too aware his month of leave was running out. 'You'll go back to your parents and I'll be sent to the road gang in the Northern Territory. But if I get some work here, maybe they'll let me stay. Then I can earn better money and we can be together.'

She chewed in contemplative silence. After the small coffee pot was empty, she went and waited outside while Annibale approached the counter and mentioned the sign in the window.

'There isn't any available work.' The manager's face reminded Annibale of the shoe salesman from whom Vitale had bought those boots, that first day he had arrived in Brisbane.

'But the sign says …'

The manager glanced around and lowered his voice. 'Look, we want dinky-di Aussies only, *comprende?*'

Francesca was waiting near a streetlight pole in a welcome pocket of winter sun. She nodded when Annibale told her the positions had all been taken but he glimpsed uncertainty in her eyes as though she'd guessed the truth. Both quiet, they walked along Adelaide Street. She noticed a drapery selling rickrack trimming more cheaply than at Stanthorpe but didn't suggest going inside and they strolled on, rounding the corner into Edward Street.

'Boccabella! What are you doing here?'

Annibale jumped and half-turned. 'Pandi? Pandi Stratu!'

They rushed at each other, almost hugging, slapping each other on the arms and back. 'Can you believe it? First the boat! Then the camp! Now here!'

Francesca took in Pandi's prematurely thinning hair, his raw-boned face and benevolent eyes. He was smiling, yet she thought he had a somewhat sad mien.

Annibale suddenly remembered her. 'Pandi, this is my wife, Francesca.'

'Your *wife*?' Pandi's eyes widened. 'Very pleased to meet you, Francesca.' He could barely conceal his amazement that his friend had married since he last saw him.

Annibale watched Francesca chat to Pandi. He felt proud of her in her smart suit, the taupe skirt matching her tailored jacket. She'd made it herself from fabric bought in a fire sale, the cut making it look more expensive. Like most women at that time, she simplified patterns to adjust for the lack of material for ruffles or tucking that came with war rationing.

Pandi turned to Annibale. 'Geez, I never thought they'd let you out of the camp.'

'I'm not really out. I got a month's leave to get married. Unless I can find some work soon, I have to go back.'

Pandi grabbed his arm. 'I'm working as a cook at the Astoria Café over there.' He pointed to an art deco façade of wood and glass on the opposite corner. 'I was just taking a break between shifts. Maybe I could fix it so you can work there too. Actually, come over now,' he said, caught up in the moment. 'I'll introduce you to Milos, the manager.'

Milos was half-Italian, half-Greek — though he was downplaying his Italian origins for the duration of the war. He'd got the job at the Astoria through his father knowing the Greek owners. His mother was descended from one of the first Italian families who migrated to Australia in the 1890s as part of the assisted immigration agreement between the Italian and Australian governments, instigated by the then Premier of Queensland, Sir Samuel Griffith. Milos' Greek family, on his father's side, had been in Queensland for three decades, worked hard, lived frugally and had risen to the middle classes. Born in Australia, Milos often took a slightly superior but fair-minded attitude towards 'newer' migrants. He sighed, stroking his moustache as Annibale explained his circumstances. The Astoria Café did need more wait staff, but the Manpower Directorate expected them to hire British-Australians over migrants, especially Italian or German ones.

Milos put up his hand to stop Annibale speaking. 'Do you think your English is good enough to read the menu?'

Annibale took the menu he held out. 'Roast lamb, T-bone steak, mixed grill, roast chicken, mutton …'

Milos nodded and took the menu back. 'I can give you both work waiting tables. I have a shortage of lady waitresses. The girls keep running off and marrying Americans.'

Annibale quickly looked at Francesca, thinking she mightn't approve, yet she appeared quite pleased with the idea.

'You'll each work two shifts each day, one from noon to two o'clock, then five until half past eleven in the evening. Six days a week.' Milos turned to Annibale. 'Now, you must go to the doctor tomorrow.'

'But I'm not sick.'

'I'm not training you up only to have you return to the camp. I have an arrangement with a doctor. He'll write a report so you won't have to go back to the road gang.'

'Not ever?'

'Just see him.' Milos scribbled directions on a scrap of paper. 'Here's the address. And don't go asking any questions.'

When Annibale turned up at the surgery, he encountered a morose doctor who silently examined him all over, pausing only to make notes.

'I don't know what he wrote was wrong with me,' Annibale said, half-chuckling, half-incredulous, to Francesca and Pandi afterwards, 'but for now I've got an extra three months leave from the camp. He said he'll keep extending it up to twelve months.'

'Milos has certain "arrangements" with influential people all throughout Brisbane.' Pandi nodded. 'That doctor eats at the café *gratis*.'

One block east of the Astoria Café was the American PX. And one block south, on the busiest intersection in the centre of town, was the AMP Building, housing General MacArthur's headquarters and military command post for the Pacific. With Queensland deemed the most likely area for invasion, American troops kept pouring into Brisbane. 'Tent towns' mushrooming at Eagle Farm racecourse, Victoria Park and the Woolloongabba cricket ground accommodated the white US troops, with the African-American servicemen segregated at Ipswich, Redbank and Wacol. MacArthur, his wife and his young son, Arthur — accompanied by his Chinese amah — were living on the top floor of Lennon's Hotel in George Street, and small crowds often gathered at the entrance to see them coming and going.

While there was much secrecy surrounding the general being in Brisbane — with newspapers reporting him as located 'somewhere in Australia' — local residents commonly saw MacArthur commuting between his hotel apartments and his office. Pandi quickly pointed out the general's dark Wolseley staff car with its long snout-like bonnet to Annibale and Francesca as it streaked past while they were waiting to cross Queen Street. They glimpsed the shadow of a man inside and saw the licence plate's distinctive four stars.

'He usually goes home for lunch,' Pandi said.

In no other Allied city in the world was the American GI presence as large in proportion to the local population as in Brisbane — the city's

330,000 or so residents ultimately playing host to around 300,000 American servicemen. And the new style of talking, eating, drinking, entertainment, music and dances the American GIs brought with them was catching on.

Seeing Annibale looking up at US flags fluttering from numerous city buildings, an Australian digger beside him sneered, 'The American village, eh?', using the condescending nickname growing in use. Australian soldiers were becoming increasingly maddened at what they saw as the Americans taking over their city and the hearts of Australian girls.

MacArthur wasn't helping the situation by giving Americans kudos for winning major battles in the Pacific, while ordering Australian troops to 'mop up' residual Japanese troops on small islands around New Guinea. A constant crackle of tension on Brisbane's city streets was palpable, and even as Pandi, Annibale and Francesca crossed the road, they heard several shouts and a commotion further down as military police waded into a stoush between Americans and Australians. Pandi suggested they stop at a milk bar before going past the ruckus and on to the Astoria.

'Last November there was a huge brawl that started outside the Australian canteen not far from the Astoria,' said Pandi as the three of them sat down at the counter, Annibale assisting Francesca onto a tall stool. 'At the time, we didn't know what was happening but later we heard several Australians were talking with a drunk American and then a US military policeman weighed in and went to hit an Australian with his baton so they attacked him.'

They ordered three chocolate milkshakes, Annibale watching as the server dipped a ladle into a drum of cold milk. 'Then what happened?'

'From the Astoria we could hear more MPs turning up blowing their whistles and Australians running down the street to help their mates. We looked outside and saw them chasing the MPs towards the PX. More Australians in the hotels nearby came pouring out and it became a free-for-all in front of the PX. Well … you know how much stuff they've got in there.'

The ground floor of the American Post Exchange was brimming with luxuries reserved for the foreigners: cigarettes, alcohol, hams, turkeys, chocolates, nylon stockings — items heavily rationed or too expensive for wartime Australians.

'It was incredible.' Pandi shook his head. 'The Australians threw rocks, even uprooted parking signs to smash into the PX. Trams and traffic stopped along Adelaide Street. A few thousand Australians rioted. Then the first gun was fired.' His eyes went wide remembering the echo of gun blasts ricocheting around the city buildings. 'We all hid out the back.' He drew his milkshake towards him, prodding its melting lump of ice cream with the paper straw before taking a long draught.

Annibale and Francesca exchanged looks. Along with most Australian residents, they hadn't heard of what people would later call the 'Battle of Brisbane', as the government suppressed or denied the extent of the incident to maintain a façade of unity between Americans and Australians. It explained the noticeable military and civilian police presence in the city. And so Brisbane, though lively with dances and entertainment, had a dangerous edge. An uneasy stalemate existed between Americans and Australians, but both remained quick on the draw — the diggers with their fists and boots; the GIs with handguns and knives. And the Astoria Café was located right where clashes kept recurring.

The Astoria Café

When the Astoria Café was opened in 1929 by two Greek brothers, it was proclaimed 'the most luxurious and up-to-date café in Brisbane'. The Freeleagus brothers built a high-rise on the corner of Edward and Adelaide Streets on the site where they had run the City Café since 1909. The new building contained shops and a café at street level, and five storeys of offices above. Painted in prominent lettering across the vast expanse of brick wall on the northeastern side of the building were the words 'Astoria Café & Sundae Shop. Ice Cream Delicacies'.

From Adelaide Street, doors opened to a lounge salon and milk bar, while the main Edward Street entrance led into the Astoria Café. Glass frontage on one side of the main entrance showcased four waffle machines, while the other housed elegant displays of pastries and confectionary made in the basement bakehouse and the ice-cream room. Inside, the dining room provided seating for two hundred and fifty, the furniture all made from silky oak. Walls, cornices and pillars were trimmed in decorative plaster, a massive ornate dome crowned the ceiling and lantern lights shining at intervals along the walls completed the setting.

At the time Annibale and Francesca began working there, the Astoria had been in business for more than thirteen years and by then the furniture was a little worn, the floor scuffed. Because of the war, meals weren't as elegant as they'd been in the thirties, but its central position and popular fare still kept the Astoria busy.

Though known as a Greek café, the meals were mostly Australian — steak and eggs, mixed grill, chops and eggs, pork fillet, chicken Maryland, battered fish — all served with two slices of buttered bread as well as salad or boiled vegetables. Staff made all the drinks on the premises. Soda fountains of syrup and carbonated water jetted forth lemonade, sarsaparilla, ginger ale, lime, strawberry, passionfruit and pineapple soft drinks. Chicory essence brewed in milk kept hot in a big urn was brought to the table in small coffee pots. Each waiter served sixteen people — two tables that sat four each and four smaller tables of two.

Annibale's wage of six pounds a week strengthened his conviction that coming to Brisbane was the right thing to do. After their first pay, Francesca realised she had received only half the amount Annibale had earned. Not quite five feet tall and having lost some weight, Francesca was tiny in her white apron and black waitressing dress, stockings and shoes, but she was steely in her resolve as she marched up to where Milos perched on a stool behind the cash register. Seeing her face, something made him stand up.

'Why do I earn less than Annibale?' she asked. 'That can't be right.'

'Oh, well, you're a lady … and a junior.' Milos was all bluster.

'I'm doing exactly the same work and hours. I think I should be paid for it.'

Her matter-of-fact disposition caught Milos off guard. He grudgingly agreed and went to the till, glancing over at Annibale, who was unaware of what had transpired.

Annibale was by a table taking the order of an American GI and his Australian date. He then went through the swinging doors to the kitchen and gave the order to Pandi, before coming back out to the counter where Milos sat once more behind the cash register.

'One chicken and one fish,' he relayed, paying Milos out of the pound with which he started each shift. The café's system required wait staff to take an order, advise the kitchen, then go to Milos and pay for the meals out of the pound or 'float' he or she started with, before returning to the table and collecting payment from the diners. If the waiter made a mistake or the diners left without paying it was bad luck, but on the other hand any tips were the waiter's to keep.

Annibale returned to the table. 'That's two and six.'

The American pulled out a pound. 'That cover it?' Annibale had already discovered many GIs were loath to grapple with the pounds, shillings and pence system of Australian currency.

'Yeah, and some change.' Annibale rummaged in his pocket.

'Nah, you keep it.'

'Thank you very much.'

Annibale came through the swinging doors to the kitchen, marvelling at the cavalier attitude of the well-paid Americans. He was earning more in tips than his weekly wage. With tongs, Pandi was lifting an old hen he had been boiling in order to soften its stringy flesh and thrust it into a vat of burnt oil to give it a golden colour — wartime restrictions necessitated being resourceful. He looked up. 'What type of fish, mullet or whiting?'

'Whiting.'

Pandi went over to the hunk of shark sitting on the bench. For whiting, he cut small, narrow fillets; if the customer wanted mullet, he'd slice slightly thicker pieces. Once he dipped and fried the flake in batter, no one seemed to know the difference.

Annibale carried the meals out to the table.

'Hang on.' The GI grabbed Annibale's sleeve. 'You call that chicken?'

'Is chicken.' They both peered at the orangey-golden morsels shrunk to the size of quail.

'If that's chicken my grandmother's a virgin. What kind of joint you running here?'

'I just work here,' said Annibale, squaring up.

Francesca shot a look from where she was serving across the room. The American shook his head and nothing more came of it.

The lunchtime rush subsided and Annibale and Pandi were in the kitchen laughing about the 'grandmother's a virgin' comment when Milos came in.

'Annibale, I want you to take this.' He handed him a black briefcase. 'Get on the tram and go over to Hope Street in South Brisbane. When you get off, sit at the tram stop and wait. A fellow will come along and swap it for another briefcase and then you get the next tram back here as quickly as possible. Fast as you can, understand?'

'Okay.' Annibale was astute enough not to ask questions.

He did exactly as Milos said and all went according to plan. When he got back to the café, Milos propelled him into the kitchen. Pandi took the briefcase, hauling it onto the bench. He clicked open the locks and lifted the lid. Annibale was amazed to see it was full of wrapped butter pats. Milos grinned. The government had rationed butter to eight ounces per person a week. He derived a small pleasure in getting around this via the black market.

'From now on you'll do the same every Tuesday after the lunchtime shift,' Milos told Annibale. 'I'll add ten shillings to your wages.'

'But I don't want Francesca knowing. She'll only worry.'

Milos nodded. 'And go back to my doctor friend. He'll get you another extension for your leave.'

In September that year, just a few months after Annibale and Francesca had started work at the Astoria, Italy signed an armistice with the Allies. The news brought with it a sense of relief, but they still could not contact their family members in Italy and had no idea how they'd fared, although it was becoming apparent many areas had copped a lot of damage or been destroyed in the fighting. Southern Italy, including the west coast of Calabria where Francesca's relatives lived, was by then occupied by the Allies. But further north, in particular around central Italy where Maddalena and Elia were, was under German occupation.

At the small kitchen table of their room in the boarding house, Francesca closed the newspaper and blew her nose into her handkerchief. Annibale felt concerned and upset himself, but seeing her tears he patted her arm and kept his demeanour matter-of-fact. 'There's not much we can do but wait until we can write to them. Come on now, give your face a wash, you can't go to work like that.' But underneath he was anxious. *The Germans still in Abruzzo surely won't react well to Italy changing sides*, he thought.

At the end of each evening shift, Annibale put all the chairs up on the tables and Francesca swept the floor. He'd just balanced the last chair on a tabletop when Milos called him to the kitchen. Annibale exchanged a glance with Francesca as she kept sweeping.

'You're the biggest of all of us,' Milos told him. 'Every night at closing I want you to check the toilets to make sure no one is inside and then lock them up.'

It came to be a duty Annibale dreaded. The toilets were outside, down a shadowy staircase near the bins, and the wartime electricity brown-outs made it even harder to see. Close to midnight, he often encountered drunks or tramps checking the café bins for scraps. Each night he stood at the doorway of the toilets, saw all the cubicle doors were open and yelled out: 'Is anybody there?' just to make sure, then locked the main door and darted back up the stairs.

On one occasion he found a cubicle door shut and thought it odd, since the last patrons had left the café almost half an hour before. The toilet doors were floor to ceiling, making it impossible for him to tell if someone was inside.

'Is anybody there?' he called out.

No one answered. The back of his neck tingled. He was sure he could feel a presence lurking. The door was slightly ajar. Perhaps it had got stuck. He walked over and pushed it open — to find an American GI pointing a gun straight at him. Annibale stumbled backwards and almost fell.

'Can't a guy crap in peace?' The GI slammed the door.

'Café's closing!' Annibale shouted, taking the steps two at a time.

The next day he still felt shaken by the incident. It was no secret the Americans were trigger-happy. At Francesca's urging, he confronted Milos.

'I don't want to check the toilets at night any more.'

Milos scoffed. 'Well, *I'm* not doing it. You want to keep your job, you'll check them.'

Annibale thought about it while he ducked in and out of the kitchen, serving tables and then suggested, 'You know, if the toilet doors had a foot gap at the bottom of them it would be easier to check if they were occupied.'

'Bloody hell, next you'll be running the joint. Am I supposed to buy new doors?'

'If you give me a saw I'll just cut off the bottom of them for you.'

Milos thought for a moment, stroking his moustache. 'Very well, but come in earlier in the morning to do it before your shift.'

The Astoria was full in the evenings. Annibale and Francesca ate their dinner at about four o'clock before again donning their uniforms, knowing they would be flat out during their second shift. They'd quickly learnt the knack of manoeuvring between the crowded chairs and tables carrying two to three plates on each arm. At night, Milos put on the wireless, playing music from the hit parade, but with all the hard surfaces in the café, activity and voices reverberated loudly, almost drowning out the songs. As evenings wore on, the air thickened with cigarette smoke and the perspiration and perfume of warm bodies.

Annibale was taking an order from an American GI and his Australian date when two Australian men strode in, one of them shouting, 'You. Yank! This is *my* girl.'

'What the bloody hell, you only get six shillings a day,' the American retorted. 'You can't even buy piss. Get out.'

Both Australians rushed at the GI, knocking him off his chair and laying into him. Immediately all the other American GIs rose from surrounding tables and went to his defence. Mates of the Australians, watching drunkenly out in the street, stormed inside. In a matter of seconds, an all-out brawl ensued. The café's wooden chairs were thrown, tables toppled and dishes smashed.

'*Annibale!*' Francesca's voice was shrill as she frantically beckoned to him from the kitchen doorway.

Annibale saw the Australian girl backing herself against a wall, petrified, and grabbed her by the arm, pulling her into the kitchen with him. The swinging doors were all that separated them from the ruckus.

'The café!' Milos wailed. 'They're ruining the café!'

'He's got a gun!' Someone shouted amid the brawl. 'Get some knives from the kitchen. We need to arm ourselves with *something*!'

Pandi and Annibale looked at each other. 'Quick!' They grabbed the buffet hutch, dragging it across the swinging doors just in time. From the dining room some of the men tried to batter their way in. Annibale pushed the kitchen worktable against the buffet hutch as well. They heard kicking against the doors. Cups hanging on hooks inside the hutch fell and shattered. The table slid forward an inch. The Australian girl screamed.

'Come on. We've got to hold it!' shouted Annibale.

He, Pandi, Milos and a couple of other waiters all pushed against the table and the buffet hutch, managing to keep the swinging doors blocked. From the other side came the sickening sounds of punching.

The Australian girl sank to her knees, sobbing. 'I was Les's girl originally but I want to go out with Gerry now.'

Francesca put her arm around her and looked up at Annibale, her brown eyes full of fear. Annibale gave her a half-smile he hoped was reassuring but suddenly an explosion of glass made them jump.

Francesca's eyes filled with tears. 'What's happening?'

'Oh no, not the front window,' Milos moaned.

'Get under the table,' Annibale told Francesca and the Australian girl. 'And stay there.' *Bloody hell,* he thought, striving to appear calm for Francesca's sake.

The men continued to hold the furniture against the doorway.

Pandi cocked his head. 'Listen, I think the police are here.'

They heard the yelling of both American and Australian military police breaking up the brawl. Annibale and Pandi pulled back the table and the buffet hutch. Milos tried to push through the swinging doors but they wouldn't budge because pieces of furniture had fallen up against them. Eventually they all emerged from the kitchen, dazed and shaken but unscathed. Pieces of glass and crockery crunched underfoot. They stepped around broken chairs and upturned tables. Two Australian military police came over to see if they were all right. Milos tried to speak, but as he looked around the room his words quavered to silence.

The café remained closed while they cleaned up and repaired furniture. When the Freeleagus brothers came to inspect the damage, Milos was vocal in his lamentation. Three days later they reopened and the Astoria was as busy as before. Considering what had happened, Annibale was amazed to see GIs with Australian girls on their arms strutting in past the long line of diggers queuing outside the tobacconist next door to pick up their packets of rationed cigarettes. But the uneasy peace didn't last long.

Widespread brawling in the street kept Annibale, Francesca and the rest of the staff at the Astoria confined inside the café until the early hours of the morning as tensions between Australian and American servicemen erupted once again.

'You've got to let him go.' The police officer's voice was blunt.

Milos looked pained. He glanced from the police officer to Annibale, wondering if someone had complained. Even though Italy had spent the best part of the past nine months fighting on the side of the Allies, most

Australians still considered Italians the enemy. It was May 1944, and with those Australian soldiers invalided out of the army beginning to return home, bosses were telling both women and migrants they had to leave their jobs to make way for the Australian men. Not that Milos had asked Annibale and Francesca to leave — which was what made him suspect a tip-off.

The police officer turned back to Annibale. 'You won't sign your allegiance to Australia?'

'If I do that, I *sign* that, it means I'm volunteering to fight in New Guinea.'

'Look, mate, you're either with us or not.'

'First you make us prisoners in camps, now you want us to fight for you?' Annibale was incredulous. 'I won't sign.'

The police officer turned to Milos. 'Well, he can't work here. Who knows what he might do, poison the food or something.'

'Oh for God's sake.' Annibale slapped his hand on the counter. 'Milos, you know I wouldn't do that.'

Milos sighed. 'I have no choice.' The deal with the doctor no longer stood; the doctor had been conscripted to supply medical services to the army. 'I'd lose all my customers if I was seen to choose Italians over Australians.' He said this for the police officer's benefit.

The police officer wrote down Annibale's details. 'This goes to Manpower,' he said. 'While Australia is at war your name is on a blacklist of migrants not to be employed in this country. Your name will be registered with the government. You must return to the town where you were picked up, supply four photographs of yourself to the police station and promise in writing not to act against the British Empire. Where were you picked up?'

'Stanthorpe. Well, Applethorpe to be exact.'

'Then you must return to Applethorpe and once there you will need to obtain permission from the police to travel out of town.' He paused, his eyes moving to Francesca, then back to Annibale again. 'You go back to the bush. Where you belong.'

Never having done anything to foment unrest or promote fascism, Annibale couldn't help feeling frustrated and a little bitter.

'We have to do as he says,' Francesca said with a shrug, although she was subdued as they said goodbye to Milos and Pandi and everyone else at the Astoria.

'We'll cross paths again.' Pandi's grin almost veiled his disappointment.

Annibale patted his friend's bony shoulder. 'Of course.'

He and Francesca were walking out the door when Milos sprang up. 'When this war is over and you're not blacklisted, if you come back to Brisbane there's a job for you here.'

Annibale's eyes ignited with feeling as he clasped Milos's hand in a hearty shake. 'Thank you. I will remember that.'

'You too, Francesca.' Milos nodded. 'Same rates.'

She went up on tiptoe and kissed his cheek.

Annibale couldn't fully express his gratitude. Milos's offer enabled him to leave with some hope. He and Francesca were quiet as they crossed busy Adelaide Street. It felt strange to be walking up the long, slow-bending hill to the boarding house with the setting sun in their eyes, at a time when they usually would be preparing for the dinner rush. They had been living in the boarding house in Spring Hill for about a year and the landlady raised her threadlike eyebrows in surprise when they explained they had to leave. Francesca gave Annibale a look but said nothing as he told the landlady they might be back one day.

'We were making good money.' Annibale sank down on his side of the bed. 'Thank God we saved most of it. Do you realise in one year with our wages and tips we've made a thousand pounds? That's a lot of money.'

Francesca was already sliding out her port from underneath the bed. She brushed off the dust and placed it open on the brown chenille bedspread. 'At least we'll be able to see the family again. I've missed Ma. Don't look like that. Maybe your father will be back, too.'

'Battle of Brisbane'

I stand before General Douglas MacArthur's desk, alone in the quietness of room 806. From 1942 until 1944, his office here on the eighth floor of what was then Brisbane's AMP Building would have been filled with the sound of footsteps, MacArthur's American accent, maps, pipe smoke, advisors, clinking glasses, his deputy ducking in from his office next door. My gaze roams the wood and plaster walls of this spacious and elegant room, the boardroom of the Australian Mutual Provident Society before MacArthur chose it for his office.

Apparently the Australian authorities, concerned about the safety of Brisbane's residents at the height of the war and the added risk MacArthur's presence would bring, couldn't persuade the general to set up his Pacific War command on the outskirts of the city. He commandeered the AMP Building on the busiest corner of the central business district (evicting all tenants), choosing it for being the largest, most modern structure in Brisbane, with several elevators and air-raid blast walls along the corridors of two floors. The building is currently named MacArthur Chambers.

Two leather armchairs angle towards the polished desk where pens slanting in a holder remain as if ready for their owner who died fifty years ago. A clean pale marble fireplace stands sentry behind the desk, a clock on the mantel. The room is not dusty but the plaster and cracked leather exhale the dry staleness of a space long disused. Venetian blinds drawn against the mid-afternoon western sun cover the bank of shut windows. Careful parting of a blind reveals the flurry of Queen and Edward Streets below — still one of the city's busiest intersections. The closed windows and stone exterior of this lofty sanctuary mute the din of the traffic. When MacArthur was here the windows would have likely been wide open, letting in the sounds of the busy city, especially during summer before air-conditioning was installed. Now he is long gone and the room has the still, quiet ambience of a tomb.

A block from here, down on a corner obscured by present-day high-rise buildings, cooking smoke once emanated from the kitchens of the Astoria Café, its dining room humming with patrons and black-and-white attired wait staff. While Nonno Anni and Nanna Francesca were waiting tables, MacArthur sat in this room making decisions that affected many other people's lives. MacArthur's office is preserved almost exactly as it looked more than seventy years ago, while many of the places frequented and often treasured by 'everyday' people have changed, faded and disappeared ...

Pacific — peaceful, tranquil, calm, gentle.
War — conflict, combat, feud, battle.
Push–pull. East–west. Sun–moon. Build–demolish.

Outside, down amid the noise at street level, I stand on the opposite corner and look up at the windows of MacArthur's office. My gaze drops eight storeys past the columns of Lockyer sandstone to where foundations and paving conceal the previous occupiers of this site. Trees, grass, dirt, rock. Cleared, rutted, compacted by muddy bullock hooves. Chained men built dwellings that were razed to ashes during the Great Fire of Brisbane in 1864, when entire blocks of the CBD were destroyed. Makeshift lodgings popped up, receiving the moniker Refuge Row. In 1871, a bootmaker's was run by George Finch, but the building was torn down in 1877. The first AMP Building, built in 1885, in a style of imposing Renaissance beauty, sister to the Treasury Building, was demolished in 1931, an act lamented by many. And then the building of 1934 gestated a museum for a general, forever covering this spot. Perhaps.

I walk back along Edward Street to see where the Astoria Café, long gone, used to be. How wonderful it would be to walk in there now and be ushered to one of the tables. When we stayed at Katoomba in the Blue Mountains of New South Wales, Roger and I made a beeline for the Paragon Café. Said to be the oldest café in Australia — trading at the same site since 1916 — it has retained its art deco Greek café form since 1926. We adored everything about it — sliding into one of the scuffed booths of Queensland maple beneath chandelier light, 1940s jazz playing, an enticing clatter coming from the back kitchen, honeyed, classical Greek figures in low relief bedecking dark-panelled walls.

Picture rails held framed photographs of celebrities who'd visited the café over the previous ninety years. We ordered hamburgers and milkshakes made in tall metal drink containers at the milk bar. Afterwards we hovered before the glass cabinet that looked the same as the one in a photograph taken in 1925, choosing handmade chocolates placed in a box adorned with a drawing of nearby Orphan Rock, the design virtually unchanged for almost a century.

The unheated back rooms were freezing on the wintry day we visited. We wandered through the tawny 1934 Banquet Hall set with linen cloths and then the 1936 Blue Room, fitted out in the style of a 1930s ocean liner with piano, sprung dance floor, cocktail bar and wall mirrors. Linking the rooms was a foyer displaying each cash register used at the café — the oldest was the most ornate and beautiful, created before utilitarian and cheaper-to-make versions took over. Fortunately, the Paragon was placed on Australia's National Trust Register in 1975, making it one of a very few of its style of café to survive. By then, the Astoria, along with thousands of Greek cafés in towns and cities across Australia, had disappeared.

The Astoria Café was on an intersection in Brisbane I've crossed many times in my life, and yet I've never taken much notice of the location, mostly unaware of the significance of the address for my grandparents. I'm uncertain what occupies the site as I walk towards it to take a look. Approaching the corner of Edward and Adelaide Streets, I stop a few metres from where people crowd to cross the two busy streets diagonally. Standing almost at the spot where the original Shingle Inn entrance used to be, I look across to the other side of the road.

A 7-Eleven convenience store occupies the corner where the Astoria Café stood. Next door is a pawnbroker. And almost in the same position as where the Astoria's doors swung open to the street is a tired entry to an eleven-storey office building. Not even the structure built by the Freeleagus brothers remains. I'm disappointed, but am surprised by just how much. Perhaps because from what I've seen of archival pictures the Astoria was splendid, it had character. It was an elegant part of Brisbane's past. And it wasn't valued. No trace remains.

 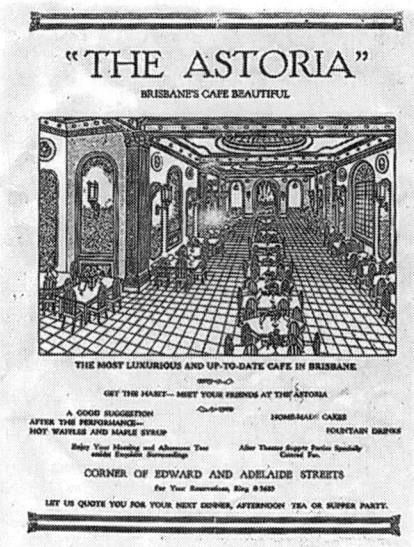

I stand out of the way of the constant streams of traffic — people behind, vehicles in front. Present day fades to images of GIs walking arm in arm with cheerful Australian girls, a group of diggers standing smoking and following the couples with their eyes. A time when women wore hats and gloves, church bells tolled regularly, young men often drank cups of tea, trams shared Brisbane roads and men kept a comb and a handkerchief in their pockets.

> ZOË: *Grandpa, were you here for the Battle of Brisbane?*
> BOB: *Too right. We chased the Yanks right down the street.*

For years, I hadn't considered that Grandpa Bob might have been present when the Battle of Brisbane occurred, though I'd mistakenly assumed Nonno Anni and Nanna Francesca were among it at the Astoria. Over time, the story of my grandparents being present when brawling Australians and Americans wrecked the café had merged to fit with the Battle of Brisbane. Only as I closely pieced together my grandparents' stories did I realise the dates didn't match up.

When the Battle of Brisbane occurred on November 26–27, 1942 — by chance encompassing Thanksgiving Day that year — Nonno Anni was still in the internment camp and Nanna Francesca in Applethorpe. It strikes me how easily anecdotes can fuse and kink over time both in the retelling and the interpreting. The incident they experienced in the Astoria Café did occur, but not until about a year after the main 'battle'. I discover that while the Battle of Brisbane was the largest riot of its kind in Australia, there were many other times during the war when fierce brawls broke out in Brisbane between Australians and Americans, both on the streets and in cafés like the Astoria. And in other states, too: there were the Melbourne riots of December 1, 1942; the Battle of Bondi on February 6, 1943; the Battle of Perth in January 1944; and the Battle of Fremantle in April 1944.

As I gaze along the street, thinking about this, I realise I happen to be standing almost at the spot where Nonno Anni and Pandi Stratu again crossed paths in June 1943, when my grandparents were on their honeymoon.

> FRANCESCA: *When we left to get married, my mother helped me pack a port and this and that. She said, 'Good luck to you, daughter …'*
> ANNIBALE: *Don't cry for that. That was a long time ago.*
> ZOË: *Well, it must have been hard for her.*
> ANNIBALE: *Well, we'd been two weeks here. My idea was to get a job in Brisbane, not go back to the camp. And then we met the Albanian, Pandi Stratu, in Edward Street. Funny, funny thing — meet him in Italy, travel together, then he went to Biloela, then we met in the camp, then here. I always think of him when I pass the corner of Edward and Adelaide Streets, you know the spot? Near the Shingle Inn.*
> FRANCESCA: *On the corner of Edward and Adelaide Street. I can never forget that.*
> ANNIBALE: *That Albanian was our luck. He got us the jobs in the Astoria Café.*

After the police blacklisted him, forcing Nonno Anni to leave the Astoria, he never saw Pandi again. Where I'm standing is the last place their paths inadvertently crossed. Years after my grandfather's death, I decided to try to find out if Pandi Stratu returned to Albania, as Nonno Anni had thought. I discovered that in 1949, not only was Pandi still in Australia, he was applying for naturalisation. Incredibly, the address he gave on his application was just two short blocks away from where my grandparents' shop stood. And yet the two men never met by chance again.

Nonno Anni and Pandi Stratu are gone. The Astoria Café is gone. The original Shingle Inn is gone. I walk on, seeking out the places in central Brisbane where my grandparents lived and worked, and where during their honeymoon they sometimes ate or enjoyed entertainment. From the boarding house and the more modest cafés and milk bars to the Trocadero with its dance floor that could accommodate two thousand, and the Regent Theatre picture palace of gilded opulence as grand as Sydney's surviving State Theatre or Melbourne's Regent — every structure is gone, demolished, seemingly erased. A battle of Brisbane pushes on, each year a little more is lost, brick by brick.

Tin Dwelling

For Annibale, being back in the country after the excitement of Brisbane felt like seeing a glow in the windows of a party and being drawn to the music and laughter but remaining outside in the darkness, unable to come closer. He stood holding a port in each hand as Francesca embraced Cesca, aware of Mico's eyes upon him.

'Oh, I *hoped* you'd come back.' Cesca shone, her arm linked with Francesca's. The women went into one of the bedrooms to unpack, chatting hungrily.

Annibale sat with Mico and Vincenzo on the back steps eating pears picked the month before, and when he asked after his father, Mico shrugged, saying that as far as he knew Vitale hadn't returned to the district. Giuseppe was back but Remilda and the girls were mostly running the farm with a couple of workers.

'Giuseppe seems changed since the internment.' Mico took out his handkerchief to wipe pear juice from his hands. 'I think it's broken him.'

Despite Italy's surrender nine months earlier prompting the release of more internees, most migrants were yet to hear news of their loved ones in Italy. They were still not allowed to meet in large numbers or keep firearms on their farms. There were Australians who'd softened somewhat towards the Italians, realising they posed no threat, but there were also those who remained prejudiced. Just a few days before Annibale and Francesca returned to Applethorpe, a Queensland Protestant newspaper, *The Clarion*, had published on May 25, 1944, an article titled 'Dago Menace Again Threatens Stanthorpe District'.

At dinner, Mico sloshed some homemade wine into tumblers and Annibale gladly quaffed the tannin-heavy drop. He felt displaced, blacklisted by the Manpower Directorate, and trapped within the watchfulness of family expectation. During the train trip from Brisbane, Francesca had announced it was time they had a baby, saying she was eighteen and they had been married almost a year now. Annibale had tried to put forward his reasons for waiting, but she'd talked over him. In most things, he got his way. On this, she refused to budge.

He'd sighed. 'All right.' Seeing her beaming face, he'd added, 'The only thing I ask is that we rent a farm. I need to have my own place rather than live with your parents. I want to make my own way.'

Her smile had faltered a little, though she nodded. 'Why not buy?'

'I think there's a ban on land sales but I can't buy until I become an Australian citizen anyway. Besides, I'd rather save our money to start a business in Brisbane one day.'

Francesca had hesitated. But she was thrilled at the same time: he had agreed they could have a baby, and she relegated all else to the back of her mind.

Within two weeks, Annibale and Francesca moved to a small farm further along Ellwood Road and around a bend from the Solano farm. They rented it from a woman whose son was away in the army. She offered it to them for twelve months with the possibility of renewal at the end of that time. It depended on when her son might return. The war had been going for five years and no one knew how much longer it might continue.

The dwelling on the property was tiny with a tin roof, tin linings and a compacted dirt floor. It had been uninhabited for years, and to make the place liveable Annibale had to secure several tin sheets that had come loose and cover what he could of the interior walls with a bolt of hessian. It was the start of winter so the frosty nights alerted them to undiscovered holes in the tin walls. They kept on hand some jute rags to stuff into the gaps and plenty of cut wood to keep the fire stoked.

Modest as it was, Francesca enjoyed making the dwelling their home. With ticking bought from Pierpoint's she sewed a cover for the mattress and swept the floors daily. She made curtains, scrubbed the bare wooden table with a cake of yellow Sunlight soap the way she'd learnt from Cesca, and got up before Annibale to cook his breakfast. Annibale bought two horses, a plough and a cart and started working the farm. He'd come inside from the fields and hang his hat on the nail by the back door, ravenous from clearing land or planting, and Francesca always had something simmering on the stove, the bread baked and ready to slice.

She'd been pining for a baby for almost ten months when she could finally say, 'I think so. I really think so.'

Annibale's face lit up. 'We'll go into town in the truck with your parents next week so you can see the doctor.'

A month or so after Francesca realised she was pregnant, word filtered along Ellwood Road from those who had radiograms or newspapers that the war might be ending in Europe. Within days, both Mussolini and Hitler were dead. German forces had surrendered in Italy, then in Germany, Denmark, the Netherlands … A week later on May 8, celebrations erupted to mark Victory in Europe Day — or VE Day, as people called it. But while the war was finally over in Europe, the conflict in the Pacific was ongoing. And for many in the Australian armed forces, including some who had survived combat in Europe and Africa, the ordeal was not yet over.

With contact still to resume with loved ones on the other side of the world this often seemed the most testing time for Annibale and Francesca. They were both impatient for and fearful of the news that lay in store for them, and at times it felt easier to focus on the upcoming addition to the family. As Francesca changed with her pregnancy, so too the dynamic within the extended family transformed, anticipation bringing with it hope. The baby was due two weeks before Christmas, still some months away, but they all looked forward to both events.

Mico regarded Annibale with new respect now the younger man was soon to be a fellow father. Soccorsa suddenly seemed older than her ten years as she helped Francesca and her mother, while Cesca relished her position as matriarch and prepared items for the baby. Francesca hoped for a girl, wanting to recapture the closeness she and Cesca shared, though she'd adore a boy for Annibale, reasoning the next baby might be a daughter anyway.

Francesca stopped riding her bicycle, instead walking up the road to visit her parents' house, Mico sometimes giving her a lift back in the truck. (Annibale was learning to drive but was yet to get his licence.) She was careful lifting garments heavy with water as she did the washing. Though mostly well during her pregnancy, Francesca loathed having to visit the outhouse more often. Their dwelling was closer to bushland than her parents' place and she was afraid of the tangle of trees and brush near the outhouse. Even at dawn when the sky was pale lavender with the coming day, Francesca was hesitant to venture out. Carrying the kerosene lantern that threw crazily moving shadows, her eyes darted as she crunched over the frosty grass.

Chopping wood at dusk was when Annibale had time to think: of the impending birth, the responsibilities to come, his own family. Each day they were learning of more towns and cities, in Italy and elsewhere, destroyed by heavy bombardment and of atrocities concealed throughout the war, in particular the concentration camps. He brought the axe down hard between a knot and limb, easily splitting the wood. His breath hung in the cold August air as he paused, considering if Maddalena and Elia could have survived the heavy bombings in Italy — and where Vitale, who had still not returned, might be. With each rapid, controlled swing, the axe head bit into the log.

Francesca glanced at the little clock her parents had given them — a quarter to ten. At that time of morning the area near the back door was a suntrap on a wintry day, and Annibale had put together a makeshift bench with some planks. She set the bread in the oven and figured she'd sit for a few minutes. She was five months into her pregnancy and her lower back ached when she'd been on her feet too long. The air was still cold, yet out of the wind she warmed her face and hands in the sun, comforted by the sound of Annibale tinkering somewhere out of sight in the way that reminded her of her father in his shed.

'Francesca! Francesca!' Soccorsa threw open the front door and came careering in, fleetingly thrown not to find her sister indoors. 'Francesca! Where are you?'

'Out the back. *Mamma mia*, what's happening? Why are you shouting?' Francesca was up, her hands outstretched. 'Is someone hurt?'

Soccorsa struggled to catch her breath, having just run down the road. 'Pa sent me straightaway. They just heard on the wireless. The war is over!'

Francesca's hands went to her mouth, her eyes filled with tears. 'Oh, are you sure? Annibale! Annibale, where are you? *Vieni qua!* The war is over!'

They walked back with Soccorsa to the Solano farm and everyone sat around the table — not eating, not drinking, just talking, through both gladness and sorrow. There was relief the war was over, in the Pacific now as well as Europe, but with it continued their anxiety to learn the fate of those they loved, straining the hope they'd held so long.

Across Australia celebrations continued well into the night and next morning. Then, as the weeks turned into months, jubilation faded as thousands struggled with learning about the death or wounding of a relative or friend. Worse was waiting to hear news of a loved one — only to hear nothing at all. The resumption of normal life had a sluggish start. Severe shortages meant rationing continued. Women were forced to give up jobs they enjoyed and were good at, and had to contend with freedoms curtailed as men returned from war. And for the many men who came back traumatised and maimed, it was a struggle to adjust to their old lives. This, in turn, affected their families.

Annibale found out they could send mail through the Red Cross, so he and Francesca sat at the kitchen table composing letters. He wrote to Maddalena, telling her he was safe and well and working on a small farm; he told her about his marriage to Francesca and the impending birth of their first child, her grandchild. Francesca wrote a letter for her mother to her grandmother, hope and trepidation adding a little shakiness to her handwriting.

And then they nervously waited for word back.

Annibale raised his head from where he was crouched harvesting cabbages, knife poised mid-air. Barely two weeks into summer and the sun was smarting through the back of his shirt.

'*Annibale!*' Francesca's voice rose.

He dropped the knife and ran back to the house. She was leaning with one hand flat on the tabletop, the other curving under the lower part of her stomach. He felt his heart beat harder.

'Go and get Papà to fetch the truck. I need to go to the hospital.'

Without a word, Annibale was out the door and legging it up the road, the soles of his leather boots crunching on the gravel. He began bellowing Mico's name as soon as he reached the driveway. Cesca's head appeared out the back door. Mico came in a half-run out of the shed.

'Get the truck,' Annibale shouted. 'Francesca has to get to hospital.'

Mico loped into the driver's seat just as Cesca came scuttling down the back stairs with her hefty purse over her arm, the skirt of her dress flapping in her haste. The two children were home for school holidays and Cesca, manoeuvring her short, corpulent form into the truck, kept yelling instructions to Soccorsa to look after her brother and continue with the housework.

For Annibale the day unfolded in a blur: the three of them bouncing on the bench seat as the truck strained down the road; Francesca waiting with her small port packed, her forced smile almost a pained grimace; the truck disappearing around the bend without him as he ran back to get the cabbages finished for the consignment in time for Martinuzzi's truck to meet the train. The hurried, mundane task: cabbage head in one hand, the thud of the knife at its neck. Packing them.

Martinuzzi arriving. Hoisting his packed cabbages up to join Martinuzzi's on the back of the truck. His friend's wide smile at the news of the impending birth. A snatched lunch of half a loaf and a hunk of hard cheese. Welcome relief in the cool flask of water to wash it down. Martinuzzi backing the truck up to the open door of the waiting train carriage. A light wind drying their sweat as they hoisted the packed cabbages inside. Martinuzzi driving Annibale straight to Stanthorpe Hospital. Annibale too distracted to take in High Street with its cars and shoppers, the early-afternoon sun beginning its slant into the west-facing shopfronts.

Stanthorpe Hospital was a long, low-set brick building, the entrance in the central, taller section capped with a small turret. Inside, the smell of antiseptic pervaded Annibale's nostrils. He spoke to a nurse in a blue and white uniform, her starched headdress reminiscent of an order of nuns Annibale vaguely remembered from Italy. She directed him to a matron at the front desk, who asked his particulars and looked up a ledger book.

She smiled. 'Mr Boccabella, you have a son.'

All that was a blur. Then he saw Francesca sitting up in the hospital bed, looking both slightly smug and shy as, a little awkwardly, she held a baby with dark hair. Everything seemed to stop still. Annibale's heart swelled.

They named him Remo, after the boat that had brought Annibale to Australia.

'Something Italian but short and easy for Australians to say,' Francesca agreed.

'Of course. We're in Australia now.' Annibale nodded, eyes not leaving his son, and for the first time perhaps in his life he acutely wished for his father's presence.

Remo had been home with Francesca and Annibale about a month when Cesca and Mico went into town to collect their mail and Cesca discovered she'd received a reply to the letter they'd sent through the Red Cross to her mother in Palmi. Sitting in the cabin of the truck parked outside the Stanthorpe Post Office, she asked Mico to read it for her, unable to wait until they got home. Unfolding the page, he saw immediately it was not from her mother but her aunt, and he looked up into Cesca's anxious, probing eyes before starting to read aloud.

Annibale came in from the fields later that day to find Francesca jiggling Remo in one arm and wiping tears from her face with a handkerchief in her other hand. 'Nonna Soccorsa died.' Her voice quaked. *'Two years ago.'*

Annibale's thoughts flew immediately to his own mother. Vitale had been so confident she and Elia would be safe in the mountains. *But who can judge the effects of a war like this?* It was more than six years since they had heard from Maddalena.

Poppies

Maddalena read the letter for the third time, and then placed it on the kitchen table, resting her hand on top. Hearing from Annibale, knowing he was safe … her shoulders slumped a little and she gave way to tears, aware Elia wouldn't be back for a little while yet. The letter tore through the stoicism she'd so carefully cultivated throughout the war … relief Annibale was well, worry he and Vitale had become separated, anxiousness for Vitale whom she'd not yet heard from, joy at her eldest being married and that, by now, she was perhaps a grandmother, but sadness and regret for missing these events as well.

She rubbed her eyes with a stiff handkerchief and blew her nose. Impelled to write back straightaway, she retrieved the writing instruments and paper she kept in a tin box on the mantelpiece. She inked the nib of the fountain pen. *The main thing is to assure them that Elia and I are alive and well*, she told herself. But after scratching out a couple of lines, she caught herself staring into space …

When the war started and Maddalena could no longer send letters to Vitale and Annibale, she strove to convince herself they were relatively safe, so far from the fighting in Europe. Initially, it seemed hard to believe conflict was taking place at all. Village life went on as normal, as it was necessary to plough, sow and harvest, buy a piglet to rear, fatten and kill for the winter, get the grain milled, worry about the rain ruining the hay.

Her mother died. Maddalena and Elia walked across the valley to Poggio Picenze for the funeral. She strode in silence, her heart numb, black coat ends flapping, relieved that Elia went ahead, that the blustery wind kept drying the tears almost as soon as they moistened her cheeks. Unable to tell Vitale what had happened or slip next door to speak to Giovanna, who'd gone to Australia by then, Maddalena found the loss of her mother hard. Elia was still too young and self-absorbed to mourn deeply or offer comfort, and she understood this. Sleep proved elusive. In the dark, silent hours, she struggled with conflicting thoughts of a mother she'd adored, but who had also let her down. Her brother now owned all the family businesses.

The war crept upon them with the insidious silence of slow-rising floodwater. Two men from the local Fascist squad came and put up posters depicting the enemy with an ear pressed to a wall and a slogan warning everyone to keep their 'lips sealed for the enemy is listening'. Village menfolk who hadn't emigrated were drafted. Boys in their teens eagerly signed up to fight on the hollow promise of gaining whatever job they wanted upon their return. Maddalena was grateful Elia was only ten. Most of the boys never returned, sent undertrained to different fronts, many with the same weapons their fathers had used in the Great War.

Women, boys and girls became a common sight working in the fields. Families helped each other at harvest time when they needed extra hands. Maddalena counted herself fortunate, Elia was old enough to chip in with farm work, she didn't have younger children to feed, and they still owned their donkey, Gina.

During the initial part of the war, like most of those she spoke to around Fossa, Maddalena continued to believe Mussolini had their best interests at heart. They had no idea how grossly unprepared Italy was for war or that Mussolini's reason for plunging them into it prematurely was that he was worried Hitler would get all the glory. As the war went on, Maddalena, like more and more people, became exasperated, particularly as it became apparent how bad Hitler was, and she questioned why Mussolini kept supporting him.

The Fascist authorities only broadcast news of Italian victories. Some villagers gleaned more information in secret from crystal-set radios. Elia had a friend in Monticchio whose father had a powerful radio that could pick up Radio Londra, a British broadcast produced in Italian, designed to give people in Italy another source of war news. He went along to listen to several broadcasts and relayed the news to his mother.

Maddalena heard about a particularly nasty Fascist squad member living not far away in Pratola. He roamed the valley with his cronies, beating up their opponents and administering large doses of castor oil. At best, the castor oil would cause severe vomiting and diarrhoea, but there were also more severe cases of it causing acute skin rashes, wild, irregular heartbeats and even death. She couldn't risk the Fascist squad catching Elia, by then thirteen, and forbade him from visiting his friend with the radio.

In the summer of 1943 several events occurred, ramping up the war in central Italy and bringing it closer to Fossa. On July 10, the Allies invaded the Italian south. A week and a half later the villagers heard distant, muffled thuds they initially thought were thunder. Large numbers of Flying Fortresses and Liberators were bombarding Rome, a direct distance of about ninety-four kilometres from them.

Two days after that, wave after wave of Flying Fortresses attacked the Abruzzese towns of Sulmona and Pratola. People came to a standstill in the laneways around Fossa hearing the ominous blast and crackle as bombs shook the countryside, this time landing less than forty kilometres to the south. The closest were exploding in the foothills of Monte San Cosimo near Pratola, where Mussolini had built Montecatini, one of the largest explosives plants in Italy, on farmland resumed from villagers who were given no compensation for the loss of their livelihoods.

Then, on July 25, King Victor Emmanuel deposed Mussolini, ordering his arrest and installing the arch-enemy of il Duce, Marshal Badoglio, as the head of the government. Believing this meant the war would be over, people throughout Italy poured onto streets, cheering and weeping, with no thought of the blackout or curfew. Mobs attacked Fascist establishments. Portraits and busts of il Duce were burnt or smashed. The Fascist squad member from Pratola was found dead on his farm the next day. In an attempt to hide Mussolini from the Germans lest they try to free him, he was taken under guard to the isolated Campo Imperatore Hotel near the highest peak of the Apennines, Gran Sasso, not far from Fossa. It was the same hotel at which Annibale and fellow Fascist Youth members had sung for il Duce during its official opening back in 1934.

Melancholy settled in, however, as people realised the war would continue. Six uneasy weeks followed. Maddalena even let Elia go back to his friend's place in Monticchio to hear what was happening via Radio Londra. The situation was changing almost daily. And then, on September 8, a day that would remain in the memory of all those in Italy at the time, the armistice was declared. Marshal Badoglio had been secretly negotiating with the Allies for some time.

Thousands of extra German troops swarmed down from the north into Italy bent on vengeance. The King and Badoglio fled to Allied-occupied Brindisi on the Adriatic coast, leaving ordinary Italians to face the danger undefended — an act of cowardice for which most never forgave the monarchy. Without any leadership, the Italian army collapsed. The Germans began shipping Italian soldiers off to concentration camps. It was not the first time the Italian government had betrayed its citizens and it wouldn't be the last.

Four days after the armistice, the Germans rescued Mussolini in a daring raid among the highest ridges of the Apennines. Maddalena and Elia, along with many others, were working in the fields when a tiny plane with a swastika painted on its tail took off from Campo Imperatore. They all stopped and straightened to watch, shielding their eyes from the sun with raised hands. Even Gina the donkey, who stood waiting with a load tethered to her back, looked up as the plane droned overhead and flicked her ears.

Mussolini tried to re-establish his authority in northern Italy but he was only Hitler's puppet, and people were already quoting the Latin maxim — *He entered like a fox, reigned like a lion and would die like a dog.*

With German forces in direct control of central Italy, it became a particularly dangerous time for all residents, especially Italy's Jewish population. Since 1938, Italy's Jews had endured systematic marginalisation and, in some cases, the confiscation or forced sale of businesses and property, but in the wake of occupation, German soldiers began rounding up and transporting Jewish people to concentration camps.

When Maddalena was coming out of church after Sunday Mass she overheard an older woman with a makeshift walking stick asking Don

Angelo why people hated the Jews. Although she never missed Mass, since the disinheritance Maddalena had had little time for the priest's opinions, yet now she lingered with several others to hear what he had to say.

Don Angelo coughed a little. 'In history it is proven that people have never liked those who choose to separate themselves from the rest of humanity.'

'What do *you* say about it, Don Angelo?'

He stared at the bent-over woman and stiffened as though slightly affronted, then relaxed. 'I would say, "Thou shalt love thy neighbour as thou wouldst oneself".'

No one was sure if Don Angelo was aware that the villagers were sheltering five Jewish families — around thirty people — in Fossa at that very moment. The group had turned up with fake documents, posing as refugees from the Allied bombings in Rome. Realising they were Jews, the villagers gave them shelter, aware that if they were discovered the Germans would most likely kill both the Jewish people and those protecting them. The families were fortunate to have fled when they did. Just a few weeks later Nazi troops swept through Rome and deported more than two thousand Jews, only a handful of whom would survive the death camps.

The coming winter promised to be hard for those in Fossa. Maddalena had barely enough to feed herself and Elia. There was no pig to kill that year. Even wheat was becoming scarce and if she couldn't buy any on the black market Maddalena had to make bread with maize flour. Within a couple of days the maize loaf became hard and coarse and if hastily bitten into could cut the roof of the mouth. *Appetito rende il cibo migliore* — Appetite makes the best food, she reminded herself, watching her teenage son, hungry from working in the fields, moisten the bread with water and wolf it down. She made sure Elia always had something to eat, sometimes skipping meals herself and occasionally fainting as a result, cursing herself for being weak as she got older. Her fiftieth birthday had come and gone that year, passing like any other day.

Maddalena's long hair now had almost as many strands of grey as brown. Working in the fields had darkened her skin and made creases around her eyes. Her hands were furrowed and becoming ropey with veins but remained strong and capable. She recalled when she was first married proudly retrieving from the hook over the fire pots weighty with polenta, ragù or minestrone, despite how poor they'd been back then. Now she looked down at the meagre broth ingredients assembled on the worn tabletop. Before the war their circumstances had been tough but she had never gone to bed without eating. Now the gnawing in her stomach frequently kept her from sleep.

After the Allies invaded Sicily, the bitter winter impeded their progress north into the central part of the mainland, and strong German defences held the Allies back behind several lines stretching across Italy. Almost a hundred and fifty kilometres south of Rome, near Monte Cassino, was the Gustav Line. The northernmost line of defence, just south of Rome, was the Caesar C line, extending from near Ostia and Valmontone in the west to Pescara on the east coast, crossing the centre of Italy at Avezzano, roughly fifty kilometres south of Fossa. It would not be until the end of May 1944 that the Allies would breach the Caesar C line.

For the eight months prior to that, the Germans exercised a particular cruelty in the area, including in the Aterno Valley where Fossa and Poggio Picenze were situated. The way the battlelines formed, the Abruzzese were among the first Italians to suffer at the hands of the German SS. The German soldiers were out of control, rounding up men and beating them violently, stealing and killing animals, raiding homes for personal items, evicting people and moving into their abodes or simply destroying them and moving onto the next village. They chose the largest house in Fossa, cast out the family and took the place for themselves. Watching through a crack in her shutters, Maddalena glimpsed Germans with guns passing by the windows of the big house near the piazza.

People across the valley were beginning to starve. The Germans deliberately ruined the few crops that were growing, massacring several unarmed villagers who tried to stop them. Women were raped. Word spread that the Germans liked their women young and clean, so many younger women ceased washing, some even covering themselves in dirt and letting lice crawl through their hair, hoping to deter the soldiers. Maddalena was grateful death had spared her mother from witnessing all this. She was losing hope of the world returning to how her mother had known it.

It was midwinter when the Germans learnt of the Jews in Fossa. The Jewish families were forced to flee during the night in snow waist-deep. They hid on an abandoned farm in a derelict house with no heat as a blizzard blasted the valley, before a woman in the nearby village of Casentino took them in, sheltering them all for six months and ultimately ensuring their survival.

The spring warmth of 1944 was welcome, bringing with it renewed hope both for the possibility of gathering food and that the Allies would be able to continue pushing north as fighting resumed. But the German menace remained. Late one afternoon in Fossa some villagers were sitting around a stoop talking when a German soldier walking past accused one of them of laughing at him. He stalked off to get another soldier, the villagers scattering. When the two Germans returned, another man, who hadn't been part of the previous group, had since come and sat down on the stoop. They shot him. Walking back along the laneway in the early-evening light, the second German soldier saw an elderly man standing in his doorway, looking out. He accused him of breaching curfew and shot and killed him, too.

The faces of the villagers were etched in desperation and shock. Most Abruzzese were self-effacing and generous, and not in the habit of using violence. But they were strong and if pushed hard they fought. It was perhaps inevitable that, with such happenings, almost fifty different partisan groups sprang up over the Abruzzo. If only they had known about each other they could have banded together.

Early one cold spring evening, as Maddalena and Elia huddled in front of a dying fire, a loud thumping at the front door made them both jump. Maddalena hurried to answer it, motioning to Elia to stay out of sight in the bedroom and keep quiet. She opened the door a crack. Several German soldiers stood in a semi-circle outside. Maddalena felt as if her heart were pounding in the back of her throat.

Poppies

'We need food.'

Maddalena pulled her shawl tighter. 'I barely have enough for myself.'

Three soldiers pushed their way in. She backed away, standing in the bedroom doorway as the Germans rifled through the kitchen cupboards. She prayed Elia would keep hidden. One of the soldiers grabbed the hunk of stale bread Maddalena had kept for their next meal and started chomping on it.

Another soldier appeared. 'I found a stable. There's a donkey and a chicken.'

'No, please.' Maddalena teetered, almost falling forward.

A soldier spun round, his pale eyes boring into her. 'You would let the soldiers defending your village starve?'

A sharp gunshot blast, a throaty haw, and then the soft thud of Gina's fall. Another shot sounded. Maddalena winced. The soldier gave her a final glare, then turned and strode out to the stable. The others followed, banging the door shut behind them.

It was not until late the following morning that Maddalena could bring herself to venture into the stable. Bones, fur, chicken feathers and a long streak of Gina's blood were all that remained, along with the remains of a fire. She thought of Gina's moist dark eyes and the way she'd often nuzzled and spoken to her with her gentle brays. She'd been a loyal donkey and part of the family for so many years.

Maddalena cleaned out the *stalla*, dripping hot tears. She felt the urgent need for Vitale, for her father, and especially for her mother. She longed to run and bury her face in her mother's skirts as she'd done as a tiny girl. But her parents were gone and Vitale was far away. She needed to look after Elia. Maddalena could only look to herself for strength.

As the first bomb hit L'Aquila, Maddalena's immediate thought in half-wakefulness was that a thunderstorm must have blown over the ridge. But there was something not quite right about the rumble. Sitting up in bed, she stilled her breathing to listen. A strange whistle sounded, like a loud bird, yet it was night-time. Goosebumps swept up her arms. The following boom ended with a crackling sound.

'*Elia!*' She rushed into the next room where he was sitting up in bed in fright. 'Quick, get up! Put your shoes on, grab your coa—.' Another boom cut off her last word as she tugged at the blanket. 'Your coat.'

In the kitchen, she hesitated. The bombs were loud, though they sounded a few kilometres off yet, still in the vicinity of L'Aquila. *Should we stay in the house or go to the stable?* Maddalena tried to think.

'Under the table.' She pushed Elia underneath, crawling in after him.

They huddled together in their coats beneath the blanket, trying not to flinch each time they heard the ghostly whistling sound, knowing an explosion would soon follow. The bombing went on, and on.

'When will it stop?' Maddalena cried out. Another bomb fell, then another and she shouted, '*Vaffanculo!*' The bombing ceased, making the obscenity seem louder, and she and Elia looked at each other. She gave a tight nod. 'That told them.' They couldn't help chuckling together in nervousness and relief.

In the quiet that followed they debated whether it was over. Then the drone of several planes sounded overhead and they huddled tighter.

Maddalena composed her reply to Annibale and Francesca, making no mention of any of this. Instead, she told them that she and Elia were safe and asked after Vitale, not comprehending how they could have been separated, not yet knowing of their internment. She didn't bring up whether she and Elia would be coming to Australia or if the others might return to Italy, saving this for when she could correspond with Vitale. It occurred to her that Vitale might already be on his way home to Fossa.

Afterwards, she draped her pilled work shawl around her shoulders, tied the ends in a knot over her chest and closed the front door behind her, heading back to the fields. Poppies sprouting among the new rows of sugar beet needed weeding. Elia was playing football in the piazza with his friends, the ball made of scrunched newspapers bound tightly with string. She decided to let him be for the afternoon. He'd worked hard during the war and although he was now fifteen and much taller than her, she still thought of him as her little one.

She strode down the hill to the valley, feeling every step in her knees. Since turning fifty-three, she occasionally had to rub warm olive oil into her joints. Maddalena was inwardly cursing having to kneel to weed the immature plants when she caught sight of an abandoned hillside covered with poppies in full bloom. Her steps slowed, the flowers holding her gaze, a sea of red and green rippling in the spring breeze. She'd never considered them beautiful before. There seemed to be so many, thousands upon thousands, and yet if each one represented a person lost in the war, the number didn't come even close.

Australia Felix

Australia Felix, n.
1. ~ *Latin meaning 'fortunate Australia' or 'felicitous Australia'.*
2. ~ *term applied in 1836 by explorer Thomas Mitchell to a region south of the Murray River (present-day Victoria).*
3. ~ *Impressionist artwork painted in 1907 by landscape artist and member of the Heidelberg School Arthur Streeton.*
4. ~ *novel published in 1917, first of* The Fortunes of Richard Mahony *trilogy, authored by female novelist Henry Handel Richardson.*
5. ~ *poem by poet Clive James.*

Nonno Anni's small stone house in Fossa stands uninhabitable since the earthquake in 2009. Heavy snowdrifts shift the tarpaulin covering where part of the roof collapsed. The snow melts onto furniture, books, framed photographs, wiring … such further damage unbeknown to those on the other side of the world until it is too late. And there will be many more winters before repairs can begin, if ever they can. Such is the tangle of red tape, politics, venality and finance since the earthquake in Abruzzo.

I walk with Roger along Fossa's streets, which are almost empty bar the affectionate cats that villagers, like my relative, Placido, often come back to feed. There has been looting in damaged houses and almost all of the copper drainpipes have been stolen from the external stone walls of people's abodes, including ours. We step around some debris and pass overgrown plants, neither of us wanting to concede Fossa will become a ghost town. We still hold hope. Before the earthquake, Fossa had not been a village on the path of natural desertion as an elderly population dwindled. It was a vibrant community of all ages, a village thriving. Hundreds of Fossa's residents remain in 'temporary' abodes down in the valley as repair work progresses slowly, waiting, hoping to return to their homes.

I close my eyes to the thick dust and disrepair and see the way my family's house used to be when I could come and stay here. Smooth tiles and walls, antique dressers. Nanna Francesca's kitsch that seemed to increase each year she came to stay. Packages from the L'Aquila market swamping the kitchen bench … pecorino, pears, artichokes, fragrant roast chicken. Wildflowers in a glass jar. Lively village sounds invited in by open windows — conversations, televisions turned up, a Fiat coughing as it resisted being started, birds tittering across terracotta roofs. I can almost sense the paisley fabric of the tablecloth beneath my fingertips; smell pasta sauce cooking, the frying pork and fennel sausages handmade at the Boccabella *alimentari*, a corner shop run by relatives, the tall pine forest Nonno Anni helped plant when he was young.

Several elderly people staying at a farmhouse down in the valley tell me that damage wrought by the earthquake reminds them of how many towns across the valley looked after the bombings of the War. Some building façades look normal and then I realise that behind all is rubble. I see collapsed houses where I know people died. And yet, though I oscillate between sadness, anger and despair, I cannot truly know how it is for those who survived the earthquake, let alone those who almost starved after the war as they carved out life among bombed-out ruins.

The stable where Gina the donkey, the chickens, and the occasional pig or sheep lived now houses bits of broken furniture, storage boxes and firewood. Even standing just inside the doorway, I can feel the coolness in the air that comes from the back wall of the stone *stalla* having been built partly into the mountain. Seven decades on, there is nothing to indicate that German soldiers sat here and ate a donkey named Gina that they'd just killed, along with a chicken. As much as this story and the other happenings around Fossa during the war upset me, I am grateful Granny Maddalena didn't keep what occurred to herself. I may never face the danger she did, but her strength inspires me to be strong, too.

ZOË: *Grandpa, what was your role when you flew in the Liberators during the war?*
BOB: *I was the navigator, love.* [He leads me into his study and pulls open a wooden drawer, and then a dented tin. He hands me what is inside. I gently open the silk maps. They are also known as escape or evasion maps and were carried by servicemen to be used in case of capture.] *You can keep those, if you like.*
ZOË: *No, I couldn't.*
BOB: *You take them, love. I know you'll look after them.*
ZOË: *Really? Are you sure? I will. I promise.* [I carefully refold them.] *What was it like?*
BOB: *In the Liberator? Noisy. Ruined my eardrums.* [He sees me glance at the eagle tattoo on his right arm, midway between his shoulder and elbow. It is dark, blurry upon his wrinkled skin.] *Promise me you'll never get one of these. Terrible things. I got it during the war. The tattoo bloke wasn't very good.*
ZOË: *What was it like — the fighting?*
BOB: [He hesitates.] *When you're in the air, dropping bombs, well … you're not face to face with the people being killed.* [He stops. I know he was in the regular army during the War before he joined the air force. I've met his close friend who was in the Z special force.] *Let's put the kettle on, eh, love? I saw you brought a nice tea bun. We'll have a cuppa and you can tell me about what you've been up to lately. How's work going?*

After he dies, I keep in a tin box my grandfather's silk maps and a typed copy of his life story entitled 'A Digest', which contains many things he wasn't able to say. He leaves his war medals to my cousin, who is ten at the time, the only boy among his grandchildren.

Marco, a photographer in his mid-forties, ushers me into the study of his parents' elegant apartment in northern Italy. Books line the walls from floor to ceiling, a wooden ladder on rails leading to the upper shelves. French doors open onto a balcony that overlooks a garden of tall fir trees. Marco's mother, Coletta, is diminutive and impeccably dressed, possessing a sweet smile. She is quite a bit younger than her husband, Sebastiano, a retired academic and psychiatrist who trembles with Parkinson's disease. When Marco introduces us I take Sebastiano's hand warmly. He smiles, communicating mainly with his eyes. The conversation shifts and gains momentum, Marco's language skills bridging the gap between the English and Italian speakers. I sense Sebastiano still watching me. He smiles.

Granny Maddalena's grandfather is the connection that makes us distantly related, a link stretching back to early 1800s Abruzzo. Sebastiano was born in the Abruzzo, but it's a long time since he has been back. Marco knows I am hoping to find out more about what it was like in Fossa and in Granny Maddalena's hometown of Poggio Picenze during the war, and he says Sebastiano has a story to tell. I turn eagerly to him to hear it; however, Marco says it is time to eat and we must go up to his apartment on the next floor. I feel a little disappointed when Coletta and Sebastiano don't come, too. I could happily spend more time with them.

Marco's apartment is noisy with the younger two generations of Coletta and Sebastiano's family. The adults wear Italian designer brands and all speak at once, yet in harmony, a group at ease from much time spent together. The children are quieter, a bit shy, but their dark eyes shine when Roger and I give them some little presents, including boomerangs from Australia.

In Marco's dining room, large photographs of Australian landmarks decorate the walls — the Sydney Opera House, the Harbour Bridge, the Great Barrier Reef, Uluru — the sights familiar to us yet somewhat exotic in an Italian apartment. 'I took these when we went to Australia for our honeymoon.' Marco grins, swiftly translating for his wife who doesn't speak any English. 'It's a pity we did not know of you then. We love Australia, but the flight there — too long. It gave me the fevers! When we arrived in Sydney I had to go straight to the doctor.'

Late at night, Roger and I walk around the quiet city centre with Marco and his wife. Marco points out modern buildings that have replaced buildings bombed during the war, lamenting the 'new, ugly' architecture. It is not until Marco and I are alone that he tells me Sebastiano's story, which happened in Abruzzo during the Second World War.

'My father lived with his family in Castel del Monte. Have you seen the movie of George Clooney, *The American*? It is set there. Anyway, in 1944 the German troops were escaping from the villages because Allied troops were due to arrive any time, and one day my father went to meet his uncles in Poggio Picenze to stay there for a few days …'

Marco tells me that at the beginning of summer 1944, when the German troops began realising they needed to escape north, they departed Poggio Picenze leaving some TNT under the bridge at the entrance of the village with a hidden detonator designed to trigger when the Allies arrived. None of the villagers could disarm it.

When Allied trucks lumbered up the road towards the bridge, a large number of the villagers, among them Sebastiano, ran towards them, waving their arms to alert them to the danger. The column of trucks kept driving forward, the Allied soldiers thinking the villagers, with all their shouting and waving, were just happy to see them. When the trucks didn't pause, several men stood in front of the bridge to create a barricade. The British officer in charge presumed the Italians were stalling them to help their ex-allies, the Germans, escape, and gave the order for his soldiers to get off the trucks with their guns ready.

He eyed the villagers. 'Out of the way! Move!'

The villagers stood still, their pleas in Italian not understood.

The officer turned to his men and shouted, 'Prepare to open fire!'

Thirteen-year-old Sebastiano, the only one in the village who knew some English, slowly walked forward, alone. 'Stop! The bridge is mined!'

'The situation was going bad, but *tutto è bene quel che finisce bene*,' Marco chuckled — all's well that ends well. 'To thank my father for saving them, for a whole week the soldiers took him on their trucks as they travelled between the village and the harbour of Pescara to get supplies for the troops, and he had some baths in the sea with them. He received also a lot of chocolate and gums.'

I smile, imagining Sebastiano, the dignified elderly man I met, as a thirteen-year-old hero, chuffed with his rewards of chocolate and chewing gum and bathing in the sea.

Marco grins. 'He was for some days the boy most admired of Poggio. The only thing was when my grandmother, Marcella, find out what happened, perhaps as always mums do, she first thinks of all the risks for her son travelling on the military trucks — you see, sometimes they were bombed by the Luftwaffe — and she gave him some slaps on his bones!'

Poppies,
lillypillies,
folk songs,
bush poems,
fireflies,
cicadas,
pane di casa,
damper,
triccheballacche,
lagerphone,
chaffinch,
whipbird,
Italian with an Australian accent,
Australian with an Italian accent.

ZOË: *Uncle Andy, did you ever go back to the town where you came from, near Lublin in Poland?* [My great-uncle looks at me, his eyes almost hidden by creased skin. His ninety-two-year-old face has seen much since the Gestapo came to his family home at two o'clock one morning and took him away when he was eighteen.]
ANDREW: *Once. When the war had finished. After I was released from Mannheim. Everyone, my whole family, k— gone. I was the only one left. So I came here. Built roads and bridges out at Adavale near Quilpie with eleven other Polish men. Went outback, fixed fences and windmills. Worked on a cattle station. I came to Brisbane to get some new shoes and your Aunty Mona, she served me in the shop — Shirley's it was. That's how we met.*

'When I went to listen to Radio Londra in Monticchio, my friend's father bolted the door and they closed all the shutters before turning the radio on.'

Sitting in my great-uncle Elia's townhouse in Brisbane, morning sun penetrating the back screen-door and illuminating the kitchen, the war and Italy seem far, far away. It has been a couple of years since Nonno Anni died and it feels both strange and comforting hearing his brother, Elia, speaking in the same accent as my grandfather, whom I miss terribly. Their voices, hands and olive skin are similar, but the brothers were quite different men.

'Fossa during the war was very poor. Couldn't buy clothes or anything. My mother, she had to keep mending and patching the ones we had. We ate chicory she picked from the mountainside, boiled up. Couldn't put the light on at night because of the bombs. I took the donkey, Gina, down to the field but she had broken shoes and didn't want to get up or lift her legs sometimes.'

Elia corroborates and expands upon the stories his mother told of their time in Fossa during the war, those stories passed on to me via Nonno Anni. The hunger seems to have stayed in Elia's mind — he says he's craved food ever since. Also the sound of the bombs, where they dropped, and the people he knew killed by them, including the farmer with the radio in Monticchio, along with his cows. As I am writing this down in a notebook, I look up to see a large lizard, about thirty centimetres long, making its way across the floor. Who knows how it got in but I look around at the fully screened windows and back door and realise it cannot get out.

'Uh, excuse me a moment, but there is a large lizard just over there.'

'Where? How the bloody hell did that get in here?'

'I'll just open the door to let it out.' I go over to do so, thinking the poor thing won't survive if it stays inside. Startled by my movement, it bolts under the kitchen table.

'Here, use this.' Elia thrusts his walking stick towards me.

The situation descends into farce, Elia yelling instructions from his chair as the lizard darts in different directions, me using the walking stick to try to encourage it outside. It seems so incongruous, considering the subject we've been discussing. Finally, I coax it onto the mat just outside the back door. The lizard sits there looking around blinking as I close the screen-door. A butcherbird swoops down, picks it up in its mouth and flies off. I cry out and feel terrible.

Elia shrugs. 'Bah.'

A nurse arrives to give my great-uncle his check-up and I go for a walk after he makes me promise to come back in half an hour. I still can't believe what happened to the lizard I'd been trying to save. If I can, I rescue spiders and geckos trapped indoors and take them outside, and every night I feed the possums that live in trees around our house. Roger and I bury them if they're killed by cars, and take in abandoned cats. How would I have lived during the war in Fossa with innocent neighbours shot by German soldiers and friends killed by Allied bombs? And yet I've felt that with each loss in my family, of which there have been many in recent years, I've become more accustomed to death, more accepting. Perhaps it is injustice that is most difficult to accept.

'You know, I slept in the room where Mussolini was kept prisoner in Hotel Campo Imperatore,' Elia says when we're back in his kitchen nook. 'Just for one night, in 1994.'

'Were you aware of Mussolini being there in 1943?' I ask. 'Of the Germans rescuing him?'

'We saw the plane take off, though we didn't know what was happening at the time. Most of the village was down in the valley, working in the fields. We all stopped and looked up and watched the plane take off and go over.'

It seems so incredible, I wonder if it is true. Then my neighbour from a few doors up, who also happens to be from Fossa and was there during the war, confirms it.

'I remember working in the field and the plane took off from the mountain. Everyone looked up, we shaded our eyes like this.' He shrugs, goes back to hosing his yard.

Later that year, both men die. With Elia's death, my family's last living link to Fossa is gone. The Italian accents are gone. Everyone in the family now has Australian accents.

Fruit Shop and Milk Bar

When the second lease on Annibale and Francesca's farm was due to end in May 1946, the woman who owned it told them they'd need to leave, as her son was coming back from the war. Annibale decided to catch a train to Brisbane, telling Francesca he'd be gone only a few days. With the war over and Annibale no longer blacklisted by the Manpower Directorate, he was free to work wherever he chose. He hadn't had the chance to get to know Australia when it wasn't at war. All of a sudden, the future became sunny. His goal to start up his own business seemed within reach, especially with the thousand pounds in the bank. However, with a six-month-old baby they wouldn't risk travelling to the city without a room and work organised.

He returned after a couple of days, full of drive and plans. 'Milos is happy to give me a job back at the Astoria. I told him I'm looking for a shop to run and he said no problem, I can leave any time. He was really good about it. Pandi's not there any more, though. Apparently he moved on when the war finished, nobody's sure where. Someone said maybe even back to Albania.' Annibale shifted in his chair, unable to sit still. 'There's a large room about to become empty back at the boarding house in Leichhardt Street. The same lady is running it. I told her I reckon we can be packed up here and in Brisbane within the next couple of weeks. I'll write to Mamma tonight and tell her not to send any more letters here, that we're moving to Brisbane.'

Francesca gently bit one side of her bottom lip and nodded, knowing this had been coming. Watching Annibale don his hat and head out to the fields, she considered how he'd grown up working the land, and yet he seemed more energised, more content in the city. She recalled him telling her his mother's family had been business people, owning a grain mill and butchery in Poggio Picenze. *Perhaps Annibale is more like his mother's side*, she thought, pondering the mild-mannered, almost diffident Vitale.

Even via Maddalena's short letter, Francesca had detected her mother-in-law's strength and bluntness.

They still didn't know where Vitale was. Carlo Benocci had run into Paolo, working at a vineyard down at Ballandean, who thought Vitale's lot of internees had been taken out to somewhere near Alice Springs. Annibale could only assume his father had picked up work and decided to stay in the Northern Territory. It had been years since they'd heard from him. Francesca calculated Vitale would be about fifty-two. She almost wished he'd return and convince Annibale to stay and work on another farm, somewhere near Stanthorpe, that they could run together.

'There's nothing I can do but get on with our own plans until I hear from him,' Annibale had told her. 'For now, Mamma and Elia will stay in Fossa and we will go to Brisbane.'

In the quiet autumn morning of the next day, Francesca waited until Annibale went to the field and headed up to her parents' farm. The gravel crunching under the pram wheels and her shoes seemed the only noise save for the call of a currawong high in a tree. When she got close to her parents' farm, an occasional chinking of metal told her Mico was in the shed, most likely working on the tractor. She was relieved he was busy and that Soccorsa and Vincenzo were at school. She parked the pram in the slatted shade beneath the back steps and carried Remo upstairs.

Cesca was in the kitchen and Francesca felt instantly warmed by her mother's greeting of surprise and joy as she wiped her hands on her apron and put them out for Remo.

'Annibale is back from Brisbane.' Francesca filled a glass of water from the tap, then turned around, sipping it as she leant against the sink and told her mother his plans.

Cesca kept bouncing Remo, meeting her gaze. In her daughter's eyes she saw perhaps resignation, but most of all a seeking of assurance. They both knew she wouldn't be back this time. She sighed. Cesca didn't want them to go but she knew Annibale wasn't the type to settle on a nearby farm. Out of love for her daughter she gave a slight shrug and feigned matter-of-fact acceptance.

'At least it's what you know from before, the same boarding house, and Annibale has a job to go to.' She inserted her knuckle into Remo's mouth as he began to grizzle.

'Yes.' Francesca seemed to straighten and nodded. 'This is true.'

'I know you'll write and tell me how Remo is growing. And of course we can still visit occasionally.' But they both knew there would be little opportunity for trips.

The fresh, sweet, earthy perfume of apples mingled with the scent of wooden crates and orange rind. Shelves, glass-fronted cabinets and a large glass-fronted display case in an L-shape, which Annibale had commissioned his friend Serafino to build, were crammed with chocolates, biscuits and cigarettes. The long refrigerated milk-bar unit hummed, emitting a constant heat at the far end. Annibale briefly ran his hand along its gleaming counter. He'd never once regretted the decision to start their fruit shop and milk bar.

He handed a few coins in change to a nurse on her lunch break and turned to the next customer. 'What would you like?'

'An orange drink, please.' The woman was holding a paper-wrapped roll Annibale recognised as one from George's snack bar, just across the road.

He leant into the four-gallon canister of orange drink in the milk bar. The electrically refrigerated unit was about ten feet long and waist-high, the stainless-steel top of one half of it serving as a counter. This section had a glass front underneath the counter where Annibale kept small bottles of Coke, Fanta and other Tristram's and Kirks soft drinks on display. The other half of the milk bar, with glass sliding covers on top, had a freezer section for ice cream and ice blocks, and a chiller accommodating four three-foot-high four-gallon canisters — two filled with milk, one with water and one with Annibale's orange drink, which was swiftly gaining popularity. He made it with two to three oranges per glass put through the vitamiser — skin, seeds and all, along with one part Tristam's orange cordial and five parts water.

He reached in with a ladle, filled a sturdy fluted glass to the brim and passed it to the woman. 'Sixpence, thanks.'

She handed him the correct money, then, seeing him glance at George's roll again, smiled and said, 'Your orange drink is nicer.'

'Thank you.' Annibale flushed with happiness. 'See you next time.' He turned to his next customer, a pimple-faced youth. 'Can I help you?'

Fruit Shop and Milk Bar

'Pint of milk, thanks, and can you tip a bit out and add some chocolate flavouring?'

'No problem.'

Young blokes often came in asking for a pint of milk with some chocolate or strawberry flavouring added to the bottle. To make room for the flavouring, Annibale tipped the creamy top off the pints into the milk canister, the secret to his milkshakes being creamier. Customers had started crossing busy Ann Street after they'd bought a sandwich at George's to buy milkshakes from Annibale. Francesca and Annibale had no plans to make rolls and sandwiches, preferring to keep their business as a milk bar and fruit shop, selling produce, drinks, chocolates, biscuits, cigarettes, chewing gum and newspapers, as well as Bex and Vincent's powders.

'Tristram's lemon squash and a Golden Rough,' said a woman in an ill-fitting hat.

Annibale finished serving her and turned to the next customer as the woman dropped her soft-drink bottle on the floor. It broke, creating a puddle of sticky glass.

'Oh no! Oh, I'm so sorry!' Her face went red and she bent as though to clean it up.

Annibale waved his hand. 'Don't worry about it. These things happen.' He reached into the fridge and got her out another bottle. 'Here you go.'

'Oh, would you like some money for that?'

'Course not. These things happen.'

As the lunchtime rush died down, Annibale ducked out the back and got the mop and bucket. He picked up the bits of broken bottle and quickly mopped away the stickiness, going back out to the courtyard to empty the bucket. In the summery heat the floor was already dry when he returned to find his next customer waiting. Annibale grinned, seeing it was one of his regulars who came in every day for a small bottle of Kirks Indian Tonic water and a packet of Vincent's powder — the sachet containing aspirin, phenacetin and caffeine. 'Mr Lawson, the usual?'

'That's right, Joe.' Lawson winked, put his money on the counter and began rolling his cigarette one-handed. He'd been driving with his arm out of the car window one day when a passing bus cut it off.

There was a loud shot and a woman coming into the shop dropped heavily onto the floor.

'*Bloody hell!*' Annibale came running around from behind the counter.

He bent over the prostrate woman as she began easing herself up on all fours.

'Are you all right? Where did the bullet get you?'

She stared at him. 'What? I tripped on the top step.'

Lawson, doubled over with laughter, spoke in a wheeze. 'A car backfired just as she tripped.'

Annibale and Francesca opened the shop for sixteen hours each day, seven days a week, just the two of them taking turns at shifts. The days and evenings took on a steady routine. When the alarm clock rang out in their room at the boarding house at five-thirty, Francesca switched it off and thrust her feet into her slippers on the linoleum floor, hoping no one had beaten her to the communal bathroom out the back. Once she'd dressed, there was Remo to tend to, breakfast to cook and dishes to wash, before she gathered bottles and nappies and headed with Annibale and Remo to open the shop at seven o'clock.

She and Annibale took turns pushing Remo in the pram from Leichhardt Street down to Ann Street. It was just the three of them in Brisbane, no other family. At twenty years of age, Francesca had a husband, a son, a place to live and a shop. *There is only one thing missing*, she thought. *A daughter*. But she knew she'd have to wait until they bought a house, and following the war there was a shortage of these.

When they arrived at the shop, Francesca manoeuvred the pram behind the curtain Annibale had hung at the back to keep Remo hidden from customers.

'I'll see if there are any decent Williams pears,' Annibale said as he headed off to the markets.

Remo had been asleep about an hour when she heard him starting to grunt and move. She hurried to count out coins in change to a customer, knowing that at any moment Remo would break into a howl.

At nine o'clock the Pauls delivery man carried in a metal milk churn and tipped fresh milk into a canister in the refrigerated milk bar. Since the delivery truck wasn't refrigerated, the milk needed time to get cold for milkshakes. Francesca asked him to top up the other milk canister as well. It had got so low that the milk left in the bottom had frozen overnight. Before he'd left for the market, Annibale had lifted the tall canister into the sink to sit in hot water to defrost. The deliveryman went back to his van and brought in a metal crate tinkling with twenty pints of milk in glass bottles with cardboard-wad tops.

Annibale returned and Francesca looked over what he'd bought. She began arranging the displays. 'I'm not touching those peaches,' she said.

Annibale looked up. 'What's wrong with you?'

'That fur on the skin.' She exaggerated a shudder. 'Gives me the heebie jeebies.'

He laughed. 'Leave them to me. You better get back anyway.'

'I'll just tidy up the chocolates.'

Francesca liked tending to the chocolates that came wrapped in coloured foil and paper or in boxes. Annibale, not a chocolate eater, complained that the chocolates got grubs in summer but Francesca insisted they stock them. Travelling salesmen — 'travellers' — came out from Cadbury and Nestlé to renew orders. From the Nestlé representative Francesca ordered milk chocolate, Coconut Rough and Old Gold dark chocolate. The quarter-pound bars sold for two shillings, the smaller versions, one shilling. For five shillings, a box of Old Gold chocolates with assorted nut and soft centres were popular with hospital visitors looking for something to give a patient. From the Cadbury man she bought Dairy Milk, Nut Milk, Fruit and Nut and a dark chocolate called Cadbury Energy. She was quite fond of the Cadbury Dairy Milk and tucked a bar into her purse before she left.

With the midmorning sun blazing on her back, Francesca wheeled Remo in the pram uphill to the boarding house. Back in their room, she ran a damp washcloth over her face then had a long drink of water. For a moment, she stood at the window, the breeze cooling the moisture on her forehead, and wondered what her family at Applethorpe was doing, then Remo gurgled in his pram and she hastened over to him. He fixed on her, his eyes like dark pebbles, and she sang a little nursery song in Italian as she changed him. Then, holding him on her hip with one arm, she grabbed the bucket of dirty nappies in the other hand and went outside to the washhouse copper. She boiled, washed, rinsed, wrung and pegged out the cloth nappies, keeping an eye on Remo, chasing him if he started his lumbering crawl towards a gap in the paling fence near the papaw trees.

After lunch when Remo finally went down for his nap, Francesca allowed herself ten minutes to sit by the window, unwrapping her Cadbury Dairy Milk, then set to cooking the tomato gravy for Annibale to have with his pasta that evening.

Annibale was busy serving when she returned to the shop at around three o'clock, so Francesca waited on the footpath keeping hold of the pram. The day was still hot and she could hear both electric milkshake mixers whirring and saw a number of customers standing at the counter drinking their shakes through straws. Gradually the rush of customers abated.

'Busy today.' Annibale put on his hat as he walked out towards her. 'If you get a chance you might get some more apples from out the back.'

'Take the lid off the gravy before you heat it on the stove or it will boil over.'

'*Va bene.*' He took the pram handle as Francesca went into the shop and began to neaten the trays of Freddo Frogs and OK Peanut Bars. 'Don't forget the nugget,' he called back.

'*Nougat!*' She corrected him, not for the first time, then realised he was teasing her. She made to throw a bar out the door at him and he ducked, laughing.

By seven o'clock Annibale was back at the shop with Remo, ready to start the last shift and close up some time around eleven. Though by the evening Francesca was tired, her steps were always a little quicker as she wheeled the pram back to the boarding house in the darkness. Annibale had left the light on in their room. She told him not to but he didn't like her entering the room in the dark.

For the next three years, their routine would be the same, with only two days off a year: Good Friday and Christmas Day.

Vita Brevis

It was just after two o'clock in the morning and Annibale was yet to sleep. He lay in the darkened room listening to the ticking clock and Francesca's sleeping breaths. Remo had had a bad dream and was now asleep in the bed between them, arms and legs splayed, taking up most of the room. Annibale rolled over, trying to create a little more space for himself. A streetlamp out the front illuminated the gauze curtains, their hems swelling and falling on a light breeze through the bottom of the sash window that was open a crack. Finally, he gave up trying to sleep and padded over to the window, looking out onto the darkened garden and empty road beyond. He thought back to the conversation he and Francesca had had earlier and knew it was time to buy a house. They had enough saved in the bank but he'd held off, knowing that to gain a house meant losing something as well.

To buy a house in Australia Annibale had to be naturalised, just like the other Italian migrants he knew who owned property. He was happy to become a British subject — it would not be until the following year, 1948, that the legal status of 'Australian citizen' would come into being — it was relinquishing his Italian citizenship, the tie to the country where he was born, where generations of his family had lived for centuries, that was difficult to bear. It felt a little like turning his back, letting his ancestors down, betraying future generations. The years had barely tempered Annibale's resentment for what Don Angelo had done. The priest had taken Annibale's future in Fossa, his inheritance, and now he was to lose his nationality, his birthright, as well. As happy as Annibale was with life in Australia, it was still hard to accept that once he took that oath he would be formally severing ties with the land in which he was born, even if it would still hold a place in his heart.

Annibale swore allegiance to a king he knew little about and Francesca began combing newspaper advertisements for properties for sale.

'I found an auction for two houses on one block,' she said to Annibale as they were finishing their coffee at breakfast.

Annibale stared at her, the thought of owning two houses instead of one appealing to him immensely. 'Where at?'

They got a tram out to Commercial Road at Teneriffe, Annibale carrying Remo, and walked until they found Wyandra Street. Teneriffe was a riverside working-class suburb in the inner city, and the house for sale at number fourteen sat about midway along the almost flat street. The house at the back on the same block had frontage onto Wyatt Street at its junction with Masters Street. Both houses were weatherboard workers' cottages on tall stumps with wooden flights of steps leading up to latticework doors on their front verandahs.

Annibale put Remo on the ground and the toddler tore across the grass on wonky legs while they looked at the houses from the outside. Behind, the gasworks' cylindrical framework dominated the skyline, and around the corner loomed numerous immense red-brick wool stores, built around the turn of century. With one eye on Remo, Francesca reminded Annibale that, due to the post-war housing shortage, it was a condition of the sale that the current tenants not be evicted for a year.

'It doesn't matter if we can't move in straightaway,' Annibale said on the tram ride back to the shop. 'We'll just stay where we are at the boarding house and at least we can be collecting rent from the houses. I'm more worried about the auction. You can't bid and my English isn't good enough to catch the man, what do you call him, the auctioneer, with the numbers. They go quick-sticks.' They got off the tram and began walking towards the shop.

'*Courier-Mail!* Get your *Courier* here,' the paperboy hollered on the corner of Ann and Wharf Streets. He was perhaps about twenty, selling newspapers there most mornings and afternoons, and was familiar to both Annibale and Francesca, though they didn't know his name.

Francesca hung back a little, holding Remo, as Annibale went up to him. 'Hey, I own that milk bar just there.' He pointed to the shop. 'I want to buy a couple of houses at an auction over at Teneriffe later today but I might not catch the numbers properly. If I give you five pounds will you make the bids?'

'Five pounds, you say?'

Francesca kept Remo with her in the shop while Annibale and the paperboy caught the tram back to Teneriffe in time for the auction.

'We can't spend more than one thousand pounds,' Annibale told him.

The paperboy nodded, his eyes bright. 'And afterwards you give me the fiver whether you buy them or not?'

'Yes, yes.' Annibale could see the auction was about to start.

He looked around at the other buyers congregating on the footpath. The auctioneer started and as the bidding got going, his pace increased. Even though by now he'd become accustomed to the singsong of the vendors' shouts at the Roma Street markets, to Annibale the auctioneer's words blurred into one another, becoming unintelligible. Occasionally the paperboy raised his hand and Annibale thought he might have caught the word eight. The paperboy raised his hand for the last time. There was a pause in the bidding. No one else raised a hand. Annibale tensed.

'*Sold!*' The auctioneer thwacked a wooden gavel against the contract.

The paperboy turned to Annibale with a grin. 'Nine hundred pounds, cobber.'

Annibale smiled. *A hundred pounds to spare.* He signed the necessary paperwork, then he and the paperboy got the tram back to Ann Street. Outside the shop, Annibale gave the paperboy five pounds, as promised. The young man doffed his hat and ambled down Wharf Street.

That afternoon Annibale noticed that the paperboy hadn't returned to the corner at three o'clock to sell the afternoon papers as he usually did, but then with a rush of customers he was too busy to think much of it.

Late in the evening when the shop was quiet and Annibale was wiping down the shelves behind the counter, getting ready to close up, two policemen came in.

'Your friend Walter Herbert is in jail. You'll need to come and pay two pounds to bail him out.'

Annibale frowned. 'What friend? I don't know any Walter Herbert.'

'He got picked up for being drunk. Says he normally sells newspapers.'

Walter was sober by the time Annibale arrived at the watch-house. He sheepishly told Annibale he'd gone to the pub for the afternoon with the five pounds. Annibale shook his head and paid the two pounds bail.

Early the next morning Walter was back on the corner, selling papers.

Riding the clutch, Annibale manoeuvred his second-hand Chevrolet utility into a spot on Ann Street in front of the shop to unload several cases of fruit and vegetables. He got out, closing the door but leaving both windows wound down, unable to resist casting a quick glance over his recent purchase. It had a timber tray, a single windscreen wiper that operated top-down on the driver's side, and a bonnet like a long nose above a grille bookended with two eye-like headlights.

'I got my driver's licence in Stanthorpe but it had expired,' Annibale later told a customer in the shop. 'When I took it into the police station to get a new one, the police officer wouldn't believe I could drive. I had to take him around the block in Roma Street before he'd renew it for me.'

A young bloke drinking a milkshake at the counter overheard. 'I might try for a licence soon. Might make it easier for work.'

'What do you do?' Annibale asked, nodding to the other customer as he left.

'I'm a signwriter. Been doing it since I left school at thirteen and got an apprenticeship out at Ipswich.' He took a long sip of his milkshake.

There were no other customers just then so Annibale folded his arms and leant on the counter. 'You paint any signs around here?'

'I wish. There's no work about lately. The rent's due. Not sure what I'm going to do. Perhaps join the navy.'

Annibale watched the young man suck on the straw as he drained the last of his drink. 'You could do a job for me,' he suggested. 'My utility truck. You could paint something on the side doors.'

'Fair dinkum?' The young man's face brightened. 'It would get me out of a spot. I'll do a great job, I promise.'

A few weeks later, after the signwriter had left, Annibale and Francesca stood looking at the enormous bouquets of fruit painted on both doors of the ute.

'Geez.' Annibale stood rubbing his chin. 'I wasn't expecting that.'

Francesca tentatively ran her fingertips across the dry paint. 'I think it's nice. Pretty.'

'You're a woman.' Annibale sighed, half-wincing at the florid fruit festooning his ute. 'Oh, well, at least it got him a bit of work to tide him over.'

Some time later at the Roma Street markets, he was buying mandarins from Len, the seller who'd dubbed him 'Joe'. Len seemed unusually withdrawn and Annibale asked him if everything was okay.

'I'm super worried, Joe.' Len shook his head. 'I've been trying to make payments on a ute I bought a while back but the market prices here have been down of late. I can't afford the instalments any more and the vehicle company won't let me get out of the contract. I reckon it's going to be the last straw. I might lose the farm.'

Annibale frowned. 'Can I take a look at it?'

Len left his son in charge and led Annibale over to where his utility truck sat parked. The ute was larger and newer than Annibale's, but it had quite a few payments owing.

'My ute isn't as good as yours,' said Annibale, 'but if you want to swap it with this one we can call it even and I'll take over the payments for you.'

Len looked astounded. 'You'd do that for me?'

Annibale shrugged. 'No trouble. Come and have a look at mine first and see what you think.'

Len took one look at Annibale's ute and stuck out his hand. 'It's a deal.' They shook hands and Len added, 'I really like the bunches of fruit painted on the sides — perfect for my business.'

Annibale couldn't hold back a brief laugh. 'That's great.'

The overhead wires bowed and cracked just before a tram came labouring along on thundering wheels. A small truck filled with white sacks — 'For Hire' in fading paint across its wooden tray — beeped as a fellow on a bicycle lost his hat. He jumped off and scooped it up, ringing the handlebar bell in thanks. Cheekily, as he put his hat back on, he tipped it at a woman in a fur stole waiting to cross the road. She nodded primly and looked around to see if anyone noticed. Vitale made no sign of having seen the incident as he walked up Ann Street in the direction of the shop. Sandstone buildings expelled office workers, late-afternoon sun casting channels of ripening light through the crossroads. His pace slowed while he lit a cigarette and then increased as he tucked the box of matches into his coat pocket. Smoke seared the back of his throat and he walked on, a tobacco-scented trail lingering after him.

During his internment, Vitale had been taken to the Northern Territory where he remained for years, working as part of the Civil Alien Corps on a road gang upgrading and constructing new sections of the Stuart Highway, chiefly between Alice Springs and Darwin. Known as 'The Track', the highway spanned almost eighteen hundred and twenty miles across central Australia. The section between Alice Springs and Larrimah, which was mainly constructed during the war, stretched a distance of more than six hundred and twenty miles through challenging dry and sandy country. Much of the labour was undertaken amid high heat and choking dust, and was made more difficult by almost continuous military traffic using the existing tracks.

Returning to Stanthorpe the month before, Vitale was astonished to hear from Mico and Cesca that Annibale and Francesca had a baby boy and were living in Brisbane. And yet he'd half-expected such news, knowing Annibale's drive. For Vitale, the years of detention and working on the labour gang in the Northern Territory had taken their toll and he wanted to return to Italy. He wrote to Annibale telling him he was going back and received a swift reply. *What do you want to go back for? Come to Brisbane. We must talk.* The words were emphatic, almost embossed into the paper.

Vitale saw Annibale first — he was transferring some oranges from a hanging scale into a paper bag. He watched him go behind the counter to get change for the coin a woman had just given him. She carried the bag of oranges down the steps towards Vitale, turned and continued walking. Vitale was stamping his cigarette out on the footpath when Annibale caught sight of him. Their eyes met. Vitale saw assurance in Annibale, a confidence that had shrugged off youthful stridency. His paternal pride rose, then coloured with a little resentment, perhaps even envy that his son had realised the dream he'd voiced on his first night in Australia.

Vitale went into the shop. 'Hello.' They began an awkward conversation but were interrupted by a customer. When he finished serving, Annibale turned to Vitale. 'We can talk over dinner back at the room. There's a little kitchen there Francesca cooks in. I'll close up here now and drive us back. I've got a ute parked round the side.'

Vitale nodded and lit another cigarette. Annibale, still not a smoker, watched him. Vitale's hat sat low, the brim just above the bushy brows that were now a little wilder and greyer. It was hard to see his father's eyes behind round spectacles smudged with fingerprints and grime. He seemed smaller, a little more bent over. *My father looks old*, Annibale thought.

Francesca dipped a wooden spoon into the large cut-off tin they used to boil pasta on the stove and fished out a strand to taste. She stirred the tomato gravy for good measure, banging the spoon on the side of the pan and telling the men she was about to serve up.

'What's the good of going back to Italy?' Annibale picked up a tall brown glass bottle and poured more beer in a tumbler for Vitale. 'We can make more money here.'

Vitale sighed. 'I found out the fares for your mother and brother would cost almost three hundred and fifty pounds. And that's the cheapest, in a dormitory arrangement.' He stubbed out his cigarette in the saucer Francesca let him use as an ashtray. 'I can't afford it.'

In the same year that Annibale had made almost five hundred pounds in wages and tips at the Astoria, Vitale had received a group certificate from the Allied Works Council in Alice Springs showing his earnings amounted to fifty-four pounds and eleven shillings.

'Listen, we'll pay for everything, the fare for Mamma, for Elia.' Annibale took a slug of beer. 'We've got the shop now, the truck, two houses. We can all live there when we're allowed to move in next year.'

The reassuring smell of pasta and *passata* drifted over as Francesca mixed them together. Vitale sensed his stomach almost tremble with hunger. He'd been living as a single man for most of his life, yet he had a wife, a family.

It was cheery under the electric light in the kitchenette with Francesca bustling about. He glanced over to where Remo stood on stout legs in his makeshift playpen, eyeing his grandfather with dark, beady eyes.

Vitale turned back to Annibale. 'Okay. I will write to Maddalena and Elia and you organise for them to come to Australia.'

Maddalena slowed to look up at the bold white lettering of the ship's name painted on the black hull at the back of the vessel: *Toscana*. It was the first post-war voyage to Australia for both the *Toscana* and the Lloyd Triestino shipping company. The *Toscana*, one of very few Italian ships to have survived the war, had been used as a troop carrier and then a hospital ship, and had undergone a complete refit inside and out before becoming a passenger liner once more. Maddalena gazed up at the black smoke gusting out of the ship's funnel.

'Ma, come on.' Elia, carrying ports in each hand, paused for her to catch up.

She muttered and hastened towards the gangway. If she hadn't been holding a bundle of shawls and other smaller bags she would have made a sign of the cross.

The ship happened to be departing Naples on October 21, Annibale's twenty-fifth birthday. Their *terza-classe* tickets stated they would arrive in Sydney on November 30, 1948 — in about six weeks. As soon as they got on board, Maddelena and Elia, who was now seventeen, were separated, she to the women's dormitory, he to the men's. Maddelena discovered her dormitory in the ship's hold was very basic. Narrow bunks were stacked in fours with only a thin metal railing on one side separating her bed from the stranger in the next one. With no cupboards or drawers, the only place to put belongings was on the concrete floor beneath the bottom bunk, and here large rats roamed, eliciting screams from a number of women when they spotted them.

Up on deck, at first it didn't seem like the ship was moving as the *Toscana* left the dock, but when people realised they were on their way the tears came. As the ship gradually drew away, it became apparrent just how many buildings had been reduced to rubble from the wartime bombings. Such a different sight from the crowded buildings and gaiety of the city Annibale had departed from almost a decade earlier. Maddalena turned her gaze to Vesuvius for some time, and then went along the decks in search of Elia.

A few days later in Port Said, the passengers crowded the decks once more, intrigued by the Egyptian harbour lined with boxy biscuit-coloured buildings and graceful minarets. They did the same in Colombo, marvelling at the number of other ships anchored nearby, the heat, the low buildings and bent palm trees. After that, there was nothing but open water until their next stop at Fremantle.

In the ship's dining room, Elia enjoyed heaping second helpings onto his plate, saying to Maddalena, 'It will be good to have more food in Australia.'

Some of the meat had been rotten before it was frozen for the voyage, making many passengers sick, though Elia and Maddalena were fortunate to avoid it. Several of the crew had also warned passengers that the water on board was too dangerous to drink, instead providing jugs of wine on all the dining tables. Other hot or cold drinks could be purchased at the ship's cafétéria. Numerous passengers went down to the engine room to boil water.

Elia befriended young men his age and disappeared for stretches to play shipboard games or cards. Maddalena sat chatting to other women. Sometimes she stood gripping the railings, the metal initially cold under her hands, and then warmed by them. She stared at the water, her hat pinned tightly to her hair wound up in a bun, the sea wind fluttering the brim but not gaining purchase.

Before she had opened the letter from Vitale, she had known her future was sealed inside that envelope. It was something of a surprise that Annibale had sent the money for their passage. Part of her glimmered with pride. For generations the Boccabella men had been farmers in Fossa; now Annibale had a shop in a city on the other side of the world. He was a shopkeeper, like her father had been.

During those solitary moments staring into the sea, Maddalena allowed herself to think back over their last weeks in Fossa. She'd sold the animals she'd managed to purchase with money Annibale had sent to her previously, but not the furniture. Offering the house to another family from the village to live in, Maddalena had waved away any talk of rent.

'Just look after the house,' she'd told them. 'That's enough. If it's vacant it will end up crumbling like some of the empty places down on Via Roma.'

She thought it best to keep the house liveable should they need to come back to it one day.

Following the last Mass Maddalena attended, Don Angelo came up to her as she stood about chatting with her friends outside the church. 'I wish you well, Signora Boccabella, and that you have a safe journey.'

Maddalena had inclined her head, the lace mantilla she wore for church sliding forward, slightly obscuring her face and the look in her eyes. Don Angelo still lived in the house of Vitale's aunt. Like Annibale, Elia had turned away from religion, but Maddalena felt God was not to blame for one priest.

Before they left, Maddalena and Elia walked across the valley one last time to Poggio Picenze to visit her parents' graves and farewell the rest of her relatives there … *But I do not want to think of that.* She fished in her pocket for a handkerchief. *Better to think of seeing Vitale and Annibale again. And my grandchild.* She knew she would never return.

Standing on the Sydney docks surrounded by the noisy, waving crowd, Vitale's face held such joyful anticipation that Francesca felt a gust of affection for him. Vitale was quieter than Annibale, not so driven, but always his own boss. He didn't live with them, preferring to rent a separate room in the boarding house. He'd got work at a sawmill by the Brisbane River.

Vitale hoisted Remo up into his arms. 'Can you see the big ship, *piccolo*?'

'Yes, Nonno! Can we get on it?'

'No, no, everyone's getting off. Soon you'll see your nonna and Zio Elia. Elia was younger than you when I left. He'll be all grown up now.'

The *Toscana* had docked almost a week late, heightening the anticipation. Francesca squinted up at the ship. Standing in full sun in the December heat, breathing wafts of ship fumes and brine, was making her woozy. She dabbed her brow beneath her hat and reached to tuck in part of Remo's shirt that had worked free. Meeting her mother-in-law for the first time, she wanted them to look their best. Vitale kept his eyes on the gangway. The passengers coming ashore all wore hats and dark clothes; it was hard to tell who was whom.

'Can you see them?' Francesca was fighting to hold her ground as the exuberant horde surged forward, taking them with it.

Vitale strained to see. 'Not yet ...'

Shouts of recognition rang around the dock as happy reunions began.

'It can't be ...' Vitale stared harder. 'I think I see them. *Dio!* Elia is a man. And there's Maddalena. Over here! Maddalena! *Vieni qua!*' He waved wildly, Remo slipping from his other arm, Francesca grabbing him and keeping hold of her son's little hand.

Hearing his shout, Maddalena looked over. Vitale looked so stooped and tanned. It was almost seventeen years since she'd last seen him. She was shocked to see the hair sticking out from under his hat was a blend of white and grey. Her gaze moved to a smiling, plump young woman with brown eyes, before resting on a cheeky-looking little boy, whom she could scarcely believe was her grandson. A whimper escaped her lips as Vitale held her.

Maddalena hastily wiped away tears and glanced around. 'Where's Annibale?'

'He had to stay in Brisbane to run the shop.' Vitale patted his pockets for his matches.

Maddalena kissed Francesca's cheeks, then lovingly pinched Remo's cheeks until he looked set to cry. Elia stood watching. Francesca noticed he was different from Annibale. Elia's eyes were blue, his eyebrows low, and when he lifted his hat he revealed a head of thick, wavy dark hair that sat high on his head, quite a contrast to Annibale's premature balding. And yet he had the same cleft in his chin as Annibale, the dimple Francesca knew her own son had also been born with.

Maddalena glanced at Vitale and turned to Elia. 'Well, here's your father.'

Francesca sensed the awkwardness between the two men. She had been eight when she'd seen her father for the first time since babyhood and Elia was almost ten years older than that. She returned her attention to her mother-in-law. Maddalena had intelligent eyes and the same strong jawline as her sons. She was slightly shorter even than Francesca, yet strength radiated from her. And Francesca knew, with the family reuniting, its dynamics were set to change.

As they walked along the dock with their backs to the ship, Francesca heard Elia say to Maddalena, 'Isn't it strange here, Ma? It feels so strange.'

Annibale closed the shop to be at the train station when Maddalena and Elia arrived in Brisbane. He could feel his chest tightening and swelling as he spied the engine with its big grille in the distance, his eyes never leaving it as it decelerated into the station, billowing steam and the smell of coal. Carriage doors were flung open. Passengers began climbing down and passing out luggage. Annibale swivelled back and forth, craning to see, frustrated with the engine steam blurring faces in the distance. Then he saw his father helping his mother off the train. Annibale's eyes filled with tears and he stumbled towards them. He drew up to Maddalena. She looked past him, scanning the platform.

'Mamma, it's me.'

Maddalena jumped with the shock. Annibale had been a boy of fifteen when she'd last seen him, now he was twenty-five.

'Oh, *oh*.' Barely able to speak, she clutched him to her.

When they eventually parted, Maddalena's gaze stayed on Annibale's face, wanting to drink it in, almost hoping it could somehow impart all he had experienced over the decade they'd been separated.

Instead, she blurted out, 'Your hair is thinning.'

And Annibale laughed.

Annibale sought Maddalena's approval in a way he'd never needed to with Vitale. In the shop he hovered as she inspected the fruit displays, the long refrigerated milk bar and the glass-fronted cabinets of chocolates and cigarettes. Vitale lighting up a cigarette distracted her. He'd never smoked in Italy — they couldn't have afforded it — yet now he seemed unable to be without his unfiltered Temple Bar cigarettes. Maddalena squinted at a row of pineapples, never having seen the fruit before. Annibale's smile began to slip; he'd hoped for more from his mother than silent scrutiny.

'I want to go up north and cut cane,' said Elia. 'You said there's good money in it.'

'It's only for six months of the year and you've missed this season, but you can go up in June.' Annibale half-turned to address Elia, though he kept watching his mother. 'Last year the cannery opened. They're always looking for people. I can take you out there.'

Maddalena swung around from the pineapples, suddenly realising that just as she was regaining her eldest son, she was about to lose Elia. For the past decade it had been she and Elia alone and she felt the impending separation in the pit of her stomach. But she hid it with a distracted nod and pointed at the pineapples. 'Annibale, you're not meant to eat these, are you?'

Elia began at the cannery in Brisbane but soon left to work on a banana farm near the south coast at Coomera. Then he headed up to cut cane around Ingham, Innisfail and Gordonvale, alternating the seasons between farm work and labouring jobs. It would be seven years before he'd return to Brisbane. Occasionally he wrote letters, sending some money towards repaying Annibale and Francesca for his passage from Italy.

In twenty-six years of marriage, Maddalena and Vitale had spent only about three years in the same country. Now both in their fifties they were thrown together once more, very different people to the ones who had said goodbye to each other in their thirties. Much had happened to change them in the years they'd been forced apart, their intimacy set adrift. Maddalena discovered she'd come to prefer sleeping alone and it took some time for her to adjust to Vitale's snoring and scent of tobacco. And yet for all the strangeness of her new situation, she felt a safeness in their being reunited.

Vitale continued working at the sawmill Brown and Broad, by the river in Teneriffe, not far from the two houses Annibale and Francesca had bought. Each evening at knock-off time, Vitale went to the Waterloo Hotel for two beers with a mate before making his way back to the boarding house at Spring Hill. Maddalena noticed that as well as smoking Vitale had a taste for beer. It reminded her of Demetrio's penchant for wine.

Sitting down to dinner, she said, 'What is this "beer" you drink? It is like *vino*, no?'

'Try it, Ma.' Annibale poured her a half-glass to taste.

She took a sip and screwed up her face, so he topped it up with lemonade and she took another mouthful. 'That's quite good, actually. Especially in this heat.'

'It's called a shandy.' Annibale smiled.

In Italy, Maddalena had had her own house and almost complete control of her affairs and finances; now she had a room in a boarding house that didn't even provide her a kitchen.

'Ma, why don't you do the cooking in our kitchenette and look after Remo, and then Francesca and I can both work in the shop all the time,' Annibale suggested.

Francesca looked up in surprise. She'd been hoping to have more babies and to stay home with Remo.

Maddalena nodded with a shrug. '*Va bene.*'

'Everything works out perfect,' Annibale said to Francesca after they went to bed. 'It will be good to have us both at the shop. It's getting so busy. And Remo will be fine with Ma. Lucky he can understand Italian and English.'

'Yes.' Francesca wanted to object, but she didn't. Instead, she would write to her mother, knowing Cesca would write back something soothing. But she lay awake for a long time after Annibale started to snore. A tear trickled down her temple into her hair.

In the morning, Maddalena knocked on the door at six and came in to cook breakfast. Francesca showed her where everything was, trying to impart her way of doing things, but Maddalena was only half-listening, already working out her own ways. They all crowded around the small wooden table and ate a family breakfast together. Annibale gazed at the bent heads and couldn't have felt happier.

Stonehenge Boarding House

> **FRANCESCA:** *I didn't have to take Remo up and down to the shop all the time once my mother-in-law used to mind him. But it took him a while to get used to his nonna, because he was three when she came out here, almost three, and she was like a stranger, you see. Remo wanted to come with me all the time. He cried and cried, and then he was all right and he loved his 'Nunna' like a mother, too.*

As Nanna Francesca tells me this she seems so pragmatic, and yet her eyelashes are wet.

> **FRANCESCA:** *Where we lived, at the boarding house called Stonehenge, there were three flats, one for us, one where two older ladies lived, and one other. The rest were serviced rooms upstairs. Some Italians from North Queensland used to come to Brisbane to see specialists and would ring up and say, 'Save us a room.' Others would stay there when they first got off the boat from Italy. There was a seat in the front yard, a very big bench one, and when Italian ladies came to stay they sometimes sat there, and my mother-in-law would talk to those Italian ladies that came, cause she had trouble learning English. Sometimes she sat on that bench for hours watching for Italian ladies to come by so she could talk to them. She'd just sit and watch people walking by in the street.*

The Granny Maddalena I knew was a lively, bold, strong person, not fazed by much, even if she always made a sign of the cross whenever she saw lightning. My father fondly remembers making gnocchi with her after school. By the time he got home she'd already have the potatoes boiled in readiness. Other times they'd sit at the table sorting through dried lentils together to remove the tiny pebbles that could damage a tooth. At sixty, she climbed a huge camphor laurel tree to help guide him down when he got stuck as a little boy. If someone stepped over a child lying on the floor Granny would cry out in her local dialect, *'Raccavallala!'* — Climb back over it! — otherwise you'd stunt the child's growth.

Yet her sitting on that garden bench, waiting, hoping to talk to someone she could understand reveals something of what coming to Australia must have wrought on her life. Granny Maddalena was fifty-five when she had to adjust to living in a boarding house in Brisbane after spending her entire life in two tiny towns not so far apart in Abruzzo. Despite the hardship she left in Italy, she most likely missed the communality of village life, the banter, local festivals, even people coming to her with their ailments. As far as I am aware, she rarely if ever practised her healing skills once she left Italy — the gift, passed down from mother to daughter over centuries, lost, and along with it her ability to communicate freely. She must have felt displaced. In the late 1940s her only option was to adjust as best she could.

I've heard some migrants say that when they first came to Australia with no understanding of English it seemed everyone around them was talking, yet they were surrounded by silence. Maddalena went on to live for thirty-three years in Australia with little English. In spite of this, she managed to communicate with shopkeepers and conduct her life within the community, rather than becoming isolated. She also had family and friends to speak to in Italian and to translate for her. Hopefully she didn't always feel surrounded by silence.

While I wish I could go back to the boarding house at 157 Leichhardt Street, Spring Hill, and sit in the garden where Granny Maddalena sat, of course it is gone. It bore the name of the English monument Stonehenge, which has survived since prehistoric times, but two concrete buildings now straddle the place where the boarding house once stood. An old photograph of it reveals a beautiful gabled house, with steep chalet-style roofs and walls of stone quarried by convicts.

I locate two newspaper articles about it, the first written in the 1930s, a little over a decade before my grandparents moved in, and the other in the 1950s, just a few years after they'd left. Both mention the colonial past of the property. Decades on, no one reading them could know of the many different Italian migrants who stayed or started their new lives in Australia there. Or that a small woman, who was once the village witch, lived there and sat in the leafy garden, hoping to converse in a centuries-old dialect from the other side of the world —

an Italian,
by a Colonial house,
built on Yuggera land.

'BRISBANE'S HISTORIC HOMES'
by F.E. Lord

At first glance, if the chimneys have not first caught one's eye, one might mistake this old gable-roofed house of stone for a church. And its likeness to a sacred edifice is further brought to mind when one enters the garden gate and the gable-roofed entrance porch, almost screened from the view of passers-by in St. George's Terrace [Leichhardt Street] by the wealth of foliage in the garden ...

The house was built about the year 1859, by [a] mason in his spare time and single-handed. He was living nearby at the time, and I daresay he obtained the stone for his home from the now disused quarries less than half a mile distant ...

Stonehenge [is] quite devoid of any species of verandah ... It is a very cool old dwelling nevertheless, and possesses a number of windows, both upstairs and down, some of them long and all deep set in the stone walls. Those downstairs are low to the ground, and, of course, open directly into the garden, and the present-day lane running between the house and the next building on that side occupied by Alexanders Ltd.

The path, paved in brick and stone, and in keeping with the old house, brings one crossways from the gate, and through the garden, with its green recesses and rustic bench ... the front door, with its coloured-glass sides … the windows of which command a fine view of the city and the enclosing hills beyond …

It is being conducted today as a boarding establishment … yet we [see] in old Stonehenge … associations with our own old horse-coach days, as well as those 'scenes far distant' to which its old stone walls and its gabled roof — once of slate, and now of iron — 'point the way'.

Excerpt published in the Queenslander, 1931.

'IT'S NOT SO HIDEOUS'
by Keith Dunstan

For my money the loveliest of them all is [Stonehenge], crammed between a car park and a dry cleaners at 157 Leichhardt Street. The walls are a rich yellow and feet thick. Nobody knows how long it has been there. The owner, Mr ——— believes that it was built by the convicts and perhaps it is 90 years old. Let us hope that the old place stays there forever. These concrete mixers are getting nearer and nearer.

The old buildings, with their thick walls, their balconies and their porphyry stone foundations, are coming down, one by one. The big bricks, with their lovely yellowy-red tones, are being whisked off and used as paving stones in gardens for the nice houses out at St. Lucia.

Excerpt published in the Courier-Mail, 1956.

Moroccan Beans

Maddalena was washing up when the sound of women's voices speaking Italian drifted through the open window near the kitchenette. Sudsy hands dripping, she stuck her head out to see several boarders sitting in the shade on the bench seat in the front yard. She dried her hands, patted her hair and, leaving the rest of the dishes in the cooling water in the sink, rushed down with Remo in tow to join the conversation.

'Oh, what a smell, what a smell!' Mrs Simpson, the boarding-house owner, came out the front entrance about a quarter of an hour later, waving her hand back and forth in front of her face. 'Is that you, Mrs Boccabella? You got something cooking?'

Maddalena couldn't understand her but suddenly realised and leapt off the bench, leaving Remo playing on the grass in front of the other women. She hurried up to Francesca and Annibale's room where she'd left her Moroccan beans cooking on the stove. The water had boiled dry and the beans were blackened and smoking in the bottom of the pot. She poured water into the pot and hid it under Annibale and Francesca's bed, then dashed back out onto the landing.

'Signora Simpson, come and see, there's nothing cooking, the stove is shut.'

To Mrs Simpson, Maddalena's frenzied Italian was incomprehensible and seemed a little mad. She kept a lookout for Francesca returning from the milk bar and had a word with her instead.

Maddalena remained on the garden bench, outwardly immersed in conversation, while Francesca took Remo back to their room to look in the kitchenette. Nothing was cooking; the dishwater was cold in the sink, a final few soapy bubbles evaporating. But Francesca's nostrils twitched, picking up a fading acrid scent. She searched around the room, finally getting down on her hands and knees — much to Remo's delight — to look under the bed.

'*Mamma mia.*' She pulled the pot towards her and saw the crusty darkened mass of fava beans.

'*Mamma mia!*' Remo mimicked.

Later, when Maddalena came in to cook dinner, Francesca showed her the pot, saying in Italian, 'Don't cook Moroccan beans unless you stay in the room to watch them.'

Maddalena grabbed the pot and dumped it in the sink with a clang. 'Right. I'll never cook them again.'

'Has a rat been at this?' A woman held up an apple to Annibale, but she was smiling.

Annibale saw the tiny bite out of the apple, the teeth marks he knew were Remo's. 'Sorry, my son is here in the shop with me this morning.'

She laughed. 'That's fine. I'll have a half-dozen Jonathans … without the bites.'

Annibale smiled, putting his hand inside an empty paper bag to open it. He picked up another apple, saw it also had a bite out of it and inwardly cursed. There were tiny bites out of almost a whole row of apples arranged at Remo's height. After he finished serving, Annibale hastily removed them from the display. He turned around to reprimand Remo and saw he'd wandered out to the footpath, had found a small hole at just the right height in one of the cast-iron posts holding up the shop awning and was peeing into it.

'Geez, he's a devil that one,' Annibale muttered, though he was trying not to laugh.

He took Remo out the back of the shop to the landing where they kept crates of soft drinks and told him to go down and play in the courtyard. Hearing a customer come in, Annibale hurried back, hoping Maddalena would swiftly recover from the flu and Francesca return from the bank.

He saw it was Mrs Delaney, who ran a boarding house on the other side of Wharf Street. 'You got any of those freestone peaches?' She wore her hat low to try to conceal her over-plucked eyebrows. 'And I need a half-dozen Golden Delicious too.'

Annibale nodded and turned away to get them. In the large mirror hanging behind the counter, he saw her glance at his back before taking several oranges and putting them into her carry bag. Annibale said nothing. Mrs Delaney was a regular customer and he didn't want her to dissuade the twenty boarders she housed from coming into his shop. Instead, he added a couple of pennies onto the cost of the fruit she bought. *Let her think she's pinching what she likes.* Mrs Delaney wished him a good day with a slightly smug smile. Annibale smiled back and turned to the next customer walking in.

'A chocolate milkshake, thanks, Joe.'

Between customers, Annibale went out the back to find Remo taking the tops off Coca-Cola bottles. '*Cripes*.' He swooped in and grabbed the bottle opener.

'They make a great sound when they open, Dad.'

When Francesca got back from the bank to take over in the shop, Annibale took Remo to the boarding house to have a rest. He unlaced his own shoes and, with his socks still on, stretched out on the bed. Remo tried to clamber onto his chest.

'Show me how you can close your eyes like Papà,' said Annibale. 'See who can sleep the longest.'

Remo scrunched his eyes shut, smiling.

'Close them properly, not like that.'

'Mr Boccabella! *Mr Boccabella!*'

At first Annibale wasn't sure if he was dreaming, but the banging continued on the door, jerking him into wakefulness.

'Mr Boccabella!' Mrs Simpson was almost screeching. 'It's your son!'

Still groggy with sleep, Annibale looked over to the other side of the bed. It was empty. He jumped up and almost slid across the linoleum floor in his socks to open the door. 'Where's Remo?'

'He's on the roof.'

'*What?*' The building was two storeys high, the roof very steeply pitched.

'The electrician was doing some work. Your boy must have gone up his ladder.'

Annibale hurriedly put on his shoes and ran around to the side of the boarding house. He looked up at the wooden extension ladder in wonder, and then swore under his breath. Remo was not quite three and a half. Almost missing one of the rungs, he rushed up the ladder to find Remo sitting calmly in the middle of the steep-pitched roof.

'Hi, Dad.'

'Remo, carefully now, come here to me.'

Remo shrugged and clambered over.

Annibale was by himself when he returned from the shop the following week to a commotion of boarders and passers-by gathered in the side yard of Stonehenge. Smoke reached his nostrils. It seemed to be coming from the wood yard next door, where workers chopped timber and put it into bags to sell as firewood for boilers for people to wash their clothes. Annibale realised with sudden alarm he could hear Maddalena shrieking in Italian. *What the bloody hell?* He pushed through the small crowd.

'What's happening? Ma?'

Maddalena was chastising Remo as she held him by the wrist.

Mrs Simpson, the boarding-house owner, strode over. 'That son of yours set the wood heap on fire.'

Annibale turned to Maddalena. 'Weren't you watching him?' he asked in Italian, glad most of the onlookers couldn't understand.

'Who's going to pay for a new wood heap, that's what I'd like to know.' Mrs Simpson put her hands on her hips. 'And he's pulled up all my new plants.'

'I'll pay for it all,' Annibale told her.

'Could've burnt the whole place down,' she went on.

'Look! *Fire!*' someone yelled in the front yard.

They all ran around to see smoke escaping from the window of Annibale and Francesca's room.

'*Remo!*'

'It wasn't me, Dad.'

Maddalena let out a shriek. 'My Moroccan beans!'

Francesca was thrilled when they all moved into the house on Wyandra Street in Teneriffe. It had linoleum and bare wooden floors, fretwork above the three bedroom doors, their own copper out the back and lattice on the front verandah. She and Annibale took the main bedroom, Remo the other front room, and Maddalena and Vitale one further down the hall from Remo. Francesca went into town and paid fifty pounds and ten shillings in cash for her own Singer treadle sewing-machine. Annibale collected it on the back of the utility truck and carried it up into the house. After returning from the shop at night, Francesca set to sewing new curtains for the windows and slips for the cane-lounge cushions.

There was cold running water plumbed to the house. For hot water to wash the dishes, Maddalena and Francesca boiled water on the stove. In the bathroom underneath the house they heated water for the bath in a gas-fuelled water-heater that perched on a wooden shelf just above the tub, dubbing it 'the Geyser', the gas piped to it from the enormous gasworks down the river end of their street. Before filling the tub, they would fire up the water-heater by lighting a small flame, then turning a lever to ignite the gas-ring to heat the water inside. The backyard copper was not connected to the gas, though, and still required a wood fire underneath it to heat. After boiling and wringing the clothes, sheets and towels, Maddalena would tuck several ears of corn, protected by their husks, into the dying embers and they would all enjoy roasted corn on the cob.

Once he learnt that the tenant in the house out the back was a widow with three sons, Annibale let her stay, despite her paying only five shillings rent a week. Ongoing rent restrictions under the Fair Rents law, dating from the Depression and war years, made it difficult to raise rents anyway. Next door, at number sixteen, lived another Italian family. When number eighteen on the other side of them came up for sale, Annibale and Vitale, who'd saved some money of his own, together bought it and the house at its rear, renting out both.

Vitale could now easily walk to work at the sawmill, and when the knock-off bell sounded, to the Waterloo Hotel. He wasn't expected home for dinner until he and his Australian mate from the mill each drank two pots of Bulimba beer in reciprocal shouts. After dinner, Vitale sat at the dining table reading the newspaper and smoking as Remo played underneath in a cubby constructed with a sheet stretched from the table to a nearby cane lounge chair. They could never sit down all together for a family dinner, with Francesca and Annibale's overlapping shifts at the shop.

Maddalena asked Annibale to buy some garden tools and together they set about putting in two vegetable patches. With offcuts of timber left under the house, they constructed a chook pen. And along one side of the house, Annibale built a structure of wooden beams and posts strung with wire, on which he trained vines of muscatel table grapes for everyone to eat. By the end of summer, tight bunches of violet grapes hung among the leafy vines, protected by sweeping netting.

After so long in the boarding house, they revelled in having more space, especially Remo. Maddalena lost sight of him within the first fortnight. She rushed around the house, slippers flapping across the hard floors.

'Remo! *Vieni qua!* Remo?'

She leant against the kitchen dresser, starting to get worried. Then the sound of giggling came from a big, empty, cardboard box in the corner. Smiling to herself, she stepped out of her slippers, crept over in stockinged feet and lifted the lid. Remo squealed with delight and jumped up.

'Come on, I need your help to pick some parsley for the *frittata*.' She ruffled his hair.

The house was about to get much more crowded, though. When Francesca's cousins from Palmi wrote to say they were coming out to live in Australia, she wrote back offering them a room until they could set themselves up. She then wrote to her mother to say the cousins were coming and, knowing both her parents couldn't leave the farm at that time of year, she asked if Cesca could come down on the bus to visit when the newcomers arrived — that way she could see the new house, too. Annibale quickly closed in half of the front verandah to create a sleep-out, and when the cousins came to stay Remo moved into it, giving up his bedroom for almost a year.

With the war over, more and more Italians were coming to Australia, reuniting with family or emigrating in response to Australian government advertisements in Italy encouraging them to come to a 'land of plenty'. Prime Minister Ben Chifley, recognising Australia urgently needed a larger population for continued development and defence, established the first Federal Department of Immigration. With Arthur Calwell as minister touting the slogan 'Populate or Perish', increased immigration and a 'baby boom' ensued. At the time, the International Refugee Organisation was sponsoring more than 182,000 people to migrate to Australia from Europe. This number of refugees, arriving over less than a decade, exceeded the total number of convicts transported to Australia during the entire first eighty years of European settlement.

Annibale and Francesca went along to hear Calwell speak at Brisbane City Hall, taking Remo with them. The event was held in the huge main auditorium and all the seats were full, people standing around the back and sides of the room. Calwell happened to be sitting near Francesca and Annibale down the front, and before getting up to make his speech asked them if he could borrow their son for a moment. When he stood up, Calwell held Remo up to the crowd and announced: 'This is the kind of migrant we want!' Annibale and Francesca exchanged astonished looks.

This occured despite both Chifley and Calwell having declared a preference for British settlers, setting an impossible goal of nine British migrants out of every ten entering the country. In reality, southern Europeans rapidly outnumbered Britons. Annibale sponsored dozens of people emigrating from Italy, inviting them to stay in the family home when they arrived. Dalgety's Wharf, where numerous Italian ships came in, was just down the road and around the corner from Annibale and Francesca's house, and many Italian migrants walked off the boat and straight to their door.

Annibale contacted Serafino, who'd helped with the outfitting of the shop, and asked him to carry out some building work underneath the house, leaving the existing laundry, bathroom and toilet as they were, and dividing the rest of the area into two rooms, one larger than the other. The bigger area was for entertaining and storage, and was where they would make the tomato sauce each year. It was a cool, shadowy spot where Remo liked to play, building structures with empty wooden fruit boxes and creating walkways for the two stray ginger cats who'd become part of the family. Annibale bought some single beds and bunk beds for the other room and it became a dormitory lodging for many Italians over the years, mostly young men, during their first months in Brisbane, a place to stay until they found their feet.

An Unlikely Racketeer

On the way to Queen Street, Francesca passed a bakery with several cakes displayed among plastic flowers on shelves in the window. A sponge cake with pale-pink icing caught her eye, perfect for supper at home that evening. She quite liked the buttery English-style cakes and decided she would come back and purchase it after she'd done the banking and been to Barry and Roberts department store to buy a cardigan and socks. It was a bright day, the kind that made her steps light. In the bank she joined the queue, taking out the bank books to have them ready for the teller. Still thinking of the cake, Francesca was oblivious to the young clerk catching sight of her and moving over to his supervisor.

Having done the banking, Francesca turned to leave the counter when the supervisor and the bank manager, accompanied by two policemen, loomed in her path.

The bank manager indicated his office. 'Mrs Boccabella, this way please.'

Other customers waiting in line stared. Anxious and clutching her bag, Francesca walked to the manager's office surrounded by the group of men who towered head and shoulders above her.

The bank manager cleared his throat. 'Mrs Boccabella, please sit down.'

She perched on the edge of the chair, holding her purse on her knees in front of her chest, casting timid looks up at the others who remained standing.

'The bank has been watching you for some time. Over a dozen different bank books all in different names, hundreds of pounds going every which way—'

'But I've been—'

A police officer held up his hand. 'Save it for the police station. You're being arrested for racketeering.'

The afternoon sun began to eat into shade from the awning over the footpath. Annibale went out to check the Central Station clock and was surprised to see it was getting close to three. Francesca had never failed to turn up for her shift at the shop and he thought back to late that morning when he'd last seen her.

'I'm going to the bank,' Francesca had told him, tucking a dozen bank books rubber-banded with money and her list of deposits into her purse. 'And Remo needs a new cardigan and I'll get some socks for you. I'll be back by two.'

'*Va bene*. Oh, Guido came in earlier — he and his wife found a house to rent. I say we take them a couple of those nice watermelons and some other food and drink to help them settle in.'

Francesca had nodded. 'I'll make some biscuits.' She caught his playful look and waved him away. 'Go on, get away with you.' She'd been smiling.

Glancing again at the clock, he was starting to feel uneasy when Maddalena turned up tugging Remo by the hand.

'Ma, what are you doing here? What's happened?'

'Two policemen came to the house but I couldn't understand what they were saying.' She handed him a piece of paper. 'They wrote this down.'

Annibale gave a start. 'Francesca is at the police station.' Straightaway, he began closing up the shop. 'Take Remo back home.'

He hurried to the station to find two police officers with Francesca, who was wringing her hands. The way she looked at Annibale unleashed a surge of protectiveness in him.

'I'm her husband, Annibale Boccabella. What's all this about?'

It had begun when two young men in dark clothes came into the shop. Wide-eyed and hesitant, they looked at Francesca. She looked at them. The shop was empty of other people. She'd been tidying the boxes of chocolates and hurried to swallow a mouthful of Cadbury squares. Suspecting the men might be from Italy, she asked in Italian if she could help them. The men broke into smiles with joyful relief. Both burst into Italian at once, finishing each other's sentences. They were delighted to discover Francesca could read and write English and asked if she would assist them in getting bank accounts set up and to deposit their wages for them.

'Of course, but you have to come back when my husband is here to mind the shop. So you both have some work?'

Word had spread among many Italian migrants arriving in Brisbane, to head to Annibale and Francesca's shop for help in getting set up in a job. Francesca took people along to the bank to help them open an account and approached businesses that she knew took on migrants for jobs like dishwashing, making deliveries and factory work. Some Australians continued to view Italians as the enemy, despite several years having passed since the end of the war, and they refused to hire them no matter how hard, or cheaply, the migrants worked. Annibale also found vacancies where he could through Italian friends who'd been in Australia for years, now established with their own businesses, often as builders, plumbers or electricians. The war had drawn a line between those who'd migrated before the conflict, and those after.

'Thank you so much for doing this for me,' a woman named Luisa said to Francesca as they sat on a tram hurtling along a flat stretch towards the Golden Circle cannery.

Francesca shook her head. 'No trouble. You already have a bit of English. We'll set you up in a job here, no trouble.'

Most stepped off the boat with little or no English, and did not have the luxury of time or circumstance to learn much before they needed a wage to support themselves.

'It's easy for the children, they learn English at school, but for me … no good,' Stefania, the wife of Annibale's friend Lino explained to Francesca when she and Annibale took a box of fruit, some bottles of their homemade *passata* and other food out to their rented house in Mitchelton. A housewife mostly at home in an outer suburb, Stefania hardly saw anyone and relied on her children to translate at the shops or the doctor's surgery. 'Lino knows more English, from being at work,' she added, 'but he is not at home much. He's always working; he has to, so we can buy our own house one day.'

Francesca nodded. 'It's easier for children. I came here when I was eight and picked up English at school, though it was hard to begin with.'

'I was going to do one of those English courses but we can't afford it.'

After the police checked everything and found that Francesca had been helping new migrants too shy, daunted or embarrassed by their broken English to venture into the bank to deposit savings from their earnings, they praised her. And the bank teller who'd suspected her apologised.

Francesca had nodded. 'I suppose it did look a little suspicious.'

Outside, Annibale muttered and shook his head but Francesca was already looking about to see where he'd parked the ute. By then the day was almost over, and though the sky still held a brightness, the cake shop she had passed on her way to the bank that morning had shut, the shelves in the window empty except for some yellowed plastic roses.

The Anzac Day public holiday was busy for the milk bar. Anzac Square was a little further along the same street and people sought drinks after standing in the sun at the war memorial. Annibale and Francesca opened early to cater to those who attended the dawn service, and they remained on the go throughout the rest of the day, especially before and after the Anzac Day parade.

Maddalena had stayed home while the rest of the family worked at the shop. She was taking advantage of the fine weather after a bout of rain to wash all the bedding, a task that took most of the day. It was unseasonably warm for late April, and Annibale and Francesca remained busy serving while Vitale sorted the soft-drink bottles out the back, bringing in more to restock the fridge as customers came in for cold drinks and milkshakes.

Shops and milk bars could only sell a certain amount of bottled soft drink due to soft-drink companies requiring the return of the empty glass bottles before replacing them with the equivalent number of full bottles. However, Annibale had a constant supply, due to a man who came in by chance one evening to buy a carton of cigarettes.

'I'm sorry, but I can't sell you a carton,' Annibale had told him. Cigarettes were still rationed and shops were restricted to a quota for seven years after the war. 'I might run out of packs for my regulars.'

The man had taken off his hat and stroked its rim, considering this. 'What about your empty bottles? Mate, I'm a bottle merchant. I can give you an unending supply of bottles for the soft-drink companies if you pay me a tuppence or penny depending on the type and sell me a carton of cigarettes a week.'

From then on they sold a lot of soft drinks, particularly on Friday and Saturday nights and public holidays, knowing they could easily get more. Taxis would pull up outside with partygoers stocking up because they knew there were always plenty of drinks at 'Joe's'.

That Anzac Day, the cold drinks were selling so fast Vitale was stacking bottles of Coca-Cola around the canisters of orange drink, milk and ice cream in the refrigerated milk-bar unit to get them cold before transferring them into the rapidly emptying glass-fronted fridge. The milk bar whirred, emanating heat. Sleeves rolled up and a half-smoked cigarette at the corner of his lips, Vitale gathered armfuls of empties left on the counter by customers and carried them out the back to sort into wooden crates labelled Coca-Cola, Tristram's, Helidon, Pepsi Cola, Cottee's and Kirks.

Catching sight of Remo playing with his toy cars on the cement reassured Vitale that the boy was fine, and he continued on his way, retrieving some bottles of sarsaparilla and lemonade from the full crates on the landing near the back steps and carrying them inside. When he returned he couldn't see Remo, but assumed he was safe in the locked courtyard and hurried back into the shop carrying more bottles. It was humid and the air was close with all the people crammed around the milk bar. Annibale worked fast, producing several dripping bottles of cold soft drink in his large hands and adeptly issuing change. Francesca had milkshakes churning on both electric mixers, while scooping ice cream and ladling milk into other containers and lining them up ready for the flavourings each customer wanted.

She spared Vitale a quick glance. 'Remo all right?'

'Yes, but I'll go and check.'

Vitale gripped the railing and swung down the short flight of back steps to the courtyard area. He came around the corner to see Remo lying on the cement and broke into a run. Remo's dark eyes were trained on him anxiously as he knelt down.

'What's happened to you?' Vitale's bushy brows crumpled in concern.

Remo grunted and shook his head, looking stiff and uncomfortable, his arms straight along his sides. Vitale turned, spying more than a dozen empty cups of ice cream and their discarded wooden-stick spoons, already attracting ants over in the corner.

'Madonna mia!'

At the children's hospital, a Doctor Clarke informed them that Remo's stomach had frozen. They were gently heating it under a steam tent and wanted to keep him overnight for observation.

'He'll be all right,' Doctor Clarke assured them, trying not to smile. 'But he ate a lot of ice cream very quickly for a small tummy.'

'We run a shop and milk bar,' Annibale told him by way of explanation. 'And being so busy with Anzac Day and all … Well, it was more than the usual tub.'

'*Fourteen* tubs.' Vitale's murmur emitted a drift of cigarette smoke.

Maddalena, who'd left the washing boiling in the copper as soon as she heard and caught a tram to meet them at the hospital, gave a tight nod. 'Little greedy.'

'Can we see Remo now?' Francesca was teary.

'Yes, end of the hall and to the right. The nurse will take you in.'

As they turned to walk away, another doctor was coming along the hall and Annibale heard him ask Doctor Clarke if he'd been 'dealing with those dagos'.

'I think you'll find Calwell wants us to call them "New Australians" now.' Doctor Clarke's tone was dry.

'Oh, that's right,' the other doctor laughed, missing his meaning and using the term disparagingly. '*New Australians.*' He shook his head and kept walking.

Annibale looked back to watch him go.

A Peters delivery man came up the steps carrying two metal canisters of vanilla ice cream, each protected by a layer of waxed paper. 'Two today, eh, Joe?'

Annibale smiled and paid him from the till. 'I'm making chocolate coated ice-cream blocks.'

The delivery man smacked his lips. 'Whacko, I'll be back later.'

A friend, Fulvio, had popped in for an orange drink while taking a break from a tiling job he was doing at the Greek's hotel nearby. 'I've just bought a rundown house at Bowen Hills,' he said, watching Annibale slot the canisters into the freezer section of the milk bar. 'You always get your ice cream from Peters?'

Annibale got out a stainless-steel syringe-like implement. 'Peters, Pauls, both.' He shrugged, plunging the implement into the vanilla ice cream to extract perfect individual serves.

'Anyway, this place at Bowen Hills,' Fulvio continued as Annibale hurriedly wedged sticks into each pat of ice cream before they began to melt, 'I'm going to do it up and convert it into flats.'

Annibale, picking up several pats of ice cream by the sticks and dunking them into a container of runny chocolate syrup that set quickly, looked up at him, intrigued.

Fulvio nodded. 'Business is good, why not expand into property? Might retire sooner.' They both laughed. 'I better get back. How much for the drink?'

'*Niente.*' Annibale stood the ice creams by their sticks inside a specially designed container and carried it over to the chest freezer. 'Let me know if the flats are a goer.'

'*Grazie.* Will do.' Fulvio almost ran into a customer coming up the steps.

Annibale manoeuvred the ice creams into the freezer. 'Be with you in a minute.'

'No problem, Joe.' The man was a regular, always wearing a tie and suit that looked a little too big for him, his hat sitting far back on his head, revealing twine-like hair.

Annibale came over, wiping the stickiness of chocolate and ice cream from his hands with a damp rag. 'How are you today, Curly?'

'Good, mate.' Curly slid onto a stool. 'A caramel milkshake with malt, thanks.'

Annibale ladled milk into a half-pint milkshake container, scooped in ice cream and measured an amount of flavouring. He added some malt from the flick dispenser and slid the milkshake container onto the electric mixer to churn while he went back to the register. Malt added an extra penny to the usual ten-pence cost of a milkshake and Curly dug around in his coat pocket to get the exact coins.

'What do you think about real estate?' Annibale put the money straight in the till, knowing with Curly he didn't need to count it. 'I mean, being a landlord?'

Curly shook his head. 'Mug's game, I reckon. You could get bad tenants who wreck the joint.'

Annibale brought over the milkshake and popped a paper straw into it. A woman came in, dressed smartly and holding a string bag containing several paper-wrapped purchases. About to order, she became distracted. Annibale followed her gaze. Curly was holding the container at an angle drinking through the straw, at the same time tipping milkshake down his tie. The woman burst out laughing. Her false teeth flew out, landing with a clatter on the counter. For a split second all three of them looked at the teeth. She swiped them straight up into her mouth and ran red-faced from the shop. Curly looked down at his tie. '*Jeezus.*'

Old-style Ice-cream Milkshake

      ❧ two scoops vanilla ice cream
      ❧ half a pint full-cream milk
      ❧ half a tablespoon powdered malt
      ❧ a dollop of liquid flavouring
         (chocolate, caramel, strawberry)

blend in a milkshake machine or electric blender until frothy

serve in a tall glass or steel milkshake container with a waxed-paper straw

Photographs of my father as a teenager fall into two groups: the earlier ones when he is not too tall and quite plump, and those taken after he'd had a growth spurt, the weight dropping away in a relatively short time. At twenty, he looks Italian film-star handsome. Yet there's something about the chubby teenager with smiling eyes that is warming, I think.

Dad laughs. 'No wonder I got so fat! When it wasn't busy at the shop, I'd make myself a malted milk, putting in extra scoops of ice cream, malt and flavouring. It was delicious.'

I smile. 'What milkshake flavours did the milk bar have?'

'Chocolate, strawberry, caramel, custard, lime and vanilla. Custard was dropped as it wasn't very popular. Eventually lime went, too. Chocolate was always the most popular.'

I hesitate, then reach for some paper and a pen sitting beside the nearby telephone. To my relief, he continues speaking as I jot down the milkshake flavours.

'We usually stuck a straw in the milkshake as we gave it to a customer. The earlier straws were made from waxed paper and you could unravel them. Sometimes if we forgot to order straws and were running out, Dad would send me down to a company in Adelaide Street to buy more. The company was called Parbury Henty and Dad would pronounce it "Parburienti".'

His faraway gaze tightens and he stops. It is quiet inside the kitchen, making the sounds outside more prominent: a neighbour raking leaves, some cars going past, insects humming.

'Dad, I know you have some resentment about the shop days but I—'

'Resentment? I don't have any resentment.'

I open my mouth to say more, then decide against it. The quiet stretches between us. And then, seemingly out of nowhere, he continues.

'Occasionally a customer would request their milkshake be served in a glass rather than the metal container. Eventually we offered takeaway milkshakes. The tall waxed cardboard cups had a giraffe on the side with the caption "The longest drink in town". Dad found this quite amusing. Around the corner there was a gym and these guys with the hugest muscles would come in for a milkshake. A few would ask us to add some powder that they brought with them. Some even asked us to crack one or two eggs into it as well.

'There were quite a few regulars who came into the shop. I remember a fellow who'd lost his arms in the war and had a pencil tied with leather around one stump to do his desk job. Even though I was still a kid, I'd started serving in the shop by then and Dad told me to make sure that I always put a straw in this man's drink. Then there were the Freemasons who came into the shop wearing unusual outfits, including regalia such as aprons and ornate collars, coming and going from their temple down the road. Another regular I remember when I was older was a high-ranking public servant who would turn up about seven pm. I think he would have a session at the Brisbane Hotel and then have his chauffeur drive him to our shop on his way home. By this time, the public servant would be quite ruddy and jolly. He was always pleasant and polite. I don't know where all the fruit went because he would always buy quite a bit.

'In the early '50s, many single Italian men who recently emigrated would end up in boarding houses in Spring Hill. After tea, they'd often walk down to the milk bar and chat. Dad was in his early thirties and enjoyed the camaraderie, often closing the shop even later than usual. Apparently an Italian priest would join in the conversations. One of the young men must have taunted the priest. Some time later, the police came to the shop and took the man into custody. Despite Dad speaking on his behalf, the young man was deported back to Italy, supposedly for being a communist.'

Dad shifts his coffee cup to move his hands on the table, the same way Nonno Anni used to when he spoke. 'Around this time there was a group of Aboriginal people who lived at the top of Wharf Street near Leichhardt Street. They would come to the shop occasionally and Dad would chat with them. He thought them a gentle people. I think they asked Dad what his name was, and when they couldn't get their tongues around Annibale they ended up calling him Neebo. Dad had so many names at the shop, it seemed. The Italians used Annibale, the Aboriginal people "Neebo", and then from the Australians he'd mostly get "Joe", but also "Bocca" or "Mr Bocc", even "Porky". We'd all been enjoying a few milkshakes by then …'

An hour later, my father is still talking. I've already filled five pages and the backs of several old envelopes with notes. Looking over them afterwards, it dawns on me that his previous reluctance to talk about the shop days hasn't had anything to do with the shop after all.

*There comes a day when you
can pick up the mosaic
box, that was out of
bounds in childhood.
No fear of capture,
careful to place it back
in the rectangle of dust,
its movement undetected.
But the hope of finding
something inside brings
with it the consequence
of what that might be.*

Annabelle and Joe

In 1977, when Nonno Anni received a British Empire Medal for 'service to the British Empire in the United Kingdom and abroad', he'd already been serving for a number of years in Brisbane as the President of ANFE — the *Associazione Nazionale Famiglie degli Emigrati*, or National Association of Migrant Families. It was a position he continued in on a volunteer basis for many decades, devoting large portions of his time and personal finances to the organisation. By a quirk of fate, the land Nonno Anni eventually found for the construction of the ANFE building was in Wyandra Street, Teneriffe, just two doors up from where he and his family lived for all those years, the place where so many migrants headed after stepping off ships from Italy. Not only the dozens of Italians he'd sponsored to migrate to Australia, but also many others he and Nanna Francesca accommodated as well.

As he could take only two people to the investiture with him, Nanna Francesca and my father went. I've seen one grainy photograph from the event. Nonno Anni stands alone, the medal pinned to his suit coat. Queensland's Government House rising behind him, stark white against a cloudless blue sky, the mid-nineteenth-century structure almost Mediterranean-looking. It seems Nonno Anni blinked as the picture was taken, or he could be squinting from the glare. I suspect Nanna Francesca took the photograph, not realising the camera strap was blocking part of the lens.

While he accepted the British Empire Medal, Nonno Anni wasn't one to covet awards or recognition, later declining a *Cavaliere Della Rebubblica*, or Italian knighthood. Perhaps the BEM told him how far he'd come since arriving in Australia with nothing but a suitcase and a will to work hard, even after being interned and blacklisted during the war. All the same, the medal remained stored away in its velvet box. And he never used letters after his name. Part of me admired his humility, while at the same time I felt proud he'd received the award.

In the supplement to the *London Gazette* dated June 11, 1977, the entry listing my grandfather among those who received the award that year appears as: 'Annibale Boccabella of New Farm. For charitable works on behalf of migrants and for Italian families.' In another official listing I find him recorded among the female recipients of the British Empire Medal — as 'Miss Annibale Boccabella'. It isn't the first time his name, the Italian version of Hannibal, is understandably mistaken for 'Annabelle' in Australia, and I can't help but smile. Perhaps he should have told them it was 'Joe'.

Antonio — Tony
Ignazio — Ian
Vincenzo — Vince
Assunta — Suzy
Lorenzo — Laurie
Giancarlo — Carl
Soccorsa — Nancy
Concetta — Connie
Agata — Aggie
Giovanni — John

As a teenager, I'm briefly excited to hear that after migrating from Italy some distant relatives have changed their surname from Boccabella to Bell. Immediately, I begin envisaging a simpler life as 'Zoë Bell', without all that having an ethnic surname entails. Nonno Anni, however, is slightly upset.

'Your name is what connects you to your history, your family,' he chides me, 'to the place they came from, where you come from.'

'But I was born in Australia.' I no doubt give him a cross adolescent look.

'But you, your blood, still comes from Italy. You should never forget that.'

Antonio Boccabella (Born Fossa, Italy 1644)
Domenico Boccabella (Born Fossa, Italy 1680)
Girolamo Boccabella (Born Fossa, Italy 1732)
Croce Boccabella (Born Fossa, Italy 1778)
Gaetano Boccabella (Born Fossa, Italy 1818)
Demetrio Boccabella (Born Fossa, Italy 1847)
Vitale Boccabella (Born Fossa, Italy 1894)
Annibale Boccabella (Born Fossa, Italy 1923)
Remo Boccabella (Born Australia)
Zoë Boccabella (Born Australia)

It was around the time I heard about the relatives changing their surname to Bell that Nonno Anni first showed me the British Empire Medal he had been awarded; then about a decade since he'd received it. Sitting at my grandparents' kitchen table I turned the medal over in my hands. 'Nanna, you should get one, too.'

'What for?' Nanna Francesca cried in a tone implying I was being ridiculous.

'You've done lots of work for Italian migrants as well.'

'*Go on!*' She thrust her hand out, bending it at the wrist. 'Set the table. The others will be here soon and I need to cook the meat before I put the pasta on.'

It later occurred to me that in the same way many thought of my grandparents' fruit shop and milk bar as being 'Joe's', despite it having no official name — it was just as much Francesca's.

The Late Shift

Nurses from the adjacent St Martin's Hospital frequented the shop to buy their extras like cigarettes and chocolates. The girls' faces were clear, their hair neatly pinned and tucked beneath their starched white headdresses. Over slate-coloured dresses, they wore white pinafores that hugged their slim waists and crisscrossed over their backs. Some of the nurses were very young, fresh out of school and still in training. They lived at the hospital and often came into the shop, at times complaining about the strict matron who oversaw the nurses' quarters.

'Hello there, packet of Three Threes and a Nut Milk.' The tallest nurse, whose two front teeth slightly overlapped, smiled at Annibale as she handed him her money. 'We see you so often, what's your name? Mister …?'

'Boccabella.'

The four nurses trilled with sunny amusement.

'Oh, we can't call you that! It's *much* too long. How about Mr Bocca?'

Annibale shrugged. 'Whatever you like.'

Francesca would come to curse Annibale for uttering such words. The nurses called him Mr Bocca for a while, but somehow they came to call him 'Mr Porky'. This extended to their calling Francesca 'Porky's wife' or 'Mrs Porky' and Remo 'Porky's son'. For all three of them, the milk bar with ice creams, milkshakes and chocolates on hand were proving too tempting.

'Thanks, Mrs Porky,' said two nurses in unison as Francesca gave them some change.

'I don't really like being called that,' Francesca murmured to Annibale, watching the young women leave. 'It's not very nice.' She tied her scarf over her head to go home, having finished her shift.

'Don't worry about it.' Annibale, able to carry some extra weight beause of his height, thought the nickname a great laugh. 'You better go. I can hear the tram coming.'

Francesca gave him an acerbic look and put her handbag over her arm.

She'd barely been gone ten minutes when a nurse ran into the shop watery-eyed and stuttered, 'T-toilet? Out in the—?'

'Straight through.' Annibale pointed to the back door and the nurse scampered out there.

After he'd served a couple of customers and the nurse had not yet returned, Annibale thought he'd better see if she was okay. He found her in the courtyard sitting on a wooden crate, framed by pegged photographs of society shoots, weddings and portraits that the photographers of WA Jones and Co across the passageway had hung to dry on a line above the washtubs. With a trembling hand, the young nurse wiped her mouth with her handkerchief.

'Are you all right?' Annibale asked.

She looked up at him. 'I'm sorry, Mr Porky. I was just a bit sick. I just had to …' She stopped and pressed the handkerchief to her lips.

Annibale upturned another crate and sat down beside her. 'Your name is … Ruth, isn't it? Tell me, what's happened?'

'I just had to tend to a dead person for the first time and it was so …'

Annibale sighed and nodded. 'Sit here and collect yourself before you go back—'

'I can't go back.' Ruth shook her head and shuddered.

'Not yet. But you'll be okay.'

'You don't understand. We get the sack if we vomit, and some of the things we have to do … It's not just me, it's the other trainees, too.'

'Tell them if they feel sick to come out here and sit down for a while, and if they need to vomit the toilet is over there. Just tell Matron you're getting a drink if you have to.' Annibale stood up. 'Now you wait for a bit and I'll get you some water.'

Ruth smiled with gratitude, her forehead wrinkling. 'Thanks. I'll let the other girls know.'

Annibale sat on a stool behind the counter. Compared with daytime, at night the shop felt brightly lit against the darkened street outside. The milk bar hummed. Occasionally he heard footsteps on the footpath, but the late hour and a blustery wind meant the CBD was almost deserted.

'Oi!'

Annibale looked up. A man paused in the doorway. His hat sat unnaturally far forward, the shadow under the brim almost completely obscuring his face. He seemed to survey the shop.

Annibale stood up, using the heel of his shoe to push back the stool. 'What do you want?'

Hearing Annibale's accent, the man said, 'What nationality are you?'

Annibale said nothing.

He sneered. 'Now, you be a good boy and hand over—'

'Out you go.' The speed with which Annibale came around from the other side of the counter caught the man off guard.

'I'll have you, bloody dago …'

Annibale grabbed him by the shirt near his collar and pushed him towards the open doorway. 'Out!'

When he let go, the man fell down the last three steps at the front of the shop. Blood streamed from the corner of his forehead.

Maddalena plunked the coffee pot down on the breakfast table. 'So he fell over and cut his head or something?'

'He just slipped in the street,' said Francesca hurriedly, giving Annibale a look.

'Ah, well, I sort of pushed him, actually.' Annibale shrugged. 'The police came but they didn't do anything.'

'Serves him right.' Vitale cracked a raw egg into his coffee, gave it a brief stir and gulped it down.

'After the markets this morning I'll go to the hardware store and buy some hammers.'

Francesca stared at Annibale. 'What for?'

'I'll hide them all around the shop. You have to be prepared.' Seeing her look, he added, 'I'm not planning on hitting anyone.'

Annibale leant on the counter and nodded as two policemen came in from the darkness of walking the beat and went straight through to the back door and out into the courtyard. He knew there were several more police officers out there, including some that were quite highly ranked. Their murmurs were low; bottles clinked. Annibale avoided going out there while they were around. The scent of alcohol drifted from them as they walked back through the shop and continued on their beat. Some kept their eyes averted as they passed, while others boldly said good evening or gave a nod.

An hour or so later, Annibale heard a hobo scrounging around in the pig bin of old fruit out in the courtyard and then the sound of the tap running. It was getting late but he let the man finish at his own pace before closing the shop and locking the side gate to the courtyard. He'd forgotten to lock it sometimes in the past and arrived early the next morning to find several drunks or homeless people sleeping there. Hearing the scrape of shoes on the front steps, Annibale looked up and smiled to see Beverley, one of the St Martin's nurses, coming in.

'Just a bar of Cadbury Energy, Porky.' She fished around in her purse. 'I'm on night shift, worse luck. I suppose you're going home soon?'

He put the chocolate bar on the counter, exchanging it for the coin she placed there. 'I think so.'

'Lucky duck. Night-o.'

Annibale rarely wore a watch and didn't have a clock hanging in the shop. To check the time he walked outside to the footpath and looked down Ann Street to the Central Station clock tower, its face illuminated at night. Sensing it was getting late, he went out to see. *Almost eleven. Time to close.* At that moment a shriek carried down the virtually empty street. He looked towards the hospital and saw a flash of Beverley's nursing cape, then a man accosting her.

'Hoi!' Annibale broke into a run. 'What the hell?'

'Fuck off, dago.' The man's speech was slurred.

'Get out of here.' Annibale slapped both his hands at once against the man's chest, pushing him away from Beverley. '*Go on!*'

The man contemplated throwing a punch, then muttered to himself and staggered off. Annibale and Beverley watched him cross the road and disappear towards Central Station.

'You all right?'

'Yes, thanks, Porky. Just a bit shaken, that's all.'

'Come on, I'll walk you back up to the hospital.'

Nurses Joan and Patricia came into the shop, manoeuvring between them a box of empty soft-drink bottles they'd collected from patients' bedsides.

Annibale's eyes crinkled at the corners. 'A little while since payday?'

The girls laughed and he counted the bottles; there was a penny refund for each one.

'Heard what you did for Bev last night,' said Joan. 'Good on ya, Joe.'

Annibale shook his head, a little embarrassed.

'More and more drunks around this end of town late at night, unfortunately.' Patricia half-suppressed a shudder. 'You know, the bloke in the grocery shop up the road has a four-gallon drum of metho he puts into empty Coke bottles and sells cheap. Don't know how he lives with himself.'

'Anyone needs me to walk them back to the hospital that's okay,' Annibale said.

'That's very kind. I'll tell the girls.'

Joan ordered a milkshake and counted the rest of the pennies into her purse. 'Better than spending a penny,' she quipped, referring to the entry fee to use any of the public restrooms around town.

'*Joan.*' Patricia hit her on the shoulder and they laughed some more.

All day it had been wet and by late evening the road outside gleamed black and empty. The rain had stopped, though the gutters still dripped and the air remained muggy and still. Annibale had just closed the evening paper when a car pulled up with two men in it. One got out while the driver stayed inside with the engine running. Annibale's senses prickled. He came around from behind the counter and stood beside one of the fruit displays. There was a shelf behind it, with one of the hammers hidden there.

The man had a baleful stare. 'Give me a carton of cigarettes.'

Annibale didn't move. 'Where's the money first?'

The man came forward. 'Give me a carton of cigarettes.'

'Money first.' Annibale's fingertips brushed the hammer behind the display.

The man came right up, eye to eye. 'Dago, in five minutes I could ruin this shop.'

'Just throw one thing and see what will happen next.' Annibale whipped out the hammer, stopping the metal head right next to the man's ear.

The man sprang back. He swore and ran out, Annibale coming after him. They pounded down the steps, the man diving into the front seat of the car. The driver, seeing Annibale with the hammer, threw the car into reverse and hastily backed up the street, the tyres spinning on the wet road and leaving a singeing smell hanging in the air.

Each week seemed to take on a certain rhythm at the milk bar, with particular evenings busier than others. Some nights midweek it was crowded with people who wandered down after dinner from the boarding houses at Spring Hill. Often on Saturday nights young couples would come in on their way to or from the pictures. It was when the shop was quiet, often on a Monday or Tuesday night, that the hours dragged and the occasional strange incident seemed to occur.

Annibale was just about to close the shop for the night when a bloke he'd never seen before staggered in drunk.

'I want some ice cream.'

Annibale picked up the metal scoop. 'Single or double?'

'*Nooo*. In my pocket.' The drunk fumbled and held his side trouser pocket open.

'You don't want it in your pocket.' Annibale's eyes flickered with amusement.

'I'm the customer and I *want it in my pocket!*'

Annibale sighed, pondering this. 'Just a moment.' He went outside, looked up and down the empty street, then came back in. 'How many scoops?'

Birth ...

'Remo, this afternoon I need you to go to the doctor's surgery with Mrs Rezzini so you can translate what the doctor says to her, okay?'

'Oh Mum, no. It's embarrassing!' Remo had gone many times in Francesca's place and he sensed it was as uncomfortable for the patients as it was for him, especially considering he was only seven.

'You have to go. I'm not feeling very well. Be there at four o'clock after school.'

'*Sì, sì, ci sarò.*' Remo kicked the toe of his leather school shoe at the floorboards of the verandah, kissed his mother on both cheeks and barrelled down the front steps.

Francesca stood on the verandah for a moment, watching him disappear up the road on his way to school.

'Will you tell him?'

She flinched, not having heard Maddalena draw up beside her. 'What?'

'That you're expecting a baby.'

'Did Annibale tell you?'

'No.' Maddalena beamed. 'When is it due?'

'September.' Francesca touched her stomach, even though she wasn't showing yet. 'There's no need to tell Remo. He's too young to know of these things. He'll see the baby when we bring her home.' At Maddalena's look, she added, 'I want a girl this time.'

Francesca was still feeling ill with her pregnancy when she was supposed to accompany Tonino, a friend of Annibale's from Fossa, to the bank to apply for a loan. She'd helped fill out the paperwork, but organised for

Annibale to accompany him instead. Tonino's English was coming along, but for such an important transaction it was best to have someone there to translate if necessary.

The bank in Queen Street was a formidable building flanked with tall sandstone columns. A bank clerk told them to wait, indicating a row of chairs outside the bank manager's office, before taking the paperwork inside the office and shutting the door. A loud clunking as a bank teller stamped several documents for another customer echoed into the soaring ceiling.

The door of the office opened and the bank manager came out, eyeing them with a frown. 'Which one of you is wanting this loan?'

'It is me.' Tonino scrambled to his feet, grabbing his hat.

'You from Italy?' The manager put his hands on his hips. 'Which part?'

'*Sì*, er, yes, Abruzzo.'

'I fought in the war and was taken prisoner in Abruzzo. What village are you from?'

'Fossa.'

All of a sudden the bank manager broke into a grin and rushed forward, his hand extended. 'I thought it was you, Tony, but I had to be sure.' He pumped Tonino's hand, turning to Annibale and explaining, 'This man helped me escape over the mountains when I was a prisoner of the Germans. I owe my life to this man.'

'I didn't recognise you,' Tonino said to the bank manager, turning to Annibale to say, 'He was unshaven with longer hair the last time I saw him.' He didn't mention that the bank manager had also been much thinner and dirtier at the time.

They all laughed, marvelling at the coincidence of crossing paths again.

Ushering them into his office, the manager clapped Tonino on the back. 'Any amount you want, I will lend it to you.'

Vincenzo and Remo crouched on their haunches, the toes of their shoes almost touching the edge of the creek as they tried to catch yabbies with pieces of string tied to bits of meat. The late-winter air was cold, but it was the middle of the day and they were in a protected spot so the sun was pleasantly warm on the backs of their woollen jumpers. There was only six years difference in age between thirteen-year-old Vincenzo and Remo, while there would be close to eight years between Remo and his new sibling.

'You should come out here to the farm more.' Vincenzo glanced at Remo's head, bowed in concentration over his piece of string. 'Maybe the next school holidays. In summer when all the workers are here, it's really fun. At the end of the day they play the guitar and the piano accordion and we have a singalong. Dad cuts up some watermelons and we sit on the back steps eating them and seeing how far we can flick the seeds.'

Remo pulled at the string. 'Why isn't it taking the bait?'

Vincenzo stood up, brushing down his pants. 'Probably too cold.' He didn't tell Remo they could lift up the stones and most likely the yabbies would be underneath. 'Come on. Come and help me catch the horse and we'll go for a ride.'

With reluctance, Remo let go of the piece of string. 'I'll help you catch it but I don't want to ride it.'

Upstairs in the house, the lunch dishes still sat on the kitchen table as the adults talked.

'I've got something for you, Papà.' Francesca rummaged in her straw bag.

'For me?' Mico's cigarette moved with his lips as he placed a box of matches on the packet of Capstans, the red, white and blue packet never far from his hand.

She got out a parcel and kissed his cheek. *'Buon compleanno.'*

Mico tugged at the bow a little clumsily and unwrapped it.

'It's from McWhirters, a department store in Brisbane, Dad.' Francesca couldn't help reaching out to touch the starched white long-sleeved shirt as Mico held it up for everyone to see.

Cesca leaned forward. 'Look at that stitching on the cuffs. Faultless.' She exchanged glances with Francesca and Soccorsa, all having previously agreed that such a shirt would be perfect for Mico to wear when Soccorsa got married.

Francesca nodded with satisfaction. 'I know it's a bit early with your birthday not until September, but with the baby due I won't be able to come out here then.'

'Maybe it will be born on Dad's birthday.' Soccorsa carried coffee cups over to the table. 'Francesca, you could name him after Dad.'

Birth ...

'Francesca's not having a boy.' Cesca was trying not to smirk.

Soccorsa looked confused. 'I thought you didn't know until the baby was born?'

Mico smiled. 'You don't.'

Cesca began pouring the coffee. 'But if sheer will has anything to do with it ... Francesca, please don't tell me you've only picked out girls' names.'

The look that crossed Francesca's face gave her away and they all laughed.

'What's so funny?' Remo bounded up the back steps with Vincenzo following.

Cesca, holding a plate of homemade biscuits, shook her head. 'I swear you two always turn up the moment food hits the table.'

They laughed more and Mico gazed around at them all, pleased. The talk flowed on without him and he was content with that. He would be fifty-three on his upcoming birthday. His thoughts drifted to when he'd been alone on the farm, birthdays sometimes spent by himself; how the days would draw out, the nights stretching even longer. Sometimes, when he'd been still in the quiet hours, there was no sound at all. He'd close his eyes and remember Palmi — the gentle splash of waves on the pebbled shore, the laughter of his brothers, his mother calling his name. Mico had always known he'd never see any of them again.

Francesca smoothed the electric iron over a shirt, glancing up as Remo hovered beside the bassinet, peering in at his little brother.

'Mum, why does he have those things on his legs?'

'It's plaster. Plaster casts. He was born a bit early. The bones in the bottom of his legs are still a bit soft, that's all.'

'How long will he wear those for?'

'About six months.' She put the ironed shirt on a coat hanger, hung it on the back of a wooden chair and reached into the washing basket to grab one of her dresses. 'We have to take him up to the hospital once a week to have the plaster casts cut off and new ones put on.'

Maddalena appeared at the back doorway. 'Come on, Remo, come and help me pluck the chicken. It's bled now.'

The men were at work and Francesca could hear Maddalena and Remo talking downstairs. Several silent tears fell upon the fabric of her dress in moist circles and she seared them away with the hot iron.

The morning of Lorenzo's christening, Annibale took Remo in the utility to the iceworks to get some ice to cool drinks for the party they'd have underneath the house later that day. Annibale picked up another block of ice, his hands slippery from the first. It slithered in his grasp, dropping with a heavy thud on his toe. He went white, unable to utter any sound at first. Sweat broke out on his brow. Eventually, he let out a long sigh and swore.

Remo dithered, wincing. 'Are you okay, Dad?'

'In a minute.' Annibale gathered himself, gently lifting his foot up and down, not game to take off his shoe. 'Let's get the rest of the bloody ice and get home.'

By the time they got back to the house, Annibale's toe had swelled.

'Oh, Annibale! But the christening?' Francesca's hands flew to her mouth, grimacing at the angry purple of his enormous toe.

'It'll be fine. Don't fuss.' He brushed her away.

Maddalena bent to squint at it. 'Should you put some ice on it?'

Annibale gave her a look.

'You won't get your shoe on, Annibale. You can't go to church in a sandal or, even worse, barefoot,' said Francesca. '*Mamma mia*, what would the priest think of us?'

'I'll just have to cut a hole in the toe of my good leather shoe,' he told her.

She bit her lip and nodded. 'You'd better hurry. We don't want to be late.'

At the church, everyone waited for the priest to appear. Annibale and Francesca had invited a crowd of their relatives and friends. The longer it took the priest to arrive, the more people started milling among the pews, talking. Lorenzo began crying for his feed and Francesca jiggled him, looking around in desperation for the priest.

Annibale leant towards her. 'If he doesn't get here soon we'll take Lorenzo over to the Salvation Army to get it done.'

'No, no.' Francesca's eyes widened in alarm. 'He'll be here soon.'

Birth ...

Father Martin finally arrived, eyes bloodshot, a little unsteady on his feet, the fumes on his breath almost overpowering them all.

The cement flooring underneath the house had been swept clean, trestle tables set up and chairs brought down from upstairs or borrowed from neighbours. There was quite a crowd. Talk and laughter rose. The women carried platters of grilled steak and oven-baked fish from the kitchen down the back steps to the tables, along with bowls of pasta, green salads and bread. Annibale had brought several crates of soft drink from the shop and put them, along with bottles of beer, into old tin tubs with the broken-up ice. He poured red wine into jugs and placed them along the tabletops and people helped themselves. Afterwards, when the christening cake had been cut and bowls of oranges half-emptied, peel scattered on plates, the singing and dancing began.

Two of the men had brought along guitars. Another had a slide trombone with a mute cork to alter the timbre, toning down its intensity for the small area. Most of the men had discarded their coats and ties and had rolled up their shirtsleeves. Some sang around cigarettes between their lips while others, like Annibale, opened their mouths wide and bellowed out the songs. The women sang too, laughing and clapping, and talking as well, passing Lorenzo around, getting up and dancing with each other or their husbands. They still did Italian folk dances, but among the younger ones some of the '50s rock-and-roll steps were creeping in, matching the rhythm of the Italian tunes.

It was 1953 and with the post-war influx of migrants continuing to stream in from Europe the resentment and prejudice shown by some Australians towards them was being exacerbated by a fear of communism whipped up by Prime Minister Menzies. But that sun-drenched afternoon, for the migrants celebrating in the cool shade beneath the house with their Italian food and Australian beer, there was only music and laughter and gladness.

... and Death

The day of Mico's funeral, the driveway of the farm was crowded with parked cars and utility trucks, the house teeming with people who'd come for the wake. They'd stood in their heavy black clothes in the scorching cemetery, on a treeless, gentle slope. Cesca's face reddened from tears and sun. Everyone wilted, stilled. Mico had been fifty-three, his death sudden. They told fourteen-year-old Vincenzo the cause was 'dust in your father's lungs'. Due to the shock, Francesca was no longer able to breastfeed Lorenzo. Soccorsa seemed to be almost clinging to her fiancé, Girolamo.

Then, the next day, the driveway was empty and the farm especially quiet. A breeze carried the soft flutter of leaves moving in the orchard and distant birdcalls, but otherwise nothing. The ground baked rigid beneath the silent, pounding heat of the sun. There was no ping of metal from Mico in his shed, no waft of cigarette smoke indicating his proximity. Time sluggishly ticked by. Annibale, Francesca, Soccorsa and Girolamo gravitated to the kitchen table from where Cesca and Vincenzo had seemed unable to move since breakfast. It was only a fortnight into 1954 and the year felt ruined.

Annibale became conscious of Cesca eyeing him. He glanced at Francesca beside her; she unconsciously clutched at Cesca's arm like a protective mother cat.

'We've written to my sister in Palmi and told her to go around and tell Mico's family. They can't hear about this in a letter.' Cesca rubbed her forehead with her fingertips. 'I have to think what to do. We're meant to harvest soon.' She looked at Annibale again and he realised that, although at twenty-nine and sixteen years younger than Cesca, she was expecting him, as the oldest male, to help with the decision-making.

'I can drive up and help, along with Vincenzo and Girolamo,' he suggested. 'But it's hard for me to leave the shop. Are you able to hire a couple of workers for the busiest times?'

'I think we could.'

Annibale nodded but he knew they were postponing the inevitable.

Soccorsa and Girolamo drove away still wearing their wedding clothes. Cesca stood waving her handkerchief, feeling a sense of resignation deep within. Since Mico's death, she'd continued wearing black dresses to honour him, although for Soccorsa's wedding she'd worn a dark fabric embroidered with small cream flowers. Cesca thought of other weddings in the district over the years at which Mico had often been among several musicians. And yet he never had the opportunity to play his guitar at any of his children's weddings.

Happiness mingled with melancholy as she watched Annibale and Francesca with their young family; her own family life seemed to be slipping away. Cesca gazed across the paddocks Mico had cleared by hand. She thought how solitary it must have been for him on the farm, until she and Francesca arrived. Now she'd lived on this spot for twenty-one years. She'd thought she'd grow old here, with Mico, their children and grandchildren nearby. *But things happen that you never thought would. Children grow up, leave, have their own lives to live.* She realised Annibale was watching her. His eyes softened, knowing. She nodded.

'Annibale, I need you to help me put the farm on the market.'

When Cesca sold the farm, Francesca and Annibale drove out to Applethorpe in their utility truck and helped her and Vincenzo pack up. With the truck piled high, they took almost four hours to drive back to Brisbane. Francesca sat in the middle of the bench seat between her mother and her husband. Vincenzo sat in the back among the boxes of belongings and pieces of furniture. With the money from the farm, Cesca had bought a modest weatherboard house with a corrugated-iron lean-to on the corner of Chermside and Kent Streets in Teneriffe, and she and Vincenzo settled in.

Fifteen-year-old Vincenzo got a job doing leatherwork, mainly making shoes, at Johnson's in Bishop Street, Kelvin Grove. The factory where he worked sat across from a tannery, which had been operating in the street since the 1800s, relentlessly pumping out the putrid smell of animal skins being processed in competion with the nearby rubber works that billowed up a reek of burning rubber. It was very loud compared to the farm. Vincenzo became mostly quiet.

Cesca was depressed and felt displaced after losing Mico and the farm, though she didn't recognise such feelings. Being in the city where she couldn't converse in English and didn't know shopkeepers or her way around as she had in Stanthorpe's High Street was intimidating. She was more isolated than she'd been on the farm, rarely venturing out without Vincenzo or Francesca to interpret for her, often asking them to run errands instead.

At around this time, Elia returned from seven years up north, looking tanned and fit, his thick wiry hair a little more unruly. The North Queensland climate seemed to have had both a galvanising and coarsening effect on him. Not for the first time, Annibale felt their differences as brothers. To him, some of Elia's tales seemed a little tall, but when Annibale murmured this to Maddalena, she took umbrage. Elia bought a house in Brisbane, Annibale suspecting Maddalena's hand in bringing this about, in the same way she conspired with the aunt of a girl from Campania to orchestrate a wedding.

Caterina's smiling eyes shone so dark they seemed almost black to match her hair, her grin impish. When she giggled, her shoulders joined in. For the photographs taken on their wedding day in January 1955, she beamed. Beside her, Elia, more at ease in work singlet and shorts, stood somewhat stupefied in his tuxedo and white gloves. Bookending the couple, Maddalena and Caterina's aunt both grinned at their achievement. Annibale felt a little perturbed by the arrangement, but then became distracted by Remo, dressed completely in white as a pageboy, tugging on his sleeve.

'I don't want to wear white girls' shoes. Can't I put my own on for the reception?'

The man with wide vivid-blue eyes and hair that began about halfway back on his head came into the milk bar from the side hallway entrance rather than the front entry that most people used. Carrying a paper-wrapped bottle of medicine, he stated he couldn't use the front steps as his back was in constant pain from a fall. He ordered a drink, telling Annibale he'd been to see Plint next door, adding he had lost faith in the doctors of mainstream medicine, who couldn't find a cure for his pain.

Harold Plint — alternative health practitioner — had moved in across the hall from the shop when WA Jones and Co, the photographers, moved out. He'd relocated from close to the corner of Adelaide and Wharf Streets, nearby. Remo had often caught the Bulimba Ferry tram home from the stop outside the Plint practice, and while waiting had sometimes caught sight through the window of an intimidating white bust, presumably of the founder of homeopathy, and jars of different coloured liquids. The mystique vanished when Plint moved into their building and they saw him mixing and funnelling fluids over the washtubs out the back.

The man lamenting his chronic back pain was named Karl, and during 1955 he became a regular patient of Plint, often coming across to the milk bar afterwards to buy a drink. As with many of his customers, Annibale provided a sympathetic ear and advice, if sought. Karl was born in Germany and had jumped ship in Brisbane in 1939. He'd spent the war in the Gaythorne and Tatura internment camps, then in the Civil Alien Corps, on four occasions escaping and being recaptured. For years, he'd tried to no avail to convince authorities that he was of no threat and hated Nazism; now he bemoaned that doctors were not listening to him either.

Karl said the pain was driving him mad, preventing him sleeping, but doctors told him he was exaggerating, two even telling him not to come back. He sipped his drink and Annibale did his best to placate him. When Karl spoke bitterly of his internment during the war, Annibale told him that he too, and his father, Vitale, had been placed in internment camps and worked for the CAC. He suggested that one had to get on with life and not dwell on things; that it had been war and you couldn't take it personally. Karl muttered and shook his head but he shrugged and said no more. The thirty-nine-year-old didn't appear any different to many who came in and spoke of their lives and complaints, and after he left the shop Annibale was on the go with the next lot of customers. No one foresaw what was to happen on December 1 that same year.

The late-edition newspapers headlined the tragedy on the front page. Karl Kast had gone on a rampage, shooting and detonating several bombs in the medical precinct up on Wickham Terrace. Just before three that afternoon, he'd walked into Wickham House and shot Dr Michael Gallagher. Leaving several bombs in the foyer, Kast then ran down the road to Ballow Chambers and killed Dr Arthur Meehan and Dr Andrew Murray, before threatening Dr John Lahz, who managed to escape. Kast then exploded another bomb and shot himself, though he didn't die until almost two hours later in Brisbane General Hospital.

It was shocking to the people of Brisbane. Such an incident had never occurred in their city before. When the paperboy thwacked the wad of papers down in front of the milk-bar counter, the blow resonated through the shop and across to Plint. Activity stalled. Everyone felt shaken. The newspapers were held up and pored over. There had been no warning signs, even for those who'd lived in the same house as Kast.

Listening to customers disparage Kast and express sympathy for the doctors killed and their families left behind, especially so close to Christmas, Annibale too felt sadness for the victims. Thinking back to the times Karl had come into the milk bar for a soft drink, he found it hard to grasp that this same person had done such a terrible deed. He would later reflect that many people continued to struggle from experiences that had occurred during the war years, and how Kast had seemed unable to move on from his internment. Ten years on from its end, the war, it seemed, was still claiming lives.

At the coronial inquiry, a forensic pathologist, Dr John Tonge, gave evidence that an autopsy of Kast revealed no abnormality of the spine. People discussing the case at tram stops, over counters and at kitchen tables felt this exposed Kast as a malingerer trying to exploit the system for compensation and to avoid work. Yet there were those who sensed something wasn't quite right, but at the time there was little idea of what that could be.

Almost twenty-five years after the tragedy, an article in the *Australian Medical Journal* cited the case, warning of the risk for doctors handling 'rare cases of severe and dangerous mental illness which masquerade as malingering'.

… and Death

On Boxing Day that same December, Annibale helped the others load the back of the red Chevrolet utility truck with cold drinks, some roast chickens and a couple of large watermelons. After several years of keeping the fruit shop and milk bar open almost every day, Annibale had decided they would close for a couple of days over Christmas and Easter. And for their annual holiday, the family would head to the beach for the day. Vitale, Remo, Elia and several of the migrants currently staying at the house climbed into the back of the open truck. Towels slung like horseshoes around their necks, they positioned themselves among the tin Eskies for the forty-minute trip to Suttons Beach. Annibale passed Lorenzo to Remo to hold on to, then helped Francesca into the back of the utility.

'Everyone set? Good.' With a grin, he got into the driver's side of the cabin, next to Maddalena and Caterina, who said she got carsick if she rode behind.

Annibale drove north onto Sandgate Road, then it was almost one long straight thoroughfare all the way to Redcliffe. The Chev bumped over the two-lane timber-and-girder Hornibrook Bridge, which stretched more than two and a half kilometres across Bramble Bay. Then they wound their way around Woody Point and along to Suttons Beach. Although it was still early in the morning, the foreshore was already crowded. They chose a grassy spot in the stippled shade of a Norfolk Pine and set out the Esky of drinks on top of an old canvas tarpaulin. Maddalena and Vitale sat on fold-out chairs in the shade while everyone else headed for the beach.

The sand was rough with bits of broken shell underfoot. Francesca was last to the water's edge, stepping around several jellyfish washed up and drying in the sun. She watched the others already splashing about in the water. The sun, gaining strength in a cloudless sky, felt hot on her shoulders. She hadn't stood on a beach since her childhood in Palmi. Just the sound of the gentle waves breaking in little bubbly ripples around her feet brought a smile. She looked over at Annibale in his dark swimming trunks, standing up to his thighs in the water and holding a squirming Lorenzo. Annibale had bathed in creeks and dams before, but this was his first time in the sea.

'Come in, Mum! It's beautiful!' Remo splashed about, pretending to be hit, then staging a fall into the water.

Francesca stepped forward. 'Careful …'

'He's all right.' Annibale was grinning. 'Come in.'

It was a perfect day for the seaside, warm, with little wind, sunlight glinting on the water. None of them could swim but they only went in waist-deep, crouching and talking, ducking under at times to cool their heads. The current lightly moved them further up the beach. Occasionally they'd look up to see where Maddalena and Vitale were sitting, then move back through the water to bob in front of them.

At noon, Maddalena waved everyone in, and they traipsed up the beach for lunch. Towels wrapped about their waists, they sat on the edge of the tarpaulin, feet caked with wet sand sticking out onto the grass. Everyone devoured pieces of roast chicken, licking salt and grease from their fingers, before biting into slices of watermelon, the sugary juice flooding their mouths. Remo and a couple of the young migrants competed in how far they could shoot black seeds from between their lips onto the grass.

After lunch, Caterina and Elia disappeared to get an ice cream, while Vitale and Maddalena went for a walk along the dry sand above the tideline, keeping their shoes on. Most of the others took another dip in the sea, but Annibale lay back on the tarp snoozing, one arm flung over his eyes. With a chuckle, Francesca took a photo as he dozed, unaware. Then she sat down next to him, watching Remo and Lorenzo building a sandcastle with a moat. There was no way the incoming tide would fill it until they'd long gone back to Brisbane.

Francesca felt so happy being at a beach again she didn't want it to end. The waves slapped with calming monotony. Children shrieked in their games along the sand. Seagulls strolled, squabbled and scooped water into their beaks at the water's edge. Presently Annibale stirred, propping himself up on one elbow to look out across Moreton Bay.

'I wish we'd brought Ma and Vincenzo along.' Francesca was wistful. 'I know they were seeing Soccorsa's family today but coming to the beach would have done Mum good.'

Annibale sat up. 'The truck was packed as it was.' He glanced at her. 'Next time, eh?'

Francesca nodded, smiling. 'Another year just about over. I wonder what 1956 will bring?' She kept looking out at the sea, realising she'd be turning thirty in the coming year. 'Perhaps we could have one more baby. I would really like a daughter.'

'No more children.'

'What? Why?'

'What if we end up with another boy? Then we'd have three little devils to deal with.'

'But Annibale …'

'No. No more.'

Francesca said nothing.

Maddalena and Vitale sauntered back up the beach and sat down. Annibale got up and stretched, avoiding his mother's gaze. Without a word, he headed back towards the water for another swim. Francesca pretended to brush sand from around her hairline to wipe the corners of her eyes, then stood up, shook out her towel and walked over to the pavilion to change. Maddalena frowned as she picked out Annibale's form in the water.

Annibale gripped the black telephone receiver, aware of Francesca hovering near his elbow in the narrow hallway. 'We're on our way.' He hung up.

Francesca spoke first. 'It's Mum, isn't it?'

The drive to Cesca's took only a few minutes, but although Annibale sped, to Francesca it seemed to take forever. 'Say again what Vincenzo told you?'

'Just that she wasn't well and had a pain in her chest.' Annibale omitted telling her that Vincenzo had been close to hysterical and pressed harder on the accelerator.

Francesca let out a cry when she saw the creamy-yellow station wagon with a red ambulance cross outside Cesca's house. She started opening the passenger door before Annibale had fully stopped. Hearing her mother wail from inside the house, Francesca hurried up the front steps.

Vincenzo and an ambulance driver were arguing just inside the doorway. 'Here she is now,' said Vincenzo, as though he had been insisting on something and wasn't being believed.

The ambulance officer looked at Francesca. 'Do you speak English and Italian?'

'Mum? Where's my mother? What's happening?' Francesca sensed Annibale looming behind her.

'She won't let us take her to the hospital,' the ambulance officer said. 'Sonny here says she complained of a pain in her chest but she won't let us examine her. We need to take her to hospital. She may have had a heart attack or be having one.'

Francesca rushed into the bedroom to find Cesca in bed, pale and sweating, her dark hair damp, long strands sticking to her face. She had pulled the sheet up to her chin to stop the ambulance officers examining her and at the same time was clutching her chest. When she saw Francesca, she seemed to register relief, but panic prevailed.

'Don't let them take me,' she begged in Italian. 'I don't want to go to hospital with them. I'm frightened. I can't understand what any of them are saying.'

'Mamma, please!' Tears were spilling down Francesca's cheeks. 'You have to go so they can make you well.'

'I'll be okay. Just feels like something heavy on my chest.' Cesca said this between gasps. 'Have they got a tablet I can take or something?'

Annibale explained to the ambulance officers that Cesca didn't know English and was frightened to go to the hospital, as she couldn't understand what they were doing to her. The driver told him they had to convince her to go or she could die. When Francesca heard this, she started begging in Italian.

'Ma, please! I can't lose you. You must go to the hospital. *Please*. I will come with you.' She grasped her mother's clammy hand.

Cesca looked terrified. Annibale saw her eyes flick from Francesca to Vincenzo to him. More pain gripped her chest. Then she nodded, eyes squeezed shut. The ambulance officers manoeuvred the stretcher into the room. Francesca, Annibale and Vincenzo moved into the hallway and then the kitchen to make way. They followed Cesca's short, sharp, rasping breaths out the front to the ambulance.

Annibale turned to Vincenzo. 'Let Francesca go in the ambulance with her and we'll follow them to the hospital.'

The ambulance officers had loaded Cesca on the stretcher into the back of the station wagon. But they didn't drive off straightaway. They stayed in a flurry of activity around her. Francesca, Annibale and Vincenzo stood on the road, watching in bewilderment. Suddenly the commotion stopped.

… and Death

One of the officers turned to them and shook his head. Francesca's knees gave way and Annibale caught her by the elbow. The other ambulance officer covered Cesca's face with a sheet. She was fifty.

'You have to look after that girl extra special,' Vitale whispered, 'now she's got no parents.'

Annibale nodded, his eyes not leaving Francesca's pale face. Two women had supported her under the arms when her legs kept buckling at Cesca's burial. She'd screamed as her mother's coffin was lowered into the ground. He'd felt helpless and redundant, Remo pressing next to him, moved by his mother's anguish. Seeing Francesca's unrestrained crying, Annibale realised he'd forgotten how close she and Cesca were.

He remembered Cesca during the last harvest on the farm. Short and stout, she'd worked hard alongside the other fruit pickers — her nephews who'd come up from Sydney for a working holiday. Cesca had been wearing a dark linen dress, the hessian harvest bag tied around her waist. A frayed straw hat with the brim folded back let the sun shine on her perspiring face. Every so often she'd coax the draughthorse pulling the cart onto which they stacked the bags of apples to move forward. To Annibale, Cesca had always seemed in good health. And yet she'd become listless since losing Mico, having to sell the farm and move to the city.

Vincenzo, still sixteen, had lost both his parents within two and a half years. Francesca was appointed his legal guardian until he reached twenty-one. She arranged for him to live with them at Wyandra Street. Remo and Lorenzo now shared the second bedroom, so the front sleep-out became Vincenzo's room. He continued his job making leather shoes at Johnson's and grieved quietly, each of Cesca's children grappling with their bereavement in their own way. After losing their parents, all three siblings experienced the upheaval, distancing and change that follows a death, especially of a binding matriarch.

During the first fortnight Cesca was gone Francesca cried often, though she kept trying to appear calm for the sake of her sons and Vincenzo, for whom she knew she must now be strong. Annibale held her one night in bed as Francesca shed more tears.

'You have to stop or you'll make yourself ill,' he murmured. 'You need to move on.'

She cried harder, thinking, *You don't understand. You haven't lost a parent, let alone two.* But she didn't voice this aloud. She mostly kept her sorrow private from then on, moving routinely about her chores yet hushed inside, her grieving making her forgetful, preoccupied, even clumsy now and then. Yet sometimes, when she was alone, she would touch her fingertips to her mother's initials embroidered on a pillowslip brought from Palmi.

A Small Thread

We sit on the orange vinyl lounge on the front patio: Nonno Anni, Nanna Francesca and me. Nonno Anni has carried out the small coffee table from inside and Nanna Francesca places a parcel wrapped in butcher's paper on top, opening it to release the scent of hot fish and chips. I'm still in my togs, faintly damp from a morning at the beach, my inflatable surf-rider leaning against the timber wall of the modest 1950s duplex. Nonno Anni bought the holiday house at Nobby Beach back in the '60s, after a cyclone caused many to sell up and leave the Gold Coast, sometimes known within Queensland as the south coast back then.

Nanna Francesca nudges me, almost knocking a chip from my hand. 'Have a scallop.'

'I don't like seafood that much.' I crinkle my sun-scorched nose.

'It's potato! Take a bite.' She is smiling.

My parents never get potato scallops with their fish and chips. I chomp into the golden crunchy batter encasing a disc of potato. 'It's delicious!'

It's curious how small pleasures temper the sadness that sometimes tremors through everyday life. I realise now that Nonno Anni saying we had to go to 'Nobby's' so he could 'cut the grass', was my grandparents' way of distracting their ten-year-old granddaughter with a day at the beach. It was a stressful time with one of my family seriously ill in hospital and perhaps that's why initially it went almost unnoticed that, sometimes, when Nanna Francesca began telling a story, it was the same story she'd told not long before.

Mico and Cesca are buried more than two hundred kilometres apart. It takes me a little while to find Bisnonno Mico's grave in the Stanthorpe Cemetery, as I haven't seen it since I was a teenager. A cold wind whips under high sun, the gravestones blinding white. I am surprised and pleased to see someone has left a transparent dome of plastic flowers upon his grave, their hue slightly faded, perhaps over a year or two. Sixty years he's been gone — longer than he lived. He has no family buried near him. No family left in Stanthorpe. Perhaps in a generation or so his grave will become one of those that no one ever visits or remembers. His full first name — Domenico — is etched into the headstone; not 'Mico', which Nanna Francesca told me her mother always called him. Some passer-by walking their dog might glance at the fading words, never knowing of the man, the life. I read the gravestones of strangers and wonder at the lives and stories behind their names. There is always a story.

Only a few generations back, my ancestors on both sides — all from the working class — would not always get a marked grave. I've stood on the outskirts of a village before a grassy field that gave no hint that my great-great-grandparents, along with hundreds of other villagers, lay buried there. Then there were those buried for a number of decades before their bodies were exhumed, their bones stored in the church bone room, the village needing more room in the cemetery. Nothing distinguishes them from their fellows.

At Lutwyche Cemetery in Brisbane, Bisnonna Cesca's grave is relatively easy to find, close to the edge of the graveyard, opposite a house with a pool. I don't know why but I'm glad she's far from the busy road at the other end. It doesn't look like anyone has been to her grave in a long time. The headstone appears time-worn but robust, traditional, from another era. Like Bisnonna Cesca herself. A working life, strong hands, her heart worn out at fifty years.

On this spot in 1956, Nanna Francesca was consumed by a grief so raw it overtook her. I could not truly understand until I'd walked a similar path, being not much older than she was when I lost my own mother, also taken early. I learnt how expectation for the future is illusory; the years don't always play out the way you suppose they might. My mother's death was much harder than I could ever have imagined, despite my thinking I was prepared. Afterwards, I assumed grief would closely bind those of us left behind. Instead, it thrust us onto completely different courses. Within a few months my father embarked upon a new life with another. For those still deep in the initial sorrow of loss, the jolt put immense strain on a rope already frayed and unravelling fast.

I came to recognise that we all cope in all different ways. I changed, too. Initially I rallied, but then crashed. Roger later told me that for a long while I'd rarely leave the house. Unable to keep up usual relationships, I discovered that people you don't expect to persevere do, while others fade from your life. No one knows all the intricacies of my soul, so it would be presumptuous of me to assume I know another's — including my father's. *The war made diverse creatures of us*, wrote Hector Dinning, and so, too, do death and grief.

In particular, my heart goes out to Nanna Francesca's young brother, Vincenzo, only a teenager when he lost both his parents so soon after each other. During his time of grief, he also had to leave his home and adjust to life in a different household, his sister as guardian. Just a few years later, while working at the factory stitching leather goods, he got the top of his middle finger caught in an industrial sewing machine, slicing it off. The doctor didn't reattach it; instead, he folded over the flap of skin, stitched it up and sent Vincenzo home the same day, the top of his finger down to the first knuckle gone. Another small grief to carry alongside the larger.

Still, we return to everyday life, as we must. To live our own story, until it, like us, disappears back into the earth, the trees, into the air, the rivers and the sea. And it is another's turn to live their story.

'Where's Annibale?' Nanna Francesca blinks, her dark eyes trained on me.

'He's out in the backyard with Roger.'

She nods, looks down at her hands on the bedspread, the same tasselled bedspread on this bed in the spare room that was here when she showed me her mother's linens from Palmi all those years ago. Her hands are bare, her plain gold wedding ring, purchased more than sixty years ago in Warwick when she was seventeen, lost. She looks up at me again.

'Where's Annibale?'

'He's in the backyard, doing some gardening.'

She nods, looks down at her hands, then up at me, straight in the eye. 'Who are you?'

I swallow hard. 'I'm Zoë. Your granddaughter. You have a rest now. I'll be back in a minute.'

In the lounge room I suck in some breaths and get my welling eyes under control. Framed photographs of Nanna Francesca's two sons and her five grandchildren come into focus, crowding the top of the glass-fronted cabinet containing hi-ball glasses, gold espresso cups, ceramic bomboniere. How she's loved us all. Three decades I've been Nanna Francesca's eldest grandchild, felt treasured and protected by her, loved and fought her, tried to resist that which is similar between us, tried to be independent rather than face her life of duty. By the time I began opening myself to her, time was already running out. The grief of her failing to recognise me still hurts each time it happens.

I can hear Roger and Nonno Anni outside in the backyard trimming the grapevines. I don't want to disturb Nonno Anni, knowing he is having a much-needed break. But I don't want Nanna Francesca to be frightened, either. She has no idea the cancer she has is terminal, the doctor advising she wouldn't understand, given her vascular dementia. Nonno Anni is honouring her long-held wish to die at home. She is seventy-seven.

'Annibale!' she calls out.

I rush back to her bedside. 'I'm here, Nanna.'

'Who are you?'

'Zoë. Your granddaughter. Would you like a glass of water? Annibale will be back soon.' It still feels strange calling my grandfather by his first name with my grandmother.

She sleeps. I clean the kitchen from top to bottom finding solace in scrubbing. All my life, Nanna Francesca has cooked in this spacious, high-ceilinged kitchen, sometimes several courses for up to forty people. I miss her food already. She lost the ability to cook some time ago, one of many incremental losses of skills in which she'd once been so adept. Incredible now to remember her not so long ago in her sixties caring for her three youngest grandchildren, who were for a time all under the age of three. And she fed, bathed and tended to my young cousins almost single-handedly and without protest for years.

I help her in the bathroom. It must be awful for her to think a stranger is aiding her. Then, as I am helping her dress, she has one of her rare moments of clarity and knows who I am. It feels like sunlight flooding the room and I kiss her cheek. She clutches my arm.

'I need help.'

'I know, Nanna, I am here to help you. I love you.'

She nods. Then she is gone again. It is the last time she ever recognises me.

Later on as she is resting, Roger and I sit with Nonno Anni at the kitchen table. He says she keeps asking him to take her to the farm at Applethorpe to see her parents. When she doesn't let up, he drives her on a short trip to the park. They don't get out of the car. Instead, he points at the grass and trees and says it is the farm but they cannot go up to the house, as her parents aren't home right now. He tells her they'll come back another day. This appeases her. My heart breaks for both of them. It is their sixtieth year of marriage — Nanna Francesca having no idea what the pieces of paper bearing congratulations from the Queen, the Prime Minister and other dignitaries are. I know Nonno Anni is bravely trying his best. The thought of her wanting to return to her childhood home makes me desolate.

More than eight hundred people attend Nanna Francesca's funeral, filling the pews and standing at the back of the church, spilling outside and crowding the open doorways. Recognition not in the form of a medal, but in warmth, breath, heart. Her glass-fronted cabinet of hi-ball glasses, gold espresso cups and ceramic bomboniere is lost in the flood, but I'm fortunate to safeguard her treadle Singer sewing-machine. I've kept the little drawers of buttons, thread, thimbles and the original receipt exactly as she left them.

I become custodian of several of her mother's linens, now close to a century old. The heavy, well-stitched fabrics I keep clean and carefully folded in a set of wooden drawers where I also store linens and the intricate hand-sewn lace that belonged to my mother, my grandmothers and great-grandmothers, both maternal and paternal, along with some pieces collected by me. The linens of seven women over four generations, all saved 'for good' — for my lifetime anyway.

Not for the first time, I touch my fingertips to my great-grandmother's initials embroidered on a pillowslip brought from Palmi — CF — Francesca Carrozza. I do so with a kind of reverence for the connection it brings to my grandmother and great-grandmother who clasped this fabric, sewed thread into it, folded it on their laps, held it up to see. Looking more closely, I notice that what I thought was a swirling design in both initials is actually a tiny pattern of intricate flowers within each curve of lettering, no larger than the crescent moon at the base of my thumbnail. It has taken me years to peer this closely and find them. The revelation feels like a gift.

Old Chums

The children sat side by side on skinny wooden benches to eat their lunches, Sister Rita waiting ten minutes before swinging the hefty brass handbell signalling time to play. Remo unwrapped the waxed paper and took a bite of his sandwich made with hunks of bread.

'What's that?' A boy, Gordon, beside him, stabbed his finger at it.

Remo's mouthful of salami and bread became gluggy and hard to swallow.

'Geez, it stinks!' Gordon clamped one hand over his nose.

'That's *wog* food,' said Janet, a girl with her hair pinned to one side.

Gordon reeled back. 'Where'd you get meat like that?'

Remo thought of Maddalena wielding a razor to shave the hair off the skin of half a pig as it lay across the table downstairs. Then there was the cleaning, cutting and dividing of the animal, his mother carefully washing out the intestines, his father fastening the metal hand-cranked mincer onto the edge of the tabletop with the attachment to direct the seasoned meat laced with fennel into the concertinaed intestine. As it filled with meat, the intestine magically turned into sausages and salami.

For months afterwards, salami and a trotter-less salted hind leg would hang underneath the house to cure, upturned tins suspended above them preventing mice from nibbling at them. Remo thought the salami tasted delicious, but then he noticed his schoolmates mostly eating sandwiches of jam, Vegemite or cheese. In particular, one girl had finely chopped egg and lettuce sandwiches on delicate squares of white bread.

When Francesca returned from the shop that evening, Remo cornered her in the kitchen. 'Mum, tomorrow for school can you make me an egg sandwich like the Australian kids have?'

Francesca shrugged. 'Okay.'

Remo was quite looking forward to lunchtime the next day, certain his classmates would forget the salami now he had a lunch like them. Beaming, he got out his sandwich. A tiny stream of oil slid down his hand. His smile wavered. He opened the wax paper and was dismayed to discover that, in her naïvety, Francesca had slapped a fried egg between two slices of bread. By the middle of a Brisbane summer's day, the bread was soaked with congealed egg and oil.

'What's *that?*' Gordon's voice escalated in alarm, drawing more attention.

'Nothing.' Remo hastily rewrapped his lunch.

Francesca was at her Singer sewing-machine, foot gently pumping the treadle as she hemmed a dress, when Remo came up beside her in his cotton pyjamas. 'Mum, do I have to go to Chinese school tomorrow? Other kids don't have to go to school on a Saturday.'

'Don't call it that, it's good you go to Italian school. You must know your heritage.'

'But Granny and I talk Italian all the time at home.'

Even though Maddalena was downstairs chatting to the Italians currently living in the understorey of the house, Francesca lowered her voice. 'She talks dialect, not proper Italian.'

Vitale glanced up from reading the newspaper and Francesca's foot skipped a beat on the treadle, almost jamming the needle. They exchanged glances, but Vitale merely crushed out his finished cigarette in the ashtray and went back to reading the paper.

'Now have you done your homework? Your father's expecting you to help in the shop tomorrow afternoon when you get back from Italian school.'

'Mum ...'

'What else?'

'I don't want egg on my sandwich any more.'

'A packet of Craven A, son.'

From early childhood Remo had recognised the cigarette packet 'with a cat on it' as a good seller. After the customer left he checked the stock of cigarettes, knowing one of the travellers would soon be coming in to take the order. The tobacco company WD and HO Wills had its offices in a building on the other side of the road, opposite St Martin's Hospital, so their salesman didn't have to come far.

Remo often placed the orders for Camel cigarettes, Three Threes (a pack of nine cigarettes), Capstan, Temple Bar, Craven A (with cork-tipped filters) and a cheap brand called Old Chums, made with an older grade tobacco that sold for one shilling and four pence. The shop also sold loose tobacco, Champion, in a pouch, and Log Cabin that came in strips, along with Tally Ho papers. The only matches sold were Redheads. Remo never really felt inclined to smoke either in childhood or when he was older, though he collected matchboxes, mostly for the pictures featured on them.

He had a box of matches in his pocket when he and Robbie, who lived nearby, walked up to the end of their street in the evening to where the trams travelled along Commercial Road.

Robbie bent sideways to scratch at a mosquito bite on his leg. 'You got 'em?'

'Yeah.' Remo pulled the box of matches out of his pocket.

'We better hurry, Rem. The ten past eight will be here soon.'

The boys put some matches on the tram track, then hid behind a nearby fence, watching through gaps between the palings, their shoes and socks dampening in the dew-soaked long grass.

'I can hear it coming.' Robbie's grin was wide, the streetlight picking out the freckles on his pale skin. 'I hope it scares the motorman.'

The tram rumbled along, getting closer. Remo chuckled in anticipation. The tram thundered past, its wheels igniting the matches and causing two loud bangs, to the boys' delight.

'Hey, you got a penny, Rem? Let's see if the tram will squash it flat.'

Remo dug into his pocket and eagerly scrambled back up to the track.

Hearing Remo drop his school bag on the floor in the bedroom, Maddalena began cutting off the end of the loaf of bread. He wandered into the kitchen, expecting her to trickle a little olive oil onto bread for his afternoon tea as she usually did, but instead she hollowed out the crust and filled it with some pasta gravy simmering in a pot on the stove.

She handed it to him. 'Be back by dark.'

After school, children pounded up the wooden steps of houses all along Wyandra Street, only to thud back down five or ten minutes later. Remo and his friends — Robbie, who was two years older, and the Moore boys from several doors down — went straight to Bartlett's wafer factory at the end of the street, where they got free reject wafers to eat, before heading to the muddy riverbank in front of the wool stores.

'Quick, the ferry's here,' shouted Robbie, prompting the boys to run and clamber on.

The barge could ferry about six cars at a time across the river between Teneriffe and Bulimba. When it sat at the terminal not in service, the boys used it as a pirate ship. It was a game they played often, and Remo had fallen into the river a couple of times, one time sinking in grey mud up to his thighs, another time cutting his foot on a piece of submerged glass.

They were halcyon afternoons, stretching from when the sun was still high until it sank low and the mammoth wool-store buildings cast long shadows, dimming the shine on the slate-coloured water. Remo was one of the gang at those moments, even if he didn't have a name that could be easily Anglicised. He could put aside all the things he'd never tell his mates — like translating for women in doctors' surgeries; foregoing the serial on the radiogram out of respect when an Italian he didn't even know had died; working at the shop; or going to Italian school on weekends while his friends were playing cricket. Things that set him — as an Italian born in Australia — slightly apart from the crowd.

Breakfast Creek was a two-kilometre walk from the boys' street. Upstream it became Enoggera Creek, while the wider downstream section to where Robbie, Remo and the Moore boys traipsed, flowed straight into the Brisbane River. They saw an old man securing a dinghy, and Robbie, as the eldest, asked if they could take it for a row.

'Long as you bring her back and tie her up here.' The man nodded as Remo and the youngest Moore brother leant over with their hands on their knees to peer into his bucket of writhing fish. 'You all hop in and I'll give you a push out.'

Even though the morning sun was strong, the four boys' faces seemed lit from within as they began rowing with the current. Robbie, being ten, shared an oar with the youngest Moore boy, who was seven, while Remo and the other Moore brother, both eight, gripped the second.

Vitale helped Annibale hasten to close up the shop. It was just after three o'clock and they never closed during the afternoon.

'No one's seen them since breakfast?' Annibale couldn't quite believe what he was hearing. His hand shook slightly as he fastened the back door.

'The police are looking and announcements are being made on the radio.'

Out the front of the house, Francesca and Maddalena stood with the mothers of the other boys, all the women trying not to panic. The other fathers had left work early, too, as had half a dozen young Italian men staying at Annibale and Francesca's, including Annibale's cousin Evandro. Everyone milled about, debating what to do. Mr Moore had a local map and divided the surrounding area into sections where the boys might be. The men split up, hurrying away by foot, bicycle or vehicle, backing up the police search. At intervals they returned — with no news — then headed back out to a different spot.

Francesca, holding Lorenzo in one arm, gripped Maddalena's arm with her other hand. 'It will be dark soon.'

Evandro thought he'd take one last walk through the gasworks before heading back to the house. The sun had set and twilight didn't linger in Brisbane. Already the sky was beginning to lose its faint pewter luminosity to darkness. He walked towards the river and was about to turn around when he saw four small figures coming through the hillocks of coal and ashes dumped around the gasworks site.

'Remo! Is it you?'

Remo's sunburnt face broke into a happy smile and he bounded up to Evandro. 'What are you doing here?'

Remo received that many rough hugs and pats his sunburn started to smart. Annibale was so relieved he didn't even go back to open the shop for the evening. Maddalena put on two big pots of water to boil the pasta while Francesca began frying cut-up pieces of their homemade sausages. Annibale fetched several bottles of beer, wine and lemonade and the house took on a party atmosphere. The half-dozen Italians from downstairs joined them and, for a little while, Remo had centre stage at the crowded kitchen table. Relishing everyone being together, he suddenly wished his parents would always close the shop before dark, so they could have dinner as a family every night.

Call This a Holiday?

When Annibale and Vitale went halves in buying two blocks of flats, converted from what had once been a couple of grand houses in Fortitude Valley, word travelled on the Italian grapevine and new migrants snapped up all eight flats. Annibale collected the rents on a Sunday morning, most tenants inviting him in for coffee and grappa. They were a mixed bunch — families, older couples and men sharing flats until they could afford the fares for their wives in Italy to travel out to join them. Most had factory or labouring work — all they could get with their limited English being their second language. They'd come from farming families, except for one man who had been a schoolteacher in Italy.

'And he acts as though he's better than the rest of us,' one of the older men, Antonio, chuckled to Annibale. 'Even though here he's doing the same work as us.'

'We're having a big party on Saturday night,' said Antonio's wife, Ginessa. 'Bring all the family. Now, will you have a coffee?'

Annibale peered around the room, looking for a clock. 'Well, I've got to get to the shop, but maybe a quick coffee …'

'Dad doesn't get into the shop until nearly lunchtime,' Remo, then eleven, complained to Francesca, annoyed that he had to open the shop early every Sunday morning and handle the St John's crowd that swarmed in after attending church, while Annibale collected the rents. 'A lot of the Grammar boys are shoplifting from us, but on my own, I can't do much about it.'

'Well, I need one day off.' Francesca kept ironing as she spoke. 'Your father will get there as soon as he finishes collecting the rents. Remo, we just have to do our bit.'

Coming towards the shop, Remo gently applied the brakes on his bicycle and smoothly dismounted while it was still moving. He wheeled the bike through the side entrance into the courtyard, propped it against the wall of the shop and bounded up the back steps. Inside, one of the milkshake machines was going and Annibale immediately told him to give the shake to a man waiting, then went back to weighing some sultana grapes and putting them in a paper bag for another customer.

'Fruit and Nut, and the paper,' said the next man and Remo reached for the chocolate bar, the customer picking up a newspaper from the stack in front of the counter.

With paperboys on many city street corners, Annibale only stocked about twenty copies, just enough for regulars. Cherry, an older paper 'boy' who sold newspapers outside the Gresham Hotel to make a bit on top of his pension, was nicknamed for his ever crimson face. He delivered each new edition of the paper to the shop throughout the day — the Late Extra and City Final editions in the afternoon, and on race days a third evening edition at around six o'clock called Last Race, with results and pictures of Brisbane's Saturday-afternoon sports, including the last horse race that day.

Annibale and Remo were both busy serving customers when Len Bleakley, the shoe repairer who had a small workshop directly above the milk bar, let down a soft-drink bottle on a piece of string with a message taped to it asking for a bottle of Coca-Cola. Usually they untied the empty bottle and replaced it with a new one straightaway but they were too busy serving at that moment. Getting impatient, Bleakley tweaked the string from above, crashing the empty bottle through the open window and into all the empties they'd lined up to move out the back. Remo groaned and quickly got him a new bottle, and then set about tidying up the mess.

It was summer holidays and the day was already promising to be hot. Sun glinted on cars passing outside, occasionally flashing light into the shop. Some of the cars were packed with families, luggage secured to the car roof or protruding from a partially open boot, heading to or from the south coast or the beaches up north.

'We camped right by the sea,' said one of Remo's friends, Dennis, who'd come into the shop for ice cream with their other friend, Malcolm. 'Every morning we went swimming and in the afternoon we played footy on the beach.'

'We went fishing out in my uncle's tinny,' Malcom joined in. 'But the best were the barbecues at night. Sometimes we had a big bonfire.'

Remo's gaze flicked between the tanned happy faces of his friends. He smiled, nodding and making interested expressions at their stories and laughter, yet after they left his face felt a little stiff. They hadn't asked what he'd been doing on his holidays, during which he'd turned twelve. They knew he'd mainly been helping his parents behind the milk bar and in the fruit shop.

One of the dressmakers from the Epstein tailors upstairs came down to buy a packet of biscuits. Then a woman wearing a sunhat trimmed with fabric flowers came in and asked for half a dozen peaches. Remo went over to the wooden case to get the fruit for her.

She watched him putting the peaches into a paper bag and smiled. 'So, enjoying the school holidays?'

'Holiday? You call this a holiday?'

She looked at him for a moment, then started to chuckle.

When Annibale purchased more flats, he needed some of Saturday as well as Sunday morning to collect the rents, carry out maintenance and do the mowing. In the shop the middle hours of Saturday stretched. Remo stared longingly out at the sunny street. He turned back to stacking the shelf with packets of Arnott's Milk Arrowroot, Scotch Finger, Iced VoVo and Nice biscuits. A burst of girlish laughter grabbed his attention as a group of boys and girls in their early teens walked past the shop. He didn't know them but they looked not much older than he was.

That morning he had mustered the courage to complain to his parents about having to work at the shop that day, pointing out, 'Laurie doesn't work in the shop.'

'He's too young,' Francesca and Annibale had both said at once.

Remo had opened his mouth to argue that he'd started working in the shop unsupervised from the age of ten, and that he'd been helping out for years before that, at an age younger than Lorenzo was now, but instead bit his lip. In all Remo's life, Annibale had never once laid a hand on him, but he had a fearful respect for his father and said nothing more.

Feeling bored and petulant, Remo made himself a milkshake, tipping in a little less milk than usual, though taking care to capture with the ladle as much of the cream on top of the milk canister as he could. Then he scooped in some ice cream, adding an extra few scoops for good measure, and poured in a liberal amount of chocolate syrup. The electric mixer protested at first, the little engine climbing to a whine, but he persevered and slurped the dense, cold milkshake through two paper straws. It tempered his resentment, just a little.

By the afternoon, the busy lunchtime crowd of customers had thinned out and Annibale, back from the flats, clamped his hand down on Remo's shoulder. 'Why don't you take off for a bit to the pictures?' He held out some money and saw his son's face brighten.

Movies became Remo's escape — *20,000 Leagues Under the Sea*, *The Court Jester*, *Gunfight at the O.K. Corral*, *Ben-Hur*. Sometimes he went on his own during a break from the shop, but often with friends. While suburban cinemas had canvas seats, the city theatres had proper plush seating, the Regent being a real treat. The boys gravitated to the back, standing with the rest of the theatregoers as the session commenced with the national anthem. When they sat down the newsreel started with its laughing kookaburras, followed by a cartoon. Then the next instalment in a serial of *The Lone Ranger* or *The Green Hornet* screened for about fifteen minutes, finishing on a cliffhanger so people would come back the next week to see what happened. Sitting in the darkened theatre, Remo's face shone in the light of the screen.

It was a muggy night and Annibale plugged in a small fan on the bench behind the counter. Although after ten, the temperature was still above seventy-five degrees Fahrenheit. The milk bar and freezer pumped out hot air as usual, making the shop even warmer. A sweet, ripe scent rose from the fruit displays. Remo came in wearing long trousers and a neatly pressed short-sleeved shirt.

Annibale looked up. 'You been to the pictures?'

Remo nodded, wandering around behind the counter to get a glass of cold water. '*Jailhouse Rock*. With Malcolm and Keith from school.'

They heard a blare of rock-and-roll music coming from a car radio and glanced out to see 'Rock 'n' Roll George' cruise by in his bulbous '52 FX Holden, lapping the inner-city streets as he always did. They looked back at each other.

'I was going to get a lift home with you, if you're closing up soon.'

Annibale smiled. 'Yeah, why not? It's pretty quiet.'

Remo helped him close up. He shut and locked the narrow hallway door, along with the back door. Then, to secure the front of the shop, together they slid into grooves four metal gates, each about five feet high and one and a half feet wide. The two gates covering the display window Annibale padlocked into position. Where the steps led up to the main entrance, he slid a wooden panel into place as Remo helped with another two gates. Even though the shop looked secure, Remo realised one of these final two gates could be removed. 'Dad, this doesn't lock. Anyone could just push it open and get into the shop if they wanted to.'

'Yeah, but they haven't. It's been like that for years, it'll be right.' They walked to the corner and Annibale turned down Wharf Street towards the river. 'I had to park the truck down the next block. It was really busy in town earlier tonight.'

At this late hour, the dark street was almost deserted. Flying foxes gently winged overhead on trajectory from the mammoth Moreton Bay fig trees on the other side of the river. Annibale and Remo, talking as they walked, didn't see the two men lurking in the shadows.

'*Hey*. You. Wog.'

The men stepped out towards the middle of the footpath. With the streetlight behind them, their faces were in darkness. Annibale moved to walk around them, aware of his twelve-year-old son beside him.

'I'll 'ave ya, yer *wog*.' The man raised his fist.

Annibale swiftly punched him first. The man went down onto the footpath.

Fists still ready, Annibale turned to the other man. '*Come on then*.' His Italian accent was thick but his English was clear.

The other man backed into a chain-link fence. It sagged inward with his weight. Annibale lunged towards him. Panicking, the man dropped to the ground and wriggled underneath the fence. He legged it across an empty lot, leaving the other man still on the footpath, moaning and gingerly touching his bloody nose.

Annibale slowly lowered his fists and turned to Remo, who was standing near the gutter. 'Let's go.'

They continued at a brisk pace towards the truck. Approaching his teens, Remo usually felt a tangle of affection, apprehension and sometimes resentment towards his father. He sneaked a glance at him, a little in awe just then.

'Remo …'

'Yeah, Dad?'

'What does "wog" mean?'

Remo hid his surprise. 'It's a bad word they now use that's kind of like dago.'

Annibale nodded. 'By that bloke's tone I thought it couldn't be good.'

In that moment, Remo saw his father's vulnerability too.

The Descant Shifts

The Australian government, alarmed that the number of migrants arriving from southern Europe was outnumbering British migrants, had instigated in 1957 the 'Bring out a Briton' campaign. Prime Minister Menzies also introduced restrictions on people like Annibale sponsoring southern European newcomers. Although the Australian government operated schemes to assist selected migrants from Italy and other European countries, its generous financial assistance to Britons meant they soon exceeded in number all other migrants. As the 1950s were drawing to a close, the surge of Italian migration to Australia that had occurred over several decades was diminishing. In the rooms underneath the house at Wyandra Street, where newcomers had so often stayed, the beds stood stripped and empty, mattresses leant up against a wall.

At about this time, Brisbane's backdrop of the gently undulating Taylor Range also changed forever with the construction of TV transmitters along the ridgetops. In daylight, they towered over the tree line, and at night they became daggers of red light punctuating the hills. Everyone was excited about the introduction of television to Brisbane in August 1959. One of the Boccabellas' neighbours was among the first to get a licence and a television set, but much to Remo's chagrin, Annibale refused to buy one.

'Annibale, get him a television set.' Maddalena shook her head. 'You can afford it.'

'You know what Remo's like, wanting to go to the pictures all the time. He'll be constantly staring at that thing.' Annibale was adamant. 'It's only a few years until he finishes his senior certificate at school. Till then he can concentrate on his exams and getting into university.' He turned to Remo. 'I didn't have the chance to finish school, like you. You could be a doctor one day.'

Remo looked alarmed. 'I don't want anything to do with blood.'

Francesca stepped forward. 'Annibale ...'

'We're not buying a television set.' Annibale's bellow silenced them all.

Vincenzo, watching the exchange, stayed out of it. But later he joined Remo sitting on the back steps after dinner. 'I'm going for a bike ride, do you want to come?'

Remo shrugged, putting spit on a mosquito bite on his elbow.

Vincenzo's voice was soft. 'There's a shop at Bulimba that leaves television sets on in their window at night.' Remo's head jerked up. 'When your father heads back to the shop we can take our bikes across on the ferry. He'll never know.'

Vincenzo and Remo drew up on their bicycles at the electrical shop in Oxford Street to find a small crowd had already gathered to marvel at the new entertainment. People not only stood around to watch, some brought chairs and supper too. Vincenzo and Remo found a spot where they could see one of the small black-and-white screens and quickly became engrossed in an episode of *Maverick*. They couldn't go every evening and risk raising suspicion but it often proved tempting to take the ferry across the river to watch whatever happened to be on the shop television — ballroom dancing, *I Love Lucy*, the wrestling.

Life was changing in Wyandra Street, too. The after-school banter of children and their running footsteps faded. For a little while the street became very quiet as houses emptied ... and then noisy as bulldozers moved in. Residents were given little choice but to move on as developers applied pressure. Low-set concrete industrial buildings began outnumbering the workers' cottages with their lattice and sash windows until there was almost no hint that they and the neighbourhood families had ever been there.

In December 1959, Annibale and Francesca bought a house on Brunswick Street in the neighbouring suburb of New Farm, two doors up from a few small shops clustering at the intersection with Merthyr Road. The house sat high on stumps with a breezeway, cement-floored bathroom, toilet and laundry underneath. Like most Brisbane houses, its roof was russet-red corrugated iron. The bay window of leadlight-glass diamonds glinted in the morning sunlight, the timber walls gleaming with fresh coats of white paint. In the front garden a poinsettia — Brisbane's floral emblem — blazed with red blooms.

They all moved in — Annibale, Francesca, Remo, Lorenzo, Maddalena, Vitale and Vincenzo — even though by then Annibale and Vitale owned several houses and blocks of flats. Annibale had also begun to buy and renovate large old houses, raising the first-floor level so underneath could be enclosed with brick and plaster, then dividing the structures into yet more flats. Sometimes Vitale and Vincenzo helped as navvies and Remo, now in his mid-teens, worked as a brickie's labourer over his summer holidays, enjoying a break from the shop.

Yet they were big jobs, and as well as contracting Italian bricklayers and plasterers, Annibale needed more labourers. Word got around at the Fire Brigade headquarters across from the shop. A number of the firemen had trades such as carpentry or plumbing, but weren't officially supposed to work when they were off duty. Nevertheless, Annibale soon found he had a team of firemen working on his flats, one member always keeping lookout and giving the tip-off if a senior fire officer was sighted. Annibale worked alongside his team, buying many of the tools, a couple of wheelbarrows and even a cement-mixer, soon battered with use.

Faced with the problem of removing old house stumps embedded in the earth, Annibale would simply tie a thick rope to the back of his Chev to drag them out. The back wheels would spin, the tyres struggling to grip the clay.

'You burn out another clutch, Joe?' a fireman chuckled, a running joke.

Annibale grinned. 'Got all the stumps out.'

One of the other firemen was an SP bookie who asked Annibale if he could rent one of the flats unfurnished. All he wanted in it was a telephone. But Annibale politely declined.

He had no trouble renting the flats, all of them furnished, mostly to young Australian couples. In the course of time children were born and brought up in them and little communities blossomed. On 'rent day' Annibale walked around knocking on each of the doors to collect the rents, and if a toilet needed fixing, the grass mowing or there was painting to be done, he did it himself.

Remo put down the pencil and closed his final senior-certificate exam. Walking towards the door to leave, he thought, *Well, I've done the best I can.*

It's out of my hands now whether I get into uni. He suppressed a smile. *But Dad will finally have to buy us a television set.*

Before he quite got to the doorway, a girl rushed in and hissed to the supervisor, 'President Kennedy has been shot!'

Shocked murmurs surged between the students who remained at their desks, still to complete their exam. Remo headed straight for the shop.

It was Saturday morning and most people were learning of American President John F. Kennedy's assassination by word of mouth. Remo found Annibale leaning on the counter, talking with half a dozen customers about it. Everyone was stunned, some shaking their heads, others holding their hands to their mouths.

'It's incredible. This sort of thing just doesn't happen,' said one man.

'They were a good-looking family with young children. He was so full of life,' mourned a woman.

Annibale inclined his head to Remo as he joined them. 'You've heard?'

He nodded. 'It's unbelievable.'

There was a pause then a man said, 'This your son, Joe?'

Annibale smiled. 'My eldest, Remo. Just finished his last senior exam.'

'So will you work at the shop now?' the woman asked Remo.

'I'm hoping to study to be a teacher.'

'He's going to go to university.' The pride in Annibale's tone was clear.

Remo smiled self-consciously.

He waited until later when there was a lull in customers and then turned to his father. 'Dad, I'm not going to work in the shop this summer like I usually do. I've got a job at the postal exchange on North Quay, helping to sort the mail ...' His voice trailed off.

Annibale looked at him for a moment; his lips twitched. 'Oh. Right then.'

On his way home for dinner on impulse Annibale ducked into the Queens Arms Hotel in James Street. He ordered a beer and stood at the bar, taking a long sip. He'd felt surprised and slightly annoyed about Remo getting a job elsewhere over the holidays but wouldn't try to stop him. He recognised Remo was beginning to assert himself as a young man and needed to make his own way, just as he had. It did make him think, though, about the future of the milk bar and fruit shop, especially with the rents coming in steadily now. Lorenzo was doing well at school and would most likely go to university too. Annibale took another draft of his beer.

'Black bastard.' The voice was menacing but soft, an almost serpentine whisper.

Annibale wasn't quite sure if he'd heard right. He looked over to see a group of white Australian men standing around a tall table, all holding beers.

'Who's this Abo think he is?'

Annibale followed the direction of their stares to an Aboriginal man dressed neatly in work clothes sitting at the other end of the bar, trying to have a quiet drink.

'They don't allow animals in the bar. Abos are fauna, aren't they?'

'Maybe we need to give this darkie a seeing-to.' One of the men pushed his cap a little further back on his head. 'Send him outside with the dogs.'

Annibale sized up the group of five men, picked up his beer and went and sat down next to the Aboriginal man. 'Unbelievable about Kennedy getting shot, isn't it?'

The man flicked a shy glance at him and looked down. 'Yes.'

Annibale sighed. 'Who knows why you'd go and do a thing like that?'

'Yep.' From experience the man remained guarded.

Annibale was aware the group of men was now directing their looks at him. 'It was warm today, wasn't it?'

'Too right.'

'Not as hot as it used to get further out west, though. There was a time I was working in a road gang out near Pikedale and, by geez, it could get hot.'

'I been out that way. Gets hot all right.'

Annibale introduced himself. 'Can I buy you a beer?'

The man looked at him for a moment, then gave a ghost of a smile and relaxed a little. 'Yep. Thanks. My name's Jack.'

One of the white men behind them scoffed. 'Both the Abo and the wog deserve a hiding, I reckon.'

Twisting slightly in his seat, Annibale gave him an intense, almost challenging look. He'd turned forty the month before, but his tall frame was muscular from his labouring work on the flats and the constant lifting of wooden boxes of soft drinks and produce at the shop. A couple of the men looked away.

After the second beer, Jack said he should head home for tea and Annibale got up to leave the pub with him. As they walked past the men at the table, Annibale was poised to act should he need to, but the group must have decided the prospect of picking on an Aboriginal bloke was less appealing when he was no longer on his own.

Cloudland

Perched on a summit in Bowen Hills, Cloudland Ballroom's vaulted entry arch soared high into the sky, its grotto of light visible for miles. Women in their best dresses and men in suits gravitated to its seductive light in cars or on foot via the funicular 'alpine' railway on the Breakfast Creek side of the hill. Francesca smoothed the cerise taffeta of her ballgown. It was the first dress she'd owned that had a metal zipper at the back, her dressmaker assuring her all the women were getting them now.

Francesca and Annibale walked into the vast, airy ballroom abuzz with conversation and a seven-piece band tuning their instruments. With its sprung floor, cloistered alcoves and upper circle of seating overlooking the dance floor and stage, Cloudland was reputed to be the finest ballroom of its kind in Australia. Decorated with sweeping curtains, greenery, chandeliers and domed skylights, there were sumptuously upholstered lounge chairs throughout. A servery down one end provided patrons with drinks and hors d'oeuvres.

The ball had been organised by successful migrants in order to raise funds for newer migrant families struggling to establish themselves. Both the music and food had an Italian theme and the band launched into a velvety version of 'Florentine Serenade', perfect for waltzing. Lights dimmed and the turning mirror ball above the dance floor added to the enchantment. Annibale — still never having learnt to dance — went off to talk with the men, while Francesca made a beeline for her friends, to tell them the proud news that Remo was studying to be a high-school teacher.

Annibale stood drinking wine and eating small pieces of anchovy pizza with some of his closest friends and others he'd just met. They spoke about the Italian Consul looking to set up a Brisbane branch of the ANFE — the *Associazione Nazionale Famiglie degli Emigrati* — and how those who wanted to be involved could do so on a voluntary basis around their other commitments. For the first time, Annibale considered closing the fruit shop and milk bar on weekends.

He felt someone tap his arm and turned to see Giovanna and Stefano Tomasi, both of course much older but still instantly recognisable. It was the first time he'd seen them since leaving Ingham in 1941 and the acute surprise was clear on his face. He could hear his own voice uttering the expected greetings, but his thoughts kept flitting through images from the past — of Savina's face, of Giovanna sobbing over Stefano's internment, and of himself throwing his port in the river and running to a train heading south. For a moment he felt like the teenager he'd been back then at the cane fields.

'We're down from Ingham for a week for Stefano to see a specialist — nothing serious — and friends of ours invited us along here to Cloudland with them.'

As Giovanna continued to speak, Annibale thought of his parents, at home that evening with Lorenzo, and how they'd have liked to see the Tomasis. Especially his mother, knowing how close Maddelena and Giovanna had been as neighbours and friends in Fossa.

Giovanna leaned in closer, her voice lowered. 'Have you heard about Savina?'

He cleared his throat. 'Uh, no.' All of a sudden he hoped Francesca wouldn't come over.

'I'm going to get another drink,' said Stefano, nodding to Annibale.

Giovanna sighed. 'Savina married and had a son, and he is, you know, handicapped, I think they call it. Then a few years later, her husband was badly hurt in a car accident. Brain damage, they call it. Savina spends all her time looking after them both.'

Annibale wasn't sure what to say. 'Poor Savina,' he finally murmured, though it seemed inadequate.

'*Sì, sì.*' Giovanna nodded, surveying the ballroom with another long sigh.

They stood there in a bubble of awkward silence. Annibale thought of the Savina he had known — young, smiling, with shining dark braids. He recalled standing on the riverbank with her. Their life together would have been very different. He wondered if they'd have come to Brisbane or if she'd have expected him to help on Stefano's cane property — trapped and unable to pursue his own dream. Neither Francesca nor her parents had tried to keep him at the Solanos' farm. The noise of the ball seemed to rise slightly and break through their silence.

'I'd better go and find Stefano,' Giovanna said eventually.

He hesitated. 'Could you perhaps give Savina my regards? Or maybe not?'

Giovanna moved her purse to the crook of her elbow. 'You had to do what you had to at the time,' she said matter-of-factly. 'Savina got over it. It was good to see you, Annibale.'

'Goodbye.' Annibale watched her move away through the crowd, unsure if she would tell Savina she had seen him.

The '60s whirled on. Music and fashion got louder, food more colourful, cars lengthened, generations clashed. The government introduced conscription for the Vietnam War, the birthdates of young men turning twenty to be drawn from a national service ballot every six months. Remo's birthdate was among those in the second ballot to be drawn later that year and he submitted his national service registration forms, prepared to do the 'nasho'. For months they waited, nerves on edge, Francesca often teary. He was fortunate not to be called up, but some of his friends were, their lives altered forever. For the first time, moving images and sounds of war came straight into people's houses via the nightly news telecasts, stunning everyone, making them more aware of what was occuring in combat.

Protest marches began occurring in the city, most violently quashed by police. Many younger people stopped standing for 'God Save the Queen' in picture theatres, to the disgust of older patrons. Inside homes across the country, conflicts waged over war, race, women's liberation. Australians became more conscious of how Indigenous people were subject to mistreatment and government control, and overwhelmingly voted for them to be included as Australian citizens for the first time in a national census.

For more than twenty years, life around Annibale and Francesca's fruit shop and milk bar had proceeded with little variation. And now suddenly it seemed like everything was changing around them. The Roma Street produce markets, which had been operating since 1884, closed down and were demolished in a bid to solve city traffic issues. Annibale now had to drive to the outskirts of Brisbane, to Rocklea, where the markets had moved to. Opposite the shop, the Fire Brigade headquarters closed down, also relocating. Dust and noise filled the air as the handsome building with its turreted bell tower and fire lookout was demolished.

In a desire to improve the view to St John's Cathedral, the Anglican Synod approved the demolition of St Martin's Hospital, despite it having been built as a memorial to those killed in the First World War and in operation since 1922. Drawn-out protests would eventually preserve part of the historic building, to be used for church administration, but the hospital was doomed. Speedometer Screenwiper Service moved out of the Anglican-owned building that housed Annibale and Francesca's shop, and the Church let the premises to a hot-food shop, in competition with the milk bar. Annibale was annoyed but determined to ride it out.

The hot-food shop, run by a staff of bikies, had a jukebox playing all day. Remo enjoyed hearing songs like Del Shannon's 'Runaway' drift into the shop but loathed having to go in early to open on Sunday mornings and find half a dozen bikies sleeping in the hallway and out on the back landing, blocking his way. The men were unkempt and intimidating, and all he could do was wait until they stirred.

Annibale managed to remain in business despite the opposition, but the next change proved the death knell: the council turned Ann Street into a one-way thoroughfare and prohibited parking along the road. Remo got booked just stopping to pick up Francesca after her shift at the shop. Straightaway, customer numbers decreased. The shop now relied solely on foot traffic, but with the fire headquarters gone and the hospital slated to close, the future didn't bode well. On weekends in particular the milk bar was quiet, and Annibale made the decision to trade only Monday to Friday and use his time on the weekends helping with ANFE.

On the last Saturday night he kept the shop open, he looked about at the fruit displays, the milk bar, and the shelves of chocolates and cigarettes. He thought back to that day in 1946 when he'd first stepped inside the empty premises that would become such a large part of their lives. *How can two decades pass just like that?* Change was something Annibale had mostly welcomed in his life. Usually it meant moving on to better things than what he had. Yet the shop was something he'd built up himself and it had prospered. He felt a tug in his heart knowing one day it would close for good, and that the time was rapidly nearing. The Anglican Synod had already hinted that the building housing the shop would be another worth losing to improve the view of their cathedral.

'The next number will be a progressive dance,' the band leader announced. 'Fellows, find a partner …'

There was a dull charge of shoes on timber as young men in black suits and thin ties rushed across Cloudland's dance floor, happy to ask anyone to join them, knowing they'd get a new partner within the first minute. At the end of the dance, Remo found himself landed with a girl who clutched a scrunched-up hanky. He tentatively held her hand, feeling obliged to dance the next waltz with her, hoping the unfamiliar tune would soon end.

He'd completed his studies at the University of Queensland the year before and now looked around the ballroom, the welcome dance for the new intake of students to the Kelvin Grove Teachers' College in full swing. Young women in evening gowns sat along the upholstered banquettes while the male students roamed back and forth deciding which girl to approach. Escorting the young woman with the hanky back to her seat, Remo noticed a classmate sitting nearby. Her floor-length dress of deep-green velvet hugged her petite figure and brought out the green of her eyes. He asked her to dance. At the end of the evening he offered to drive her home to her parents' house at Red Hill. Her name was Sandy.

For some time, Francesca had been encouraging Remo to date the daughters of her Italian friends; she and Annibale influenced by an adage common at the time that most cross-cultural marriages ended in divorce. But many of the next generation believed times were changing. And Remo had fallen in love with an Australian girl. Annibale and Francesca would ultimately come to be very fond of their daughter-in-law, but those early days proved challenging for everyone, particularly Remo.

After graduation, he was posted out west to teach in Goondiwindi, while Sandy stayed in Brisbane and taught at Hendra. Still, they became engaged to marry upon his return.

Annibale stood gazing around the empty shop. He had sold the fridges, milk bar and all the trappings. Without them, the walls and bare shelves looked battered and sad.

'Twenty-three years,' Francesca sighed, coming up beside him. 'Lots of memories. It's a shame the building will be demolished …' Her voice drifted off as she walked over to the shopfront to look out at the street.

Annibale glanced at Lorenzo, who was kicking at something on the floor. 'Come on, help me get this down.'

Francesca watched Annibale and Lorenzo lift down the large mirror that had hung on the wall behind the counter for two decades. In the bottom corner was a Beatles sticker that Remo had put there as a teenager. Francesca wished he could have been there to see the shop close. It had been a part of his life since he was a baby. She thought back to when it had just been the three of them in Brisbane and they first opened for business. Her eyes welling with tears, she sighed and went out the back, pretending to survey the courtyard one last time.

When he returned from his honeymoon, Remo rushed to the site hoping to see the shop one last time, but it was too late. He stopped still, standing alone on the footpath. The building was already half-demolished.

Elder Wisdoms

From the street there is nothing to indicate that a fruit shop and milk bar ever existed at 365 Ann Street, Brisbane. I pause at the spot it once occupied, in the shade of an office block of concrete and glass. A garden bed of trees and shrubs stands roughly where Nonno Anni and Nanna Francesca spent so many hours standing behind the counter. By chance, an orange-tiled staircase leads towards the modern building in almost the same place a few wooden steps led into the cool dimness of my grandparents' shop.

The milk bar and fruit shop was such a large part of their lives from 1946 until 1969, yet there is only one picture of the entire family standing in front of it, taken in the mid-1950s. Even then, just the front part of the shop can be seen rather than the entire building. Nonno Anni holds Lorenzo, a toddler. Nanna Francesca, dressed in black, mourning the sudden loss of her father, doesn't have her usual smile for the camera. My father, aged about eight, is squinting in the strong sunlight, one sock up, one down. Bisnonno Vitale and Granny Maddalena stand out of the way in the background, not realising they're both part of the picture, too. Behind are signs for Coca-Cola and Tristram's, and a glass case displaying portraits tacked up by the photographer down the hallway. A wire newspaper stand holds a *Telegraph* poster with the headline: 'Residents Complain: Girls' Easy Access to Army Camps', which makes us laugh years later.

If it weren't for a photograph accompanying a small newspaper article printed in the 1960s, I would never have seen what the building housing the shop looked like. To me, the two-storey corner structure with sash windows, awnings of iron, a pitched roof and a chimney has a lot of character. The article has nothing to do with the shop, concentrating on an outfit calling itself the 'Queensland Cultural Civic Centre', by then occupying one of the rooms on the floor above, in between the boot-repair workshop and the tailor. When I ask my father about this tenant that appeared upstairs in the '60s, he recalls it was unclear what went on there but that many people considered it may have been 'a bit dodgy'. The newspaper article seems to imply the same.

OUR 'CENTRE OF CULTURE'

Is this the face of culture in Brisbane? It stands at the corner of Wharf and Ann streets, Brisbane. Entrance to the Queensland Cultural Civic Centre shown above is through a hallway in this building, beside a milk bar. On the building, a hand-painted sign hangs awry. Inside, up a flight of steps, a sign on a door says: 'If we don't hear the doorbell please ring 31 3181 from the public phone just outside'.

(The Queensland Cultural Civic Centre no longer functions as a public organisation. A proposed Government subsidy for it came to nothing. Another organisation, the Queensland Foundation for Cultural Relations, has since been allotted this subsidy.)

The *Sunday Mail*, November 27, 1966

Considering the only picture I can find of the building that contained my grandparents' milk bar and fruit shop appears in an article under the heading, 'Our "Centre of Culture"', I have to smile. While the heading had nothing to do with their modest business — one among thousands of milk bars and fruit shops across Australia — perhaps some small truth lies within the irony of the title. Almost every town and city suburb had its version of this type of shop and even now, for many, the words 'milk bar' conjure nostalgia for possibly simpler, friendlier times, for an Australia once familiar and still treasured. Looking at the photograph makes me wish I could step back into such an era even for a short time, and yet it would be naïve to think that everyday life in the past was idyllic.

The exposure of the photograph barely allows me to make out the signs at the front of the shop, these ones advertising Coca-Cola and Kirks. I see a hint of the fruit displays, but the milk bar is concealed by shade cast by the footpath awning. When this photograph was taken, somewhere in the shadows Nonno Anni and Nanna Francesca were working behind the counter of their milk bar. I am so close, yet barred by the impenetrability of time and the thinness of ink on a yellowed piece of paper.

Because relatively few photographs exist of the shop, inside or out, the descriptions I piece together rely largely upon the vivid recollections of Nonno Anni, Nanna Francesca and my father, and layouts of the shop's interior and the building that Dad draws for me. Each time I see him now he tells me a little more of his experiences growing up and working there.

'The firemen used to come from the headquarters across the road to our shop to buy snacks and drinks and have a chat. This was when there were no fires and they had long periods with not much to do. I remember the men had blue shirts and the officers wore white shirts and ties. A number of them became woven into the fabric of our lives. Often during the school holidays a show was put on that demonstrated the skills of the firemen. There were water hoses, foam hoses and loud clanging bells as engines raced in to handle the fire. It was very exciting, for kids especially.'

He speaks spontaneously, without any trace of his previous reluctance, sometimes brushing his arms as goose bumps rise with his memories. 'Another time, I remember Apollo, the strongman. He was like a strongman in a comic book, wearing the typical tight outfit with a singlet strap coming over one shoulder and showing half a bare chest. The street outside the shop was crowded with people hyped up by a fellow speaking through a loudhailer: "Ladies, gentlemen and children …" As Apollo placed a leather piece in his mouth and tightened his teeth around it, the other end was attached to a Mack fire engine. Apollo faced the engine as if squaring off against an opponent. Bending backwards, he started taking the weight of the engine, ever so slowly at first. As he used his strong legs, gradually the engine moved and we all cheered while he continued for three or four yards.'

I take in his stories in the same way I spent three decades listening to my grandparents' stories — at the kitchen table, on the back steps, driving along in the car, by the stove. And I make sure I ask more questions now. It wasn't until some years after my grandparents died that it occurred to me that often I was learning from them without realising it at the time; they themselves seemingly unaware too of what they were imparting. Not just with their stories but also through experiences they provided.

The dress Nanna Francesca brought me back from Italy feels a bit scratchy around the collar. We sit in a lounge room of gleaming white tiles. It is a Sunday — visiting day — when Nonno Anni and Nanna Francesca drive to different people's houses to visit, taking me along if I happen to be staying over. Being a child, I'm not expected to say much, so while the adults talk I sit and observe — and absorb. I look around at figurines on doilies. My piece of sponge cake on a china plate tastes like almonds. I don't have coffee like the adults; instead I'm given a crystal glass of lemonade, the soft drink cold and sweet in my mouth.

Through the window, I see a young man loitering near the garden shed. He is the son of the widow we are visiting, yet he looks lost in his own backyard. I ask to go outside to play but Nanna Francesca says no, glancing out at him. The woman smiles sadly and Nonno Anni goes out to the yard instead. I see him clasp the shoulder of the young man who hangs his head. He might be crying but I cannot be sure. In those days I never saw men cry. Nanna Francesca whispers to me not to bother the young man, 'because he has the shellshock'.

For some reason I associate him with the Second World War, but years later I realise he must have fought in Vietnam. Back then, nobody spoke about that war, denying the young men, many of them conscripts, acknowledgment and assistance. I was too young to know that young man's name, but never forgot him, standing lost by the shed. I worry for him still. My own father was so very fortunate not to have had his birthdate picked in the second national service ballot, drawn on September 10, 1965. They selected the day right before his birthday.

If I happen to be staying with my grandparents on 'rent day', Nonno Anni sometimes takes me along with him to collect the rents. My buckle-up shoes patter on the gravel of the back lane to the first block of flats, my short legs trotting, determined to keep up with my grandfather's strides. The rent book and a cloth bank bag stick out of Nonno Anni's KingGee pants pocket.

He wears his usual navy work singlet. Though he's in his fifties, the muscles in his arms remain defined, his skin deeply tanned. The milk bar and fruit shop has been closed for a few years by now.

As we approach the block of flats from the back, glimpses of the original grand Queenslander can be seen among the cladding and rendered walls — gables, balustrades, chimney pipes that lead nowhere — spectres of a former life. Warm from the sun, Nonno Anni and I walk into the downstairs hallway where open doors at either end let a breeze gust through, stirring the faint reek of old cooking oil, alcohol and damp fur. The worn cement floor is coated in the same deep-red Pavol floor paint Nonno Anni used in the shop.

I quietly trail him as he knocks on the front door of each flat, calling, 'Hello! Rent!' Over the years, as the buildings deteriorated, the tenants changed from young couples and families to single men, Aboriginal people and the elderly poor, right down to those practically destitute, suffering from alcoholism or disabilities. I see an old man smelling of grog with his belt buckled too loose and a gappy smile. Then there is a woman in a floral dress with very large hands and feet and a deep voice. A young Aboriginal man hands Nonno Anni several weeks' rent, saying, 'Thanks for letting me catch up, Joe. I was caught a bit short.' A diminutive elderly woman wearing too much mauve eye-shadow, her pale skin pasty, tells me she remembers when I was 'just a wee small thing' and offers us a cup of Bonox. There is a middle-aged man with a drooly smile whose arm remains bent, his hand almost clawed up in his shoulder socket. His speech is impaired, his movements jerky. An emotion unrecognisable to me at that age — compassion — wells up. After he closes his door and we walk on along the hallway, I'm still thinking of Toby and look up at Nonno Anni.

'Doesn't he have a mum to help him?'

'He did,' says Nonno Anni. 'But she got old and died. Toby doesn't have anyone else, poor bugger.' He pounds on the next door. 'Rent! Rent!' His sudden bellow makes me almost jump out of my skin. 'This bloke hasn't been around the last few weeks on rent day and I haven't been able to catch up with him. He's a bit of a bad egg.'

I don't know what a bad egg is, but I am learning.

I tug Nonno Anni's sleeve and ask if I can play in the backyard. He agrees, saying he won't be long. I hear him knocking on the next door as I skip down the hall towards the back. The smell of urine assaults my nostrils near the open doorway to the men's shared bathroom. From the hallway, I catch sight of an emaciated man kneeling on the floor, bent over a toilet with the black seat up, his back keeping the cubicle door ajar. I stop stock-still. The man senses my presence and turns his gaunt face towards me, wiping vomit from around his mouth.

'Fuck off.' His mutter is slurred. 'Fuck off outta here.'

'Zoë?'

I turn, not realising Nonno Anni had been keeping an eye on me. His voice is gentle but firm. 'Go on, go outside and play on the grass, I'll be there soon.'

There is a Hills hoist in the backyard but I don't feel inclined to climb and swing on it as I do at my grandparents' house. Crouching, I watch a skink dart for cover underneath the row of cement laundry tubs, then I look up at the flats. I think of the house I live in with my parents, a workers' cottage on a steep street in Red Hill. I know it isn't large or fancy but it is clean and doesn't smell, except when something nice is cooking. There is soft carpet, a big old sofa I can clamber all over, a colour television, my makeshift 'town' of cardboard box houses on the verandah for my plastic thumb-size people, and a record player. When Dad plays the record with the green apple in the middle, I watch it go round and then get up to dance. I feel grateful I don't have to live in one of Nonno Anni's flats. Being young, I am yet to grasp fully why, but I am starting to appreciate some have more fortunate lives than others.

Decades later, authorities and developers often hassle Nonno Anni about the flats, which are on prime inner-city land in an area undergoing gentrification. 'I could knock them down and build fancier places and get a lot more rent,' he says to me. 'But where would all these poor buggers live? I couldn't do it to them.' The man he had become was far from the Fascist youth of the Mussolini regime.

Nonno Anni is in his eighties when he comes across a man living in his car in the back lane. He tells him to park the car in the yard of his flats for safety, and then offers him a job mowing the lawns and a flat to live in. More than fifty years after newly arrived migrants would come and stay at his house, Nonno Anni is still in the habit of offering refuge to those needing to find their feet.

'Your grandfather was like a father to me,' the man tells me a few years after Nonno Anni's death. By then the fellow is renting my grandparents' house, has a partner, a child and a job at the produce markets my grandfather drove to daily for years. 'He gave me a chance when no one else did, turned my life around. That's why I called my son Joseph — to name him after Joe.'

Behind the floods, the land becomes lush.
Wildlife thrives. Great scores of birds move in drifts,
winging white, catching sunlight against a blue, blue sky.
Over time acceptance settles for what has been lost,
and gained, and once again life begins to bud.
Although often it is an uneasy settling,
a slippery shroud that threatens to shift.
After such inundating rains, the sun's warmth
is welcome, and then hot, and pervasive.
Lushness turns to dry.
Late one afternoon, the sky turns orange and
flecks of ash snow the backyard.
And so it begins, again.

4th June, 2011

Dear Zoë,

We are writing to tell you how much we have enjoyed Mezza Italiana. *The book was given to me for a birthday present from one of our daughters who thought I would find the story interesting. (She did not realise that for the first 18 months of her life she lived in one of Mr Bocc's flats in Spring Hill.) I laughed and cried at the tussle you initially had with your Italian Nanna and how through your Italian grandparents and your travels to their homeland you came to appreciate and understand just what migrants undertake when they leave their homeland to make a new life in another country.*

My husband Jim first met Mr Bocc in 1960 when he was a 1st year medical student at 'Union College' on Wickham Terrace very close to the milk bar owned by your grandparents. He and lots of the students frequented the shop for soft drinks and fruit salad and ice cream.

Towards the end of 1963, Jim told Mr Bocc he was getting married and Mr Bocc said he had just finished renovating a block of five units in Spring Hill and he could go and have a look and if he was interested choose one.

So began our married life at 56 York Parade, Spring Hill. Coming to Melbourne from Scotland when I was 12 years old and having a Dad who was, to put it mildly, a very plain eater, we had never eaten spaghetti bolognaise. Mr Bocc told me how to make the sauce, planted a rosemary bush at the front fence and supplied me with a couple of bottles of [their homemade] tomato puree. I can tell you Saturday nights were Bolognaise nights and we supplied the sauce, and certain medical students and their nurse friends supplied the red wine and my spaghetti bolognaise became very popular ...

When Donna was born you can imagine things were quite stretched in the money department with a new baby and text books all on Jim's scholarship money. His cheque covered eight weeks but usually didn't arrive until the ninth week, which left us pretty short. Mr Bocc would come around every Saturday morning to cut the grass and collect the rent. Jim would ask if it was okay if he paid him twice next week as we didn't have the rent money. Mr Bocc would put his hand in his pocket and draw out a wad of notes and say, 'How much do you want?' Jim would explain he didn't want to borrow any money but thanks anyway.

We lived in the flat for three years until Jim graduated [at the] end of 1966. He had a job as a 1st year intern starting [in] 1967 at Princess Alexandra Hospital. Mr Bocc moved us and our few bits of furniture in his old maroon coloured ute to Annerley and wouldn't take the last week's rent from us. We were very grateful for his kindness in the three years we lived at Spring Hill.

Many years later, on one of the days I was working for Jim, Mr Bocc appeared in the rooms. He had an appointment with a specialist and was looking at the Directory Board when he saw the name Dr James Antony and came [in] to say he knew a Jim Antony. I recognised him as soon as he spoke and Jim and I had a lovely time talking. He told us about the [ANFE] club and how he and his wife no longer returned to Italy because the journey was too far but his family visited his old family home in Italy. It was great talking to him again and as he was leaving, I said, 'I still make the bolognaise sauce the way you taught me.' He turned back and said, 'Put a bit of basil in it,' and I said I do.

Sometime later we saw his funeral notice in the paper and went to the service. We were moved by the tributes bestowed on him for his wonderful dedication to helping others. We also realise now that it was you, Zoë, his first grandchild, who spoke so lovingly about him. Jim has often said that Mr Bocc was one of the nicest men he had ever met, and because of your book, Zoë, we definitely want to visit Fossa to see for ourselves where it all began for Mr Bocc and his mezza Italiana grandchildren.

Once when we thanked Mr Bocc for his help and kindness to us, he said, 'When you help someone when they need it, they never forget you.' How very true ...

Kindest regards and best wishes,
Jan Antony

I hold the letter to my chest and cry. It has been almost five years since Nonno Anni died. Reading Jan's letter is wonderful in that, for a brief time, it is almost as if he has come alive again. For decades, I've been collecting my grandparents' stories and here is one from my grandfather's life that I had not known about, a gift when I'd long thought there were no more to receive. I'm not sure I can ever convey to Jan just how moved and grateful I am.

There is also poignancy in that at the specialist appointment Nonno Anni attended after speaking to Jan and Jim, he was diagnosed with the cancer that would eventually take his life.

I write back to Jan immediately, and we continue to exchange letters. A year or so later, I receive a letter with several photographs enclosed. Jan and Jim are in Fossa.

Orange Drink — 6d

My father hands me a jar of red capsicums he has roasted and preserved in olive oil. 'I got a huge bag of cappos cheap at the fruit shop down the road.'

'Dad, this is lovely, thank you.' I rotate the jar in my hands, admiring the way he's placed sprigs of herbs and chopped garlic so they can be seen through the glass. 'I'll put the kettle on.'

He sits at the kitchen table, absently picking up and flicking through a library book, something on his mind. I take out the cups. A bird chirrups, jumping between tree branches just outside the open kitchen window. The kettle boils. He puts the book down.

'I wanted to thank you …'

I look up, surprised.

'… for getting me talking about the shop days again. You made me realise there were many good times at the shop, special times. I probably came across as having resented working there, but I realise in many ways I was fortunate. That shop has so many stories to tell.'

I feel a surge of love for my dad and thank him too for entrusting me with his stories. Just as I will be forever thankful to Nanna Francesca and Nonno Anni. Learning how my family lived, the three generations before me, in Italy and Australia — their challenges, successes, what they went through — makes me feel humble and grateful. I can't help getting a bit teary, and seeing this, Dad shakes his head and chuckles, knowing how sentimental I am.

I carry our tea to the table. 'What made you feel that way, do you think?'

He sighs. 'Mum and Dad were always busy running the shop while I was growing up, you know. I wish they could have closed it at night so we could have sat down to a family meal together. And by the later years, at times it got so quiet on weekends — I remember as a teenager sometimes sitting at that counter for hours and it was as dead as a dodo but Dad insisted we open seven days a week, even after they'd made enough money to buy the flats. Dad was always working. I wish he could have spent more time with us.'

I want to say something but hesitate, unsure if I should trust my own reflection on this or whether I have any right to voice it. 'Perhaps he didn't feel he needed to be there for you so much because his own father couldn't be around when he was growing up …'

Dad is quiet, seeming to digest this. I know I'm treading a fine line here, having had a less fraught relationship with Annibale as his granddaughter than my father did as his elder son.

'I hadn't thought of that.' He is being fair.

Working as a schoolteacher my father may not have earned as much as some fathers, but he mostly got home when I did on school days and often made time to play games in the backyard when I was young. My parents also ensured we always had a family meal together, even on the nights we had to eat at five o'clock so Dad could get to the night school by six o'clock to teach an evening class. I now realise why that family meal with all of us together meant so much to him.

'I think the other thing about working at the shop was that it set me apart from all the other kids when I was growing up,' Dad says. 'We could never go on holidays because we always had to keep the milk bar open. And friends would come in talking about the places they'd been away to and all the fun things they did. And here I was working at the shop every holiday. We didn't have a regular family life like others. We were the migrants — always working. I just wanted to fit in, be normal, you know?'

I stare at him. 'Do you realise that all my life you've teased me about how, when I was a kid, I wouldn't learn Italian cause I wanted to be "normal"?'

He chuckles a little sheepishly. 'I know. You might have gotten that from me.'

I'm sad to realise that our childhood laments are echoes of each other.

He stands to leave, reverting to his impulse to avoid talking further. But at the front door he doesn't rush straight off, and I sense that when he is ready to talk more he will. For now, he lightens with a smile and gives the side of my face an affectionate pinch.

Epiphany Eve

The long wooden table
creaks with dishes, elbows,
a slap during laughter.
Voices surge in song and tale.
My head rests into softness,
sweet with talc and perspiration.
The comfort of an ample bosom.
Throats dry and cheeks wet.
A smaller table, fewer dishes.
Moon sets in a dawning sky.
Standing barefoot upon earth,
the fortitude of those who
walked before me
rises through my soles.
Into my soul.

'How could I have forgotten how tall the mountains are?'

Nonno Anni saw the Apennines again for the first time thirty-five years after he left Fossa to come to Australia. In 1975 my grandparents, both in their fifties, took their first proper holiday — a trip around the world, including to their childhood homes in Italy.

'I was determined to see my grandmother's house in Palmi where I lived as a child,' Nanna Francesca tells me. 'I had to have just one look, you know?' I nod. 'I felt sad. It was just a pile of rubble. Everything, everyone gone.'

No one she asked could tell her what had happened to it.

I touch her arm and she lets me, just for a moment, before brushing me away and shaking her head, smiling with tears in her eyes. To me, it seems she often gets the tougher road and yet she always trudges on, always with acceptance, compliance, her circuit of duty.

'It seemed like the entire village came out into the street when we arrived in Fossa.' Nonno Anni shakes his head, marvelling.

And having stood in that lane myself, I can almost hear the clunking-open of shutters and doors, footsteps on stone.

He shows me a photograph of his return — Nonno Anni is in his travelling suit, kneeling on the cobblestones surrounded by dozens of villagers, many reaching out to place a hand on his shoulders, his arms, his back. The emotion on his face is pure. They never forgot him, enveloping him back into their community upon his return even though several decades of poverty, migration and the war had forever split the village. A period short in historical terms but long for those living through it — there would forever be those who went beyond the mountains, and those who stayed encircled by them.

'I couldn't believe it … Don Angelo, the priest who had taken our inheritance and my aunt's house, was still the parish priest. Ninety-nine he would live to be.' Nonno Anni sits back, broad hands flat on the table. 'He had this look on his face and came up to me with his hand out to shake mine. "Welcome back," he said, in front of the whole village. Most knew what he had done. I looked down at his hand and I just couldn't shake it. Instead, I said to him, "If it wasn't for you I wouldn't have had to leave." I couldn't have said that in 1939.'

I notice the priest isn't in the photograph.

'You never got the house back?' I ask, more with a faint hope of justice than any expectation of it.

'Nooo,' Nonno Anni slaps the table. 'And what's worse, in the time since my mother and Elia left in 1948, our land was taken as well. Some legal word they say about taking back property in the absence of heirs of the owner. I don't know, "ascheat" or "escheat" — more like a "cheat", I reckon. I spoke to the mayor and he said they thought none of us was coming back, and since the land had been vacant for years they decided to acquire it for someone else. I asked him why someone didn't write to ask us in Australia first. He said they didn't know where to send a letter. But that's rubbish. They could have asked someone. My mother kept in touch, writing letters with lots of people in the village. First Zia's house and land were taken, and then our land. If it's not the Church, it's the bloody government. It's lucky we had people staying in the house or we could have lost that, too.'

No wonder that on his first night back in Fossa, Nonno Anni sat and talked with friends at one of their houses until first light, and there was no wine left in the *cantina* afterwards.

'It was the ham we were eating,' he says hastily. 'It was a very salty ham.' He glances at me. 'You know, at dawn I was walking along the lane back to the house when I looked up and all the houses seemed to be falling forward and then jerking back and I thought, bloody hell, I come back after all these years and there's an earthquake …'

Nanna Francesca pushes back her chair. 'There was no earthquake,' she says with her usual matter-of-factness, getting up to clear the coffee cups and disappearing into the kitchen.

None of us could know then that a decade later a real earthquake would hit the village after virtually a century with little more than the occasional tremor. Neither of my grandparents would be alive by then to know of it.

Nonno Anni looks back down at the spread of old photographs on the table. He picks out another one and hands it to me. Although it is in black and white, I know the sign over the footpath with the words 'Milk Bar' is red and white, and either side of it 'Sweets' and 'Fruit' are in black. I can almost see the bright colours of the tin signs attached to the walls outside the shop: 'Orange drink — 6d', 'Peters', the red of 'King Size Coke', the blue and yellow of 'Vincent's Powders'. A paperboy hollers outside on the corner. From a window above, the boot repairer is lowering on a string an empty bottle with a note taped to it.

A fresh breeze flows into the shop where several people gather along the counter drinking milkshakes, strangers yet they chat and laugh with gentle courtesy. There is a tang of cut pineapple from the fruit salad mingling with the fresh scent of oranges whirring in the vitamiser. On the counter, a fluted glass stands in readiness. A man with an Italian accent weighs some pears in the hanging scale. His wife tells their young son to bring in some more sarsaparilla from out the back.

Nonno Anni gives me a nudge. 'You know, when I first came to Australia I knew that my life was going to change forever.'

'I can imagine.'

*For migrants of all cultures and circumstance,
those who welcome them with open hearts,
and the traditional custodians and elders,
both past and present, in particular those from
country where many events written about took place ...
with acknowledgment and respect.*

Compendium of Structures
as at time of publication

In Australia ...
- 'Stonehenge', the house at 157 Leichhardt Street, Spring Hill, Brisbane, built circa 1859 of convict-hewn stone, was demolished in the late 1950s, the stone walls said to have been taken to homes in the suburb of St Lucia for use as paving. High-rise buildings stand in its place.
- The Astoria Café building on the corner of Edward and Adelaide Streets, Brisbane, was demolished and replaced with an eleven-storey office block in 1955.
- The fruit shop and milk bar at 365 Ann Street, Brisbane, near the corner of Wharf Street, in a building owned by the Church of England, was knocked down in 1970. The demolition, instigated by the Anglican Synod, was originally to 'open up' a view of St John's Cathedral. A high-rise now stands in its place.
- St Martin's Hospital, Ann Street, constructed in 1922 and closed in 1971, was also approved for demolition by the Anglican Synod to open up the view of the cathedral. The 'Save St Martin's Hospital' movement and persistent public outcry preserved part of the hospital building, which now has a National Trust listing and is used for church administration purposes.
- The Regent Theatre, built in 1929, was considered the finest entertainment building ever constructed in Queensland. Vast numbers of people frequented and treasured the Regent for decades, and tens of thousands fought fiercely to keep it. Despite years of protests and heritage listing, all but the foyer has been demolished. What remained was further damaged by redevelopment in 2012,

including the original exterior gargoyles being deliberately smashed for 'ease of removal'. The gilded plaster sunburst that once surrounded the enormous ceiling chandelier was hacked into pieces during demolition. The pieces were exhibited as part of a Queensland Museum display in 2013.
- The Trocadero Dansant opened in 1923 with a sprung dance floor to fit 2,000, and alcoves furnished in mission oak. It later became a technical college and was razed in the 1970s to make way for a rail bridge across Melbourne Street.
- The Roma Street Produce Markets (1884–1964) were demolished.
- Brisbane's Fire Station headquarters (1908–1964) on the corner of Ann and Wharf Streets was demolished. Cathedral Square now exists in its place.
- The workers' cottages of Wyandra Street, Teneriffe, were knocked down and replaced with commercial buildings between the 1960s and the 1980s.
- The Newstead gasworks no longer exists but the gasometer framework (originally erected at Petrie Bight in 1873) stands as part of a commercial and residential development.
- Cloudland Ballroom, an iconic Brisbane building cherished by thousands, was demolished (despite its National Trust listing) during the night of November 7, 1982. A residential unit complex replaced it.
- The farmhouse and shed in Ellwood Road, Applethorpe, still stand, although the orchards are gone.
- Pierpoint's department store and blacksmith in Stanthorpe is gone. The Arcadia theatre building remains.
- Pigott's department store in Warwick no longer operates, although the building with 'Pigott's' on the façade still stands, and is divided into smaller shops.
- The family house at 897 Brunswick Street, New Farm, inundated by floodwater in 1974 and 2011, now houses a business.
- The house where Cesca and Vincenzo lived at 17 Chermside Street, Teneriffe, still stands.
- Flats owned by Annibale and Francesca in Brunswick Street, Lower Bowen Terrace and Sargent Street, New Farm, remain.

- After the flats at Baxter and York Streets in Spring Hill and the duplex at Nobby Beach were sold, new owners demolished and replaced them with residential and/or retail developments.

In Italy ...
- The house in Palmi, Calabria, was found in 1975 to be a pile of rubble.
- In Fossa, Abruzzo, the house built around 1692 suffered significant earthquake damage in 2009, as it did in 1915 and 1703, but it remains standing ... for now.

Author's Note

I knew from when I was a teenager that I would write about the lives of my grandparents, Annibale and Francesca. At the same time I felt nervous about doing their stories justice. I first formally interviewed my grandparents almost twenty years ago, and in between other work, I composed three accounts of their lives, both in fiction and non-fiction forms. Sometimes curious things occurred … When I was writing their stories as a novel, I told Nonno Anni I'd created the fictitious character of an aunt who would leave her estate to the Catholic Church. He stared and asked who told me that had happened. I was equally stunned, since no one had spoken to me of it. I realised then that this book could only be presented as the true story it was.

This meant I would have to face the parts that were difficult to write about, that would have been easier to gloss over in fiction. I'm not sure I fully appreciated how epic this geographical and emotional journey would be. While at a distance of up to a century it was necessary for me to compress or elaborate on elements, change several names and disguise characters (such as Milos) for the usual reasons, the stories remain as told to me by those who lived them. Due to the sheer abundance of stories collected from the transcripts of many hours of taped interviews, I unfortunately couldn't include everything.

Annibale and Francesca continue to be an inspiration to me — their strength, forbearance, successes and shortcomings, and their wisdom gained from years of experience. In writing this book my intent has been to preserve their history with respect for them and for those who were part of their lives.

Acknowledgments

I am very grateful to all those who shared parts of their lives, skills and knowledge to contribute to the creation of this book.

My grandparents, Francesca and Annibale, my father, Remo, and my husband, Roger, I thank more than I can express — *con immenso amore e gratitudine.*

Thank you to my agent, Selwa Anthony, to Brigitta Doyle, Mary Rennie, Madeleine James, all those at ABC Books/HarperCollins, and Amanda O'Connell and Kim Swivel for their impeccable care, expertise and insight.

To Kerri (Thomson) Tannahill (1961–2012) — my aunt — who transcribed the interview tapes, and to Megan Grenenger for the author photograph — warmest thanks for your kindness and generosity.

Sincere thanks to all those who provided information through interviews and official sources — Vincenzo Solano, Elia Boccabella, Robert Thomson, the Urbani family, Lorenzo Boccabella, Queensland State Archives, National Archives of Australia, Australian War Memorial, State Library of Queensland, National Library of Australia, Millmerran and District Historical Society, Stanthorpe and District Historical Society, Italian Historical Society, and not least, those who cannot be named for confidentiality reasons.

Special thanks to Jan and Jim Antony for generously giving permission for their letter to be reprinted in this book.

And to those who have fought to preserve natural places and heritage buildings in times past, thank you for saving the places you could and for enduring the heartbreak of defeat for those you couldn't.

Zoë Boccabella was born in Brisbane in 1973. For many years, she worked as a writer, in media liaison and as a researcher for universities, government and the police service, as well as freelance. She also worked in several restaurants and a delicatessen. Zoë has a Bachelor of Arts in literature and sociology, a Master of Philosophy, and has studied scriptwriting. Since childhood, she has loved to write, attempting her first novel, 'Tragedy Island', at age seven. These days Zoë is drawn to collecting spoken histories and the stories of migrants, and writes both memoir and fiction. She loves cooking handed-down family recipes as well as creating new ones, and also enjoys gardening and painting.

zoeboccabella.com

Also From Zoë Boccabella

Growing up in Brisbane in the 1970s and '80s, Zoë Boccabella knew if you wanted to fit in, you did *not* bottle tomatoes, have plastic on the hallway carpet or a glory box of Italian linens. Though she tried to be like 'everyone else', refusing to learn Italian and even dyeing her dark hair blonde, Zoë couldn't shake the unsettling sense of being 'half-and-half' — half Australian, *mezza italiana* — unable to fit fully into either culture, or merge the two.

Years later, she travels to her family's ancestral village of Fossa in Abruzzo and discovers a place that is the stuff of fairytales — medieval castles, mystics, dark forests, serpent charmers and witches. As Zoë stays in the house that has belonged to her family for centuries, the village casts its spell. She begins to realise the preciousness of her heritage and the stories, recipes and traditions of her extended Italian family become a treasured part of her life. Then the earthquake hits …

Honestly written, sprinkled with recipes and laced with love, *Mezza Italiana* is a heart-warming journey into the soul of Italy, and into a family you'll never forget.